Texas Music

Texas Music

Rick Koster

ST. MARTIN'S GRIFFIN
NEW YORK

☆ Contents

☆ Introduction

THROUGHOUT THE AGES OF THEOLOGICAL AND PHILOSOPHICAL debate, agnostic and atheistic scholars have long pointed to the fact that Jimi Hendrix was born outside of Texas as a significant argument against the existence of a benevolent God. If He is truly just, they reason, Hendrix would hail from Oak Cliff or South Austin—some place Texan, for sure—because Texas is *the* guitar state, and one of its few flaws as a Home to Music in general is that Jimi wasn't born within its borders.

Still, it was in Dallas that Hendrix traded forty bucks and an old wah-wah pedal to a youthful Jimmie Vaughan in exchange for his classic Vox wah-wah, and it was on *The Tonight Show* that Jimi extolled the virtues of Houston's Billy Gibbons as a destined-for-greatness axmeister.

I reflect on these minutiae at the outset of an admittedly subjective history of Texas musicians because it was during my early seventies Rock Kid persona that I first began a fascination with Texas music through its incredibly rich guitar heritage—storied rock and blues heroes like Johnny Winter, Gibbons, T-Bone Walker, and Freddie King, as well as younger club stalwarts like Eric Johnson, Bugs Henderson, John Nitzinger, Stevie Ray Vaughan, and Rocky Athas.

Exposure to these artists, naturally, led to an awareness of more stylistically varied players and music, and my record collection gradually expanded beyond the parameters of rock and blues (and beyond the architectural space limitations prescribed by just one bedroom). As I began seeking out other forms of music, I realized, for example, that in my grade school days my parents had introduced me to the great Texas country-and-western tradition; over the course of their weekend parties (which ritually started on Saturday afternoons and rapidly took on the Dionysian scope of Mardi Gras—in both duration and liquid saturation), the sounds of Ray Price, George Jones, Willie Nelson, Ernest Tubb, and Buck Owens would float through the house into the bed where I was supposed to be asleep, slowly establishing a comprehensive root network deep in my subconscious.

I hated C&W at the time but, by early college, I realized with shock that I'd come to love those old tunes—which was not an easy thing for am eighteen-year-old longhair to admit to his Uriah Heep–addled friends. Shortly thereafter, Willie Nelson and his Cosmic Cowboy movement sprang up in Austin, establishing among other things that fans of all music could peacefully coexist. From there, I easily made a series of short, simple steps to the discovery of jazz, classical, and R&B albums. I eventually became a fan of not just acts like King Crimson, Ted Nugent, or the Beatles, but Claude Debussy, Doc Watson, Dave Brubeck, Gil Scott-Heron, the New York Dolls, Patsy Cline, the Neville Brothers, *Pippin*, Cole Porter, the Ramones, Fishbone, Rusty Wier, and Parliament—all in the same universe at the same time. At that point, the realization that I loved all kinds of music was probably the first important step on the lunatic path that would ultimately result in this book.

The second was the discovery that, for every musical style represented in my eclectic record collection, someone from Texas not only was damned good at it, but had probably expanded and significantly enhanced the possibilities of that style.

In fact, the point of the whole project is that Texas has perhaps the most diverse and colorful tradition in American musical history. One would be hard pressed to argue that any state (or city) has made as many significant contributions to as many forms of music as Texas has. True: other states have fine musical legacies—Louisiana (with its New Orleans jazz and R&B, and a statewide Cajun/zydeco tradition) and Tennessee (Memphis blues and Nashville's dazzling array of country music in all its permutations) come immediately to mind, but their respective notoriety is generally associated with one or two distinctive styles of music, or with one or two particular cities.

For that matter, many American cities are affiliated with music: Seattle is now famous for grunge and alternative rock; Cleveland is a blue-collar heavy metal town; Chicago is a blues mecca; Detroit originated Motown soul; and San Francisco's organic rock scene mirrors the sensibilities of the entire Bay Area. And, of course, Los Angeles and New York—prime entertainment and media centers—boast a thriving musical enterprise simply because of their status as show biz towns.

But it's arguable that no one state or city can compare with Texas for the sheer depth and variety of significant musicians. There are several reasons why Texas has such a rich melodic legacy: the state's multifaceted geography, pinballing weather, and colorfully quilted ethnic cultures have certainly helped, not to mention a spirit of fierce autonomy borne of Lone Star rebellion and perseverance. Plus, as many of its writers and artists have attempted to describe, something intangible and magical happens here. There is ample evidence to support the theory that Texas makes the artist her own, or, as one of novelist Pete Gent's characters observed, "I love Texas, but she makes her people crazy."

All these things, then, are ingredients in the great cosmic recipe which has evolved into a peerless coterie of brilliant musicians, singers, players, and composers associated with Texas soil. And for every *famous* Texas musician—Blind Lemon Jefferson, Charley Pride, Van Cliburn, Ornette Coleman, ZZ Top, Barbara Mandrell, etc.—there are dozens, even *hundreds* more Texas players that are just as good. And, hopefully, most of them will be found herein.

But that's been a big problem, too. Great musicians multiply in Texas like plague rats, and by way of covering my own ass a bit, right up front, let me say that from the time the first draft of this book was finished till the end of the second draft, I'd come across some four dozen artists who had been left out the first time and who deserved to be included—and so on with each successive draft. I finally accepted that it's a never-ending phenomenon and, to that extent, my choices were to either keep revising, keep expanding the page count, and consider it a perpetual work-in-progress, or just suck it up and arbitrarily draw the line. Which, with the sage assistance of my kind and goodly editor, Jim Fitzgerald, I have at last done.

The artists who *are* included are all significant in their own right and, with luck, the great majority of those musicians who deserve to be here are. Deepest apologies are, of course, humbly extended to anyone left out—and, sadly, that there will be some is inevitable.

A few more quick notes. Although during my journeyman's musical career as well as during the research for this book I have traveled the state extensively, I grew up in Dallas. As such, my perspective as a Dallasite is, well, ingrained. This in no way means I favored Dallas musicians. (On the contrary, I strove mightily to ensure that deserving musicians were included whether they came from Austin, Pecos, Galveston, Lufkin, or wherever.) I suppose all I'm trying to say is that having spent extensive time around a particular scene puts a by-definition spin on one's experiences. An Austin writer might well include many of the same people, only with the world-view of one who grew up hanging out at the Armadillo and Antone's as opposed to Big D's Mother Blues and the Longhorn Ballroom. I'm not certain that it makes any significant difference, but it seems somehow correct to mention it.

Second, though this is necessarily a subjective exercise, the idea is simply to glorify those things about Texas musicians that are wonderful and unique. I did not exclude anyone because I personally don't like their work. While occasionally I have marveled over one or another artist's rise to fame (yes: Meat Loaf and Vanilla Ice are included in that subgroup), I nevertheless included them because they are from Texas and they made a mark in music—for better or worse.

Third, a brief note on the format and tone. Early on in this long process, I found that a peculiar narrative voice emerged in my head. Nothing mystical was going on—no divine intervention or Ouija board guidance—it was just that my own muse took on, over time, as I hammered away at the computer, a vague, third-person quality, as though I were actually jotting down notes verbatim from some genial, slightly drunken college professor. While this should in no way suggest that I consider myself professorial—or the Ultimate Authority on the subject at hand—it was important to me that the tone of the book be conversational and accessible as well as educational; this is *not* a textbook or an academic exercise, but, with luck, an insightful and amusing valentine to Texas music and its practitioners.

I have also perhaps emphasized a few aspects of Texas musicians more than others. To return to the guitarist motif I referenced at the start of this introduction, I've singled out a lot of guitar players for close scrutiny because, of the myriad brilliant performers on a variety of instruments that you'll find in these pages, there are more per capita, seminal, shake-the-foundations-of-song, bad-ass guitar players than one could find in any state in the United States—or, for that matter, on most continents. I've profiled not only those that are acknowledged big deals, but included a baker's dozen or so you've probably never heard of that are as unique and special in their own way as musicians like Gatemouth Brown, Charlie Christian, or Pantera's Dimebag Darrell Abbott.

This doesn't mean I think the guitar is more important than any other instrument, just that the sheer volume of great Texas players is particularly noteworthy. (Check out the chapters in the Jazz section on sax players for another concentration of virtuosos on a given ax.)

I've also highlighted a bunch of artists and songwriters who aren't famous—but should be. For every Geto Boys, Tanya Tucker, Lightnin' Hopkins, or Boz Scaggs, there is an intimidating number of relatively unknown Texas artists deserving of national attention and beefy royalty checks. Music, though, as most any nightclub road-dog can tell you, can be a cruel, fickle mistress. To most of us who toiled for years in obscurity, it would be realistic to anthropomorphize Music as having the face of Vendela, the temperament of Shannon Doherty, and the principles of Ma Barker. And for whichever cruel reasons, sometimes She simply just decrees that deserving folks get left out. I've profiled several such artists who deserve better.

Finally, since the differences between musical styles like folk and rock or country and folk are closer to blurred, impressionistic shadings than actual, indelible lines of demarcation, it was occasionally difficult to stick an artist in a clear-cut category. Is Peppermint Harris a blues guy or an R&B guy? Was Moon Mullican a western swing pianist or a father of boogie woogie rock 'n' roll—or both?

The answers in such instances, of course, are that the artist in question simply happened to be famous and talented at more than one genre—and for the sake of convenience, I included those musicians in a particular category depending on my own associations with their work, or if they were overwhelmingly famous in one style. Therefore, while one could argue that Joe Ely is a rocker, Jimmy LaFave a folkie, and Jimmie Dale Gilmore a country guy, each has made music that could arguably fit in any of those formats. When in doubt, check the index.

I'll conclude this exhaustive preamble by saying that, when I started this book, I thought I knew a lot about Texas music. Ha! I was astoundingly naive. Over the last two years, I have listened to a staggering amount of incredible Texas music that I never knew existed at the outset of the project. It would be a lie to say that I've actually heard bits of music by all the artists listed herein, but I don't actually know that such a thing is possible—at least in any comprehensive sense.

Again, that's the point: It's a fact that there is probably more great Texas music than one can comfortably listen to in a lifetime. But that doesn't mean one shouldn't give it a helluva try. In the words of Willie Shakespeare (or was it Willie Nelson?): " 'Tis a consummation devoutly to be wished."

☆ Acknowledgments

THIS BOOK IS FOR MY WIFE, EILEEN, IN APPRECIATION OF HER love, talent, and sacrifice in order that I might sit at a computer all day and listen to tunes. Thanks, kiddo, for keeping the wheels on, and for postponing your own dreams so that I might pursue mine. *I'm thumbing a ride with your heart. . . .*

Much love and good *gris-gris* to the surviving Kosters: to Thelm, I remain in awe of your infinite Super Mom powers and endless financial grants—the sum of which the NEA could not even conceive—and Mic, I'm perpetually grateful for your cogent medical and literary advice, your deep goodness, and for rescuing my various guitars from certain pawnshop death; mucho appreciation also to Bob and Joyce and the madcap Jenkins clan, whose collective and wily Welsh ways are the stuff of great kindness; health and power to the Dukeman and Sheehan families; and may the long path meadows run in perpetuity for Puppy Brown and Vivienne (Miss Moose).

Big thanks to the Malone "brothers," Danny Frank and Paul Scott, whose guidance and wisdom have been unerring, and whose respective talents are staggering; Kathryn Jones and Cheryl Malone for research tips and timely ideas; ECM and Sarah for benevolence the likes of which would've astonish Mother Teresa; Tim Choate and Brett Blackwell for defining friendship; Carl Daniel for quenching the (literal and cerebral) thirst; and not forgetting that every day's Halloween with the Sundry All-Kook Squad: Steve Pace, Dave Schulz, Jeff Elble, Drs. Larry Williams and Tandy Freeman, Johnny "Blind Lemon Arachnid" Mosier, Patrick and Mark Gaudin, the Matthews "brothers" (Harold and Ross), Ol' Jeem Dalton, Andy Timmons, Steve "Whip" Colwick, Chris Todora (and all at Parkit Market), Gary "He My Catcher, Pauper" McGuire; and other pals and benefactors in all nearby galaxies whom I may have forgotten. "If we offend, it is with goodwill. . . ."

I'm buying the Red Hooks for the Couldn't Have Done It Without 'Em Dept.: my visionary agent, Dave Smith, and his omniscient assistants, Shelley Lewis and Seth Robertson: and, at St. Martin's, my editor, Jim Fitzgerald, whose patience and skill are beyond mortal comprehension; Cal Morgan, the Professor Longhair of publishing, for delivering the paperback deal; and to Dana Albarella for angelic shepherding and John Karle for the sweet hype. And to Fred Sanders and Roland Guierin, Andy Timmons and Mike Medina, Tom Faulkner and Adrian Cabello, Jim Suhler and Tim Alexander, Josh Alan, and ATTIC—thanks for the help during inauguration week.

A toast, as well, to Ron McKeown, James Bland and Scott Newton for photographic and critical contributions beyond generosity; and thanks for all-around good work and inspiration to Bob Compton; Stoney Burns and *BUDDY Magazine*; James Lee Burke; Robin Yount; Jimi H.; the Brothers Finn and Neville; John Kennedy Toole; James Booker; Cowboy Mouth; Rhynes & the Hammer; Nektar for *Remember the Future*; Dan Jenkins, Lew Shiner, and Laurence Gonzales for three novels that inextricably link Texas and music: *Baja Oklahoma*, *Glimpses*, and *Jambeaux*, respectively; Peter Gent; the Boston Red Sox; and Matt Weitz, Robert Wilonsky, and the *Dallas Observer*.

Special, hold-on-to-my-life-raft praise for those individuals who guided me, Virgil-like, into those abandon-all-hope areas where my "expertise" was particularly thin: Casey Monahan of the Texas Music Office; Mark Elliot (jazz); Mark Rubin (Tex-Mex and ethnic); Peter Relic (hip-hop); Kevin Coffey (Western swing and country); Mario Tarradell (Latin); Sumter Bruton (blues, R&B, and jazz); Tim Alexander (conjunto and zydeco); Duane Turner (rap and hip-hop); Mike Hyrka (various historical scenes); Tim Schuller (blues); George Gimarc (new wave and punk); Redbeard (rock); and Kim Herriage, Keith Rust, and Bobby Greeson (at-large pithiness).

Thanks, too, go to all the guys I played with over the years (the road, indeed, goes on forever—and the bar tabs never end). I always found Safety in Ernie "Area 51" Myers, Nick "I'm *Not* Elvis" Shannon, "Bad" Bob Moersen, Dave "Stone Man" Stone, "Long" John Lange, "Young" Steve Powell and Corky "the Corkster" Ray; Joe Kim and Mickey Don of the Otter People; Larry and Russell Phariss and Nutty Ron Wilson from Broxton; Charles "Huge" Vessels; Chuck Herriage and Winfield "Skip" Devlin from Metroplex—and Texas musicians everywhere, particularly those whose genius inspired me all these years. Hopefully, you're somewhere in the pages that follow, whether you owe me money or not.

Free chowder for the New England contingent: Michael and Betsy Barker, Milton Moore, Kristina Dorsey, Tom "Hot Sauce" Crosby and the Bank Street Roadhouse folks, Tim "Cold One" Cotter, Dan Waters, Lance Johnson, Matt Berger, Barb and Chris Poirer, Jacquie and the Family Glassenberg, Skip Weisenberger, Steve Slosberg, Dan "Take Me Back to New Orleans" Pearson, the Dutch Tavern, and all at *The Day*.

And a quick but fervent prayer for the musicians/friends who didn't make it: Jamie DeWitt, Larry Rollen, Wade Michaels, Art Bear, and Mike Munday. Rest peacefully, brothahs. . . .

Finally, to R. L.: Thanks, Pop, and may you walk with like-minded giants in a world without end. . . .

☆ Part 1: Country

☆ One: Singing Cowboys and Range Songs

▼

I N THE BIG PICTURE OF COUNTRY MUSIC, IT'S THEMATICALLY DIF-ficult to reconcile George Jones singing "He Stopped Loving Her Today" with rollicking pirate songs, but in fact the original country music evolved in no small part from sea chanties that had been lyrically altered to reflect the concerns of early cowboys. Make that yo ho ho and a longneck bottle of beer.

But the phrase "country and western" is dichotomous for a reason. The evolution of the singing cowboy was a musically different proposition from the rural "string band" sound which was country music. And it would be necessary for both to evolve before they could collide and make it possible for a Billy Ray Cyrus to exist and prosper.

First things first. By the time of the Texas Republic, a vast influx of adventurers, chiefly from the existing southern states, headed west to hunt buffalo or to join up with any of a number of "trail" organizations that herded longhorn cattle and horses up the Chisholm and other trails from Texas to markets from Denver and Cheyenne to Dodge City, Kansas, and Sedalia, Missouri.

The numbers of these cowboys grew with the vast influx of post–Civil War people who streamed into Texas. From 1870 to the new century, it is estimated that twelve million head of cattle were moved out of Texas to points north and west. Similarly, with plains fairly packed with buffalo, no shortage of hunters headed from the Southeast to help wipe out the species.

Inasmuch as modern conveniences such as I-10, Hooters franchises, and tape players were decades from existence, the cowboy who wished employment on brain-numbingly monotonous cattle drives had best possess more than just the ability to ride and rope a cow or chase down and skin a buffalo. He'd better be able to tell a joke or possess whistling and singing skills.

A lot of the early cowboys were either directly from the British Isles or perhaps one or two generations removed, and the music they brought to the plains was frequently in the form of briny songs o' the sea or English and Irish folk ballads which were favorites in the New World during the eighteenth and nineteenth centuries.

Still, tunes about bagpipes and seaweed didn't cut it out on the western plain, so the cowpokes began to ad-lib words appropriate to their situations. These efforts also mixed with the migratory slave blues and ethnic folk songs which were by that time getting comfy in Texas, and all these influences simmered together in a vast *guisado* of music that became the cowboy song.

Professor John A. Lomax, a Texas folklorist, was the first person to cata-logue these tunes, most of which were attributed to "anonymous," in a 1910 book called *Cowboy Songs and Other Frontier Ballads*. And while this brought such songs as "Bury Me Not on the Lone Prairie," "The Streets of Laredo," and "The Old Chisholm Trail" to national attention, it was "Home on the Range" that was the first real chart topper of the cowboy songs.

Lomax first heard the tune from an elderly black man in San Antonio who'd been a chuck wagon cook on the trail drives and later opened his own tavern—which if nothing else demonstrates that the old gentleman truly possessed the soul and ambition of a musician. Lomax printed the song in an early edition of *Cowboy Songs*, where it festered for over two decades before sheet music arrangements brought it to a national radio audience. It was reportedly a favorite of President Franklin Roosevelt, though it is not true that he based the economic formulae of the New Deal on the song's chord structures.

But "Home on the Range" was not the first cowboy song to be recorded. It is generally acknowledged that Carl Sprague's "When the Work's All Done This Fall," out in 1925 on New York's Victor Records label, takes that honor. Sprague was authentic, too, having grown up on a ranch outside Houston. All in all, Victor released twenty-eight of Sprague's efforts, and in turn the label created an entire catalogue of cowboy singers.

"Longhorn Luke" was another bona fide cowboy who parlayed a genuine singing talent and an intimate familiarity with Lomax's source book into a career in the burgeoning entertainment world. Luke's real name was Jules Verne Allen, from Waxahachie, who as a regular performer on San Anto-nio's WOAI radio station developed quite a following in the late 1920s and early 1930s.

But while the nation's interest in the "singing cowboy" wasn't exactly dormant, it took Hollywood to turn the incidental phenomenon into a full-bore craze. As the story goes, Gene Autry was drinking a milkshake in Schwabs drugstore when . . .

Actually, the first instance of a singing Texas cowboy on the big screen was probably in 1930, when Ken Maynard appeared in *Songs of the Saddle*. Maynard subsequently starred in a number of singing westerns during the thirties, when, in a precursor to the porn industry, trifles like plot and music were secondary to action.

Gene Autry changed all that. He was born in 1907 near Tioga, Texas, and overcame the fact that his first name was actually Orvan. (Gene was his middle name.) Though he learned guitar early and played in the Fields Brothers Marvelous Medicine Show during high school, Autry was working in a telegraph station in Oklahoma when Will Rogers came in one day to send a telegraph.

Rogers, who claimed never to have met a future owner of a baseball franchise he didn't like, encouraged Autry to pursue his artistic inclinations. Ever mindful of Jimmie Rodgers's success, Autry secured work at Tulsa radio station KVOO and started calling himself "Oklahoma's Singing Cowboy."

In 1929, after a series of New York auditions, Autry began recording for a variety of record labels (chiefly Victor, but also Okeh, Columbia, and Grey Gull), under a variety of professional names and occasionally with a singer/songwriter/guitarist named Jimmy Long. The two wrote a song called "Silver Haired Daddy of Mine" which sold over five million copies.

Autry's recording success eventually persuaded Hollywood to give him a chance, and he secured a part in a Maynard western called *Old Santa Fe*. That went well, and after another film with Maynard, Autry starred in a twelve-part serial called *The Phantom Empire*.

Thereafter, with his trusty horse Champion, Autry starred in numerous films that would not only make him a movie star but also the biggest singing star in the galaxy. Autry's musical legacy was all-encompassing, too. From border ballads to prototypical western swing to pop, Autry performed them all with aplomb.

His rendition of "The Yellow Rose of Texas" is accepted as *the* version, while holiday fare such as "Rudolph the Red Nosed Reindeer," "Here Comes Peter Cottontail," and "Here Comes Santa Claus," all million-sellers, supplemented cowboy hits like "Tumbling Tumbleweeds" (1935), "Back in the Saddle Again" (1939, and no, it's not the Aerosmith song), "You Are My Sunshine" (1941), and "At Mail Call Today" (1945).

Autry paved the way for other Hollywood cowboys, among them Eddie Dean, Rex Allen, Tex Ritter, and Roy Rogers. In later years, Autry became a solo example of how to build a financial empire, channeling his singing and acting profits into a nest of radio and television stations, a hotel chain, and ownership of the California (now Anaheim) Angels.

But in all that he's done, Autry's finest legacy is his establishment, across America, of a symbolic image of the Great and Golden West. It was a glittering thematic vista which would be mined by several others of the singing cowboy ilk, but the only one who approached Autry's popularity was Woodward Maurice "Tex" Ritter, who was born in East Texas near Murval in 1905. While his status as an actual cowboy is dubious, his studies under Oscar Fox, John Lomax, and folklorist J. Frank Dobie at the University of Texas certainly instilled in Ritter a solid theoretical background.

He attended Northwestern law school for a year, then returned to Texas to sing on KPRC radio in Houston. A stint in a traveling musical variety troupe took him to New York, where he actually carved out a modest career on the Broadway stage, appearing in five early thirties productions, including *Green Grow the Lilacs*.

Ritter capitalized on his Texas roots, though, running through a series of New York radio programs such as *Cowboy Tom's Round-up*, *The Tex Ritter Show*, and *The WHN Radio Barn Dance*. He made his first records there for ARC but, having established Western Chic in New York, decided to move to Hollywood in 1936. *Song of the Gringo* was the first of over seventy films Ritter made, and he also began recording nonstop for Decca, scoring a hit with fellow Texan Cindy Walker's "Jingle, Jangle, Jingle."

But it wasn't until 1942, when Ritter signed with the newly formed Capitol label, that his recording career picked up speed. Big hits were "There's a New Moon over My Shoulder," "Boll Weevil," "Blood on the Saddle," and "Deck of Cards," the latter a triumph of corn in which a soldier escapes a court martial execution by detailing the history of the Bible using a deck of cards. ("Deck of Cards," incidentally, was written by another cowboy singing star, T. Texas Tyler, so named in spite of the fact that he was born in Arkansas, educated in Philadelphia, became famous in Hollywood, and died in Missouri.)

While Ritter's film and recording popularity had declined somewhat by the end of the forties, he won an Academy Award for his theme to the film *High Noon*, and continued to tour and star on radio successfully for a number of years. He also sired comedian John Ritter, but his vast body of quality work surely makes up for that procreational faux pas.

If Autry and Ritter were the superstars of the Texas singing cowboy contingent, there were several others who were significant contributors to the movement.

Bosque County's Foy Willing founded the Riders of the Purple Sage after successful careers in New York and Texas radio. The act formed in Hollywood, with members plucked from the Hollywood Barn Dance (which included two other Texans, Jimmie and Eddie Dean). The Riders rapidly became a popular act that recorded for such labels as Decca, Capitol, Columbia, and Majestic, with hit songs like "Ghost Riders in the Sky" and "Cool, Cool Water."

Bill Boyd and the Cowboy Ramblers, Cowboy Slim Rinehart, and Monte Hale were other Texans who combined singing ability and cowboy personas into film work, as was Tex Owens. It was Owens who wrote and sang "Cattle Call," a massive 1935 smash for Decca (and, later, for Eddie Arnold), and his sister, Texas Ruby, was one of the prominent members of the sorority of "singing cowgirls" which enjoyed significant popularity in a time before political correctness.

Louise Massey was perhaps the most famous of the cowgirls. Originally a member of the Musical Massey Family, Louise's popularity eventually resulted in a new billing for the group: Louise Massey and the Westerners. In addition to Louise's self-penned hit "My Adobe Hacienda," the group is credited with being among the first to jazz up traditional cowboy fashion and consciously exploit a "western" image.

There would come a time when the singing cowboy genre would meld with the more traditional country music bubbling in rural communities, and this mixing would result in "country and western." Goebel "The Texas Drifter" Reeves was the singer who probably played the biggest role in connecting the two musical forms. Born in Sherman to well-off parentage, Reeves nevertheless opted for the traveling hobo life. His songwriting combined the travelogue elements of the trail-riding cowboy with the hard times aspect of country music, and songs such as "The Cowboy's Prayer," "Hobo's Lullaby," and "Bright Sherman Valley" established him as a major songwriter. But it was "Big Rock Candy Mountain" that broke him nationally, and his subsequent appearances across the country opened ears to the possibilities of Reeves's new style.

Still in all, Reeves was most proud of the yodeling instructions he gave to a young, aspiring songwriter. His name was Jimmie Rodgers, and he would become the Father of Country Music.

☆ Two: Texas Shapes Early Country

OUNTRY (OR "HILLBILLY" OR "STRING BAND") MUSIC ORIGI-
nated in rural territories of the Deep South and up the East Coast, and
blended ethnic and newly minted American folk music with various developing societal and provincial considerations. Utilizing a core format of
banjo, guitar, fiddle, and vocals, and tossing whatever available supplemental instrumentation might exist into the mix, country music espoused the
conservative religious and familial doctrines indigenous to isolated rural
communities everywhere—in three chords or less.

Indeed, though the players were often dextrous to the point of virtuosity,
the song structures were simplistic and the subject matter rather limited.
There was generally no attempt to elevate the material to the level of the
musicianship (though such a process would evolve with Kinky Friedman
several decades later). Still, change was in the works, and it started when
pioneers moved west and took country music to Texas.

A substantial influence would come from Mexico, whose centuries-old,
accordion-flavored *conjunto* music made its way north of the border with
soldiers and workers from early in the days of the Texas Republic. German
and Eastern European communities also settled in Texas, and their traditional polkas and waltzes, while relying on similar structure and instrumentation to *conjunto*, yielded remarkably different results. The Texas territory
was also a lucrative area for newly freed slaves, whose relocation brought
country blues into the mix, and zydeco became prevalent in southeast Texas
when Louisiana Cajun settlements began to cross boundries.

All these musical forms would gradually intermingle with the migratory
hillbilly sounds to result in a radically altered country music, though the
process was continually evolving and is ongoing today.

Throughout this change, the "new Texans" established their communities
and, since high school football hadn't been invented yet, they took considerable local pride in their top fiddlers and guitar pickers. Competitions
cropped up between villages and, as a result, a transplanted Arkansan named
Alexander "Eck" Robertson, who learned fiddle while growing up in Amarillo, would become the first country recording artist.

In 1922, Robertson and his partner, Henry Gilliland, won a fiddling
contest at a Confederate Veterans reunion in Richmond. They decided to

try and capitalize on their success and headed to New York. Costumed as though for Halloween—Robertson in cowboy duds and Gilliland in the butternut brown of a Confederate soldier—they gained admittance at Victor Records and somehow persuaded the honchos therein to let them record. It came to pass, then, that on June 30 and July 1, Robertson and Gilliland cut the first six country tracks ever. One of them, Robertson's own "Sally Goodin," was actually released in April of 1923. When Robertson played the track, along with another tune from that first Victor session, "Arkansas Traveler," on Fort Worth station WBAP, he effectively became the inaugural recording artist to go on the radio to promote his own tunes—an admirable ploy which for some reason did not earn him the title "The Father of Payola."

By that time, WBAP had conceived the *Barn Dance* show, which ignited a flurry of country radio programming across the country. Several Texas string bands secured airplay and popularity, including the Solomon and Hughes Band, the Peacock Fiddle Band, the Shelton Brothers, the East Texas Serenaders, and Prince Albert Hunt—many of whom would host their own local and regional radio programs.

The first country megahit occurred in 1924 when Texan Vern Dalhart released "The Prisoner's Song," backed with "The Wreck of the Old '97." Intriguingly, Dalhart (born Marion Try Slaughter in Jefferson), had originally wanted to be an opera singer. Born of gentried-but-fallen stock, the young Mr. Slaughter worked as a cowboy on the trail between Vernon and Dalhart, thence coining his nom de plume, before entering the Dallas Conservatory of Music.

He then headed to New York and sang in churches and vaudevillian shows while auditioning for operas. He actually obtained roles in *Girl of the Golden West* and *H.M.S. Pinafore* but, when it became apparent that he was not going to be the world's next great tenor, Dalhart started recording for the Edison label. From 1916 through the early twenties, Dalhart freelanced for any label that would turn on a tape recorder while he happened to be in the room. He worked under dozens of pseudonyms (one biographer counted 110!) and in a variety of styles including pop songs, arias, and patriotic war tunes, but his first verifiable recording was the lamentable 1915 Edison release "Can't Yo' Heah Me Callin' Caroline," rendered in heavily stylized black vernacular.

So, while Dalhart had experience with southern musical styles, it was more a happy coincidence that he happened upon the "The Prisoner's Song" and "The Wreck of the Old '97." Frantic to ignite his lukewarm career, Dalhart took note of the growing popularity of hillbilly music and approached the executives at Victor Records and begged them to let him try a few of the country tunes he remembered from his youth.

Victor was as desperate for a hit as Dalhart, and despite the stigma of hillbilly music as moronic, eventually agreed, and the "Prisoner"/"Old '97" single sold millions of copies and made Dalhart a star. His 1927 rendition of "Home on the Range" further perpetrated the growing respectability of country music, and Dalhart, relying on the recurring disaster motif established by "The Wreck of the Old '97," recorded several like-minded follow-ups, including "The Death of Floyd Collins" and "The John T. Scopes Trial." He also liked "The Wreck of the Old '97" so much that it is estimated he rerecorded the song more than fifty times, in a variety of personas, over the years.

Though he sold over seventy-five million copies of his estimated five thousand releases, Dalhart's career was essentially over by 1933. He would occasionally record comeback attempts, most notably for the Bluebird label in 1939, but by the time of his death in 1948 he was working as a desk clerk in a hotel. Still, Dalhart's urbane tastes and considerable education gave the country music scene a certain legitimacy as it struggled through its infancy.

Any further necessary push came from Jimmie Rodgers, known at various times as "The Singing Brakeman," "The Father of Country Music," "The Mississippi Blue Yodeller" and "No, Not the Rodgers with Hammerstein." Rodgers's status as a Texan is largely a health-induced afterthought (mortally stricken with tuberculosis, he moved to the dry climate of central Texas a scant four years before he died), though his influence on the development of country music proper was such that it couldn't help but change things in his adopted state.

From Mississippi, of "railroad" stock, Rodgers actually was a brakeman until his ill health necessitated a lighter workload. He struggled with a variety of amateur and low-paying show-biz gigs, not the least of which was as a black-face minstrel in a traveling medicine show.

Then, settling in Asheville, North Carolina, in 1926, vocalist/banjoist Rodgers formed a hillbilly-styled band called the Jimmie Rodgers Entertainers (also featuring guitarist Jack Pierce, banjoist Claude Grant, and Jack Grant on mandolin and guitar). In a matter of weeks, the band achieved sufficient regional notoriety on radio to set out on a tour of the Southeast, with the eventual target being an audition for Victor Records' Ralph Peer at a portable studio he was setting up on the Virginia/Tennessee border.

For whatever reason, the Entertainers imploded, and Rodgers ended up auditioning solo. Peer liked what he heard, and Rodgers recorded for his first release "Soldier's Sweetheart," a sentimental ballad he'd written for a pal who'd died during World War I, and "Sleep, Baby Sleep." The latter featured Rodgers's distinctive and plaintive yodel—in itself an instrument equally capable of exuberant whimsy and profound and mournful loneliness.

The songs were released in October 1927, and Rodgers's first royalty check amounted to twenty-seven dollars; one assumes that his subsequent yodel on hearing that news was of the melancholic variety. Still, critical reaction was swift and enthusiastic, and shortly thereafter Victor brought Rodgers to New Jersey to record several more songs.

The first release from that session was "T for Texas" (retitled "Blue Yodel" by the record label), featuring an octave-jumping yodel. It became a million seller—and at last Rodgers had made it.

For the next six years, until his death, Rodgers was the prototypical superstar. He recorded 110 sides in all, including thirteen more of what became known as the "Blue Yodel" series. In 1929, Rodgers had another million-seller with "Brakeman's Blues," and starred in a short film, *The Singing Brakeman*, whence one of his nicknames came. Furthermore, Victor backed the singer with an interesting variety of musicians, from jazz to bluegrass to Hawaiian players.

Pursuant to the drier air which would ease his worsening tubercular condition, Rodgers moved to Kerrville, Texas, in 1929. He toured as much as his debilitating malady would allow (which wasn't much). He generally traveled the South headlining vaudeville-flavored tours, and in 1931 accompanied Will Rogers on a tour of northeast Texas to benefit flood victims.

In 1932, costly medical treatments necessitated that Rodgers relocate to San Antonio, where he appeared twice every week on KMAC radio. Finally, in the spring of 1933, incredibly ill, Rodgers summoned the courage to return to New York City for what he surely knew would be his last recording sessions.

Victor actually provided a cot in the studio, to which Rodgers would frequently retire while he summoned sufficient strength to try yet one more take. His last song, "Fifteen Years Ago Today," was completed on May 24 and, after a visit to Coney Island two days later, Rodgers fell into a coma and died.

Though one could characterize Rodgers's legacy in terms of courage, charity, yodeling, songwriting, or any of a number inspirational virtues, it is absolutely certain that he gave form and vision to a theretofore amorphous music now known as country and western.

It is perhaps ironic that the next key ingredient in C&W's evolution would be the repeal of Prohibition and the triumph of the honky-tonk. The time was ripe for a celebratory fusion of musical elements which would become western swing.

☆ Three: The Dawn of Western Swing

WESTERN SWING IS THE BLUE-RIBBON CHILI OF MUSIC, A SA-
vory, bubbling blend of numerous, ever-changing ingredients, and it
is unlikely that it could have developed anywhere else but Texas.

By the 1920s, though, all signs were right in the Lone Star State. Between
the new dance hall string bands; cowboy songs; German, Cajun, and Tex-
Mex accordion music; the blues (and its kicking-in-the-womb offspring,
rhythm and blues), Texas had several of the important components for
western swing already simmering.

Also essential to the recipe was a societal development *not* exclusive to
Texas: the miracle of jazz. It was an improvisational musical from which
gained early notoriety in New Orleans' Congo Square and which was popping up across the United States in a variety of substyles from Dixieland to
big band.

As such, several of these dance bands began supplementing their renditions of "Ol' Dan Tucker" with pop standards, Tex-Mex ballads, or black
music, and the amalgamation was proving irresistible.

And so, while it's difficult to say precisely which moment commemorates
the birth of western swing proper, it is a matter of record that in 1929, a
brash young barber named Bob Wills, late of Ham's Barber Shop in Turkey,
Texas, moved to Fort Worth and met Herman Arnspiger. It seems Wills
could play the fiddle a bit, and Arnspiger the guitar, and later that year,
when they formed the Wills Fiddle Band, the seeds for what would become
the Texas Playboys were planted in a particularly fertile patch of history—
and that which would shortly be known as western swing would have one
hell of a spokesman.

James Robert Wills was born on March 6, 1905, near Kosse, Texas, in
Limestone County. It is not true that he sprang from the womb fiddle and
flask in hand and stogie clenched in a devilish grin, but most other rumors
enmeshed in his substantial mythology are probably verifiable.

Under the tutelage of his fiddle-playing father, Wills became versatile on
fiddle and mandolin at an early age. He played in square-dance bands during
a wild youth, and before he was out of his teens, his passion for travel,
drink, and all forms of music was well established.

By his early twenties, he'd graduated from barber college, gotten married and relocated to Turkey, Texas. He regularly participated in a variety of hotly contested fiddle contests throughout West Texas, New Mexico, and Oklahoma—in which his toughest competition usually came from his father or Eck Robertson (noted earlier as the first actual country recording artist).

Still, Jim Rob was far too ambitious to spend his life and talent in fiddle contests or cutting the locals' hair in Ham's Barber Shop and, shortly before the stock market crash of '29, he abruptly headed to Fort Worth. He played briefly at WBAP and in a black-face medicine show, and since the latter already had a performer named Jim, Wills became "Bob." Arnspiger caught Wills's act at a medicine show performance, struck up a conversation, and the two decided to form a band. The Wills Fiddle Band, as the outfit was called, rapidly became a popular dance-hall draw, but they were quick to expand the parameters of the genre.

Wills's searing fiddle work and impish stage persona made the group instantly identifiable and, as a leader, he was a veritable musical librarian; the band was able to switch rhythms and styles with alacrity, and any dance music—be it "race," Dixieland, or pop—might easily find its way onto their song lists. There were instrumental innovations happening, as well.

But if Wills's role in the birth of western swing was important, his moniker, "King of Western Swing," is probably not an entirely just title.

In fact, Milton Brown may well deserve it more than Wills. It was Brown, a former cigar salesman who signed on as Wills's lead vocalist in 1930, who would be responsible for many of the innovations and defining characteristics of western swing; he was the first to coalesce the instrumentation and repertoire into a recognizable style; and too, under his guidance, improvisation would become a standout highlight of the music.

In fact, back when Brown first joined the Wills Fiddle Band, the group began to experiment with even wilder arrangements and an exploding stylistic repertoire. In August, WBAP hired them to do a show sponsored by the Aladin Lamp Company. In an interesting coincidence, the band changed its name to the Aladin Laddies and, between the radio exposure and regular gigs at a dance pavilion called Crystal Springs (frequented by, among others, noted dance enthusiasts cum murderers Bonnie and Clyde), their reputation mushroomed.

In a similar radio maneuver the next year, when they switched to rival station KFJZ to do a morning show for the Burrus Mill and Elevator Company (whose major product was Light Crust Flour), the Laddies became the Light Crust Doughboys. For the next eighteen months, under the guidance of W. Lee "Pappy" O'Daniel, the Burrus Mill general manager–turned–Light Crust Doughboys emcee and head wizard, the band's popularity expanded well beyond the listening area afforded by KFJZ. O'Daniel started the Texas Quality Network, which was a radio network that had outposts in Dallas, Houston, and San Antonio. As part of the TQN maneuver, O'Daniel shifted the Doughboys' airwave base to WBAP.

In early 1932, the Light Crust Doughboys recorded two songs for Victor, straight-ahead country dance tracks (save for Brown's Jazzy/bluesy vocal turns) called "Sunbonnet Sue" and "Nancy Jane," and for reasons probably related to Burrus Mill policy, the band was referred to on the rare sides as the Fort Worth Doughboys.

But a rift was developing between O'Daniel and Brown. For one thing, O'Daniel was beginning to foster political aspirations and started to utilize his emcee status to proselytize during the band's radio broadcasts. And though O'Daniel built a rehearsal and recording studio at Burrus Mill for the Doughboys, his decree that the band could no longer play the lucrative dance circuit caused Milton Brown to quit and put together a rival outfit, Milton Brown and His Musical Brownies, which was soon broadcasting over KTAT.

It was perhaps the biggest moment in the evolution of western swing. Within two months, Brown had added twin fiddles, tenor banjo, piano, and slap bass to his instrumental lineup. As a pop singer in a string band, which had never really happened before, Brown pointed the music in the direction of swing.

At the time Brown left the Doughboys, Wills wanted to quit as well, but was too intimidated. Instead, he settled on a youngster named Tommy Duncan as a replacement. But when O'Daniel fired Arnspiger and began to complain about Wills's affection for stout drink (which occasionally resulted in Wills showing up late for a gig or missing one altogether), the situation became intolerable.

Wills took his tenor banjoist brother, Johnnie Lee, vocalist Duncan, guitarist Arnspiger, and formed the Texas Playboys (the original lineup of which also included bassist/steel guitarist Kermit Whalin, and rhythm guitarist June Whalin). After short stints in Waco and Oklahoma City (necessitated largely by the popularity of Brown and the Musical Brownies in Fort Worth and Dallas), they settled in Tulsa and began broadcasting noontime shows over the fifty-thousand-watt KVOO which rapidly became required listening throughout Oklahoma.

Pursuant to his expansive musical curiosities, Wills added horn and reed players, and the band's ranks swelled to thirteen by 1935. They signed with Brunswick Records that year, added steel guitar innovator Leon McAuliffe, and over the next several years recorded prototypical and invaluable western swing, including Wills's own 1940 tune "San Antonio Rose," which became their signature song.

"San Antonio Rose" sold over a million copies, and the Texas Playboys soon found themselves superstars. They appeared in eight movies, toured relentlessly, and Wills's ebullient cries, "Ahhhh-ha!" or "Take it, Leon!" were ritual calls to fun throughout the Southwest.

Though the band broke up during World War II, they re-formed after the war and continued to work, albeit with numerous personnel changes. Wills suffered heart attacks in 1962 and 1964, and the latter drove him to break up the best damn fiddle band ever. In 1968, he was inducted into the Country Music Hall of Fame.

But in 1973, despite a series of strokes that had commenced in 1969, Wills reconvened the band one last time. The occasion was a United Artists recording session in Dallas for which Wills would oversee a Playboys memorial album. Unfortunately, Wills suffered yet another stroke during the sessions. Merle Haggard kindly stepped in to help complete the project, but it was Wills's final trip into the studio: In 1975, the original Texas Playboy, whose sage advice was that we "stay all night, stay a little longer," did that big two-step into the beyond.

And lest ye think the Light Crust Doughboys band was nothing more than a convenient musical trampoline from which Bob Wills and Milton Brown high-jumped into history, remember that the Doughsters are *still* performing.

It's true that, after first Brown and then Wills left (and took various members with them), Pappy O'Daniel was forced to frequently restock the depleted band, and on occasion did so with his own kids. But regardless of personnel, the Doughboys were a terrific band, utilizing jazz sophistication and incredible arrangements. Through their daily radio program, they became extremely popular, which was a bit of a catch-22 situation: Obligated as they were to appear on daily live radio broadcasts, their travel was limited to gigs from whence they could get back to the studio in time for broadcasts.

Eventually, O'Daniel went on to a career in politics, and the Burrus Mill sponsorship and radio program necessarily ended at the outbreak of World War II.

The Light Crust Doughboys have persevered, though, and a list of players who've worn the Doughboy colors is staggering, including Leon McAuliffe, Knocky Parker, Leon Huff, Smokey Montgomery, Hank Thompson, and Cecil Brower, the latter of whom was the first real western swing fiddle player (classically trained, he set the standard for everyone who came along afterward); the current lineup still includes tenor banjoist Montgomery.

Much of the band's recorded legacy (originally on Vocalion labels) has been rereleased in a variety of accessible packages, and the Doughboys still tour the United States and internationally to generations of fans.

It should be mentioned that several of the graduates of the Texas Playboys, the Musical Brownies, and the Light Crust Doughboys went on to careers of moderate success on their own or in pretzel configurations with other alumni. Johnny Gimble, Leon McAuliffe, Leon Huff, Johnnie Lee Wills, and Jesse Ashlock were just a few who kept the pulse of western swing pounding through the years.

And of the dozens of western swing bands that rapidly cropped up on the heels of the aforementioned Big Three, regional strongholds began to develop throughout Texas that lasted until well after the war years. In Fort Worth, besides Brown and the Doughboys, there were the High Flyers and O. C. Stockard's Wanderers.

CRIMINALLY OVERLOOKED ARTIST
Milton Brown

☆

A Stephenville native who was born in 1903, Brown's tutelage in the Wills Fiddle Band and with the Doughboys had served him well, but when he broke off and started the Brownies, he returned the favor in spades.

In addition to added instrumentation and the improvisational aspects of Brown's band, he constantly looked for ways to improve the sound. He'd spend hours in Fort Worth's Kemble Furniture and Record store, listening to discs of obscure blues and pop singers and jazz and southeastern string bands, fusing all of that input in some great melodic cauldron in his brain.

The original Musical Brownies lineup included brother Durwood Brown on guitar, fiddlers Jesse Ashlock and Cecil Brower, pianist Fred "Papa" Calhoun, and bassist Wanna Coffman. The band started to record for the Bluebird label in April of 1934, then switched to Decca in 1935. While Brown eschewed the horn sections later favored by Wills, the Brownies nevertheless embraced a wildly improvisational style and, with the addition of jazz guitarist Bob Dunn in 1935, became the first country-rooted act to utilize an electric guitar. (It's interesting to note that country guitarist Zeke Campbell was the first musician to record with an electric guitar—not jazz great Charlie Christian, as is so widely believed.)

The Brownies had several big-selling singles—both jazz and country—and became a huge draw at the Crystal Springs Dance Pavilion. Though the music was still called Texas fiddle music, by the Brownies' Crystal Springs era what they were playing was the prototypical form of western swing. Their popularity was enormous, and the band began traveling throughout Texas and into Oklahoma, performing a heavy schedule of fanatically attended dances wherever they played.

That they were the most popular band in Texas was not open to discussion, and Brown's place in history might well have exceeded that of his good friend and rival, Bob Wills—but in 1936, returning from a gig at the Crystal Springs Pavilion, Brown blew a tire and ran into a telegraph pole. The speedometer was found frozen at 93 mph, and Brown's passenger, a sixteen-year-old girl, was killed instantly. Brown survived the crash and was transported to a hospital, but died shortly thereafter. Though the Brownies stayed together, they never really overcame the tragedy, and when their recording contract was up in 1938, the group called it quits.

Though their recorded output was limited, the Texas Rose collection *With His Musical Brownies 1934* and MCA's *Pioneer Western Swing Band (1935–1936)* ably demonstrate the significance of Milton Brown.

In Dallas, Roy Newman, and Pinky Dawson and the Merry-Makers (featuring Ronnie Dawson's dad) were popular. In San Antonio the Tune Wranglers, Jim Revard, and Adolph Hofner and the Night Owls held court.

Houston and the Gulf Coast had a scene: the Bar X Cowboys, Blue Ridge Playboys, the Village Boys, and the Modern Mountaineers were big draws, as were Port Arthur/Beaumont's P.A. Jubileers.

In Waco and central Texas, acts like the Lone Star Playboys and Doug Bine's Dixielanders were favorites, and just south, in Austin, Jesse James and Dolores and the Blue Bonnet Boys headlined dance halls.

And of course, in West Texas, where it all more or less began, Amarillo's Sons of the West and Billy Briggs, and Pecos's Bob Skyle's Skyrockets all carried on the tradition.

But there were more than just local favorites, too. Singer/guitarist/songwriter Bill Boyd was a Fannin County native whose Cowboy Ramblers band recorded over three hundred songs for RCA during their enduring career. Boyd was born in 1910 and performed in Alexander's Daybreakers, a more traditional country outfit that ultimately transformed into the Cowboy Ramblers. Among the band's hit were "Spanish Fandango," "The New Spanish Two-Step," and "Lone Star Rag," and an early Cowboy Rambler was the astonishingly gifted fiddler Jesse Ashlock. Jim Boyd, the bandleader's brother, was himself a member of the Light Crust Doughboys.

Throughout the bulk of his career, Bill Boyd was a mainstay on Dallas's WRR, and he continued to record until 1950, at which time he retired and luxuriated in the miasma of his good works until his death in 1977.

Ex-Brownie Cliff Bruner led a terrific band, too, the Texas Wanderers. Building on a traditional country stock with wild doses of blues and jazz, the group (also booked as Cliff Bruner's Boys) is particularly famous for two hits, "It Makes No Difference Now" and "Truck Driver's Blues," which is particularly notable as giving birth to the "trucker song" phenomenon.

Still, it's hard to be angry with Bruner: The fiddle master, who started playing in his mid-teens with early swing pioneers Leo Raley and Cotton Thompson, remains a wizard of the genre. Further, his Wanderers included two particularly outstanding musicians, Aubrey "Moon" Mullican and Bob Dunn.

Mullican, whose talents at piano, guitar, and organ were employed in a variety of musical styles, might well fit in any chapter in this book. His musical education was in church and brothels, and he gravitated to swing as the music originated. After stints with Leon "Pappy" Selph's Blue Ridge Playboys and with Bruner, Mullican began to record solo material for the King label. He had moderate chart success—but his music was far closer to what would be rock 'n' roll than anything country. Over the years, his rollicking, masterly, overlapping piano musings resulted in a variety of country, boogie, and rockabilly recordings (for King and Decca) and earned a reputation as a true innovator.

Dunn, too, was a remarkable musician whose fame, though, never matched Mullican's.

And while the popularity of Western swing has ebbed and flowed over the years—and will probably never again reach its level of favor during the thirties and forties—each successive decade has sported at least one Texas band that carried the torch onward.

Undeniably, one of the most successful western swing band of the fifties and sixties, the group that bridged the originals with modern times, was Hank Thompson and the Brazos Valley Boys. Thompson was born in Waco in 1925, mastering first harmonica and then guitar. He gravitated to country music as a kid, hanging out at his neighbor's house and listening to her Vern Dalhart and Carter Family records.

In the early forties, he anchored a local radio show on WACO, which dubbed him with the fortunately short-lived moniker "Hank the Hired Hand." After a stint in the navy, he briefly attended Princeton, Southern Methodist University, and the University of Texas, then returned to central Texas to play music. He secured another radio gig, this time at KWTX, and gradually fleshed out his core C&W band, the Brazos Valley Boys, until he had a full-bore western swing outfit.

Thompson's first hits for Capitol were in 1948, when he released "Humpty Dumpty Heart" and "Today." These were only precursors in a career in which Thompson would have chart hits in five different decades.

His biggest song, a 1952 rendition of Carter/Warren's "The Wild Side of Life," stayed at number 1 for fifteen weeks—and Thompson had hit on what would be a recurrent motif throughout his Hall of Fame run: honkytonk songs. "On Tap, in the Can, or in the Bottle," "A Six Pack to Go," "Smokey the Bar," and "Hangover Tavern" were but a few of his paeans to alcohol, and despite his western swing style, the tunes helped popularize a predominant phase of all country music: the barroom lament and/or celebration. Life is Liquid seemed to be the message, and it's one which is completely ingrained in C&W tradition.

Beer-fueled or not, Thompson and his Brazos Valley Boys cruised the nation's highways, winning thirteen consecutive Best Western Swing Band awards and selling millions of records. After Thompson left Capitol for Dot in the mid-sixties, record sales leveled off. Still, Thompson and the Boys explored the world (and record labels, surfacing with an occasional hit on MCA, ABC, or Churchill), and he continues to carry that western swing banner today, even as we head toward the millennium and younger generations take up the tradition.

Although there were slow years in the western swing story, the early seventies musical renaissance that transformed Austin and, ultimately, the entire country-and-western community, would heighten public awareness of Milton Brown's love child. Merle Haggard's 1970 LP, *Tribute to the Best Damned Fiddle Player in the World*, started a new enthusiasm for the music and, ironically, it was Wills's final session—the 1973 Texas Playboys me-

CRIMINALLY NEGLECTED GUITARIST

Bob Dunn

While most guitar fans still drool over the likes of rock stars like Deep Purple's Ritchie Blackmore, few know that a western swing steel guitarist from the thirties and forties named Bob Dunn is one of the true magicians of guitar history.

Born in Fort Gibson, Oklahoma, in 1908, Dunn was raised by a breakdown fiddler father to love music. At an early age, Dunn became obsessed with Hawaiian music, got a steel guitar in his teens, and began to practice virtually around the clock. As the twenties were also the great Jazz Era, Dunn also began to incorporate the extemporized lines of horn heroes like Jack Teagarden to his crystal clear Hawaiian runs.

An itinerant musician, Dunn traveled throughout the twenties, playing in a variety of jazz and blues bands and in various vaudevillian shows, and in 1932 came through Fort Worth, where he was introduced to Milton Brown and His Musical Brownies. After a studio jam in which he astounded the musically amazing Brownies, Dunn came aboard. As one of the pioneers of amplified steel guitar, his rainbow-colored, hot jazz leads added much texture to a band that already set out new musical boundaries every time they played—and Dunn himself fell in love with Western swing music.

After Brown died, Dunn played awhile with Roy Newman (for whom he recorded on a number of excellent Vocalion sides), then hooked up with another ex-Brownie, Cliff Bruner, in his Musical Wanderers. When the Wanderers split into two factions, Dunn founded his own band, the Vagabonds, which recorded for Decca in the late thirties, then played in a number of bands and on countless sessions throughout the thirties and forties.

By 1950, tired of the grind, Dunn opened his own music store in Houston, which he ran for twenty years before he died of lung cancer in 1971. His legacy as a technical wizard is undeniable, and his musical ideas exploded like fireworks every time he sat down to play.

morial album—that supplemented Haggard's record in western swing and also revived the sagging careers of those former Playboys like McAuliffe, Smokey Dacus, Johnny Gimble, Leon Rausch, and Johnnie Lee Wills.

But it wasn't enough that Hank Thompson and a few of the old original guys were dusting off the still-viable form. Any ongoing art form needs an infusion of youth, and the dawning "progressive country" movement spontaneously generating in Austin would result in two youngsters enamored of the old music.

A terrific fiddler named Alvin Crow, who was born in Oklahoma and spent his youth in Amarillo, soaked up all manners of music indigenous to the West Texas lifestyle. He formed a dance-swing band called Alvin Crow and the Pleasant Valley Boys, which relocated to Austin in 1971 and became a major force in the new cosmic cowboy transformation taking place. While their recorded output is scarce and hard to find, their self-titled album on Long Neck Records is an out-of-print treasure.

The other western swing act that would invade Austin was Asleep at the Wheel. The brainchild of Philadelphia's Ray Benson, Asleep at the Wheel formed in Paw Paw, West Virginia, as a straight country band, then began to expand, both figuratively and literally, relocating to the San Francisco area in the late sixties. As Benson added members, the focus of the band basically embodied a hippie approach to traditional western swing.

None other than Willie Nelson saw the Wheel in the Bay Area and suggested they ought to check out Austin, and the band relocated to central Texas in the primordial early seventies. It was the perfect mating of ideology and fate, and the Wheel rolled into the mix effortlessly.

Though Benson has been the one constant in a band that has had about eighty different members (and almost as many different record deals), Asleep at the Wheel has been a consistently interesting band. Benson's vision admirably mixes the western swing tradition with newly developing musical components—in the exact spirit that enabled western swing to evolve in the first place.

It can probably be said that anyone who ever played for the Wheel was damned good or he/she wouldn't have been there, but some of the standout members have included Chris O'Connell, ex-Playboy Johnny Gimble, Leroy Preston, Lucky Oceans, and multi-instrumentalist Tim Alexander.

Finally, in refreshing combinations of the old guard and the new pups, a variety of western swing bands continue to perform at clubs and festivals throughout Texas. Leon Rausch plays with his own band, the Texas Panthers, and at various Texas Playboys reunions.

Former Brazos Valley Boy Tommy Morrell is the glue behind a loose amalgamation known as the Time Warp Tophands, which occasionally includes Rausch as well as former Asleep at the Wheel vocalist Chris O'Connell, and Houston's River Road Boys are still active.

O'Connell also has Ethyl 'N' Methyl, her own western swing duo with Maryann Price (formerly of Dan Hicks and his Hot Licks), as well as a swing-influenced jazz sextet, the Mood Swing Orchestra. Modern-day warriors like Don Walser and Wayne Hancock dabble in swing as well, and will be discussed in greater detail in a later chapter.

Perhaps the most interesting of the resurgent swing bands is the Dallas outfit Cowboys and Indians. An outfit of Gen-X-aged kooks of varying educational and musical backgrounds, Cowboys and Indians is absolutely *not* a novelty band. Under the guidance of Erik Swanson—an NBA-sized singer/guitarist/songwriter who is an avid student of traditional western swing and whose only regret in life is that he wasn't born in time to drink beer with Bob Wills and Milton Brown—Cowboys and Indians is the real thing, a brilliant throwback group that would've been stars sixty years ago and might yet today. Their one independent CD, 1995's *The Western Life*, available through Crystal Clear Records, is astonishing.

☆Four: The Honky-Tonk Tradition

B Y THE LATE FORTIES, COUNTRY MUSIC BEGAN TO FURTHER SUB-
divide. The genre's first big spin-off, western swing, was spinning itself
out, and a new form evolved to take its place. Called honky-tonk, this fresh
country style provided countless three-minute soundtracks to a beer-soaked
generation of hard-livin', hard-workin' folks of decidedly rural and conservative demeanor.

The repeal of Prohibition had spawned no end of friendly taverns in
which people, cautiously optimistic after first the Depression and then
World War II, had drained their collective spirit, could blow their pay-
checks with gleeful alacrity. And the competition between bars for the
drinking dollar resulted in *mucho* live music—in turn providing hundreds
of new gigs for bands. That the songs written by these artists during that
time quickly evolved to reflect the fighting, drinking, infidelity, and sundry
other good times going on was only natural.

Jacksonville's Al Dexter (a wisely considered pseudonym for someone
born Albert Poindexter), the leader of an early country band called the
Texas Troopers, cowrote with James B. Paris what was probably the first
country song to actually utilize the term "honky-tonk": 1937's "Honky-Tonk
Blues." A shrewd observer of barroom life, Dexter also penned the million-
selling "Pistol Packin' Mama," only one of several hits he wrote for the
Vocalion label in the forties, and incidentally one from which *Your Hit
Parade* censored the word "beer."

But if Dexter inadvertently gave name to a new movement, Floyd Tillman was its first champion. Tillman was the tumbleweed-voiced electric
guitarist who graduated from western swing stints with Adolph Hofner, the
Mark Clark Orchestra, and the Blue Ridge Playboys to add his considerable
innovations to honky-tonk.

Tillman, an Oklahoman who grew up in Post, Texas, was an effortlessly
competent writer of pure honky-tonk songs. His "Slippin' Around," "Each
Night at Nine," "I Love You So Much It Hurts," and "Gotta Have My Baby
Back" were all big sellers for labels like Decca and Columbia—and prime
fodder for a technological development that further fueled the popularity of
the honky-tonk sound: the jukebox.

A remarkable device that rapidly made its way into bars everywhere, the jukebox not only introduced new artists and songs to fans, it provided a primitive internet of music connecting fans across the country. So when truck drivers or traveling salesmen landed in new territories and hit a road-house, the first thing they'd do (after ordering an inaugural cold one, any-way) was check out the jukebox.

This in turn helped propel the expanding number of radio stations ex-ploring country-and-western formats. As such, Nashville, the mecca of country music, found in honky-tonk a genuine musical force, and with the fertile training ground that had developed in Texas, both jukeboxes and country radio stations sported great numbers of Texas honky-tonk artists.

Names like Lefty Frizzell, Ray Price, and Ernest Tubb were more than familiar, and many consider these Texas singers the essential triumvirate of honky-tonk. All three were philosophers who studied at the college of coun-try music, drank from the fountains of Jimmie Rodgers, western swing, and Hank Williams—and in that spirit developed their own inimitable styles.

Tubb perhaps best embodies the honky-tonk ethic. While his voice lacked the range and operatic quality associated with Price or Jim Reeves, his heart, conviction, and instantly identifiable baritone were unquestion-ably genuine—and, subsequently, the songs he wrote and sang communi-cated directly to working-class people. Tubb frequently said that clarity of thought and individual style were the two most important things for a song-writer to have, and he had both in abundance.

A devotee of Jimmie Rodgers, Tubb was born in 1914 in Crisp, Texas, and, though he didn't start playing until his late teens, by 1934 he was singing on San Antonio's KONO.

The following year Tubb met Rodgers's widow, who not only gave the young singer her late husband's favorite guitar, but also pulled the strings that resulted in his first record company audition, a session with RCA in October of 1934. Perhaps in gratitude, and maybe just because Rodgers was such an inspiration, the two songs Tubb opted to tape at that initial session were "The Passing of Jimmie Rodgers" and "Jimmie Rodgers' Last Thoughts."

But he wasn't an overnight success. Over the next few years, he played countless bars, appeared on any radio station that would let him sing, and worked a variety of nonmusic sales gigs. In 1938, after the death of an infant son, Tubb was driven to write a memorial song called "Jimmy Dale." The tune was later described by Willie Nelson as one of the saddest songs ever recorded, and was probably the turning point at which Tubb really began to develop his own style.

He scored a recording contract with Decca, a new radio show on Fort Worth's KGKO, and one of those kooky mill sponsorships which seem inextricably connected with the coltish years of country music. Universal Mills was the outfit, and as the makers of Gold Chain Flour, they knighted Tubb as the Gold Chain Troubadour, from whence E. T.'s enduring "Texas Troubadour" nickname would shortly evolve.

In 1940, he released his first Decca side, "Blue Eyed Elaine," and began working the bigger taverns and clubs in, uh, earnest. In 1942, one of his own compositions, "Walking the Floor Over You," sold millions of copies and led Tubb to a 1943 membership in the Grand Ole Opry. That year, he also became the first country artist to appear at Carnegie Hall.

Tubb's booming voice was utterly distinctive, and with a work ethic that had him and his Texas Troubadors band on the road three hundred nights a year, it was no wonder that his star quality is of the enduring kind. He appeared in several films and placed tunes on the charts in robotic fashion ("Let's Say Goodbye Like We Said Hello," "Drivin' Nails in My Coffin," "Tomorrow Never Comes," "Mr. and Mrs. Used-to-Be," and "I Love You Because" were just a few of his hits).

Tubb worked tirelessly for almost five decades, was a 1965 inductee into the Country Music Hall of Fame, and carved a legacy which should be de rigueur study for C&W fans everywhere. Said study would require of the novitiate only one or two listens to E. T. to instill an automatic reaction. If the listener has any soul at all, he/she will immediately crave the smoky setting of a dark bar, a smooth, characterless draft beer, and the urge to shatter any Garth Brooks CDs within reach.

Though Tubb passed away in 1984, his name has become synonymous with honky-tonk, and latter-day country guitar hero Junior Brown captures the Texas Troubador's essence in one of his best tunes, "My Baby Don't Dance to Nothin' but Ernest Tubb."

A former Golden Gloves boxer from Corsicana named William Orville "Call Me Lefty" Frizzell was another whose contributions to honky-tonk are staggering. After shrewdly calculating the benefits of music as opposed to pugilism, Frizzell hung up the gloves and was playing in bars by the time he was seventeen.

Frizzell had an emotional tenor voice that could whine wonderfully, adding a seriously overwrought quality to his dance tunes and barroom ballads alike. By 1950, he'd signed with Columbia and hit it big with his rendition of "If You've Got the Money, I've Got the Time" and "I Love You a Thousand Ways." The songs stayed on the charts for weeks, and Frizzell subsequently ingrained himself with honky-tonk audiences by landing four singles in the top ten simultaneously, a record that will probably never be broken. (In the early eighties, Michael Jackson was called "the Lefty Frizzell of Modern R&B"—or maybe not.)

Frizzell also found a home at the Grand Ole Opry, a situation that never hurt record sales and, throughout the fifties, sixties, and into the seventies (when he switched to ABC Records), he continued to record hits like "Saginaw, Michigan," "Watermelon Time in Georgia," "Long Black Veil," "She's Gone, Gone, Gone" and "Falling," the latter a 1975 song that debuted on the charts only two weeks before Frizzell succumbed to a stroke.

His voice was an acknowledged inspiration to a hall of fame fan club of artists, including Merle Haggard, George Jones, John Anderson, Dwight Yoakam, and Willie Nelson, and Frizzell will therefore remain as timeless as the music he helped create.

The third of the original Texas honky-tonk stars was Ray Price, whose smooth, powerful voice was an interesting vehicle with which to belt out the late-night booze anthems he recorded in the first part of his career.

Price was born in Perryville in 1926, graduated from high school in Dallas, and had planned on becoming a veterinarian until music seduced him. Whatever animal science may have lost, though, was more than ably compensated when "The Cherokee Cowboy," as Price came to be called, unleashed his beautiful croon in dozens of popular jukebox standards.

After he made a regional name for himself in the late forties on Abilene's KRBC and performing on Dallas's Big D Jamboree, Price moved to Nashville and was signed to record for Bullet Records. The association didn't work particularly well, though, and it wasn't until he went to the Columbia label in 1951 that his status as a honky-tonk hero began to form.

At the time, two of Price's running buddies were Lefty Frizzell and Hank Williams, and when Price recorded a song by the former and assembled a band populated by ex-players with the latter, all elements for stardom were definitely in place.

He joined the Grand Ole Opry, and by the end of 1952 had recorded his first two hit singles, "Don't Let the Stars Get in Your Eyes" and "Talk to Your Heart." But it was only after Williams died on New Year's Day, 1953, that Price emerged from his mentor's significant shadow and became a pure honky-tonk voice. Starting in 1954 and continuing for about twenty years, country radio was aflame with Ray Price. His band, the Cherokee Cowboys, became a prep school for future country stars, with no less than Willie Nelson, Johnny Paycheck, and Roger Miller all doing time therein.

But it wasn't just his band or his world-class voice, either. Price's selection of material—poetic but minimum-wager beer joint songs that touched the core emotions of men and women alike—solidified his role as the premier honky-tonk singer of his time, and his status as an arranger and innovator were also of major importance. He crossed walking 4/4 bass lines with steady, cornpone applications of fiddle and steel guitar, then utilized the mixture behind classic honky-tonk fare like "Crazy Arms" and "Please Release Me."

The innately danceable style became so standard within the industry that it was known as "the Ray Price beat," and subsequently fueled a never-ending stream of hits like "I've Got a New Heartache," "City Lights," "Soft Rain," "Make the World Go Away," "Touch My Heart," and "The Other Woman"—songs that provided the musical score to an entire generation of nightclub fanatics. Price recorded tunes for every conceivable drinking joint soap opera, and it wasn't unusual for couples to have danced to Price at their high school proms, during their courting years, at their wedding, and throughout the long slide toward divorce—at which time they'd cue up Price hits like "Burning Memories" or "For the Good Times," and weep copious tears into their beer bottles.

The latter song, incidentally, was probably the one that cemented Price's gradual segue from pure honky-tonk singer to more of a country pop stylist. He'd released a wonderful, string-heavy arrangement of "Danny Boy" in 1967—a version that ranks with fellow Texan Don Walser's as two of the finest ever recorded—and though some of his old-line fans bitterly accused him of selling out, it's a fact that Price's voice, intelligence, and range were such that some form of artistic experimentation was inevitable.

From the early seventies, then, Price pretty much abandoned the cowboy image and trod the stage in a tux or black suit, peppering his set lists with as many pop standards as country hits. He has also hopscotched record labels over the succeeding years, and though his once-mammoth sales figures have dropped dramatically, an occasional hit slips through the cracks to remind us what a remarkable talent he is. Of particular note is 1980's duet album with his old pal Willie Nelson, San Antonio Rose, and Price is reportedly writing an autobiography that will surely be of interest to any fan of country music, honky-tonk or otherwise.

Yet another country great who was born with an acutely bizarre name and was forced to resort to a nickname in order to become famous was Alvis Edgar Owens, Jr., whom the world knows as "Buck."

Buck Owens was born in Sherman, Texas in 1929, and shortly thereafter his family headed west to California in a Steinbeckian attempt to offset the ravages of the Depression. They only made it as far as Arizona, and it wasn't until 1951, after Owens had established himself as a terrific guitar and mandolin player, that he made it to Bakersfield, California. It was there he would sire "The Bakersfield Sound," a West Coast strain of raw honky-tonk that was pure in twang and steeped in tradition.

Owens started as a top-notch session musician, and only fell into the role of a singer by default, in a club band situation. It was a development that obviously clicked. In 1957, he was signed by Capitol, and over the next few years, with his band the Buckaroos, he scored several top five hits. In 1963, "Act Naturally" became the first of over twenty songs by Owens that went to number one, others of which included "Love's Gonna Live Here Again," "Tiger by the Tail," and "Waitin' in the Welfare Line." Owens also charted over the years with a series of duets, first with Rose Maddox in the early sixties and, later, with Susan Raye. Too, Owens is familiar from his years on the long-running television series Hee Haw, which he hosted with Roy Clark.

By the mid-eighties, though, Owens had effectively retired, and it wasn't until a new generation of hardcore youngsters—chiefly Dwight Yoakam— who were nurtured on Owens's nasally, whining, and totally wonderful songs, came of age, that Owens came out of retirement. In 1988, he and

Yoakam had a hit with Owens's "Streets of Bakersfield," cementing the Bakersfield Dude's spot in the 100-proof hall of legends' liquor cabinet.

A contemporary of all these artists who lent a gentle, somewhat dignified air to the alcohol-triggered pure country of the honky-tonk movement was Jim Reeves. Born in Galloway, Texas, in 1923, Reeves parlayed an early interest in Jimmie Rodgers and an eminently listenable voice into a solid career as a country pop singer, underlining the point that not every country musician who performed in the fifties and sixties followed the honky-tonk hard line.

Which is not to say Reeves didn't have a bit of raw C&W bubbling in his veins. After all, he made his first radio broadcast over a Shreveport, Louisiana station at the tender age of nine. Oddly, had it not been for a freak ankle injury, it's possible Reeves would've been a major league baseball player; the St. Louis Cardinals actually signed him out of the University of Texas.

Post-injury, Reeves worked as a radio announcer, and one night in Shreveport in 1952, working on the *Louisiana Hayride* program, he had to fill in when Hank Williams was a no-show. In the audience was the owner of Abbott Records, who gave Reeves a record deal on the strength of his substitute performance.

Though his first two songs, "Mexican Joe" and "Bimbo," went to number 1 in 1953, and it was clear Reeves's clear baritone had a winsome quality, it was also obvious that his vocals were too mellifluous to grind out honky-tonk, so he was among the first to take Nashville in a more sophisticated pop direction.

In 1955, Reeves joined the Grand Ole Opry, signed with RCA, and the hits began to roll in assembly-line fashion. He charted over forty top ten hits, including "He'll Have to Go," "Welcome to My World," "I Love You Because," and "Angels Don't Lie."

He toured South Africa, where he remains a huge-selling artist, and Britain, and Reeves's momentum seemed unstoppable. In July of 1964, though, Reeves perished in an airline crash—but even death couldn't halt his success. He had six songs released posthumously that went to number 1, several top ten hits in the seventies, and even "Take Me in Your Arms and Hold Me," an all-corpse duet with Patsy Cline crafted through the wonders of technology, went top ten in 1981.

While some complain that Reeves's mellow stylings cheapened the essence of country music, his work actually served to pry a crowbar into the rigid jaws of Nashville structure—and if that development would in turn be abused by those with less talent and vision, it shouldn't reflect on Gentleman Jim Reeves, whose talent, conviction, and character remain above reproach.

Following rapidly on the two-steppin' heels of Frizzell, Reeves, Price, Owens, and Tubb was a second wave of honky-tonkers, including two visionaries whose efforts to live up to the lifestyle nearly eclipsed their work: Willie Nelson and George Jones.

Jones was born in 1931 in the Big Thicket community of Saratoga, Texas, and it's not true that he was a no-show at his own birth. That propensity came later.

An interest in music was present from the start. His mother played piano and his dad the guitar, and after dropping out of school in his teens, Jones learned guitar and secured an afternoon radio gig on Beaumont's KTXJ. Still, he had no career plans involving music. There were other options, including house painting, baseball, and the military—all of which Jones tried—but his hobby of singing part-time in nightclubs began to grow on him.

He also possessed remarkable range and a singularly plaintive way of twisting a phrase, and the young singer caught the ear of Pappy Dailey, the enterprising owner of Houston's burgeoning Starday label. In early 1953, Starday issued Jones's first single, "There Ain't No Money in This Deal," and his encore effort, 1955's "Why Baby Why," actually landed on the charts.

Jones cut several subsequent country and rockabilly sides with Starday before moving to Mercury in 1957, and within two years had gone to number 1 with a song written by fellow Texan J. R. "The Big Bopper" Richardson: "White Lightning." Jones's career bottle-rocketed.

A staggering succession of hits followed and, similarly, so did a succession of liquor bottles and wives that kept Jones, well, staggering. Borrowing from the thespian strategy called method acting, Jones (by that point known as the Ol' Possum) seemed determined to lend autobiographical authenticity to all of his songs—and since they were invariably about women, bars, jukeboxes, and hangovers, his personal well-being declined even as his legend grew.

Songs like "Window Up Above," "She Thinks I Still Care," "If My Heart Had Windows," "The Race Is On," and "Walk Through This World with Me" were instant classics, and when you turned on the radio and heard that voice, you could smell whiskey cooking in his brain and feel the pain emanate from the speakers.

Jones married Tammy Wynette in 1967, and the royal couple of country music cranked out more hits, even as Jones lost all control. Despite the fame and adulation, Jones was having record label problems (he'd left Mercury and reupped with Dailey again, this time with the latter's Musicor label), booze problems, and behavior problems. His penchant for showing up hours late at concerts—if he showed at all—gave the Ol' Possum a new nickname, No-Show Jones, and within the industry he was viewed as a Hank Williams waiting to happen.

Miraculously, though his and Wynette's marriage didn't survive, Jones did. At some point in the eighties, not wishing to have a film of his life made called *Leaving Las Vegas*, Jones wised (and sobered) up.

He continued to release albums—solo and in a generation-hopping series of duets—and remains a productive and living warrior on behalf of contemporary and traditional honky-tonk music. Oh yeah—and if he'd never done another thing, his 1980 single "He Stopped Loving Her Today" is flat out the greatest country song of all time.

Through the nineties, Jones railed with justification that mainstream country radio was shutting him and other older artists out. That CDs like his were pretty damned good and got zero airplay is sturdy evidence. Jones hangs on—musically and otherwise—despite a near-fatal solo auto accident in which he ran into a bridge pylon (and in which a less-than-full vodka bottle was found in the car), and recent albums like *Cold Hard Truth* and *I Lived to Tell It All* kick the hell out of most Nashville product today.

Another survivor is Willie Nelson: the quintessential country music outlaw, a pony-tailed bard who conquered both Nashville and Austin and re-created them both in his own wickedly grinning image. And though Nelson is most often associated with Austin's progressive country/redneck rock movement, his status as a melodic chronicler of barroom dramas was well established long before then.

He was born in Abbott, Texas, in 1933, and essentially raised by his grandparents after his parents split up. Grandpa had the sense to show young Willie a few chords on the guitar, and the youngster took to country music at once. He was playing in his sister's band at thirteen, and in a supremely revealing gesture, helped her husband book Bob Wills into a beer lodge at nearby Lake Whitney.

Despite the auspicious beginnings, Nelson had to wait until he finished high school and served in the air force before his musical career took wobbly flight.

He also worked as a disc jockey for several Fort Worth radio stations, then hit the road, landing a deejay shift in Vancouver. There, at twenty-four, Nelson recorded his first single, a self-written, self-produced, self-promoted effort called "No Place for Me," backed with "The Lumberjack," penned by old pal Leon Payne.

But when stardom didn't come calling, it was back to the Texas workaday world, where he hustled vacuum cleaners and encyclopedias. Throughout, Nelson continued to write songs. In Houston, he played bars at night, pulled a Sunday morning radio shift, and released two more singles for Pappy Dailey's Starday Records.

Then he began to sell a few of the dozens of songs he wrote, albeit for a mere pittance. "Family Bible," for example, he sold for fifty dollars, and "Night Life" for one hundred and fifty. Though both became huge hits and Nelson's name wasn't on either tune, he was at least emboldened by the knowledge that he could write hits—and the door began to open.

Nelson scored a bass-playing gig for Ray Price (despite the fact that he couldn't play bass), and Price recorded and had a hit with "Night Life."

Then Faron Young released "Hello Walls," and Patsy Cline recorded "Crazy" and "Funny How Time Slips Away."

Then Nelson himself cut "The Party's Over," and his reputation as a singer began to equal his status as a songwriter. Still, his voice and appearance were slightly off for Nashville. And though the songs were hits, there was something *different* about them, too. There was a lot of blues in Nelson's material, along with a popster's sense of haunting melody, and Nashville didn't quite know what to do with him.

Irritated and never the sort to wait around until he could calculate how he might fit in, Nelson said to hell with it and headed back to Texas. Austin was a mellow town with a laid-back vibe, and Nelson figured he could pick a little guitar and smoke a little herb and figure out what the hell to do. And when he relocated and decided to throw a celebratory Fourth of July picnic in Dripping Springs, Texas, in 1973, Nelson had effectively ended the era of honky-tonk and was about to give a facelift to the C&W community at large.

But honky-tonk had had a grand run. And plenty of Texans contributed over the years besides the aformentioned giants. Roger Miller, Charlie Pride, and Red Stegall were all significant players in the genre as well.

Miller, born in Fort Worth in 1936, followed stints as a ranch hand and army jeep driver in Korea by landing in Nashville. There he did the old play-my-songs-for-anyone-who'll-listen routine, also working as a bellhop and playing fiddle for Minnie Pearl and drums for Faron Young. By the late fifties, though, he had written well over a hundred songs for the likes of George Jones and Ernest Tubb.

And when Ray Price scored a huge 1958 hit with Miller's "Invitation to the Blues," the songwriter's own career took off. In 1960, he signed with RCA, and recorded hits like "Two Worlds Collide." Three years later, his annoyingly infectious "Dang Me" went to number 1 (and to number 7 on the pop charts) and established the blueprint for future Miller hits: quasi-humorous, endearingly goofy songs with effortlessly catchy melodies. "Chug-A-Lug," "Do Wacka Do," "You Can't Rollerskate in a Buffalo Herd," "Kansas City Star," and "Engine, Engine No. 9" were just a few Miller songs that blasted onto the charts with regularity in the mid-sixties.

But "King of the Road," from 1965, was his watermark. By then a superstar, Miller began to diversify not only his artistic aims but his business interests. He started a hotel chain, wrote a musical called *Big River* (based on the writings of Mark Twain), and hosted a television show—all the while continuing to record two decades worth of semi-hits for labels like Mercury, Columbia, Elektra, and MCA. Miller died of lung cancer in 1992.

Charley Pride, aka the Jackie Robinson of C&W, would deserve inclusion here even if he weren't great (though he is). If any institutional color line could be said to be more brutal than another, that of country music—long a bastion of bigotry, redneck intolerance, and southern cracker ignorance—would certainly qualify.

Oddly enough, the Mississippi-born Pride, who has long resided in Dallas, would happily have followed Jackie Robinson into the major leagues. But though he bounced around the minors for several years, before and after military service, Pride eventually sang a song on a Montana radio program hosted by Red Sovine and Red Foley. The two stars were sufficiently impressed by Pride's voice to arrange for him an audition with Chet Atkins's RCA outfit.

Atkins signed the young singer, and his first single, "Snakes Crawl at Night," came out in 1965. The tune was released without cover photos or any accompanying publicity that might indicate to radio programmers that Pride was a—gasp—"Negro." In support of the song, Pride joined a tour package headlined by Willie Nelson, and when the Redheaded Stranger pulled Pride onstage at Dallas's Longhorn Ballroom and kissed him on the lips, Pride's entry into the lily-white world of country music was, symbolically, at least, assured.

A dynamic entertainer with a smooth baritone delivery, Pride has subsequently charted thirty-six number 1 hits (including "Just Between You and Me," "It's Gonna Take a Little Bit Longer," "Is Anybody Goin' to San Antone?", "Kiss an Angel Good Morning," and "Honky Tonk Blues"), won several CMA awards, and been inducted into the Grand Ole Opry. Like Price and Reeves before him, Pride's honky-tonk sound grew progressively "poppier" over the years, but he remains RCA's most successful country seller since Elvis Presley.

Many other Texans experienced country music fame during the honky-tonk era—just not to the extent of the aforementioned Big Guys.

Goldie Hill, born near Karnes City in South Texas in 1933, had a major hit with "Don't Let the Stars Get in Your Eyes." The song went top five for Decca in 1953, and Hill shortly thereafter joined the Grand Ole Opry. She toured with and eventually married Carl Smith, and had another hit with 1959's "Yankee Go Home."

But after marrying Smith, she seemed more interested in their horse ranch than belting out booze tunes and, aside from sporadic forays into the studio, one of which produced 1969's "Loveable Fool," Hill faded from C&W notoriety.

Similar to both Arthur and Hill was Texas Ruby, a hard-drinking, chain-smoking, effortlessly profane honky-tonk belter—in other words: great fun. Born Ruby Owens in North Texas in 1908, Texas Ruby, as she came to be called, had early on a love of country music and a foghorn baritone which scored her work in her mid-teens.

She gained national recognition at the Grand Ole Opry, singing with Zeke Clements and His Bronco Busters, and on radio programs, but it wasn't until after the war, when she signed with Columbia, that Ruby hit the big time. She wrote a lot of her own material—fine tunes about brawling and cheating and drinking—such as "Ain't You Sorry That You Lied," "Blue Love in My Heart," and "Soldier's Return."

Charline Arthur

☆

Though Patsy Cline and Wanda Jackson are the most renowned examples of women who can sing honky-tonk, neither was from Texas. But that they were influenced by an East Texan named Charline Arthur is undeniable. Arthur was a prototypical honky-tonk singer whose belligerent attitude was a blueprint for future country outlaws, and whose libidinous stage moves were replicated by a young Mississippi singer with whom she occasionally shared the stage: Elvis Presley.

She was born in 1929, in a boxcar, the second of twelve children born to a Pentecostal preacher. (Her given name was Charline Highsmith.) Her mother played guitar and, when Charline expressed an interest in Ernest Tubb, Mom got her a cheap plastic guitar and Charline taught herself all the Texas Troubador's material.

At fifteen, she left home to travel in a medicine show, and by 1949, the newly married Arthur (her husband was Jack Arthur) was singing in bars. She eventually became a radio deejay, singing on her own program, and got the attention of Colonel Tom Parker, who managed to get her signed to RCA Records.

Unfortunately, Arthur was such a behavioral migraine that her recording relationship with the label's Chet Atkins, for whom she recorded several excellent but overlooked sides in the fifties, was never pleasant. Still, her talent was undeniable. The first woman singer to wear pantsuits onstage, and utilizing a stage act that was totally wild, Arthur was a true commodity. Songs like "I'm Having a Party All By Myself," "Burn That Candle," and "Leave My Man Alone" established her persona as a hard-drinkin,' party-enthused bad girl, and had it not been for her stubborn attitude toward Mr. Atkins, she might well have been a huge star.

As it is, she slowly drifted back into obscurity, and Arthur spent the remainder of her life singing in hardcore booze halls. Today, tragically, her work can only be found on an obscure collection, Welcome to the Club, on Germany's Bear Family label, but her vocal influence on Cline and Jackson, and her stage moves impact on Elvis Presley are undeniable. She passed away in 1987.

After two LPs, she and Fox moved to Houston and starred on popular radio shows throughout the fifties before Ruby settled into semi-retirement. In 1963, she perished in a house fire.

Johnny Bush, a Houston native born in 1935, is a former drummer for both Nelson and Price who finally came out from behind the kit to front his own band. Though he once shrewdly advised Nelson that he ought to give up trying to sing, Bush nevertheless recorded one of Willie's tunes, "You Ought to Hear Me Cry," for Stop Records in 1967. After subsequent successes with "Undo the Right" (1968) and "You Gave Me a Mountain" (1969), Bush signed with RCA and the next year had a monster smash with another Nelson song, "Whiskey River."

Oddly, given his joking admonishments about Nelson's singing, the big-voiced Bush then experienced serious voice problems. Fortunately, he's recovered. In recent years he's recorded a western swing album (which was originally available on IRS) and is currently finishing an LP of traditional honky-tonk at Nelson's Pedernales studios, and negotiations are under way with a new label to release both records.

David Frizzell, younger brother of His Leftyness, is another honky-tonker of note. Born in Arkansas in 1941, Frizzell grew up in Texas, toured with Big Bro's band throughout his teens, and had his own recording contract by the time he was eighteen.

Though he released several albums for a variety of labels, it wasn't until he teamed up with Shelly West that David hit it big. The two recorded "You're the Reason God Made Oklahoma" as part of Clint Eastwood's soundtrack for *Any Which Way You Can* for Warner/Viva Records in 1981. They scored several more duet hits before Frizzell experienced solo success with a series of early-eighties tunes very much in the honky-tonk tradition: "I'm Gonna Hire a Wino to Decorate Our Home" and "A Million Light Beers Ago" being prime examples. In the meantime, he and West continue to record sporadic duet successes, including 1985's "Another Dawn Breaking over Georgia."

Jeannie C. Riley, born in Anson, Texas, in 1945, will forever be remembered in the great scrapbook of country music for her 1968 hit, "Harper Valley P.T.A."

She moved to Nashville directly out of high school with a music career her sole aim. She managed to release one single for the less-than-famous Little Darlin' Records, getting a chance to record a tune Tom T. Hall had written about a wild-livin', miniskirt-wearin' single mom in a small town, showing up the community's stodgy hypocrites for what they were. The tune, of course, was "Harper Valley P.T.A.," and it shot to the top of the C&W charts, crossed over and went number 1 on the pop charts, sold millions of records, and earned Riley a Grammy award as well as country music's Single of the Year.

The Biz absolutely made certain that she live up to the song's image—both in subsequent material and in performance—but the truth was that Riley was not at all like her new persona. After some rough years and less than healthy attempts to cope, Riley turned to gospel music. She's since recorded both spiritual and secular records (for such labels as MCA/Dot and her own God's Country), and while the mad stardom of her early hits is over, she continues to make music which is, at least, true to her own beliefs.

Perhaps one of the most overlooked of the latter-day honky-tonk warblers is Moe Bandy. A Mississippi-born singer who grew up in San Antonio, Bandy scored a recording contract with Satin Records while only nineteen. He had his first hit in 1974 for GRC, "I Just Started Hating Cheatin' Songs Today." After several more chartsters, Bandy moved to CBS for 1975's "Hank Williams, You Wrote My Life," then quietly logged more than thirty-five top ten singles, notably two duets with Joe Stampley, "Just Good Ol' Boys" and "You Always Leave Me Holdin' the Bag" (the latter of which, despite currying little favor with feminist groups, was a hysterical novelty song).

It was perhaps that aspect, furthered by hit singles "Bandy the Rodeo Clown," "Where's the Dress" (again with Stampley), and "Tell Ole I Ain't Here, He Better Get On Home," which eventually took a toll on the singer's reputation. The public began to view him in a silly, monodimensional fash-ion—which was in fact not accurate. Thus a superb 1989 album, *Many Mansions*, which concerned a variety of noncomic topics such as homeless-ness, didn't attract the attention it deserved.

Radio abandoned him, and though his theater at Branson, Missouri is one of the more popular in that strange town, it seems somehow inappro-priate that Bandy—one of the finest honky-tonk singers ever—shouldn't be more visible to country audiences.

Boxcar Willie, born Lecil Travis Martin in Sterratt, Texas, in 1931, is a bizarre veteran of the honky-tonk era. With his singing hobo shtick and mega-star popularity in places like Scotland, the Box Man has eschewed the traditional Nashville process, selling millions of albums through late-night TV commercials. Why not?

Finally, Fort Worth's Gary Morris is a product of the honky-tonk era whose music transcended a variety of country styles. He spent most of his formative musical years in Denver, became a favorite of Presidents Carter and Bush, and eventually scored a record deal with Warner Brothers. He charted several singles with his distinctive amalgam of pure country and folk/pop melodies, including, in the eighties, three consecutive number 1 hits: "I'll Never Stop Loving You," "100% Chance of Rain," "Makin' Up for Lost Time (the Dallas Lovers' Song)."

At the same time, Morris nurtured an acting career on both stage and screen, and he continues to work in all varieties of show business.

☆ Five: Progressive Country and the Austin Spirit

BACK WHEN WILLIE NELSON WAS TRYING TO MAKE IT AS A country singer—he was already earning a six-figure annual income as a songwriter—he released an album for Liberty (now out on United Artists) called *Country Willie Nelson*. On the cover, clad in faded overalls and a plain white T-shirt, Nelson grins goofily at the camera, looking, perhaps, like a casting call-back for the role of some corn-dusted goofus on *Hee Haw* (a part that would in fact be filled with eerie resemblance by Junior Samples).

The essence of the cover was to type Nelson as a farm-raised good ol' boy, the sort embraced by Nashville and the Grand Ole Opry in the Minnie Pearl mold. The strategy was typical of the Nashville mafia that ran country-and-western music, a disturbing and ruthless operation which nevertheless sought to mold its artists in images that today would be wrought by Tipper Gore.

The problem though, was that Nelson didn't give a rat's ass about the old-line Nashville establishment. And, though the overalls *were* Nelson's, and efforts to fit in on his part indicated an early desperation to "make it" which has been paralleled by countless artists, Nelson and Nashville were ultimately not meant for each other.

It took years for the big split to happen—during which time Willie would struggle with toeing the line—but as his status as a performer grew, so did his penchant for rebellion. An affection for marijuana and certain aesthetics borne of the sixties upheaval in rock 'n' roll were twisting Willie's concepts of art and lifestyle, and few of these character and musical evolutions fit in with the Nashville view of how things should be.

But ultimately, it wasn't so much that Nelson and his renegade pal, Waylon Jennings, were rocking the boat. It was that they couldn't handle the way the actual business of country music was being run by the likes of RCA head and Nashville icon Chet Atkins (for whom Nelson and Jennings recorded). So, at last, Nelson sidestepped Nashville and went to New York and signed with Atlantic Records—becoming the first country artist ever signed by the label.

The resultant album, *Shotgun Willie* (1972), was a radically different record, bursting with kooky energy and exploding in numerous directions, none of which sounded remotely like the glossy product Nashville was famous for cranking out. Nelson's own humorous title track fit in perfectly with cover tunes like Bob Wills's "Stay All Night" and Johnny Bush's "Whiskey River," and the whole package was refreshingly different.

It was followed almost immediately by a concept album, *Phases and Stages*, a wonderfully structured record detailing a painful divorce from the perspective of both husband and wife.

These records were like a creative rebirth for Nelson, and since his Nashville home had burned down shortly before he jumped labels, the time seemed right to move back to Texas. He chose Austin, the laid-back state capital nestled in the hill country, home to the University of Texas and center of the fruitful Texas music scene.

Austin in the early seventies was mellow to the third power, a curious amalgamation of students, hippies, ne'er-do-wells, and politicos—characteristics that might frequently be found in the same individual—and if any one location was the symbolic headquarters for the Austin attitude, it was an old national guard armory turned live music cavern called the Armadillo World Headquarters.

The club opened in 1970 under the guidance of manager Eddie Wilson, house artist and general maintenance dude Jim Franklin, and a vague organization of hippie pals, and its booking policy reflected the beatific philosophy of its management (which viewed the Armadillo as less a business venture than a giant playpen for stoners). Blues, rock, country, *conjunto*, folk bands, and musicians of every description played there, and the amazing and utopian result was that all manners of formerly antagonistic subsets— bikers, hippies, rednecks, acid heads—found themselves dancing, drinking, getting high, and laughing together.

It was the ultimate coexistence, lacking only a musical figurehead. Earlier that year, Nelson had headed up an outdoor show at Dripping Springs called the Dripping Springs Reunion, which was a financial disaster, but an eclectic lineup including Loretta Lynn, Tex Ritter, Kris Kristofferson, Waylon Jennings, Billy Joe Shaver, and Leon Russell had created an energy and vibe that seemed to flow promisingly enough. So when Willie played his first show at the Armadillo on August 12, 1972 (with the quintessential Willie Nelson band: his sister Bobbie on piano, bassist Bee Spears, guitarists Jody Payne and Grady Martin, percussionist Billy English, harmonica wizard Mickey Raphael, and drummer Paul English), the spirit of the Dripping Springs seemed to have found a home and, thereafter, the phenomenon known as progressive country, redneck rock, and/or the cosmic cowboy movement began to percolate.

The following year, Nelson staged the first of several annual Fourth of

July picnics, again at Dripping Springs (the locations would vary over time). In a little more than a year, the lycanthropic mutation of country and rock had become readily apparent on the streets of Austin. The sight of a long-hair wearing a cowboy hat and fine-tuning his Lone Star beer–induced buzz with a joint was not only accepted, it was an image to aspire to. Attendance by said folk at Nelson's picnics would become mandatory, and the event was for years a Dionysian rite of summer that typified the new Austin mentality and its Live Free and Party philosophy.

Of course, by that first picnic, Nelson himself bore no resemblance to the cover of *Country Willie* from years before, and his braided pigtails became as much a symbol of outlaw country music as his effervescent smile and his tattered Martin guitar.

Inasmuch as Atlantic had folded its country department shortly after *Phases and Stages*, Nelson signed with Columbia, and it was at that point that he began to record a string of brilliant albums that typified the entire era. Another concept record, 1975's *Red-Headed Stranger*, a story about the Old West featuring the huge-selling "Blue Eyes Crying in the Rain," was clearly the album that established Nelson as a bona fide country superstar.

The next year, he teamed with several of his Austin and Nashville pals— Waylon Jennings, Jessie Colter, and Tompall Glaser—to release *Wanted: The Outlaws*, which boasted the Nelson/Jennings duets "Good-Hearted Woman" and "Mamas Don't Let Your Babies Grow Up to Be Cowboys." The album went platinum, Nelson and Jennings would win a Country Music Award for Best Duet, and the resultant Outlaws tour blew the doors open for progressive country to "go national."

Being the figurehead of the entire movement was a full-time job, but Nelson managed to handle his duties with grace and admirable goodwill. Throughout the rest of the seventies, Nelson toured constantly, the annual picnics were certifiable big times, and his records were often adventurous and of undisputed quality. He and Jennings recorded *Waylon and Willie* in 1978, an effortless million-seller, and anyone in the contiguous United States who hadn't been aware of the duo's outlaw personas before certainly was by now.

Nelson could do no wrong—a situation strengthened by the consistent high quality of his work and the unerring brilliance of his business decisions. He released two tribute albums, 1977's *To Lefty from Willie* and 1979's *Sings Kris Kristofferson*, and encored with a collection of Nelson's ten favorite songs, *Stardust*. The idea of the latter album was reportedly frowned on by CBS, a situation that bothered Nelson not at all. Including the title song and standards like "Moonlight in Vermont," "Someone to Watch Over Me," "Georgia on My Mind," and "Blue Skies," *Stardust* was stupendously successful, selling over three million copies, and once again demonstrated Nelson's instinctive superiority over the C&W big shots.

In 1979, as the progressive country movement began to burn itself out and the Armadillo World Headquarters eased into its last year of existence,

Nelson made his film debut alongside Robert Redford and Jane Fonda in
the critically received *Electric Horseman*. Nelson had become bigger than
the movement he created, and the only possible solution was to keep moving, artistically and figuratively. He continued to maintain a base of operations in Austin, but he also secured a ranch in Colorado, a golf course and
a recording studio on the Pedernales, and continued to dip his fingers into
dozens of lucrative pies.

Though he would encounter tax troubles in the eighties, even the wily
IRS couldn't thwart the indomitable Nelson, who finally reached a settle-
ment with the agency, and his creative legacy would continue to sparkle.
Numerous recording projects have shone in the nineties—none more so
than the brilliantly dignified *Teatro*, which came out in 1988 and more than
proved the songwriter is still a force to be reckoned with.

THE NAME THAT KEPT POPPING UP WITH NELSON'S DURING THE
entire progressive country heyday was, of course, Waylon Jennings. Born in
the West Texas community of Littlefield in 1937, Jennings was a disc jockey
by the time he was twelve and an accomplished guitarist by his late teens.
He moved to Lubbock in 1958 to do another deejay gig, and made the
acquaintance of Buddy Holly during one of the station's *Sunday Afternoon
Dance Party* programs. Shortly thereafter, Jennings signed on as a Cricket,
playing bass guitar, and Holly actually produced Jennings's first recording,
a take on the Cajun classic "Jole Blon."

It was also Jennings who gave up his seat to J. P. "The Big Bopper"
Richardson on the ill-fated flight that killed Holly and all aboard in February 1959. Thereafter Jennings shakily relocated to Arizona and switched
allegiance from rock 'n' roll to country.

Blessed with a distinctive and powerful baritone voice which could astonish in its ability to render ballads tenderly or belt out hardcore C&W with
an abrasive tequila-and-cactus-needles quality, Jennings formed a backing
group, The Waylors, grew a Mephistophelean beard, threw out every item
of clothing in his wardrobe that wasn't black, and in the course of a few
years acquired quite a reputation as heading up a stone-serious country band.
Chet Atkins signed Jennings to his RCA label and brought him to Nashville
to record—whereupon Jennings ran into the same attitudinal problems Nelson had encountered. Though a number of releases did respectably enough
throughout the balance of the sixties, including two hit singles, "Walk On
Out of My Mind" (number 5) and "Only Daddy That'll Walk the Line"
(number 2, both 1968), Jennings grew tired of Nashville's cookie-cutter
mentality of record making and simply circumvented the bullshit by heading
to New York to negotiate his own deal with the label honchos.

In the face of Jennings's reputation for pill ingestion and his stubborn
and increasingly adamant insistence that he record with his own band (another Nashville taboo), the Old Guard finally threw up their hands and

allowed the black-clad rebel to record his own way. The result was 1973's *Honky Tonk Heroes*, which was, intentionally or otherwise, a spiritual companion piece to Nelson's *Shotgun Willie* and *Phases and Stages* albums.

On *Honky Tonk Heroes*, Jennings utilized the songwriting talents of another Austin songwriter, Billy Joe Shaver, and the focus of the tunes shifted from traditional country fodder to introspective and lonely themes. The connections to the whole progressive country scene were too significant to ignore, and when Nelson talked Jennings into playing at the Armadillo, their status as the dual personifications of outlaw chic was set.

There followed the aforementioned *Wanted: The Outlaws* album, after which Jennings became the closest thing to a rock star working the C&W market. His string of hit singles during that period was astounding, and included "Bob Wills Is Still the King," "Are You Sure Hank Done It This Way?" (both 1974), "Suspicious Minds" (1976), "Luckenbach, Texas (Back to the Basics of Love)," and "Wurlitzer Prize" (both 1977)—all the while interspersing CMA awards, gold, platinum, and number 1 albums (*I've Always Been Crazy*, *Mamas Don't Let Your Babies Grow Up to Be Cowboys*), and duets and tours with Willie and like-minded mutineers.

At last, though, the "outlaw" tag grew to such outlandish proportions as to embarrass Jennings, at least partially. In 1978, he recorded "Don't You Think This Outlaw Bit's Done Gone Out of Hand," proving that he had a self-effacing sense of humor as well as a propensity for writing the longest song titles on earth (until a British angst-infected pop star named Morrissey would come along in the eighties, anyway).

Still, even with the C&W rebel concept on the wane, Jennings would close the decade as a reliable hit machine, churning out two number 1 songs before the end of the decade with "Amanda" and "Come with Me."

Despite the fact that Jennings's official base of operations had always remained in Nashville, and while he would eventually change lifestyles and settle in the sedentary C&W Social Security haven of Branson, Missouri, Jennings's membership in and contributions to the redneck rock movement are significant and undeniable. Of late, Jennings has been particularly inspired, and his recent CDs *Backtracks* and *Closing in on the Fire* are of competitive quality.

IF NELSON AND JENNINGS WERE THE KING AND JACK IN THE face cards of progressive country, then surely Jerry Jeff Walker was the joker. A transplanted songwriter born in Oneonta, New York, in 1942, Walker (given name: Paul Crosby) spent his itinerant young adulthood as a quasi-folk songwriter, marinating his liver and brain cells in towns across the United States. He played for a brief time in a rock band called Circus Maximus, which recorded an album for Vanguard, but shortly thereafter he decided he wanted to travel the country as a solo songwriter.

It was the same sort of education that seasoned Jack Kerouac's muse, and when Walker wrote a song in the late sixties called "Mr. Bojangles," a wonderful and haunting song about a street dancer he met in the Orleans Parish jail that perfectly captured the innate dignity and humanity found even in society's bottom-feeders, Walker's reputation as a songwriter began to match his legacy as a bacchanalian performer. His material began to take on country characteristics, particularly in his sympathies for drunken losers with starry eyes, and if his voice sounded like it had arthritis—a diametric opposite of the smooth tenors of C&W stars like Ray Price or Jim Reeves— it was instantly identifiable and had a certain dipsomaniacal charm.

Walker had settled in central Texas in the mid-sixties, after hitchhiking through Houston and Dallas and hating them. The Austin music scene and the laid-back nonchalance of hill country communities like Fredericksburg, Wimberley, and Kerrville were particularly appealing.

Walker released *Driftin' Way of Life* for Vanguard in 1969 (an evocatively composed set of autobiographical tunes) and, after the Nitty Gritty Dirt Band had a top ten hit with "Mr. Bojangles" in 1970, Walker was signed to MCA. He recorded *Jerry Jeff Walker* in 1972, a slap-dash record relying heavily on the material of West Texas song wizard Guy Clark and a group of studio musicians comprised largely of Michael Murphy's band.

Clark's "L.A. Freeway" was an instant classic, a perfect three-minute tune that captured the essence of the Beautiful Oaf, a fun-time loser always one step ahead of the bill collector and repo man. Along with Walker's "Hill Country Rain," the album was unlike anything recorded by mainstream C&W, a detour from the expected journey-through-life gig bought into by most of young America, and it seemed to emphasize the concept that a beer-drenched holding pattern and a porch hammock weren't bad things.

All the while, Walker was endearing himself to nightclub crowds around Austin with the backing group he'd purloined from Murphy, which would come to be called the Lost Gonzo Band (Gary P. Nunn, Bob Livingston, John Inmon, Kelly Dunn, and Donny Dolan).

In 1973, Walker, preferring the loose and liquid environs of the club experience to the sterility of recording studios, persuaded the label to let him record in the friendly confines of Hondo Crouch's bar in Luckenbach.

The resultant album, *Viva Terlingua*, boasted another Clark classic, "Desperados," and a tune by Dallasite Ray Wylie Hubbard called "Up Against the Wall Redneck Mother," and the LP so perfectly captured the essence of Walker's lifestyle and philosophies—the envy of every young Austinite of legal drinking age—that its status as an indispensable record remains today.

Still, much like the whole Austin scene in the seventies, Walker was about maintaining an easygoing and decidedly nonambitious status quo. He continued his erratic performance schedule—terrific when he was sober, clownlike and occasionally pathetic when he was drunk—and recorded a yearly series of mostly dog-paddling records over the next few years: *Walker's Collectibles* (1974), *Ridin' High* (1975), *It's a Good Night for Singing* (1976),

A Man Must Carry On (1977), *Contrary to Ordinary* (1978), and *Too Old to Change* (1979).

The records continued to sell moderately well to Walker's hardcore following, and he was able to work his persona on sporadic tours throughout the United States into the early eighties. Ultimately, Austin's liquid minstrel is doing as well as ever by virtue of two shrewd nods to the future. Walker sobered up and through a craftily managed Web site and a never-ending supply of new and old product, sells a lot of stuff.

BY 1974, ALL OF AUSTIN WAS IMMERSED IN THE PROGRESSIVE country concept. One radio station, KOKE-FM, was created simply as a soundtrack to the progressive country experience, and along with the Armadillo, clubs like Castle Creek, the Pub, the Cricket, the Texas Opry House, the Split Rail, the El Paso Cattle Company, and the Broken Spoke became live-music hangouts catering to the music. And if it could be said that Nelson, Jennings, and Walker would ultimately comprise the scene's attitudinal holy trinity (and even that is arguable given Jennings's infrequent appearances in Austin), there were several significant artists who certainly qualified as cardinals.

And to belabor the religious analogy, one of the more spiritual of the Austin songwriters was Michael Martin Murphey, who utilized in his tunes the recurring theme that Austin is heaven on earth. Born in Dallas, Murphey at one point studied to be a Baptist minister before opting to write tunes. He plied his trade for Screen Gems in Los Angeles, in Colorado mining towns, and in the record company service in Nashville before he finally brought his family back to Texas in time for the progressive country upheaval. In fact, the title of his second album, *Cosmic Cowboy Souvenir*, lent a phrase to one of many pseudonyms for the music of the time, whose practitioners were called cosmic cowboys.

Murphey was something of a hero by the time he moved to Austin; his tunes had already been recorded by the likes of Flatt and Scruggs, the Monkees, Kenny Rogers, and the Nitty Gritty Dirt Band. Too, he bore no small resemblance to *Jeremiah Johnson*–era Robert Redford, sang in a plaintive voice that might crack in the higher registers (but in doing so gave his work a certain earnestness), and his songs combined a hippie spirituality with clever lyrics and pleasant and simple melodies.

His 1972 A&M release, *Geronimo's Cadillac*, worked the honky-tonk country field with a definite left-leaning awareness of environmental and Native American concerns, and 1973's *Cosmic Cowboy* was in itself a paean to the nirvanic qualities of Austin and the hill country.

He switched labels in 1974 to Epic, for whom he recorded *Michael Murphey*, and moved back to Colorado. In 1975 he released *Blue Sky, Night Thunder*, which cemented Murphey's movement away from what had already become "traditional" progressive country. Murphey segued into a smoother, more orchestrated sound typified in the monster number 1 hit "Wildfire," a stirring ballad about a girl and a horse—a musical salad made up of the sentimentality of Bobby Goldsboro's "Honey," the sad pet concept of Ol' Yeller, and the piano theme from The Exorcist.

Murphey has since relocated to Santa Fe, New Mexico, has released several more albums including 1987's terrific River of Time and a series of CDs and books of cowboy and Old West–motifed songs and has had huge hits like 1982's "What's Forever For." He also heads up Michael Martin Murphey's WestFest, one of the nation's finest country music festivals, every year in Vail, Colorado.

ON THE OPPOSITE SIDE OF THE RELIGIOUS COIN WAS KINKY Friedman, a decidedly sacrilegious Jewish songwriter who was a graduate of the University of Texas and particularly popular with a collegiate audience possessed of a certain black humor about the world in general.

With his band, the Texas Jewboys, Friedman danced around the periphery of the Austin scene, preferring instead to hang out in New York and Nashville. He recorded for the Vanguard label, for whom he released Sold American in 1971, and while the music was marginally accomplished country, it served as nothing more than structural background for his twisted, hilarious, and often brilliant lyrics—most of which seemed to be contrived to offend people.

Friedman moved to ABC for 1974's Kinky Friedman, and then to Epic for 1976's Lasso from El Paso, but nothing really changed. "They Aren't Makin' Jews Like Jesus Anymore," "Get Your Biscuits in the Oven and Your Buns in the Bed," "The Ballad of Charles Whitman"—all were calculated to get horrified reactions out of people. But for all of Friedman's sarcasm, he had a following. There was something about his hoarse, Dylanesque voice and leering Groucho mannerisms that were completely different from the longhaired cowboys competing against him in record stores.

In the end, it was the sublime idiocy of the songs that captured a theretofore neglected slice of the progressive country pie: the segment that had stopped taking themselves too seriously. Though Friedman has essentially retired from music to write a series of amusing, quasi-autobiographical mystery novels, a 1992 greatest hits CD, Old Testaments and New Revelations (Fruit of the Tune Music) is an excellent collection for the curious.

And inasmuch as artists like Nelson, Jennings, Gary P. Nunn, and Guy Clark had already said everything there was to say about progressive country's lyrical mother lodes (heartbreak, drinking, and loneliness), Friedman had the shrewd wisdom to seek the uncharted territories of redneck rock's outhouse. After all, surely no one will ever top Friedman's "Old Ben Lucas," the greatest country song ever written about snot.

* * *

ANOTHER SUBSET OF PROGRESSIVE COUNTRY LUMINARIES WAS
the one comprised of the guys who *wrote* a lot of the most famous redneck
rock tunes for folks like Waylon and Willie and Jerry Jeff, and occasionally
experienced a hit or two themselves—but for one reason or another never
became top o' the charts stars.

If he'd never done another thing during his time in our solar system, Ray
Wylie Hubbard would forever be famous as the guy who was cursed to write
the anthem of the progressive country movement: "Up Against the Wall
Redneck Mother."

Hubbard rightly considers it a curse because it doesn't matter how many
inspired tunes he might write (and he's written plenty), or if somehow he
discovers the cure for AIDS—people will always screech for "Redneck
Mother."

In fact, the song was a throwaway tune written before the progressive
country movement ever got rolling, based on a true-life exierence in which
the longhaired Hubbard tried to buy some beer from a transplanted Okie
woman running a store in Red River, New Mexico. She questioned Hubbard's hippie appearance and patriotism (bolstered by the guardian presence
of her silent, crew-cut, and absolutely Frankensteinian son), and the songwriter returned from the encounter with a song in his heart and a case of
beer under his arm.

At first, Hubbard interspersed the song during performances only when
musicians were changing broken strings or vomiting, and it was during
one such occasion that Jerry Jeff Walker heard the tune and witnessed
the subsequent riot it caused—and insisted immediately on recording the
piece.

In spite of the welcome royalty checks wrested from the tune, it still
hangs like a decaying albatross around Hubbard's neck, particularly in light
of the sluggish pace of his own career. True, back at the dawn of the Armadillo World Headquarters, Hubbard and his country-punk Cowboy Twin-
kies were quite popular, with Hubbard riding the crest of a wave of alcohol
and touring the country with Willie Nelson.

They released a self-titled album in 1975 for Reprise with a fine single,
"Bordertown Girl," and followed that with an album for Nelson's Lone Star
Records, 1978's *Off the Wall*. When that label folded, Hubbard put out
1979's *Something About the Night* on Renegade, and though the LP featured
what actually may be his best tune, "Texas Is a State of Mind," album sales
weren't exactly overpowering.

Hubbard battled gamely throughout the eighties, but when alcohol began
to win the day, he had to pull back and sober up. He emerged in the early
nineties freshly clean and newly inspired, and released two marvelous independent albums, 1993's independent *Lost Train of Thought* and 1994's
Loco Gringo's Lament (both now available on DejaDisc). Hubbard continued
to work and write steadily, and his material continues to improve. The
commitment paid off: Hubbard signed with Rounder/Philo in 1997 and

CRIMINALLY UNDERRATED ARTIST
Lloyd Maines

There is almost no aspect of Texas country music that hasn't been profoundly influenced by Lubbock pedal steel guitarist/producer Lloyd Maines. Long a twangist of note on the pedal steel, Maines got started in the production end of the business in 1978 by twisting the knobs on Terry Allen's immortal *Lubbock (On Everything)* and has since produced more albums than could probably be calculated by Alfred North Whitehead (if he were still alive).

He started out playing with his three brothers in a band appropriately called the Maines Brothers, who released several albums between 1978 and 1991—and all along toured with the likes of Joe Ely and Robert Earl Keen, did scores of session gigs (with artists from the Dixie Chicks, David Byrne, and Bruce Robison to Wilco, Uncle Tupelo, and Radney Foster), and honed his considerable production skills. (Keen, Richard Buckner, Ray Wylie Hubbard, Charlie Robison, Jerry Jeff Walker, and Chris Wall are just a representative few.)

As a pedal steel stylist, Maines is smooth, mournful, and witty—displaying just the instincts that would make, well, an excellent producer. As hundreds of artists can attest to: he's all hands and ears and taste.

issued two superb CDs for the label: *Dangerous Spirits* and *Crusades of the Restless Knights*.

Billy Joe Shaver, born in Corsicana and raised in Waco, is a songwriter whose acumen utilized the poet-as-drinker motif and has written for a staggering collection of artists: Elvis Presley, Jerry Lee Lewis, the Allman Brothers, John Anderson, Bobby Bare, Johnny Cash, Tom T. Hall, and Kris Kristofferson among them. And of course, every song except one on Waylon's legendary *Honky Tonk Heroes* was written by Shaver.

He was perfect for the progressive country image, including a colorful series of nonmusical background jobs in a sawmill (where he lost a finger-and-a-half), as a farm worker, in the navy, and as a used car salesman. But he wrote songs as well, and eventually tried Nashville, where he slowly earned a reputation as a terrific writer. Songs like "Black Rose," a tune about an interracial marriage, or the lushly evocative "Georgia on a Fast Train," were so much more literate and intriguing than the usual Nashville pap that Shaver should have been a star.

Finally, as the progressive country movement took hold, Shaver signed with Monument Records and, in 1973, released the Kristofferson-produced *Old Five and Dimers Like Me*. He jumped to Capricorn for *When I Get My*

Wings (1976) and *Gypsy Boy* (1977), then moved to Columbia for several more albums during the eighties. But although his LPs always received critical hurrahs, none sold particularly well, and his forte has remained songwriting. He was signed to Zoo/Praxis in 1993, for whom he released *Tramp on Your Street* later that year, then followed with a gritty, high-energy look back at his earlier work on *Unshaven*, which was the debut of a country power trio called Shaver that includes his son Eddy on lead guitar. Two scorching CDs, the live *Shaver* and a New West release, *Electric Shaver*, and an acoustic gospel record called *Victory* are well worth owning.

Kris Kristofferson is another brilliant writer whose career hasn't been helped particularly by his decidedly nonangelic voice. Born in Brownsville in 1937, Kristofferson is probably the only important country songwriter to have been a janitor *after* he was a Rhodes scholar. A frustrated novelist who also did time in the army, the oil fields, and flying helicopters, Kristofferson went the requisite Nashville songwriter route—a pursuit he was about to abandon when Roger Miller recorded his song "Me and Bobby McGee."

At once, Kristofferson was an in-demand guy, and wrote particularly literate hangover and loneliness tunes like "Sunday Morning Coming Down" (a hit for Johnny Cash) and "Help Me Make It Through the Night" (big for Sammi Smith). Still, though he hung out with the likes of Nelson and Jennings, and his aura and material fairly reeked of Austin, Kristofferson was never particularly visible on the progressive country scene.

In any case, his albums were cool, particularly 1970's *Kristofferson*, 1971's *The Silver-Tongued Devil and I*, and 1972's *Jesus Was a Capricorn* (all Monument). But when Kristofferson's frog-with-a-four-pack-a-day habit voice kept him from becoming a radio star, he simply channeled his good looks and Mensa brain toward Hollywood and became an actor. He also married country singing star Rita Coolidge, and though their separate and combined careers have ebbed and flowed, anyone with Kristofferson's stark and emotive songwriting ability will never go hungry.

Steve Fromholz will never be called taciturn. A self-described "up and coming, middle-aged stand-up folksinger specializing in free-form, country/folk/rock, science fiction, gospel-cum-bluegrass opera Cowjazz music," Fromholz is the same guy who defines the difference between a folksinger and a savings bond: after forty, a savings bond matures and starts earning money.

Similarly entertaining are Fromholz's songs. He was born in Temple in 1945, met and played with Michael Martin Murphey while the two were students at North Texas State University, and formed a short-lived duo with Dan McCrimmon called Frummox. They released one album in 1969, *From Here to There* (Probe/ABC), which featured Fromholz's immortal "Texas Trilogy," a three-song mini-opera comprised of "Daybreak," "Trainride," and "Bosque Country Romance," and which has remained Fromholz's signature piece.

After a stint in Stephen Stills's band and an unreleased solo album for

Michael Nesmith's Countryside label, Fromholz moved to Austin in time to become a huge part of the redneck rock agenda. He signed with Capitol and cut *A Rumour in My Own Time* (1976), generally regarded as a classic of progressive country. Two follow-ups, 1978's *Frolicking in the Myth* and 1979's *Jus' Playin' Along* (the latter on Willie Nelson's Lone Star label), fared poorly, and Fromholz began a post–cosmic cowboy career wherein he plays golf, writes plays, acts a bit, and goes whitewater rafting whenever possible.

He still pursues music whenever it occurs to him, and in 1995 recorded *The Old Fart in the Mirror,* a mixture of Fromholz classics and new songs in the same whimsically weary vein revered by his small but rabid coterie of fans.

Rusty Wier, whose Brett Maverick hat, copper beard, and demon's smile were just part of his irrepressible stage presence, came to the Austin progressive country scene through a circuitous series of rock bands. Originally a drummer, Wier, who grew up in Manchaca and went to college at Southwest Texas State, played in two of Austin's seminal sixties rock bands, The Wig and the Lavender Hill Express.

When rock didn't pan out, though, Wier opted to become a folksinger. To his own surprise, by the early seventies, he was enormously popular, on his own and with pals John Inmon and Layton DePenning in the trio Rusty, Layton and John. Building on an enormously likable stage persona, Wier continued to draw crowds even as the progressive country built up around him. Eventually, he formed a band and went to Nashville a time or two on near-miss excursions.

Oh well; back home, his boyish enthusiasm and consummate bar band polish continued to work. By then, the scene was bubbling: Michael Martin Murphey had brought his act to town, Willie was in charge, B. W. Stevenson was recording for RCA, Jerry Jeff could do no wrong artistically, and Steve Fromholz had "Texas Trilogy." Every night was like a musical slumber party, and the consensus was that, for Wier, success was inevitable.

Sure enough, ABC-Dunhill came calling. Wier took Inmon and DePenning to L.A. and with a variety of session guys recorded *Stoned, Slow, Rugged,* a magical album of country/folk with heavy rock overtones. Bolstered by a Murphey tune, "Five O'Clock in the Texas Morning," the album sold strongly across the country.

Wier jumped to 20th Century for 1975's *Don't It Make You Wanna Dance?*, featuring the hit title song and Weir's personal Austin anthem, "I Heard You Been Layin' My Old Lady." Another label switch ensued, and Weir recorded *Stacked Deck* for Columbia in 1977. It was at that point that the scene began to stagnate, and Wier's contributions became less frequent. Still, he tours with semiregularity, and everywhere he goes they call out for two songs: "Don't It Make You Wanna Dance?" and "I Heard You Been Layin' My Old Lady." Most old folksingers would tell you that that ain't a bad legacy.

The most enigmatic of the redneck rock brigade was bear-sized B. W. "Buckwheat" Stevenson. Frequently clad in overalls and a hillbilly hat, with his pale cherub's features obscured by a werewolf beard, Stevenson sang in a floating tenor voice at once melancholy and sweet, which was particularly incongruous with his hulking presence. And, though he was a frequent performer and collaborator in Austin circles, he actually lived in Dallas.

He was a graduate of Adamson, the same Oak Cliff high school that brought us Michael Martin Murphey and Ray Wylie Hubbard, and after aborted stints at NTSU and in the air force, Stevenson cut his teeth singing folk in Dallas clubs like the Rubaiyat.

A captivating writer from early on, his forte was balladry and soaring melodic sagas of lost and unrequited love. He released an album for RCA in 1972 that contained several terrific Buckwheat originals, including the heartbreaking "On My Own." With typical logic, though, the record company selected "Say What I Feel," an uptempo Murphey tongue-twister, as the first single, and it stiffed.

RCA employed a similar strategy on 1974's *Lead Free*, from which an obscure tune called "Shambala" was chosen as the single. Though it actually dented the *Billboard* charts, Three Dog Night, the biggest-selling rock act in the world (and a band that relied heavily on cover material) needed yet another hit. Upon seeing that "Shambala" actually had legs, the Dogsters rushed out *their* version—which quickly long-jumped past poor Stevenson, who in turn went to Texas to mire in his new obscurity.

But RCA was just taking care of biz, and they still had plans for Stevenson. They kept him away from the degenerate influences of Austin, insulating him in saccharine environs like Hollywood and Nashville, and cranked out product. The next album boasted a hit in the title song, "Maria," which Stevenson at least cowrote, and the damned thing actually went top ten.

There followed 1977's *Calabasas*, which RCA also had big plans for, but somehow they short-circuited. Ever unsure of what exactly he was supposed to be, Stevenson moved to MCA for 1980's *Lifeline*, which was in fact what he would soon need. Stricken with cancer, his health declined rapidly and he passed away shortly thereafter.

If Stevenson was enigmatic and tragic, Willis Alan Ramsey was eccentric and mysterious. A pleasant, handsome recluse, Ramsey was born in Alabama and moved to Austin where he wrote two classic songs, "Northeast Texas Women" and "Muskrat Love." The former is a textbook Austin in the Seventies composition, and the latter is lamentably associated with the treatment given it by the Captain and Tenille (though, face it, it *is* a song about rodents).

Ramsey released one obscure but brilliant record, *Willis Alan Ramsey*, for Shelter in 1972, then drifted into the mists of his own self-induced twilight.

In a scene typified by camaraderie and much musical incest betwixt bands and writers, Gary P. Nunn was absolutely the most important sideman in

Austin. Though most frequently associated with Jerry Jeff Walker's Lost Gonzo Band, Nunn is an outstanding singer/songwriter who eventually struck out on his own. And his "London Homesick Blues" (known by feebs as "I Wanna Go Home with the Armadillos") ranks, along with Guy Clark's "Desperadoes" and "L.A. Freeway," just below Hubbard's "Redneck Mother" in the Flagship Song of Progressive Country sweepstakes.

A prolific writer who's had hits for the likes of Willie Nelson and Rose-anne Cash, Nunn eventually left the Lost Gonzo Band (after *they* left Walker), and went solo with his own backing unit, the Sons of the Bunkhouse. He relocated to Oklahoma in the late eighties, and independent LPs such as *Border States* and *Guacamole* are still available.

Two other Texan country artists experienced noteworthy success during the progressive country era, but weren't actual members of that fraternity: Mickey Gilley and Johnny Rodriguez.

Rodriguez, who was born in Sabinal, Texas, in 1951, was a former altar boy who formed a rock band when he was sixteen, and was playing lead guitar for Tom T. Hall when he was twenty.

Shortly thereafter, Hall, who was blown away by Rodriguez's voice, got the youngster a deal with Mercury Records, and his first single, "Pass Me By," was a top ten hit in 1972. He was awarded the ACM Most Promising Male Vocalist award, encored in 1973 with three number 1 releases, and suddenly found himself a huge star.

Rodriguez's style echoed the more pop end of the C&W spectrum, and throughout the seventies he scored several hits each year. After a bad fall broke his sternum and collarbone, Rodriguez experienced vocal as well as marital problems, and though he recorded for several labels in the eighties and continued to chart an occasional hit, it was thought that his career was probably over.

Still, in 1993, he released the well-received *Run for the Border*, and with a surge in Hispanic music coinciding with Rodriguez's propensity for singing in Spanish, his career appears to be on the upswing.

Mickey Gilley, notable as Jerry Lee Lewis's cousin and as the former owner of Gilley's (at one time the world's largest honky-tonk), should also be remembered as having sold several million records.

After having been drawn into the music business by his cuz, Gilley recorded for a few small labels as well as for Texas's legendary producer Huey Meaux before opening the Gilley's club in 1970. Four years later, he recorded a single for his own jukebox, and the B-side, "Room Full of Roses," became a hit. Playboy Records, distributed by Epic, picked up the record, which climbed all the way to number 1.

Gilley, whose honky-tonk piano style and warm voice made for a winning combination, began to real off a string of consecutive number 1 singles which was astonishing. The awards swirled like confetti, and Gilley continued to rack up hit after hit, including the chauvinistic barroom verity, "Don't the Girls All Get Prettier at Closing Time."

Despite all the hits, Playboy went under and Gilley jumped to parent label Epic, for whom he recorded ten more number 1 singles by 1986. By mixing pop, classic Buddy Holly–style rock, and mainstream C&W, Gilley had a style that seemed impervious to trends.

Finally, by the end of the decade, Gilley's luck seemed to abate a bit. He closed his nightclub and, though his records continued to sell steadily, the long run of top ten hits came to an end. Ever the visionary, though, Gilley became the first artist to open his own theater in Branson, Missouri, where he continues to thrill fans by the thousands.

ALL IN ALL, THE REDNECK ROCK ERA WAS A HIGHLIGHT IN country music history, for the songs as much as for its colorful, irreverent, and truly free purveyors—and in particular for the camaraderie that wrapped the scene and the entire Travis County community in a decade-long cannabis-smoke cocoon. Besides the aforementioned heroes, artists such as Greezy Wheels, Calico, Commander Cody and the Lost Planet Airmen, Balcones Fault, Asleep at the Wheel, Alvin Crow and the Pleasant Valley Boys, and Mother of Pearl were all active and integral in the never-ending circus.

If, to its participants and admirers, the whole progressive country phenomenon seemed over with too quickly, well, maybe such a movement should, by definition, remain short-lived. Only through brevity can such a happy accident retain its vibrancy, freshness, and spontaneity—and in any event, the sheer pace of the madness would've killed 'em all by now, anyway.

☆ Six: Post-Redneck Rock and the Rise of Young Country

NOT ALL OF THE ESTIMATED SIX HUNDRED THOUSAND TEXANS who decided to become country singers during the seventies necessarily wanted to join the ranks of the redneck rockers. A few, like Johnny Rodriguez and Mickey Gilley, kept a Texas sensibility without actually being card-carrying Austinites. Others literally toed the Nashville line; they secured haircuts regularly and managed to go weeks without feeling the jumpy and drill-bit-through-the-cortex anxiety of a cocaine hangover.

After all, while progressive country was a significant musical and cultural development in Texas, and its artists sold a lot of records, it wasn't as though Nashville closed up shop while Waylon and Willie practiced their heathen ways.

In fact, in Nashville it was business as usual. And there were plenty of Texans around to help out.

Artists like Barbara Mandrell, Johnny Lee, Larry Gatlin and the Gatlin Brothers, Kenny Rogers, Tanya Tucker, and Don Williams were selling *beaucoup* records without spending an inordinate amount of time, for example, on the Armadillo World Headquarters stage.

IT TURNED OUT THAT KENNY ROGERS, THE FORMER FOLKIE who left the New Christie Minstrels to "groove out" with the First Edition, had yet one more stylistic mutation up his sleeve: He decided to abandon psychedelic rock and go mainstream country in the middle seventies. It was a perspicacious career move; MIT cannot find a mathematician who can calculate how many hit records and CMA awards Rogers has subsequently amassed.

It all started in 1976 when UA signed Rogers to a contract. A 1977 song, "Lucille," arrowed straight to number 1 on the country charts and, as would virtually all of his singles, crossed over to pop success. Rogers was out of the starting blocks like some platinum-plated sprinter. With his prematurely silver beard, an eternally cheerful bear-hug demeanor, and a sand-dune and honey croon, Rogers is architecturally designed to please Middle America.

As such, in the last fifteen years, it would be difficult to examine a country sales chart without easily locating Rogers's name. (Just look next to the bullet.) A few of his hits were remakes of earlier rock successes ("Reuben James" and "Ruby, Don't Take Your Love to Town"), but he could probably have sold a sing-along version of *The Tibetan Book of the Dead*. An all-inclusive list of his hit singles, albums, and record labels would be sleep-inducing in its length, but songs such as "Daytime Friends," "She Believes in Me," "Lady," "Every Time Two Fools Collide," "Coward of the County," and, of course, "The Gambler" are representative.

Made-for-TV movies of *Coward of the County* and *The Gambler* were also phenomenally successful, with several artistically questionable sequels made of the latter. Suffice to say that Kenny Rogers is a one-man industry with his own personal eighteen-hole golf course—a status symbol of ludicrous proportion.

TANYA TUCKER, WHO WAS BORN IN 1958 IN SEMINOLE, WAS A star by her fourteenth birthday. Her father was a country music enthusiast who was flabbergasted by his daughter's rendition, at the age of eight, of "Your Cheatin' Heart," and he set out on a quest to get Tanya heard by Nashville honchos.

After her dad financed a series of demo tapes and she sat in with a variety of C&W luminaries at county fair–type performances, Tucker fell under the tutelage of noted Columbia producer Billy Sherrill. She was then thirteen.

Though Sherrill tried to convince her that a girl (scout) next door tune like "The Happiest Girl in the Whole U.S.A." would be an appropriate first single, the youngster adamantly insisted on the more randy "Delta Dawn"— which promptly cometed into the top ten. She encored with numerous 1973 hits, including "What's Your Mama's Name" and "Blood Red and Going Down," and the suggestive and controversial content of 1974's "Would You Lay with Me (in a Field of Stone)" generated massive international sales and transformed the teen diva into a superstar. Sales weren't hurt by the fact that Tucker had a world-class voice and the soon-to-be-vixen looks associated with a slightly naughty junior high cheerleader who sneaks cigarettes during game time-outs.

In 1975, Tucker severed ties with Sherrill, inked a million-dollar contract with MCA, and grew up in the nation's tabloids even as she strung together an impressive list of top ten hits stretching to the end of the decade (including "San Antonio Stroll" (1975), the number 1 "Here's Some Love" (1976), "It's a Cowboy Lovin' Night" (1977), and "Texas When I Die" (1978).

For a while, Tucker hit a professional lull wherein her high-profile romances with people like Don Johnson, Andy Gibb, and a bizarre engagement to Glen Campbell seemed to garner more headlines than her music. She continued to make records, including an ill-considered hard rock experiment called *TNT* (1978), and after several more MCA albums and hits like 1980's "Pecos Promenade," she signed with Capitol in 1986. The first LP for that label, *Girls Like Me*, contained three hits including "I Won't Take Less Than Your Love."

She jumped to Liberty the next year, producing the particularly solid *Love Me Like You Used To* album, and in 1991, released the platinum-selling *What Do I Do with Me* album, which scored four radio hits. "Down to My Last Teardrop" was nominated for a Grammy, and Tucker was named the Country Music Association's Female Vocalist of the Year.

Tucker continues to crank out hit records like 1995's *Fire to Fire* and 1997's platinum *Complicated*, the latter of which boasted a Top Ten hit in "Little Things" and earned her a Country Music Award for Female Vocalist of the Year.

DON WILLIAMS IS SURELY THE MOST FAMOUS SON OF FLOYdada, Texas. His lengthy and fruitful career started in his teens when he formed the pop/folk act Pozo Seco Singers (whose 1966 smash, "Time," was the biggest of several hits they recorded before disintegrating in 1971).

After a stint as a furniture salesman, Williams relocated to Nashville in a country songwriting capacity, and when few producers or artists expressed interest in recording his work, he decided to sing 'em himself. *Don Williams Vol. 1* came out in 1973 on the independent JMI label (now available on MCA), and his third single, "We Should Be Together," cracked the country top ten. The song's success earned Williams a deal with Dot (later taken over by ABC, which in turn fused with MCA), and began a spreading, forest-fire run of hits.

Williams has a molasses baritone voice and a slow-as-childhood delivery, and his demeanor and battered, curl-brimmed cowboy hat have inspired folksy, "best pal" loyalty in the huddled masses of C&W fandom (his nickname is, appropriately, "the Gentle Giant"—though it is not true that the eclectic British progressive rock group Gentle Giant is nicknamed "the Don Williams").

His inaugural single for Dot, "I Wouldn't Want to Live if You Didn't Love Me" was his first number 1 hit, and there followed a steamroller line of successes. What was not to like? Williams has perfected the pretty-melodies-as-Valium art of soothing songcraft, and "You're My Best Friend," "Tulsa Time," "Til the Rivers All Run Dry," "Some Broken Hearts Never Mend," and the anthemic "I Believe in You" are probably the finest and best-remembered of his hits.

With several CMA awards to his credit, including 1981's Best Male Vocalist and Album of the Year (*I Believe in You*), and recent successes like

1998's *I Turn the Page* (on Giant), the mellow machine that is Don Williams shows no inclination to follow any trends or waves other than his own.

HOUSTON'S BARBARA MANDRELL WAS PROBABLY THE ANTI-redneck rock maven. Born in 1948, the multi-instrumentalist and singer brings a slick, almost Vegas-style approach to country music. She was playing pedal steel in the Mandrell family band by the age of eleven, learned guitar, bass, banjo, and saxophone through her teen years (touring as a steel player for no less than George Jones), and was recording for the small Mosrite label by the late sixties.

In 1969 she signed with Columbia and released a version of Otis Redding's "I've Been Loving You Too Long," a choice that would typify Mandrell's willingness to cross country with soul, R&B, and showroom pop. A string of singles eventually turned up a top ten hit, 1971's "Tonight My Baby's Coming Home."

She was inducted into the Grand Ole Opry, signed in 1975 with ABC/Dot, and over the next few years enjoyed a string of successful singles before her first number 1 hit, 1978's "Sleeping Single in a Double Bed." Mandrell's versatility and squeaky clean blond good looks were keys to her heartland success, and a bubbly Christian image and devotion to physical fitness pretty much assured her followers that she wasn't rolling spliffs with Willie Nelson. Though much of her material hinted at the cheatin' side of life so essential to a well-rounded C&W catalogue, Mandrell insisted that it was her pure image and solid values that made it all right to sing a few infidelity/barroom songs—because her fans would know what Barbara stood for.

It was a sound theory and, by 1980, she had reunited with her sisters for *Barbara Mandrell and the Mandrell Sisters*, a family-style national television variety show that increased her fan base exponentially. (Sisters Irene and Louise were the peripheral sisters, and Louise, who recorded solo for Epic and RCA, has enjoyed several top ten hits without actually breaking through to major-act status.) Only when the stress of nonstop work threatened her singing voice did Mandrell ultimately short-circuit the show.

Still, her records continued to sell (she scored four more number 1 hits before 1984: "Years," "I Was Country When Country Wasn't Cool," "Till You're Gone," "One of a Kind Pair of Fools"), she made frequent television guest appearances, and all seemed well until a near-fatal auto accident in 1984.

After an arduous and emotional recovery, though, Mandrell returned to work. She continues to record, she plays a hundred shows a year, and *Get to the Heart: My Story*, an autobiography, hit the *New York Times* best-seller list and remained there for months.

* * *

ANOTHER TEXAN WHO OCCASIONALLY UTILIZED HIS SIBLINGS
during his career is Larry Gatlin, who was born in Seminole in 1948. A
former scholarship football player at the University of Houston, Gatlin employed a strong gospel music background to enter the entertainment industry when he'd finished his gridiron chores for the feisty Cougars.

He was singing in the Imperials, a gospel group, in 1971 when Dottie
West caught his act in Vegas as part of a show headlined by sausage-king-
cum-balladeer Jimmy Dean. At West's encouragement, Gatlin sent her a
tape of several original compositions, and she in turn sent him a plane ticket
to Nashville. He began to eek out a living as a tunesmith, eventually landing an artist's contract with Monument Records in 1972.

He was joined in Nashville by his brothers, Rudy and Steve (both of
whom are nice enough guys who have managed to cling to the slimy walls
of show biz principally through nepotistic advantages similar to those enjoyed by Barbara Mandrell's sisters). Larry began to record tunes with and
without his brothers, and in 1974 released his debut album, The Pilgrim. In
1975, his "Broken Lady" went top five and won a Grammy for Song of the
Year.

The Gatlins began to experience success as a touring commodity, and
Larry went to number 1 with "I Wish You Were Someone I Love" in 1977.
A string of top ten hits followed, and Gatlin and the Gatlin Brothers Band
(as they were by then billed) jumped labels to Columbia. In 1979, they
released their biggest hit, the number 1 giant "All the Gold in California,"
scored several more chart successes, and in 1983 hit the top again with
"Houston."

The group remained hot throughout the eighties, but by the end of the
decade, Larry's affection for cocaine and liquor grew to be a significant
problem. He's since dried out and written an autobiography called All the
Gold in California. Though the Gatlin Brothers don't tour much anymore,
they record sporadically, act in regional theater productions, and hold court
at requisite out-to-pasture theaters from Branson to Myrtle Beach.

JANIE FRICKE IS NOW A PROUD TEXAS RESIDENT, BUT, BORN
and educated in Indiana and a former folkie-turned-jingle-singer, becoming
a C&W star probably wasn't something she thought much about during her
teen years.

Still, after traveling the country as a post-college hireling in the jingles
biz, she ended up in Nashville in the mid-seventies. After settling in a
routine of lucrative commercials and background session work—including
hits for everyone from Elvis to Jim Reeves—the former Joan Baez wannabe
raised the eyebrows of honchos with her contributions to a string of hits for
Johnny Duncan and subsequently scored her own record deal with Columbia—which was something she'd never even thought about.

Her marvelous voice and addictive stage presence was too much for the suits to ignore, though, and her second single, a duet with Duncan called "Come a Little Bit Closer," went Top 5 in 1978. She won the CMA's Top New Female Vocalist award that year, which started a fairly routine system of nominations and awards to go with a stream of high-charting hits.

Though it's true her producers struggled to find an identifiable niche of material to fit her versatile voice in the early years, her live shows were superb and she's since settled into a consistent style resulting in numerous quality albums (including LPs like 1982's *It Ain't Easy*, 1985's *The First Word in Memory is Me*, 1986's *Black and White*, and 1988's *Saddle the Wind*).

In all, Fricke recorded almost twenty LPs for Columbia before the big shots deemed it time for newer stars, and Fricke relocated to a ranch outside Dallas. She continues to dabble in the industry, though, and has released both gospel and secular records for smaller labels. In 1999, Fricke's extraordinary voice and body of work are capably represented on the *Anthology* CD, released on the Renaissance label.

JOHNNY LEE WAS A MICKEY GILLEY SIDEMAN WHO RAN THE house band at the infamous Gilley's nightclub (most familiar to non-Texans as the setting for the John Travolta film *Urban Cowboy*) when the bossman was out on tour.

Born in Texas City in 1946, Lee got into music while still in high school, heading up the Future Farmers of America–sponsored Johnny Lee and the Roadrunners. The band broke up after high school, and Lee scored the Gilley gig after a stint in the navy. During the mid-seventies, Lee experienced mild success with a few singles ("Sometimes," recorded in 1975 for ABC/Dot, then 1976's "Red Sails in the Sunset" and 1977's "Country Party," both on GRT).

When, during the filming of *Urban Cowboy*, Travolta heard Lee sing a song called "Looking for Love," the actor insisted it be included on the soundtrack. Full Moon/Asylum released "Looking for Love" as a single, and it promptly went to number 1 on the country charts and number 5 on the pops. Lee, of course, was promptly signed to the label, and the resultant *Looking for Love* album scored three other massive hits, including another number 1 tune called "One in a Million."

For the next few years, the handsome, mellow-voiced Lee was as incendiary as anything in country music. He married diminutive Charlene Tilton, star of the television show *Dallas*, and continued to have chart success into the mid-eighties with songs like 1982's "Cherokee Fiddle" and chart-toppers "Yellow Rose" (with Lane Brody) and "You Could Have a Heart Break" (both 1984).

Eventually, Lee and Tilton broke up amidst the sort of tabloid attention typically slavered over by the very audience that comprises the demographic country music fan, and Lee voluntarily slowed his career in an effort to stay out of the foul glare of publicity's spotlight.

*   *   *

WHILE THE AFOREMENTIONED MAINSTREAMERS CONSTITUTED
the bulk of non–cosmic cowboy artists working the C&W charts during the
seventies and eighties, there arose by the end of the Reagan years a bizarre
and wildly successful phenomenon in Nashville that has become known
variously as Young Country, Hat Acts, and Young Guys Who Look Like
Chippendale Dancers with Nashville Record Deals.

This movement is not without merit—and in fact a great many of its
practitioners are fervent country music fans with polite and genuine respect
for their predecessors—but young country is also heavily influenced by two
important developments. The first is the fact that a lot of these youngsters
grew up on rock radio; Garth Brooks makes no mistake of his adolescent
fascination with the bombast and production of Kiss, for example, and as
such a lot of the material on mainstream country music radio is nothing
more than mainstream pop music sawdusted with fiddles and pedal steel
guitar. Similarly, country record production has borrowed heavily from the
higher-tech innovations of rock music, which is particularly evident in dom-
inant big drum sounds, electronic keyboards, and crunchier guitar tones.

The second difference has been the increasingly slick and hydra-headed
hype machines that are in constant overdrive throughout the entertainment
industry. Would Billy Ray Cyrus, for example, have a contract if he looked
like Quasimodo instead of a cover model for romance novels? Decidedly
not. Virtually every country artist signed since the late eighties is a PR
person's dream. But that doesn't mean that a they're a talentless lot. Au
contraire. All it means is business is business—and to that end, talent is a
valuable ingredient in product, too.

Interestingly enough, young country started when a bunch of younger
artists like George Strait and John Anderson were just as sick of Nashville's
cream-cheese country as Waylon and Willie had been. But where the outlaws had wanted to purify country through their bacchanalian rebellion,
Strait wanted to reform Nashville from within the existing power structures.
His affection for Bob Wills and Merle Haggard was genuine and impassioned, and he was convinced that similar music could be marketed within
the current Nashville format, to the economic and artistic benefit of all.

It could in fact be said of Strait that he is the father of the phrase "hat
act"—not because he came up with the slogan, but because when he released his first national album back in 1981, the fact that he actually wore
a cowboy hat was anathema to what was happening in country music at
the time. Superstars like Ronnie Milsap and Kenny Rogers were working a
crossover look that precluded anything overly redolent of the cowboy aesthetic and in fact reeked of hotel lounges and cruise ships.

Strait was born in 1952 in Pearsall, Texas. He didn't get seriously into
music until the service, when he filled idle hours teaching himself to play
Hank Williams songs on the guitar. After army duty, Strait came back to

Texas, enrolled in Southwest Texas State to study agriculture, and formed the band that would become famous as the Ace in the Hole Band.

After graduation, juggling daytime ranch gigs with moonlight tours of South Texas honky-tonks, Strait cut a few ineffectual tracks in Houston for Pappy Dailey's D Records. But it wasn't until he was eventually discovered by former MCA promotions man Erv Woolsey that Strait made the leap to the big time.

His debut MCA album, 1981's *Strait Country*, was an appropriate pun. Strait's strong suit has always been western swing, raw honky-tonk, and time-honored country balladry. Next to the Velveeta being churned out at the time by the likes of Kenny Rogers, Strait's turn-back-the-clock music was so outdated and forgotten that it had become fresh again.

Though he came off like a print ad for a western wear outlet, the look was obviously sincere and meshed well with his pleasant, capable, but never overly histrionic voice. And with the Ace in the Hole Band relying on fiddles rather than Sno-Kone-sweet string arrangements, his first single, "Unwound," charted at number 10. His third single, "Fool Hearted Memory," a 1983 release from the soundtrack to the film *The Soldier*, was his first number 1 hit—over the course of the next few years to be followed by *thirty* more.

A study in *The New Country Music Encyclopedia* points out that Strait's career path was so perfectly constructed that, throughout most of the eighties, one could anticipate a new Strait hit on the charts at precise four-month intervals. Among the tunes from this amazing run are "Amarillo by Morning," "You Look So Good in Love," "Does Fort Worth Ever Cross Your Mind," "The Fireman," "Ocean Front Property," "All My Ex's Live in Texas," and "Check Yes or No." And that schmaltzier corn songs like "Marina del Rey" and "Blame It on Mexico" have also been part of Strait's never-ending hit parade, well, he'll be the first to admit that he *likes* songs like that—in moderation, anyway.

Such material constitutes such a small percentage of his overall output that his qualifications as the guy who brought country back to country are secure. Perhaps the finest evidence of this is the four-CD boxed set released in late 1995 by MCA, *Strait Out of the Box*, which includes seventy-two songs—nearly every one prime evidence that, while George Strait rarely writes his own material, his work as an interpreter, a historian, and a damn good country singer is virtually peerless.

BY THE MID-EIGHTIES, AFTER STARS LIKE RANDY TRAVIS, Dwight Yoakam, and John Anderson validated Strait's efforts to inject Nashville with a few doses of authenticity and tradition, the trickle that would be young country had become a stylistic adjustment, if not a full-blown flood of twang and Stetsons.

Rodney Crowell's only aim in life was to become a country songwriter—a calling which, by his definition, does not require a cowboy hat. Nevertheless, through chronology and substance, Crowell is an important link in the segue from progressive to young country.

Born in Houston in 1950 and playing drums in his father's honky-tonk band by the time he was eleven, Crowell astutely concluded it wasn't easy to write country hits from a trap kit and learned guitar.

He moved to Nashville in 1972, hung around legends like Townes Van Zandt and Guy Clark, and spent two years as a well-respected sideman in Emmylou Harris's Hot Band (during which time she recorded several of his songs).

He finally went solo, signed with Warner Brothers and issued 1978's critically respected *Ain't Living Long Like This* album. Unfortunately, Crowell's smooth voice, roots-of-rock backbeat, Ivy League good looks, and winning way with a chorus didn't necessarily connect with the record-buying public. He followed with two more floundering efforts, *Rodney Crowell* (1981)) and *But What Will the Neighbors Think* (1982), which produced mid-level hits like "Stars on the Water" as well as big-selling tunes *when recorded by other artists* like Bob Seger, Crystal Gayle, and Jimmy Buffett—but Crowell couldn't break through himself.

He married Roseanne Cash, produced two hit albums for her, and tried to reconcile himself to the fact that his father-in-law was Johnny Cash. Finally, after switching to Columbia, Crowell had a hit with 1986's *Street Language*, and his next record, 1988's *Diamonds and Dirt*, shattered country music records with *five* number 1 self-penned singles ("I Couldn't Leave You if I Tried," "She's Crazy for Leavin'," "It's Such a Small World," "After All This Time" and "Above and Beyond").

Suffice to say, Crowell hasn't had any subsequent problems with fan acceptance, and LPs like *Life Is Messy* (1992), *Let the Picture Paint Itself* (1994), and *Jewel of the South* (1995, the latter two on MCA) have done nothing to tarnish his reputation as a superb, intelligent singer-songwriter.

In '97, Crowell released an AOR CD with his backing band called *The Cicadas* on Warners. A cross between Crowded House and Nashville, it's an amazing record.

ANOTHER NON-HAT DUDE WHO IS NONETHELESS A CONTEMporary of those very young country artists is Radney Foster, who looks like the male lead in any movie made of a John Grisham novel. Born in Del Rio, Texas, Foster first gained fame as part of Foster and Lloyd, the country/ pop duo responsible for three best-selling albums (1987's *Faster and Llouder*, 1988's *Foster and Lloyd*, and 1989's *Version of the Truth*) that netted five top ten singles including "Crazy Over You" and "What Do You Want from Me." The pair seemed to match an affection for the Beatles and the Righteous Brothers with their love of old-line country, and it was a synthesis that obviously worked well.

Unfortunately, they didn't. After they split up, Foster fished around and landed a deal with Arista, and in 1992 released *Del Rio, Texas, 1959* (the title of which refers, of course, to chronological and geographical aspects of his birth). The record featured "Just Call Me Lonesome," one of the best country songs of the decade. Combining time-honored lyrical treatments of solitude with a fine two-steppin' rhythm and Foster's Marshall Crenshaw–meets–Paul McCartney tenor, the song was an instant hit.

To that end, whether it's his pop influences or just a skewed way of looking at the standard C&W songwriting format, Foster is a particularly fine writer, and CDs like *Labor of Love* (1995) and *See What You Want to See* (1999) are solid efforts. Foster imbues traditional country concerns with wit and tension, and subsequently stretches further than the average pap-constructor collecting checks on Songwriter Row. As such, that Radney Foster is collecting checks as a contemporary C&W singer/songwriter is refreshing indeed.

MEGA-SELLING POP-TWANGERS MASON-DIXON ALSO GERMI-nated in Texas. Originally a Lamar University (Beaumont) acoustic duo comprised of bassist Frank Gilligan and Texas native and guitarist Rick Henderson in the late seventies, the group found guitarist Jerry Dengler playing in Odessa, Texas, and hit the road with an ever-changing cast of drummers.

After signing with Texas Records, the group hit the country charts in 1983 with a cover of the Police's "Every Breath You Take." They continued to gain ground and attention, charting a few more hits, and eventually inked a deal with Capitol in 1988. Two CDs for the label, *Exception to the Rule* and *Reach For It*, have done respectfully, and the charity-helpful band continues to slowly build a fan base. Henderson eventually left Mason-Dixon, replaced by another Texan, Terry Casburn.

HOLLY DUNN IS ANOTHER ARTIST WHOSE CAREER PLAN DID not involve the "free your mind and your bottle of beer will follow" attitude of Austin C&W. Born in San Antonio in 1957, Dunn is a college honors graduate who helped pioneer what few songwriting/production opportunities were available to women in country music in the late seventies.

A songstress with a decided affection for the Beatles and Carole King, and who followed her brother Chris to a staff writer's gig at CBS Music in Nashville, Dunn achieved a gradual success when artists like Sylvia, Louise Mandrell, and Terri Gibbs began recording her tunes.

But boasting a clear, angel's voice and intelligent, preppy good looks, it was inevitable that Dunn would be signed to sing her own songs. After a brief artist contract with the ill-fated MTM Records (which included top ten hits with "Daddy's Hands," "Only When I Love," and a duet with

Michael Martin Murphey, "A Face in the Crowd") as well as a 1987 CMA
Horizon Award for Most Promising Newcomer, Dunn signed with Warner
Brothers and recorded *The Blue Rose of Texas*. A single off that LP, "Are
You Ever Gonna Love Me," went to number 1, and Dunn's status as a singer
was firmly established.

Ironically, given her work for "suffrage" in Nashville, "Maybe I Mean
Yes," her 1991 single off the *Milestones* greatest hits album, created a furor
with women's rights groups who interpreted the song's meaning as an en-
dorsement of date rape. Dunn yanked the tune and has carried on with
three superb albums: *Getting It Done* (1994) on Warner Bros., and *Life and
Love and All the Stages* (1995) and *Leave One Bridge Standing* (1997) on
River North.

THOUGH HE WAS BORN IN NEW JERSEY IN 1962, CLINT BLACK
grew up in Houston and is therefore forgiven. Even more significant, his
career as a singer/songwriter and aficionado of straight-from-the-bull-chute
cowboy hats qualifies Black as the missing link between George Strait and
the new generation of young country dudes who, smelling of Brut and driving graduation-present pickup trucks, motored directly from their high
school proms to careers in Nashville.

Given his diminutive size, Black was forced to alter plans to become an
astronaut and, instead, learned guitar and harmonica, formed a country band
and began writing tunes with the group's lead player, Hayden Nicholas.
After several years on the South Texas bar circuit, Black was discovered by
Bill Ham, manager of ZZ Top, who secured a deal with RCA.

The first LP, 1989's *Killing Time*, exclusively sporting Black or Black/
Nicholas tunes, had *five* number 1 songs: "Better Man," "Nobody's Home,"
the title track, "Walking Away," and "Nothing's News." Not only was this
a record-shattering debut, it was no fluke.

True, Black's crinkled, puppy dog good looks and belt-it-out tenor voice
were custom-designed for country stardom. But the *songs* were terrific. Black
and Nicholas have managed to work the time-honored themes of cheatin',
drinkin', and lost love in poetic and different ways, and the quality has
consistently held up over the course of such hit LPs as 1990's *Put Yourself
in My Shoes*, 1992's *The Hard Way*, 1993's *No Time to Kill*, and 1994's *One
Emotion*, which featured a single cowritten with Merle Haggard, "Untan-
gling My Mind."

Inasmuch as Black is virtually the Gen X of country stars (he readily
admits that, until he was already a star, his "country" of choice was George
Strait or Merle Haggard rather than Bob Wills or Willie Nelson), his ability
to mix the eternal qualities of country music with the matinee idol properties seemingly required by the new fan qualify Black's run as a Nashville
kingpin as deservedly limitless.

*   *   *

RONNIE DUNN, THE MORE PROLIFIC MEMBER OF PERENNIAL AWARD winners/always multiplatinum Brooks and Dunn, is another Texas kid, having been born in Coleman in 1953. A former student of both psychiatry and divinity—which presumably served him well in the cutthroat C&W music industry—Dunn was leading the house band in a Tulsa honky-tonk when he won first prize in a national talent competition and landed in Nashville for a recording session.

He also became a songwriter with Tree Publishing, where he met and began composing with Kix Brooks, a Shreveport native. Performance was a natural extension of their collaboration, and they quickly scored a contract with Arista. Their first four singles—the title cut of their first CD, "Brand New Man," "My Next Broken Heart," "Neon Moon," and the insufferable "Boot Scootin' Boogie" all went to number 1—and the album sold over three million copies.

The formula—catchy, slightly corny, pro forma jukebox music—stayed true, and presumably any CD they release will rocket straight to the top of the charts. They will also win every "best duo" award offered—by any organization—and, if the success of 1998's "If You See Her" is any indication, these trends will continue forever.

IN CORNIER TIMES, AS WHEN GEORGE JONES WAS KNOWN AS "the Ol' Possum," Hal Ketchum would probably have been nicknamed by record label PR hacks "The Handsome Carpenter." After all, before music stardom, Ketchum paid the bills with his carpentry skills, and his handsome visage is not unlike *Miami Vice* era Don Johnson. Fortunately, he's just called Hal.

He was born in New York in 1953, and learned to play drums and wield a claw hammer while in his high school years. A free spirit of somewhat intellectual inclinations, Ketchum bounced around various honky-tonks and construction sites before settling in Gruene in the Texas hill country. Ketchum frequented the Gruene Dance Hall—a venerable training ground for folks like Robert Earl Keen—and was subsequently inspired to add the guitar to his eclectic list of skills.

He wrote dozens of songs and played around the Austin area, releasing *Threadbare Alibis* on the Watermelon label in 1986. On one of his sporadic forays into Nashville, Ketchum actually signed a publishing deal, and shortly thereafter was picked up by Curb Records.

His first major label release, 1991's *Past the Point of Rescue*, featured hits such as the amazing title track, "Small Town Saturday Night" (number 1), "I Know Where Love Lives," and a remake of the Vogues' 1965 pop hit, "Five O'Clock World." The latter song was emblematic of Ketchum's strengths, which are typical of the emerging young country tendency to combine pop sensibilities with the traditional Nashville framework.

The difference is that Ketchum does it better than most, with unabashed sincerity, a gift for songcraft, and an obvious affection for rock, folk, and country—and the certain conviction that the three can coexist comfortably. As the success of representative CDs like 1992's *Sure Love* (Capitol), 1994's *Every Little World* (Curb), and 1999's *Awaiting Redemption* (Curb) attest, Ketchum's right.

ONE OF THE FINEST OF THE UNDER-THIRTY GANG TAGGED with the young country label is Atlanta, Texas's Tracy Lawrence, who was born just a few years after John Lennon claimed the Beatles were more popular than Jesus. Lawrence decided by sixteen that he wanted to be a country singer, and by twenty was playing in a variety of bands throughout Texas, Oklahoma, Louisiana, and Arkansas. In 1990, he decided to embark on that inevitable pilgrimage to Nashville.

It took only about a year for Lawrence to sign with Atlantic, and in less than five years he'd established himself as a major force in contemporary country music, selling over five million copies of four albums (1991's *Sticks and Stones*, 1992's *Alibis*, 1994's *I See It Now*, and 1995's *Tracy Lawrence Live*) and scoring eleven chart hits.

But despite his meteoric artistic rise, Lawrence has had to overcome substantial personal adversity: He was shot four times while being victimized in a robbery on the day he finished recording his first LP; he endured a protracted legal imbroglio with former business partners; and his wife was severely injured in a furnace explosion in which she also miscarried the couple's first child.

Still, Lawrence is positively Nietzschean in his "that which does not kill me makes me stronger" perseverance. With his saucer-brimmed cowboy hats and shoulder-length auburn hair framing a kindly, Michael Keaton face, Lawrence is clearly a fan favorite. His reedy, twangy voice boasts a terrific range, and his material—whether heartfelt balladry like "Sticks and Stones" or "Between the Moon and You," or two-steppin' stompers like "Renegades, Rebels and Rogues"—oozes an authenticity not often found in young country product.

With *Time Marches On* (1996) and *The Coast Is Clear* (1997), Lawrence continues to chronicle the themes of faith and recovery.

LEE ROY PARNELL, WHO WAS WELL ESTABLISHED AS A SONG-writer before he became a star on his own, grew up in a home of rich musical diversity. Born in Abilene in 1956, Parnell ingested large helpings of western swing and New Orleans—style R&B at an early age, and when, at the tender age of six, he sang on the radio with family pal Bob Wills, he seemed destined to make his mark in music.

Immediately upon graduation from high school, Parnell headed to the verdant musical pastures of Austin, played a brief stint as one of Kinky Friedman's Texas Jewboys, formed his own band, and set out to become a star. He worked the road for twelve years, honing his singing and song-writing, and finally made the move to Nashville in 1987. He scored an immediate publishing gig, formed a new group and set up shop at Nashville's Bluebird Cafe—which is sort of the Music City talent scout equivalent to young literary lions attending Bennington College.

Before long, artists like Marcia Ball, Pirates of the Mississippi, Jo-El Sonnier, and Johnny Lee began covering his smooth, country soul tunes, and it wasn't long before Arista collared him.

Parnell's debut album, 1990's *Lee Roy Parnell*, featured seven songs cow-ritten by the artist, including "Crocodile Tears" and "There Oughta Be a Law." A popular live performer who sports a Jon Voight in *Coming Home* look, and whose concerts bring out the Texas rockin' side of his personality, Parnell downshifted styles for his second record, 1992's *Love Without Mercy*. Featuring a more aggressive, slide guitar—steeped sound, the LP had three top ten hits: "Love Without Mercy," "What Kind of Fool Do You Think I Am," and "Tender Moment."

Parnell is an exceptionally varied and prolific artist. Whether documenting his live show, as with 1993's *On the Road*, recording with *conjunto* wizard Flaco Jimenez (1996's Grammy-nominated instrumental album *Cat Walk*), or moving toward the millennium with such forward-thinking discs as 1999's *Hits and Highways Ahead*, Parnell is one of country's true virtuosos.

THINK OF COLLIN RAYE AS THE ALAN ALDA OF NEW COUNTRY: A painfully sensitive guy with a gorgeous tenor voice and a sizable collection of platinum hits.

But though his forte has always been balladry, Raye selects material that is an intellectual cut above the "cryin' in my whiskey 'cause my wife hot-wired my pickup truck and moved to Bakersfield to seduce Merle" mentality that has traditionally comprised the essence of such songs. To that end, Raye even looks like a brooding film star—a vague cross between William Hurt and Craig T. Nelson.

Raye was born in Arkansas in 1960, but now considers Greenville, Texas, his home base. His parents were both country musicians of some regional repute, and Raye and his brother followed suit. After high school, they played in country bands in Washington, Oregon, and Nevada and, after an L.A. record honcho heard Raye fronting his own band in Reno, a deal with Epic was consummated.

In 1990, Raye released *All I Can Be*, which spent three weeks at the top of the charts and spawned the smash single "Every Second" and the gorgeous weeper of transcendent devotion, "Love, Me."

His two follow-up albums, *In This Life* (1992) and *Extremes* (1994) were plentifully stocked with heartfelt love songs, though the latter seemed to place a bit more emphasis on uptempo country stompers. But it was the slower stuff that really connected, and "My Kind of Girl," "Little Rock" (a terrifically moving song about alcoholism), and "That Was a River" were hits off the platinum albums. Raye found himself a headlining star with a devoted following, a status he utilizes in his frequent work for charitable foundations and good causes. In 1995, Raye released *I Think about You* and in 1998 put out *The Walls Came Down*, an album that more or less echoes the thoughtful, melodic motif of his earlier work.

MARK CHESNUTT WAS THE FIRST OF THE YOUNG COUNTRY gods to break out of Beaumont, along with Tracy Byrd and Clay Walker. The double-ugly area seems an odd spot for such a talent garden (George Jones hailed from the neighborhood, Johnny and Edgar Winter are Beaumont natives, and Janis Joplin was from twin city Port Arthur), and cynics suggest that it must have something to do with the reeking petroleum industry miasma that hangs over the region like a massive and perpetual mushroom cloud.

Maybe so, but to Chesnutt, who was born there in 1963 and is now a huge star who could probably live anywhere in his choice of galaxies, Beaumont is still home. His father, Bob, was a country singer who released a number of independent singles in the late sixties and early seventies, and at a young age Mark expressed interest in following in his daddy's bootsteps. The inclination was to go to Nashville, but the Old Man told Mark he could get everything he needed, career-wise, and stay in Beaumont.

And though Chesnutt worked East Texas honky-tonks for twelve years, his dad was right. Chesnutt recorded a song for a local label called "Too Cold at Home" which stirred up interest at MCA. They signed the singer, planning to release the song as a single and build some support before putting out an album. Wrong.

"Too Cold at Home" was a huge success, and Chesnutt rushed out an album by the same name in 1990. By the spring of 1991, he'd had additional chart success with "Brother Jukebox" and "Blame It on Texas." The sophomore effort, *Longnecks and Short Stories*, featured the hit "Bubba Shot the Jukebox," proving that the Bono-looking entertainer wasn't afraid to work a recurring motif.

By 1995's *Wings* (on Decca), featuring "King of Broken Hearts," Chesnutt had so cemented his place in the country top ten that he may never leave.

TRACY BYRD IS ANOTHER VETERAN OF THE HARD-DRINKIN' EAST Texas honky-tonk scene, an old-school stylist who grew up knowing that his gigs were dependent on keeping folks two-steppin'. As such, his albums for MCA have been heavy on the energy and focused on the myriad possibilities of the neon night.

A country fan virtually since birth, Byrd was born in 1966 in the Beaumont suburb of Vidor. After singing at high school talent shows, he began playing in area bars and then entered serious training at Cutter's, the same nightclub from which Mark Chesnutt's stardom was launched. In fact, the two often shared the stage, and it wasn't long after Chesnutt hit nationally that the infant-faced Byrd began making trips to Nashville in the hope of getting his own shot at the big time. On his second visit, Byrd caught the ears of an MCA A&R guy and signed on the dotted line.

His first record, 1993's *Tracy Byrd*, was a throwback to the days of Ray Price, George Jones, and Bob Wills, and Byrd's versatile baritone exudes pure country in every warbled note. "Holdin' Heaven" was a big enough hit to make Byrd's name reasonably familiar, and when, the following year, he put out *No Ordinary Man*, it was time. Featuring the dance-hall faves "Watermelon Crawl" and "Lifestyles of the Not So Rich and Famous," the album was off to a good start, though Byrd was in danger of getting tagged with a "novelty song" reputation.

But he pushed for a ballad as the next single, the uncharacteristic "Keeper of the Stars," and it became a huge hit. The album has since neared double platinum, and ensuing CDs, such as *Big Love* (1996) and *I'm from the Country* (1998) were sufficiently hit-clustered to necessitate a greatest-hits package in 1999.

CLAY WALKER IS THE YOUNGEST OF THE SO-CALLED BEAUMONT Triumvirate, and though all three are irrefutably huge stars, Walker's ascendancy has perhaps been the quickest.

Born in 1970, Walker followed the Beaumont blueprint established by Chestnutt and Byrd—which is basically to have at least one parent play an instrument in a country band, immerse yourself in the C&W tradition at an early age, and blow off any spinal surgeon aspirations and jump directly into the honky-tonks ASAP after high school.

With an appealing versatility, captain-of-the-football-team good looks, and a shrewd business perspicacity, it wasn't long before Walker signed with Giant Records. His first album, 1993's *Clay Walker*, went platinum on the strength of the number 1 single, "What's It to You?" His sophomore effort, *If I Could Make a Living* (1994), sold respectably, and in a confident and (for country music) highly unusual strategy, Walker hit the road as a headlining act, networking the United States in a variety of venues.

The gamble was a terrific success, generating even more percolating CD sales, and by that time Walker had readied *Hypnotize the Moon*, a quasi-concept LP about the myriad forms, meanings, and implications of love.

Nearing the end of the century, all five of Walker's CDs have gone platinum, and he drew fifty-five thousand fans to the Houston Liverstock Show and Rodeo in 1998. Though diagnosed with MS in 1996, Walker shows no signs of letting up.

AS HARD AS IT IS TO BELIEVE, THERE ARE EVEN NEWER TEXAS country acts—and apparently, all of them except one are over fifteen years of age.

The fifteen-year-old would be one LeAnn Rimes, who lives in the Dallas suburb of Garland and who is possessed of a bigger-than-life, Patsy Cline-esque voice. In fact, at thirteen, after she signed with MCA/Curb Records, she immediately scored a hit with "Blue," a song Dallas disc jockey Bill Mack had written for Cline years earlier. (Cline had reportedly been getting ready to record the song at the time of her death.)

Her first album, Blue, has gone quadruple platinum, resulting in untold popularity, Grammy, and CMA awards, and her label releasing a CD of early recordings—how early can you get?—called Unchained Melody—the Early Years. Under the suspect guidance of her manager/father, Rimes has pinwheeled even more product into the marketplace including a corn-tossed album of pan-proceleusmatic material called You Light Up My Life—Inspirational Songs—a collection that sounds as though it were conceived of by her dad, John Philip Sousa, and Pat Robertson—and the Sitting on Top of the World CD, a mishmash of pop and country that would be better served if the title song was the same one Cream wrote.

Throughout these efforts, Rimes sings wonderfully and has collected several trophy rooms' worth of awards; she's absolutely the real thing. With her fetching, teen-princess looks, she's already been shepherded into the movies, performing in an ABC made-for-TV film called Holiday in Your Heart. Whether this pursuit is her own or another shortcut to residual checks, who can say? She has all the promise in the world—now, if her handlers and the nation's tabloid mentality will just let her sing . . .

Doug Supernaw, who looks like a high school football coach and claims he goes through life in a state of "petrified adolescence," hails from Houston and attended St. Thomas there on a golf scholarship. A closet country songwriter who admired Vern Gosdin, Supernaw eventually gave up thoughts of a PGA career and hit the road as a wild, good-timin' C&W star-to-be.

He was signed by BNA and in 1993 released Red and Rio Grande, which included his own hit song, "Reno." His next LP was the amusingly titled Deep Thoughts from a Shallow Mind, and in 1995 he signed with Giant Records and put out You Still Got Me, which contains the smash "Daddy Made the Dollars (Mamma Made the Sense)." In August 1999, he released Fadin' Renegade.

Jacksonville's Neal McCoy, who looks like Lorenzo Lamas's sidekick, Sixkiller in the syndicated series *Renegade*, is a flamboyant live performer with a vibrant smile and a radio-ready voice. Though his Atlantic debut, 1990's *At This Moment*, didn't do much, the title song from 1994's *No Doubt About It* went to number 1. Later CDs, particularly *You Gotta Love That* (1996) and *Life of the Party* (1999), indicate a consistency of formula and the likelihood of long-term success.

Ricky Lynn Gregg, from Longview, is a former lead guitarist for the rock act Head East (a band known chiefly for sustaining a career for twenty years on the strength of one song, "Never Been Any Reason"). Gregg, though, grew up sneaking tunes like Merle Haggard's "Swinging Doors" into Top 40 sets, so it wasn't surprising that he eventually grew tired of singing the line "Save my life I'm going down for the last time" and returned to country.

While he looks not unlike a Cher video for "Half-breed" (due no doubt to his Cherokee heritage), Gregg is actually a pretty talented country guy. Signed to Liberty Records, he's released two critically lauded LPs: 1993's *Ricky Lynn Gregg* and 1995's *Get a Little Closer*.

Virginia native Kelly Willis spent her formative years in the D.C. area before relocating to Austin as the front voice for a rootsy/rockabilly outfit called Kelly and the Fireballs. She fell under the mentorish wing of Wagoneer *brujo* Monte Warden and began to explore a purer country muse. With a new batch of original songs, her angel's voice, and the filmstar looks of Suzy Amis, Willis began to split her time between Nashville and Austin and soon landed a deal with MCA.

But despite three gorgeous records for the label (*Well Traveled Love, Bang Bang,* and *Kelly Willis*) it wasn't working. She jumped to A&M for the *Fading Fast* EP, but though folks in Nashville agreed she had talent to burn, her comfort level with the whole industry wasn't happening. She returned to Austin, married the brilliant singer/songwriter Bruce Robison, and signed with the smaller (but artist-supportive) Rykodisc. *What I Deserve* (1999) may actually garner her just that. The reviews have been wall-to-wall ecstatic, and appearances on Conan O'Brien and David Letterman have boosted the Public Awareness factor substantially.

With her distilled original material and a shrewd capacity for picking great cover material, Willis has made the upward hop from mainstream country to the alt-country campground. It's a smart move.

Fort Worth's Ty Herndon may yet become the star he was well on his way to becoming when it happened. The chiseled-featured singer/songwriter signed with Epic in 1993 and in 1995 released *What Matters Most* (the title song of which went to number 1). Then, in Fort Worth, ironically enough, to perform at a Texas Police Association conference, Herndon was arrested for allegedly exposing himself to an undercover cop and for possession of methamphetamine.

To its credit, Nashville has taken a low-key approach to the incident, and Herndon, whose musical skills are substantial and undeniable, may yet rebound from charges that ten years ago would've ruined *any* C&W artist's career, guilty or not. Herndon is slowly rebuilding momentum through solid efforts like *Big Hopes* (1998) and *Living in a Moment* (1996)

Even fresher troops marching out of the Nashville studios include George Ducas, Le Ann Womack, Deryl Dodd, Lonestar, former sitcom star Crystal Bernard, Little Texas, and the estimable Linda Davis.

One group that shouldn't be overlooked is the Dixie Chicks, who will never have to balance their checkbooks again after the unparalleled success of *Wide Open Spaces*, their 1998 major label debut for Monument Records. By the time *Fly*, their sophomore Monument album, was released in August 1999, *Wide Open Spaces* had sold over six million CDs, which is enough so that every person in Waco would have sixty copies. Every human on earth also knows the chords to "I Can Love You Better" and "There's Your Trouble," two of the more popular singles from the juggernaut.

The Dixie Chicks have won the (FILL IN WHATEVER YOU WANT) award, appeared on (FILL IN WHATEVER YOU WANT) television shows and magazine covers, and appropriated Courtney Love's wardrobe whilst lacing their fruit-smoothie country pop with the virtuosic sounds dating back to the group's original street-corner busker days as a bluegrass outfit.

Now composed of vocalist Natalie Maines (the daughter of Lubbock pedal steel/producer legend Lloyd Maines, Natalie's world-class voice was the ingredient missing all along) and the sister team of Marty Seidell (fiddle) and Emily Erwin Robison (she's married to brilliant Texas singer/songwriter Charlie Robison and plays guitar, dobro, and mandolin), the Chicks are now experiencing the expected critical backlash in their home state. After all, they aren't pure bluegrass anymore and, along the way, original members Laura Lynch and Robin Lynn Macy were fired or quit (choose one).

These personnel maneuvers were probably somewhat acrimonious, but, hey, Pete Best was probably bitter, too. It happens. And if a lot of the fans of older indie albums like *Thank Heaven for Dale Evans*, *Little Ol' Cowgirl*, and *Shouldn't a Told You That*—delightful, pure records all—are still pissed off at Natalie and that the band "went Nashville," I suggest trying to get in touch with one of the current band to tell 'em.

In fact, *Wide Open Spaces* is a commendable country album, and if in the eyes of Wal-Mart Nation the Chicks have become more about *Entertainment Tonight* gossip fodder—Will they make movies with Hugh Grant? Do you think they drink or smoke cigarettes?—well, that's fame. But there's some good music happening, too.

★ Seven: Renegade Traditionalists and Country Punk

FRANK SINATRA MIGHT THINK HE DID IT HIS WAY, BUT HE NEVER hung out with Junior Brown or Steve Earle. On the other hand, Frankie may well have hung out with Lyle Lovett, in which case the Texas singer-songwriter with the Eiffel Tower hair could have told Ol' Blue Eyes a thing or two about "doing it his way."

Such is the collective, free-will decision of a band of outlaw Texas country artists who took a hard, critical look at the Velveeta product that has so pervaded Nashville and C&W radio for several years. Recognizing, well, *none* of it as having anything to do with Lefty Frizzell, Milton Brown, George Jones, or even Willie Nelson, these new warriors have circumvented the suits in the pursuit of honky-tonk verities—often at the expense of more lucrative careers and opportunities.

The result has been one hell of a lot of terrific music.

Lyle Lovett is, in fact, probably the most high-profile of these new traditionalists. Born in the Houston suburb of Klein, Texas, in 1957, Lovett spent his youth in a self-indoctrination program in the tumbleweed country/folk of Guy Clark, Townes Van Zandt, and Willie Nelson.

At Texas A&M, he obtained degrees in both German and journalism and spent large amounts of time sitting on the beer can–cluttered front porch of a student rental house with fellow undergrad Robert Earl Keen. Fueled by an ongoing procession of coeds passing by en route to class, the two strummed acoustic guitars and began writing songs.

After matriculation, Lovett began working an ever-expanding club circuit, honing his bride-of-Frankenstein haircut and his king of irony tenor even as his musical influences broadened to include western swing, big band, and Cole Porter–era pop. He played throughout Europe for a few years, while ostensibly pursuing graduate studies, then returned to Houston in 1984.

When established artists like Nancy Griffith and Lacy J. Dalton began covering his songs, Lovett headed for Nashville and, on the basis of a four-tune demo, first scored a writer's deal and, in 1986, with a boost from Guy

Clark, a recording contract with MCA/Curb. The eponymous first LP was released later that year. A fun-house mirror collection of alternately acerbic, gentle, profound, and bemused takes on romance and relationship, four songs from the album hit the charts ("Farther Down the Line," "Cowboy Man," "God Will," and "Why I Don't Know").

The follow-up, 1988's *Pontiac*, was a masterpiece of bluesy, jazzy tunes that fit into C&W parameters only just barely. The album had three more hits, though, one of which was a classic song in what was becoming Lovett's brainy and eccentric brand of country noir, "She's No Lady" (the chorus of which explains, "She's no lady, she's my wife").

With 1989's *Lyle Lovett and His Large Band*, the artist left all pretense at fitting into any Nashville stereotypes behind. It wasn't enough that Lovett's odd, Mr. Potato Head features were topped with That Hair, or that he appeared onstage in hip designer suits. With a massive horn section and gospel choir backing him, the singer's image was becoming decidedly non–Kenny Rogers even as his music became more experimental. *Lyle Lovett and His Large Band* was essentially a country-flavored Valentine's card to the big band era. The album peaked on the C&W charts at number 10, but there had to be a substantial number of Bubbas scratching their heads in bewilderment when they listened to it for the first time.

Not coincidentally, Lovett was beginning to attract the attention of the sort of hip, eclectic, public radio audience that might listen to artists like Everything But the Girl, the Neville Brothers, or Keith Jarrett. As if mulling over his ever-mutating demographics, and in leisurely obeisance to his own adventuresome muse, Lovett took three years to put any new product into the stores: 1992's *Joshua Judges Ruth*. As the punningly biblical title suggests, the CD is redolent of sonic gospel influences, despite a set of lyrics that are stark, brooding, desolate; anything but inspirational. It was a well-crafted record, but the listener couldn't help but feel that Lovett was a lonely, solitary, and melancholy guy.

So it was probably a good thing that he decided to take a brief thespian turn as a solid supporting part in *The Player*, a lauded Robert Altman film satirizing the movie industry. Not only did Lovett get to hang around with Tim Robbins and Whoopi Goldberg, he also met Julia Roberts when she performed in a cameo role.

As everyone in our tabloid-infused society knows, Lovett and Roberts became an item, got married, and subsequently led the world's paparazzi on several months of jet-setting speculation and Beauty and the Beast sightings.

Lovett's honeymoon album, *I Love Everybody*, which furthered his new status as a cerebral country alternative in accomplished fashion, came out in 1994 and made it to number 26 on the pop charts.

Lovett's 1996 *The Road to Ensenada* ushered in the post-divorce-from-Julia years, not that that's important other than as a possible creative catalyst for the brilliant record. Two subsequent discs, *Step Inside This House* (an astounding collection of cover tunes Lovett chose to honor fellow-

Texan songwriters) and *Live in Texas* (with "live" rhyming with "give") are predictably great.

If Keen and Lovett used their English and journalism backgrounds as literary springboards to songwriting careers, Steve Earle took a decidedly contrary path, inspired by Willie Nelson, to whom Earle is eternally thankful for making it okay for teenage white guys to like rock *and* country.

Though Earle was born in Virginia in 1955, his family had strong Texas roots and had permanently landed in San Antonio by the time the kid was in grade school. From postinfancy on, Earle was determined to become a rock star, and was touring Texas clubs with a guitar-playing uncle by the time he was sixteen. A Willie Nelson show in which the Red-Haired Master soothed a potential riot between rockers and rednecks, utilizing only his music and a few well-spoken comments, intrigued Earle, and he started to write songs in a progressive country vein.

The first of his twelve hundred or so marriages temporarily short-circuited the road concept, but, after Earle met Townes Van Zandt, the two became pals and Earle had his first big-time songwriter connection. Van Zandt hinted that songwriting in Nashville might be more lucrative than the Houston coffeehouse circuit, and it wasn't long before Earle was hawking his tunes in Tennessee, hanging out with folks like Van Zandt, Guy Clark, and Rodney Crowell.

Earle met with little success, though, retreated into Mexico to work on his writing, and returned to Nashville in 1979. He managed to score some nightclub gigs and sell a few tunes (another one, "Mustang Wine," was nearly recorded by Elvis Presley), but again grew frustrated and returned to San Antonio, where he formed the inaugural version of his band the Dukes.

At that point, the ever restless and volatile Earle had blown through marriage number two and was cultivating a serious substance-enthusiastic lifestyle. After the Dukes had toured the club circuit awhile, Earle found himself back in Nashville in 1981. He scored a gig as a songwriter at a publishing company and cowrote "When You Fall in Love," a big hit for Johnny Lee.

The cash windfall enabled Earle and his Dukes to record an EP, called *Pink and Black*, which so piqued the curiosity of Epic that he was offered a recording contract. A pair of singles attracted zero attention, and Earle left Epic and signed with MCA.

The first MCA single, "Hillbilly Heaven," turned some heads, but it was Earle's debut LP, 1986's *Guitar Town*, that brought him international acclaim and established the songwriter as a captivating melding of hippie political rhetoric, Jimmie Rodgers humanism, Hank Williams debauchery, and Bruce Springsteen–plays-rockabilly song structure. Along with two other newcomers, Dwight Yoakam and Randy Travis, Earle was kicking a hole in the staid wall of country music.

Guitar Town sold remarkably well, scored two hit singles ("Someday" and "Goodbye's All We've Got Left"), and paved the way for 1987's *Exit O*

CRIMINALLY UNDERRATED ARTIST
Robert Earl Keen
☆

While noted for many things (most of them unpleasant), Texas A&M was never a noted musical mecca—at least not until Lyle Lovett and Robert Earl Keen hit town. And after the two serenaded one another on that crusty and now-legendary front porch, moved from pizza parlor gigs to folk clubs, then went their separate ways after college, Keen took a decidedly different route to fame from his more high-profile buddy.

A Houston native who was born in 1956, Keen borrowed a sister's forgotten guitar in his early teens and, by the time he got settled in college, was content to split his time between studies and picking folk and bluegrass songs with Lovett and Keen's fiddle-playing roommate, Bryan Duckworth.

After obtaining a beer-fueled English degree, Keen moved to Austin, working for the Texas Railroad Commission and trying to horn in on the progressive country movement. Unfortunately, the movement was already dead.

Keen carried on, evolving a singular brand of country songcraft on the folk circuit and copping Best New Songwriter honors at the 1983 Kerrville Folk Festival. Along the way, he released an independently financed record called *No Kinda Dancer*, first distributed in 1984 by the Philo label.

He also met and became friends with Steve Earle, then an ascending bottle rocket in a select circle of newly acclaimed Nashville tunesmiths. Earle's advice was that Keen get his ass to Nashville at top speed, a suggestion with which Keen complied. It was a disaster.

Music Row honchos couldn't hear the hooks in Robert Earl's barbecue 'n' bordertown vignettes, and after a few years of failure, Keen retreated to Bandera in the Texas hill country, convinced he'd never make it. He managed to secure a weekly gig at the nearby Gruene Town Hall and expanded his solo folk frame of reference by forming the Robert Earl Keen band (with former college sidekick Duckworth on fiddle).

He began to draw a steadily increasing crowd, and his growing body of tunes started to attract the attention of other songwriters. Joe Ely, Kelly Willis, Eddie Raven, and Nancy Griffith recorded his work and, after inking a publishing deal, Keen signed with a respected North Carolina indie label called Sugar Hill.

They rereleased *No Kinda Dancer*, then followed up in 1988 with *Live Album*, playing to Keen's strength as an *in vivo* performer. In 1989, a studio album, *West Textures*, came out, and Keen's reputation as a seriously great songwriter began to take off.

While his voice is decidedly nonoperatic, as though a saddle burr is caught in his throat, it is a nevertheless effective vehicle for his material—

songs that are like musical sex acts between Carson McCullers and Marty Robbins, with occasional commentary by Jeff Foxworthy.

A Bigger Piece of the Sky, from 1993, with incredible material like "Corpus Christi Bay" and "Whenever Kindness Fails," was Keen's first totally satisfying record, though it merely served as a prelude to 1994's Gringo Honeymoon—a genuine candidate for one of the greatest Texas country records ever.

Keen's tunes—set in honky-tonks and scrub-dotted vistas that sprawl out beneath a sky that stretches from horizon to horizon—are populated by border town desperadoes, Saturday night pickup truck romantics, trailer-trash kinfolks, and melancholy wanderers driving lonely roads looking for the past. Keen tiptoes a tightrope between humor and wistfulness, setting and insight—all the while sounding like your best pal telling you a kooky story about something that happened since he'd last seen you.

Nashville doesn't want or need that sort of poetry or authenticity; it's too genuine. Fortunately, a committed national subsidiary, Arista/Texas, signed Keen. After No. 2 Live Dinner, a superb coda for Sugar Hill, Keen stepped up with two major label home runs, Walking Distance and Picnic.

album. It marked the start of Earle's serious rebellion period—though it seemed harmless enough when he blew off the accepted Nashville session players routine and utilized his Dukes on the recording dates.

The new album featured the hit songs "Nowhere Road" and "Sweet Little 66," but Earle's flagrantly mutating appearance and demeanor were causing Nashville to step back a bit. He no longer looked like a slightly malevolent Fonzie, but rather a full-blown, meth-cookin' biker.

Copperhead Road, from 1988, completely alienated Nashville, if for no other reason than it was a rock record. But it was a damned good rock record: a giddy, spinning-out-of-control batch of songs about wild, lost years; hurting and desperate Vietnam vets; and urban white outlaws cruising the highways of the lost. Accordingly, whatever airplay it got was on rock stations, and the record peaked at number 56 on the pop charts.

As interesting as that was demographically, Earle's behavior was becoming increasingly erratic and confrontational; family and friends knew the star had been a heroin addict for years, and if his status as an artist hadn't suffered, the years of abuse were taking their physical and psychological tolls.

A well-publicized fight with a Dallas cop resulted in a fine and probation, but was merely a surface indicator of the dark turmoil swirling in Earle's tattooed brain. The Hard Way (1991) was a bleak, guitar-soaked extension of Copperhead Road, and a live follow-up later that year, Shut Up and Die Like an Aviator, was notable chiefly for the psychological implications of the title and for the fact that Earle's once earnest, raspy vocals now sounded like his voice box had been run through a tree shredder.

Over the next few years, as the crack busts and altercations mounted,

Texas Guitarist Who Changed Music History

Junior Brown

Onstage, in his Joe Friday outfit and straw cowboy hat, forty-three-year-old Junior Brown seems as likely a guitar hero as Don Knotts. But when his hands blur like hummingbird wings over his guit-steel (his hybrid of a traditional electric guitar and a pedal steel), something magnificent and intergalactic happens—and somewhere the ghosts of Jimi Hendrix and Ernest Tubb are smiling.

Brown was born in New Mexico and, after a brief flirtation with teaching himself rock guitar, actively supplemented those skills by listening to acknowledged masters of Hawaiian, bluegrass, and surf tunes, then mixing it all in with his first love: hardcore honky-tonk music.

He played in a variety of roadhouse and country bands (on both traditional guitar and pedal steel) throughout the seventies and eighties, including Alvin Crow and his Pleasant Valley Boys, Asleep at the Wheel, and Rank and File. He even served a stint as an instructor at Oklahoma's Hank Thompson School of Country Music.

But it wasn't until his frustration at trying to hop from lead guitar to pedal steel caused him to invent a double-neck contraption combining both instruments—called the guit-steel—that his own act came together. He mastered the instrument and, having relocated to the fertile Austin music community, began performing around town and writing his own material—wry, alternately humorous and thoughtful country tunes as raw as a West Texas winter morning. Delivered in a honking baritone and peppered with his outer-space, shred-*und*-twang guit-steel ravings, his material eventually coalesced into an independent album called *Twelve Shades of Brown* (1991) which caused enough of an uproar in the staid offices of Nashville that, surprisingly, Curb Records signed him up.

They rereleased *Twelve Shades* in 1993 and quickly followed it up with *Guit with It*. A monstrously cool record that rocked Nashville, the CD featured "Guit-Steel Blues," a twelve-minute, medulla-scrambling instrumental, and two instant classics in a totally unfashionable throwback style—"My Wife Thinks You're Dead" and "Highway Patrol"—the latter of which actually became a hit.

The five-song EP *Junior Brown*, from 1995, only fueled the flames, as did 1996's *Semi-Crazy*. The justified hype crested with 1998's *Long Walk Back*.

Earle lost his record deal and became a shuffling zombie on the streets of Nashville. Finally, a prison sentence and an end-of-the-line rehab stretch apparently screwed some sense into his head. In 1995, clean and free, Earle released the acoustic *Train a Comin'* on the tiny Winter Harvest label. It's a stripped-down, gentle record, as pure and tentative as a child's first joyous steps, as revealing and impressive a record as Earle had yet made.

Until 1996's *I Feel Alright*, that is. The first CD on E-Squared/Warner Brothers (Earle's own imprint label), *I Feel Alright* is the kid on *Train a Comin'* growing up with a healthy appetite, feeling feisty and curious about our strange world yet retaining some creepy psycho-memory about a twisted hell he visited in a dream.

He continues to up the bar. In 1997 he came out with the miraculous *El Corazón*, an almost impossibly consistent CD, then followed with a bluegrass-flavored collaboration with the Del McCoury Band titled *The Collection*. It refuses to leave your CD player.

For all the rebellion represented by Keen, Brown, Lovett and Earle, Don Walser hasn't rebelled against anything. He simply refuses to acknowledge 99 percent of the country music made after, oh, 1965—at least that borne of Nashville marketing departments.

To be sure, the sixty-something Walser weighs about three hundred and fifty pounds and will never be mistaken for Hal Ketchum or Bryan White—and that's fine with him. He was, after all, making country music—*real* country music—decades before Garth Brooks ever bought his first Kiss record.

Walser grew up in Lamesa, a panhandle town between Lubbock and Big Spring. He spent his teen years working eighty-plus hours a week as night manager in a cottonseed mill. His companion during those long evenings was a radio blaring the Grand Ole Opry and a variety of C&W and western swing shows. Hooked, Walser learned guitar, discovered he had a wonderful voice and a celestial ability to yodel, and went to work at assimilating the music of his heroes: Hank Williams, Jimmie Rodgers, Ray Price, Ernest Tubb, and Lefty Frizzell. Walser slowly began to gig throughout West Texas and New Mexico, supplementing a day job with the national guard by gradually expanding his network of gigs until he'd performed around the world.

In 1964, Walser released an indie single, "Rolling Stone from Texas," which *Billboard* rewarded with a four-star review—and which went nowhere.

Twenty years of national guard and nightclub gigs later, Walser moved to Austin and landed in the middle of the town's open-minded country scene like a dust-blown Pavarotti executing a cannonball in a tiny swimming pool. He assembled his Pure Texas Band and became a regular attraction at Henry's Bar and Grill, where they educated a variety of new country and classic rock fans on the exalted history of *real* country music. A few cassettes remain from that period, imbued with reverent covers of

West Texas classics as well as fine original material from Walser and his writing partner, J. Pat Baughman.

Through talent and perseverance, Walser has become something of a legend in a town rich in musical ore. After winning Best Country Band, Best Male Vocalist, and Best Texas Band in *Music City Texas*'s Insiders Poll for several years running, Walser began to draw a bit of national attention.

In 1994, he signed with Austin's Watermelon Records and released a full-length CD, *Rolling Stone from Texas*, a magical record of two-steppin', Saturday night barn dance glory. To hear the Pure Texas Band blister through their taut arrangements is to know how it was meant to be done, and to hear the grandfatherly Walser's gurgling fountain of sweet melodies and ethereal yodeling is to know how they sing in heaven.

Watermelon also released a two-volume *Archive Series*, and a 1996 album of new material called *Texas Tophand*, then, in 1998, Walser signed with the original punk label, Sire. *Down at the Sky-Vue Drive-In* came out later that year, and *Here's to Country Music* was scheduled for a fall '99 release.

INSPIRED BY THE LIKES OF WALSER, AS WELL AS THOSE GEN-erations from Willie to Lyle who revere the integrity and possibilities of country music, a talented crop of artists has taken solid root in Texas.

Wayne "the Train" Hancock is not the brother of Butch Hancock, no matter what I might have said in the first edition of *Texas Music*. I stand by my comment that he's a neat highball of Jimmie Rodgers, Hank Senior, and Bob Wills.

He spent time in a self-imposed prison of liquor and self-pity, scrabbling by in a West Dallas ghetto before heading to Austin, where he found so-briety and kindred musical souls. His dusty, nasal whine and gee-whiz tunes about Being a Poor White Guy (Which Is Okay 'Cause I've Got a Fun-Lovin' Mama) are just corny and sincere enough that they're utterly charm-ing. His first two albums (*Thunderstorms and Neon Signs* and *Wild, Free & Reckless*) were brisk and intriguing.

Lubbock's Kimmie Rhodes established herself as a songwriter for big-timers like Trisha Yearwood and Wynonna Judd, but her affection for her home state and the freedom to write and record what she pleases has char-acterized her own singing career.

She, of course, has business contacts in Nashville, but Rhodes decided the hill country outside Austin was a more refreshing musical center. Dis-covered by Willie Nelson, Rhodes recorded an entire album at the legend's Pedernales Studio. Obviously, Rhodes can write killer tunes; unfortunately, the sparse, acoustic quality of her own arrangements and a willingness (and talent) to allow her sparkling voice to roam freely across stylistic pastures has confused Nashville.

She's released three records on a European label (1981's *Kimmie Rhodes and the Jackalope Brothers*, 1985's *Man in the Moon*, and 1989's *Angels Get the Blues*), but it wasn't until 1996 that Rhodes scored a major deal here in the States. Newly signed to the Houston-based Justice label, Rhodes released a triumphant *West Texas Heaven*.

Rosie Flores, who was born in San Antonio and grew up in San Diego, has brought significant life to the so-called alternative country movement. As the leader of an all-female SoCal band called Rosie and the Screamers, Flores molded roadhouse country, poetry, surf tunes, and rockabilly into an upstart but reverent form of hardcore C&W.

In 1987, she signed with Warner/Reprise and released *Rosie Flores*, for which she scored a significant critical acclaim as a guitarist/singer/songwriter. She moved to Austin the next year, then got a deal with HighTone Records, for whom she recorded 1992's *After the Farm*, a brilliant album ladling her hill country song recipes with Buck Owens's Bakersfield gravy.

In 1993, Flores's *Once More with Feeling* made her a household name among C&W stars, and her grassroots following continued to grow. With 1995's rambunctious *Rockabilly Filly*, the singer blows the walls down with a consistent set of dance-happy, catchy modern country tunes, whipped by her she-devil voice and quicksilver guitar lines. She continues to accelerate like some barroom rocket ship: in successive years, she's released *A Little Bit of Heartache* (with Ray Campi), *A Honky Tonk Reprise* (consisting of unreleased tracks from the late eighties), and the kickin' *Dance Hall Dreams*.

One of the premiere roots/country bands is the Derailers, whose own roots are in Tangent, Oregon. It was in the Pacific Northwest that guitarist Brian Hofeldt and singer/songwriter Tony O. Villanueva met and bonded over Buck Owens records.

After Villanueva moved to Austin in 1989 and was able to persuade Hofeldt to follow him a few years later, the Derailers (with an ever-changing rhythm section) were born. Central Texas instantly heated up a few degrees and hasn't cooled off since.

Their original tunes splash jiggers of pure rockabilly and western swing over prototypical Buck Owens, and, in conjunction with their wildfire stage show, the Derailers qualify as the amphetamine of Austin's honky-tonk resurgence. They've put out two albums, 1995's *Live Tracks* (on the Freedom label) and the 1996 Watermelon release, the Dave Alvin–produced and more-than-aptly-titled *Jackpot*.

It's conceivable that Dale Watson grew up in Houston wishing Merle Haggard would die—but only so the Hag's spirit would enter Watson's body. In that spirit, young Dale formed the Classic Country Band virtually before his voice changed, and had an independent single on the Gilley's jukebox by the time he was twenty.

After visiting Rosie Flores in L.A., Watson was astonished that country acts out there were playing original music, and hightailed it west at top speed. With a batch of ode-to-happy-hour songs, a croon that sounds like Ricky Nelson after swilling some of Ozzie's gin, and a Wilburn Brothers

CRIMINALLY UNDERRATED BROTHERS
Bruce and Charlie Robison

Quick: Would you rather be Charlie Robison because of whom he's married to or Bruce Robison because of whom *he's* married to—or either one simply because they're such gifted country singer/songwriters?

Both are Houston-born, Bandera-raised former college basketball players who turned to music as a less-painful way to hang around babes and because not many basketball gigs came with all-the-beer-you-can-drink clauses. And also because they loved the broad implications of Texas music. After playing in a variety of bands (some together) the two separately began to focus on their singer/songwriter personas.

Charlie's debut indie release, *Bandera,* is deceptively simple in its terrific depictions of everyday situations gone awry. He then signed with Sony/ Lucky Dog and, in 1998, came out with *The Life of the Party,* a raw country record as diverse in mood and texture as the state itself. Both CDs are also funny as hell, demonstrating Charlie's acumen for wit-laced philosophy.

Similarly, Bruce's self-titled first CD is on the same Vireo label as Charlie's *Bandera*—and in an appropriately fraternal development, is also signed to Sony/Lucky Dog. *Wrapped* was his first record for the label, and what it lacks in Charlie's darker, one-liner worldview, it makes up in a Frostian appreciation for the joy and sadness of the workaday world. The follow-up, *Long Way Home from Anywhere,* came out in the summer of 1999 and sounds like James Taylor singing Robert Earl Keen songs.

Oh, yeah: Bruce is married to Kelly Willis, and Charlie's wife is the former Emily Erwin of the Dixie Chicks.

---

haircut and wardrobe, Watson was promptly snagged by Curb Records. But when a philosophical dispute arose over whether Watson's songs were "positive" enough, the deal fell apart. A stint as an assembly-line tunesmith in Nashville wasn't fruitful, either, and Watson headed back to Texas in the hopes that Austin would provide some answers. It did.

His no-horseshit reverence for C&W history and a penchant for writing genuine tunes attracted the attention of roots label HighTone, for whom Watson recorded the popular and totally superb *Cheatin' Heart Attack* in 1995. *Blessed or Damned,* the 1996 follow-up, featuring a duet with Johnny Bush, is a logical progression.

Watson may have hit his career tape-measure homer with 1997's *I Hate These Songs*—as brilliant a honky-tonk record as exists in the nineties— and *The Truckin' Sessions,* which came out the following year and is a proper homage to songs of the big rigs.

An Austin singer/songwriter who could pass for Watson's brother, stylistically as well as genetically, and who deserves mention here, is Monte Warden. In fact, in the mid-eighties, Warden's star-spangled Porter Wagoner suits and neo–Marty Robbins songs were arguably the genesis for Austin's second progressive country movement.

Warden headed up two fine bands at that time, Whoa! Trigger (rockabilly) and the Wagoneers (pure country), but shifted gears in the nineties to a style more reminiscent of Buddy Holly or the Everly Brothers. He released two fine CDs for Watermelon (*Monte Warden* and *Here I Am*), and in 1998 signed with Asylum. His first for the label, *A Stranger to Me Now*, is a tender and heartbreakingly great CD chronicling the dissolution of his marriage.

Conversely, Corpus Christi–born Ted Roddy, long a rockabilly curator, has only recently maneuvered his muse in a pure and distilled country direction. His 1995 debut for HighTone, *Full Circle*, is as promising as any Texas country album in recent memory.

There are plenty more noteworthy participants currently bucking the Nashville line in this genre. Houston native Jack Ingram, a former SMU student who decided he was more interested in being Jerry Jeff Walker than Joe College, built a statewide following playing for tourists and sorority and fraternity guys in Dallas's Adair's saloon. After two wildly successful indie albums, he recently inked a major deal with a new Nashville label, Rising Tide Records.

Artists who unequivocally *deserve* major label deals are Don McCalister, Jr., Cornell Hurd, Jeff Hughes, Ronny Spears, Ed Burleson, Chaparral, the Millionaire Playboys, Tommy Alverson, Libby Bosworth, Marti Brom, Chris Wall (whose *Tainted Angel* and *Honky Tonk Heart* CDs are necessary listening), and, in particular, the wonderful western swing revisionists, Cowboys and Indians, and Donny Ray Ford—a Dallasite with the voice of George Jones, the songwriting acumen of Merle Haggard, and an ability to hoist a longneck whilst warbling his own honky-tonk classics that would surely please both.

WHILE ALL THESE PERFORMERS REPRESENT THE SPIRIT OF THE Generation X country purists who have striven mightily to avoid the commercial and shallow Nashville approach, an entirely different set of new country artists has evolved, too, and this second tide of upstarts came from an odd and totally unexpected direction: punk music.

In the mid-eighties, after the first punk offensive, in which the Mohawk and safety pin set sought to destroy all things decadent in what rock 'n' roll had become, practitioners in turn had to mutate in order not to step on their own sodden feet. As such, they began to fuse punk with, well, *any* form of music in their primal attempt to piss somebody off.

Ergo, it was inevitable that some angry young men would have the perspicacious idea to thrash their way through a set of Hank Williams and Buck Owens songs. Thus, "cowpunk" was born.

Probably the first notable example of it in Texas was through a band called Rank and File. The group rose from the ashes of two early San Francisco punk bands, the Nuns and the Dils, the former of which was founded by a San Antonio–born, California-bred singer/guitarist named Alejandro Escovedo, and the latter containing two brothers, Chip and Tony Kinman (guitarist/vocalist and bassist/vocalist, respectively).

After those bands disintegrated, Escovedo and Chip Kinman, both in New York City at that point, formed Rank and File to play country music; their rather amateurish, punk-trained instrumental abilities (or lack thereof) created the "cowpunk" style by accident—they simply weren't good enough musicians to play C&W correctly, and their natural, punkish anger and raw enthusiasm carried over into the new hybrid.

In 1982, joined by Tony Kinman, the band relocated to Austin, added drummer Slim Evans, signed with Slash (the noted punk label), and released *Sundown*. The album was an overwhelming critical success, although the immediate reaction among the punk crowd was bewilderment and anger.

Shortly thereafter, Escovedo, who was feeling too much a sideman, left Rank and File to form with his brother, Javier Escovedo, the True Believers, which would become the darlings of Austin's new alternative music scene. *Sundown*, then, remains the sole testimonial to the birth of cowpunk in Texas music, but it wasn't long before a crop of inspired and brilliant bands picked up the thread.

Killbilly, a Dallas group whose fusion of bluegrass and shred metal was the brainchild of guitarist Alan Wooley, was by far the most successful of the upstart country conceptions. Wooley, whose roots were in a seventies rock band called U.S. Kids and the new wave White Shapes, came up with the idea of Killbilly and actually recorded an entire cassette in his bedroom in 1986. He sent the tape to deejay Craig "Niteman" Taylor at Dallas's KNON, who was so blown away he called Wooley to invite the band into the studio to play live. When Wooley fessed up that *he* was the band, Taylor told Wooley that he, Taylor, could sing and play harmonica, and why didn't they make Killbilly a reality. So they did.

For the next seven years, Killbilly slowly established an international following and blew the opportunistic doors open for acts like Uncle Tupelo to reach an audience. Playing a scalding brand of music that crossed Bill Monroe with Motörhead, Killbilly released two cassettes, 1990's *Alive from the City of Hate in the Lone Star State*, on Denton's 4 Dots label, and an indie release the following year called *Bootleg '91*.

As the group toured across America and Europe, they attracted the attention of Flying Fish Records, which signed them and released 1992's critically huzzahed *Foggy Mountain Anarchy*. A 1994 CD on Crystal Clear Records (also with international distribution) was called *Stranger in This*

Place, and almost placed the band in a position to become, perhaps, an Asleep at the Wheel of modern bluegrass. Unfortunately, the financial burden of seven consecutive years in the red finally thwarted the band's momentum, and they broke up early the following year. Though over sixty musicians signed Killbilly time-cards during their run, the essential members, besides Wooley and Taylor, included drummer Mike Schwedler, bassist Richard Hunter, banjo man Stephen Trued, and Harris "Stealth" Kirby on mandolin, guitar, and vocals. Other luminaries who at one time or another played with Killbilly included Steve Lutke, the superstar banjoist for Vassar Clements, South-by-Southwest Music Festival honcho Louis J. Myers, and a variety of players who would surface in similar projects down the line.

Two players who served time in Killbilly, Danny Barnes and Mark Rubin, went on to form Austin's Bad Livers, whose name might seem a description of Hank Williams, Jr.'s medical prognosis, but is actually a reference to the physiological fact that, whereas a good liver filters out all impurities from the bloodstream, a bad liver simply lets everything through.

Which is, stylistically, exactly what the Bad Livers signify—at least so far as one could expect from a trio whose instrumental lineup includes banjos, mandolin, guitar, and vocals (Barnes); standup bass, tuba, and vocals (Rubin); and sundry other instruments as needed.

The Bad Livers formed in 1990 as a means for Barnes to record a funky, for-friends-and-family-only Christmas tape of eccentric arrangements of bluegrass, folk, and gospel material, and the tape became an underground collectors' item.

Gradually, as their spirited rock arrangements of dusty hillbilly and folk standards evolved, the Bad Livers became hugely popular throughout Texas as well as popular club draws on the college circuit and on international alternative music tours.

After the Bad Livers signed with ¼ Stick Records, they released a cassette version of Barnes's original Christmas tape, titled *Dust on the Bible*, and followed in 1992 with a full-length CD/album/cassette called *Delusions of Banjer*.

Later that year, an EP of radio broadcasts, *The Golden Years*, was issued on gold vinyl. Finally, in 1994, the Livers released *Horses in the Mines*, on which the emphasis shifted from their creative adaptations of acoustic standards to their own material. Two later CDs, *Hogs on the Highway* and *Industry and Thrift*, find the boys honing their unique craft. They also composed and performed the soundtrack for *The Newton Boys*.

The Cartwrights, a promising neo-honky-tonk band comprised largely of ex-punks and ex–new wavers, released one independent CD, 1994's *Ponderosa Fabulosa*, which is an obscure triumph of modern-day barroom wit and melody, but the band imploded too soon.

Some Dallasites considered the Old 97's a *Tiger Beat* version of the Cartwrights, inasmuch as they found influences in traditional country music

and were formed by former teen folkie/popster Rhett Miller, a guitarist/
singer/songwriter whose fragile good looks dazzled young chicks when he
was written up in *Seventeen* in the late eighties as a musical hunk-to-be.

But with bassist/vocalist/cowriter Murry Hammond, drummer Philip Pee-
ples, and guitarist Ken Bethea, the Old 97's are anything but a New Edition
for the Wrangler set. Sure, they look good, but their brand of Dwight
Yoakam Joins Big Star tunes are the real thing. After two enormously successful CDs for Chicago's Bloodshot label, 1994's *Hitchhiking to Rhome* and
1995's *Wreck Your Life*, the band signed a multialbum deal with Elektra in
the summer of 1996.

A year later, they came out with *Too Far to Care*, a transcendent CD
whose songs sounded like Andy Partridge if he'd grown up in Lubbock.

Other retro-Haggards from alternative sources deserving note are/were
the junkie-tonk band Tex and the Swinging Cornflake Killers, Liberty Val-
ance, Roy Heinrich, Mark Luna, Hank & Patsy, Homer Henderson, Sons
of the Desert, the Sisters Morales, and the Shakin' Apostles. Even newer
cowpokesters are forthcoming: Austin's mere babes Reckless Kelly (*Acoustic
Live at Stubbs* and *Millican*), Owen Temple, Roger Creager, the Lucky
Pierres, Eric Geyer, Amy Atchley, and the Groobees, an Amarillo band
most famous (for the time being) as having written the title cut of the Dixie
Chicks' *Wide Open Spaces* CD.

Steve Kolander, Jesse Dayton, and Stacey Earle deserve special note.
Dayton (*Raisin' Cain*) adds a roots-clustered vibe to his tavern-seeped tunes.
Kolander blends Buddy Holly and Hank Cochran to magical effect on *Pieces
of a Puzzle* and *Scoot Over, Move Closer*. Earle, the sister of Steve Earle, was
a staff writer in Nashville before her bro encouraged her to work for herself.
Simple Gearle is her first solo effort, a roots/folk gem in cowgirl clothing.

☆ One: Buddy Holly and the Fifties: The Birth of Texas Rock

A CYNIC MIGHT SAY THAT ROCK 'N' ROLL IS WHAT HAPPENED when a white guy decided he would play black rhythm and blues—which was in fact the case when Bill Haley and the Saddlemen covered Jackie Brenston's "Rocket 88" in 1951.

Though the phrase "rock 'n' roll" had long been utilized in blues songs as a euphemism for protracted bouts of "the nasty," and references to "rockin'" had cropped up in precisely those R&B recordings Haley sought to emulate (Roy Brown's 1948 tune "Good Rockin' Tonight," for example), it wasn't until Haley and the Saddlemen sold 75,000 copies of "Rock This Joint" that a fevered thirst for rock 'n' roll began to grow in white America. And when the Saddlemen recorded "Crazy Man Crazy" in 1953, and it became the first rock song to make the *Billboard* charts, the whole concept was about to become a phenomenon.

The Saddlemen would change their name to the Comets and score several rapid-fire hits, including, of course, "Rock Around the Clock," but fate decreed that Elvis Presley would become the first real rock star. Haley, despite his record sales, was a dumpy, balding guy relegated to metaphorical mop-up duties; if Elvis was the king of rock 'n' roll, Haley was, perhaps, the janitor. It was a situation that would haunt Haley throughout his ever-dwindling career. He relocated to Harlingen, Texas, and though he continued to sell records and perform on nostalgia tours and has-been packages, he eventually grew bitter and drank heavily. Toward the end of his life he was diagnosed with a brain tumor, his behavior became erratic and delusional, and he finally succumbed to a heart attack in 1981 at the age of fifty-five.

Back at the dawn of rock, however, between Elvis's penthouse and Haley's boiler room, there was plenty of opportunity for would-be rock stars, and Lubbock's Buddy Holly would soon fit the bill in a shimmering way. Born Charles Hardin Holley in 1938, he studied violin and piano at an early age, but switched at seven to guitar, inspired by the sounds of Jimmie Rodgers, Hank Williams, and a variety of country and gospel radio.

He formed a high school band, the Western and Bop Band (with Bob Montgomery and Larry Welborn), which nabbed a half-hour Sunday afternoon radio show on local station KDAV, on which they were billed as Buddy and Bob. Welborn was replaced with Don Guess, and in 1956, Decca signed the band, now called the Three Tunes, as a country act (a misspelling in the contract resulted in Buddy's more familiar "Holly" surname).

A few singles were released, including an early version of "That'll Be the Day," but country radio yawned. It was just as well; the C&W concept became an afterthought in Holly's mind after the Three Tunes opened a show for Elvis at the Lubbock Youth Center.

Holly immediately wanted to rock. He formed the Crickets with drummer Larry Allison, guitarist Niki Sullivan, and bassist Joe Maudlin, and with that alliance two major rock precedents were established: The now-accepted two guitars/bass/drums format came into being, and Holly began to write his own material.

Decca wasn't impressed with Holly's new visions, though, and after fruitless sessions in Nashville with noted producer Owen Bradley, the band returned to Lubbock. In early 1957, Buddy Holly and the Crickets drove to nearby Clovis, New Mexico, to the studios of producer/songwriter Norman Petty, where they cut a rock arrangement of "That'll Be the Day" and several other tunes.

Petty signed on as Holly's manager, and the new tracks convinced Decca that Holly had more possibilities as a rock artist. A subsequent meeting with all concerned resulted in a unique and complicated marketing strategy: Holly would record as a solo artist for Decca's Coral subsidiary and as the front man for the Crickets on another Decca label, Brunswick.

The blueprint worked. "That'll Be the Day" was a number 3 hit for Holly, while the follow-up, "Peggy Sue," credited to the Crickets, sold over a million units and necessitated the band's first national tour. By 1958, they'd charted "Oh, Boy!," "Maybe Baby," "Think It Over," "Early in the Morning," "Rave On," and "Fool's Paradise," and had toured England to the appreciation of fans like John Lennon, Paul McCartney, and Eric Clapton—all of whom would go on to own several houses as a result of their Holly-inspired attempts at songcraft.

There was a reason for Holly's appeal. Think of him as a savory, multi-layered musical lasagna, served up in magnificent, two-minute explosions of hum-along genius. In every tune was the charm of Holly's TV weatherman appearance, the life-is-a-perennial-sock-hop theme, a gentle confidence that attracted rather than repelled, and the buoyant image of his genuine performance enthusiasm.

In fact, it is probable that Holly would have curried favor indefinitely with the burgeoning rock audience. But in October 1958, upset at discovering Norman Petty's name listed as cowriter on several of his songs, Holly split from Petty and the Crickets and moved to Greenwich Village, where he married Maria Elena Santiago. Holly did some recording in New York, but, in financial limbo over the managerial imbroglio, Holly agreed to go out on a Winter Dance Party Tour of the Midwest in early 1959.

Performing with Holly on the tour were ex-Cricket guitarist Tommy Allsup and Waylon Jennings. Weary of bus travel, Holly and some of the other featured performers in the show, Richie Valens and J. P. "The Big Bopper" Richardson, chartered a plane after the Clear Lake, Iowa, concert. In an event immortalized years later in Don McClean's "American Pie" as "the day the music died," the plane crashed a few minutes after takeoff, killing all aboard.

As with any popular musician who dies prematurely, Holly's legacy of demo tapes, unfinished studio tracks, and former bandmates all popped up for commercial consumption in a variety of cobweb configurations. At the time of his death, "It Doesn't Matter Anymore" was released, and *The Complete Buddy Holly Story*, a nine-record set, and the 1978 film *The Buddy Holly Story* pretty much covered the territory.

The Crickets, with a variety of personnel changes, played on into the sixties, and two, Larry Allison and Sonny Curtis (who joined up after Holly's death), had moderate solo success.

One of the victims in the crash that killed Holly was J. P. Richardson, another Texan, who was born in Sabine Pass in 1932. A career disc jockey who started as "The Big Bopper" at Beaumont's KTRM just out of high school, Richardson became one of the region's most popular radio personalities.

Weaned in the mid-fifties from his early C&W predilections to the rockabilly of Elvis and Jerry Lee Lewis, Richardson's secret ambition was to be a pop hero. He began assimilating demos of songs he'd started writing during a brief stint in the army and, by 1957, had enough interesting material that he attracted the attention of Mercury's Shelby Singleton, who signed Richardson along with fellow Texans Johnny Preston and Bruce Channel.

Richardson cut two straight country singles under his own name, then, as the Big Bopper, released a novelty record he'd written called "The Purple People Eater Meets the Witch Doctor." It was the B-side of the disc, though, a rockabilly original called "Chantilly Lace," that became an international hit.

In 1957–58, the Big Bopper had other hits with his own compositions, including "Running Bear," "Little Red Riding Hood," and "Big Bopper's Wedding," though he wouldn't live long enough to see Johnny Preston score a number 1 hit with "Running Bear" in 1960.

Richardson, meanwhile, developed a stage show based on the Bopper persona, and became a popular attraction on a number of traveling rock packages. It was on one such tour that, feeling ill and not up to a long bus ride, the Big Bopper begged a seat on the plane carrying Holly and Richie Valens.

* * *

IF THE BIG BOPPER'S POTENTIAL AS A WRITER WAS NEVER
sufficiently developed to have indicated precisely what his future held, another Texan emerged in the fifties with incredible writing potential, and
the transcendent voice of a playful angel: Roy Orbison.

Born in Vernon, Texas, in 1936, Orbison received a guitar for his sixth
birthday. By eight, he had secured a regular Saturday morning slot on
KVWC's *Amateur Hour* and, within two years, was hosting the program.

After his family moved to the West Texas oasis of Wink, Orbison played
in a high school band called the Wink Westerners, a self-described western
swing outfit that in fact played everything from Webb Pierce to "Moonlight
in Vermont."

The Westerners metamorphosed into the Teen Kings, an outfit that attained the lofty status of local television celebrities. In 1955, Orbison utilized that fame to get backstage at Fort Worth's Panther Hall to meet Elvis
Presley. But it wasn't until he became pals with Pat Boone, while they were
both students at North Texas State University, in Denton, that Orbison
started to make the musical transformations that would lead to massive
success.

Boone, already a pop star on the Dot label, encouraged Orbison to experiment more with the rock and rockabilly sounds emanating from Sam
Phillips's Sun Studios in Memphis, home to Elvis, Carl Perkins, Jerry Lee
Lewis, and Johnny Cash. This wasn't the first time Sun had been mentioned
to Orbison. Cash had already recommended Orbison to Sam Phillips after
the two singers appeared on a regional TV show together. Though Phillips
didn't act at the time, Orbison's name stayed with him.

After backing Boone as a rhythm guitarist on a studio date, Orbison
himself received a chance to record with Norman Petty at the very same
Clovis, New Mexico studio that had launched Buddy Holly.

Now billed as Roy Orbison and the Teen Kings, they recorded "Ooby
Dooby," a quasi-rockabilly tune from their repertoire written by a duo of
NTSU upperclassmen named Dick Penner and Wade Moore. A friend of
Orbison's, an Odessa record store owner named Cecil Hollerfield, knew Sam
Phillips from the early days of Sun, and entreated him to give "Ooby Dooby"
a listen.

This time Phillips was impressed, and "Ooby Dooby" sold three hundred
thousand copies when released in 1956. Orbison relocated to Nashville,
became pals with Elvis (who talked him into buying a Cadillac with his
first Sun royalty check), and, in addition to his Sun contract, signed to
write songs for Acuff-Rose publishing. One of his first attempts, a tune he
wrote for his wife called "Claudette" (which was appropriate since that was
her name), became a big seller for the Everly Brothers. But while his reputation as a writer grew, his recording relationship with Sun proved less
than fruitful, and in 1959 Orbison moved over to Monument Records. His
career as a rockabilly artist was effectively over, but that was okay; he was
about to become a spectacularly successful pop star.

*   *   *

THERE WERE, NATURALLY, OTHER TEXANS ACTIVE IN THE blossoming rock 'n' roll scene. The Champs, a group of West Coast session men recording on the Challenge label, included Rankin's Chuck Rio on sax, Sidney's Jim Seals on guitar, and Cisco's Dash Crofts on guitar and mandolin. Their 1958 instrumental, "Tequila," hit number 1, sold over six million copies, and won a Grammy award. The band charted several more songs into the early sixties, but none matched the success of "Tequila." Seals and Crofts went on to form the Dawnbreakers and, of course, in the seventies, had terrific success as the cash-generating soft-rock duo.

Fort Worth's Robert Byrd achieved brief success working under the nom de rock Bobby Day. Though he worked with Johnny Otis, Day is most famous for his 1958 song "Rockin' Robin," which he recorded for Class Records and which went to number 2 on the charts. Day also released "Little Bitty Pretty One" for Class, and as lead singer with the Hollywood Flames, a top twenty hit with "Buzz Buzz Buzz." Day's "Over and Over" would be a number 1 seller for Brits the Dave Clark Five in 1965.

Ray Peterson, who was from Denton, had an Orbison-like four-and-a-half-octave vocal range and a similar affection for ballads. After singing to amuse fellow polio patients in the Warm Springs Foundation Hospital, Peterson started working in clubs and eventually relocated to the West Coast. RCA signed him in 1958 and released "Let's Try Romance." A few similarly indifferent singles followed, but Peterson scored big with a 1959 version of Baker Knight's "The Wonder of It All." A string of hits followed, including "Tell Laura I Love Her" (1960) and "Corinna, Corinna" (1961).

Two other panhandle musicians followed in Buddy Holly's golden footsteps. Buddy Knox and Jimmy Bowen (from Canyon and Dumas, respectively) formed Buddy Knox and the Rhythm Orchids and, in 1956, entered Norman Petty's Clovis studio. In a session memorable for Petty's use of a cardboard box instead of a drum kit (the better to deal with the infernal noise of an actual kit), they cut Knox's "Party Doll" and Bowen's "I'm Stickin' with You." Originally issued back-to-back on the same local single, both tunes were released separately on New York's Roulette—and sold over a million copies each.

Jesse Belvin, from San Antonio, was a singer/songwriter who had a studio jones that considerably predated Brian Wilson. He cowrote "Earth Angel," which was a 1955 hit for the Penguins, and in 1956 recorded four separate vocal tracks to create the illusion of a band. He called his "group" the Cliques, and the song, "Girl of My Dreams," sold respectably. He also scored with "Good Night, My Love," but his incredible potential was snuffed out in an auto accident which also killed his wife.

Rockabilly, the potent cocktail mixing country and blues that started it all, had its proponents long after the defections of Holly and Orbison. Most notable were Ronnie Dawson and Sid King and the Five Strings. Dawson, born in Dallas in 1939, was a teen star who released his first single in his early teens, "Action Packed" backed with "I Make the Love" on the regional Backbeat label. Known as the Blond Bomber, the youngster had a bigger hit with "Rockin' Bones," on Rockin' Records. Both singles sold well enough to attract the attention of Dick Clark. Clark called to offer a contract with his Swan Records as well as an appearance on *American Bandstand*, but the payola scandals rocked the record industry and stalled Dawson's career—temporarily.

Sid King was born Sidney Erwin in Denton in 1936. His early musical years were steeped in country, and he led a band called the Western Melodymakers. But as rockabilly became a force, King changed the name of his band to the Five Strings and moved into the new territory.

A 1954 single for Starday, "Who Put the Turtle in Myrtle's Girdle," drew the attention of Columbia Records, and the Five Strings signed a contract. Though they released several sides for the next half-decade, it was as live performers in Europe that the Five Strings really held court. Rockabilly was huge overseas, and King and company toured for years on the strength of their driving rhythms. Sid's brother, Billy, the band's lead guitarist, was a terrific influence on rockabilly guitarists, and in his own home state made a huge impression on no less than Ronnie Dawson and the Reverend Horton Heat.

Both brothers continue to tour Europe periodically, and there are plans for a CD of old an new material, but, they pay the bills cutting hair in their Cutting Shop in the Dallas suburb of Richardson—which is also a virtual museum of rockabilly. Plus, you can get one of those really cool fifties haircuts from the guys who actually pioneered the look.

Two other north Texas rock frontiersmen still crank it out: Fort Worth's Mac Curtis and Dallas's Gene Summers. Curtis was a wee sixteen when he signed a rockabilly contract with King Records, for whom he released three singles. He also appeared on Alan Freed's *Rock 'n' Roll Revue* at the Paramount Theater in New York before halting his career with a three-year military stint. Post-army, Curtis worked as a broadcaster before relocating to L.A, in 1971, where he jump-started his career by signing with the Rollin' Rock label. As with many of these performers, Curtis's records continued to do brisk business in rockabilly-happy Europe, and he's continued to play overseas regularly. Recently, Hightone Records has released *Rockabilly Uprising: The Best of Mac Curtis*, a more-than-worthy CD documenting Curtis's ever-youthful spirit.

Summers, who was also infected with the new virus called rock 'n' roll, formed bands out of high school and was soon appearing in a variety of North Texas clubs in support of Chuck Berry, Gene Vincent, Connie Francis, and several other burgeoning stars. He also recorded numerous local sides, including 1963's "Big Blue Diamonds," which hit the national charts. Continually active throughout the sixties and seventies, Summers also became the subject of an intense revival in Europe, where he continues to perform systematically. He's released dozens of albums for dozens of domestic and foreign labels, including a new compilation scheduled for release by Dallas's Crystal Clear Sound.

In any case, as the decade drew to a close, Roy Orbison was about to become an international voice to be reckoned with. And in the shadow of Buddy Holly's death, it was not yet possible to see the gathering tide that would betoken the very British invasion he helped inspire.

☆ Two: Texas Rock Grows Up and Crawls

A S WITH MOST OF THE COUNTRY, THE NEW DECADE STARTED blissfully enough in Texas. It would be almost four years before the state was indicted en masse as "the killer" of an American president, and even longer before the Beatles swept onto our shores like an infantry with their deceptively cute haircuts and a new way of doing things.

And despite incidental triflings like the Cuban missile crisis, the musical infant that was rock 'n' roll was digging around and taking root in the American consciousness. In the direct aftermath of Elvis and Buddy, the gentle croonings of Roy Orbison represented the last calm before a substantial storm. Orbison, a quiet, sweet guy with a shoe-polish pompadour, blindman sunglasses and a corpselike pallor, had said all along that he preferred to sing ballads, and so he did—like no one before or since.

The Orbison flood started innocuously enough in 1960. He wrote a song he hoped to pitch to Elvis or, failing that, the Everly Brothers. But the King slept through the demo session, and the Everlys politely passed on the tune. So Orbison recorded the song himself. It was "Only the Lonely," which sold over two million copies and reached number 2. And over the next four years, Roy Orbison would inundate American and British charts with his soaring, ethereal voice and a stream of wonderful songs including "Blue Angel" (number 9, 1960), "Running Scared" (number 1, 1961), "Crying" (number 2, 1961), "Dream Baby" (number 4, 1962), "In Dreams" (number 7, 1963), "Mean Woman Blues" (number 5, 1963), and "Oh Pretty Woman" (number 1, 1964).

He toured Europe with the as-yet domestically obscure Beatles in 1963, and though it appeared Orbison was invincible, a set of personal tragedies in the latter part of the sixties—his wife was killed in a 1966 motorcycle accident, and two of his three sons would die in a house fire in 1969—would retard his initial momentum. And though his career would meander and twist for twenty years, enormous popularity would again return, in peculiar ways, much later than anyone would have imagined. . . .

Star-time wouldn't last nearly so long for another alumnus of Norman Petty's studio in Clovis. Jimmy Gilmer, an Illinois kid whose family relocated to Amarillo in his youth, had studied piano and formed a pop band in 1957 while a student at Amarillo College. In the early sixties, while at

Petty's, he met an existing group called the Fireballs (bassist Stan Lark, guitarist George Tomsco, and drummer Eric Budd) who'd tasted the cheap liquor of regional popularity with songs like "Torquay" and "Bulldog."

Newly rechristened Jimmy Gilmer and the Fireballs, they recorded "Quite a Party," which landed in the top thirty, and then went to number 1 with the most popular tune of 1963, "Sugar Shack." Though they charted two more minor hits in 1964 and experienced touring success here and abroad, Gilmer and the Fireballs split up in 1965. The Fireballs resurfaced in 1968 with "Bottle of Wine," but Gilmer wisped into obscurity.

And the original Clovis outfit, the Crickets, Buddy Holly's surviving band, continued to crank it out for the Brunswick and Coral labels. With ex-Holly guitarist Sonny Curtis and singer Earl Sinks joining the original Cricket rhythm section (bassist Joe Maudlin and drummer Larry Allison), the band actually turned out some pretty nice records, including the original versions of "More Than I Can Say" and "I Fought the Law."

In 1961, they switched to Liberty Records and instituted Jerry Naylor as their new vocalist, but the resultant records didn't do much. At that point, though the members changed frequently, the Crickets managed occasional airplay and maintained their legend status overseas well into the decade—though without ever approaching Holly's actual genius. A collection of the post-Holly stuff called *The Liberty Years* came out on EMI America in 1991.

Other pre-Beatles musical happenings abounded in Texas, and Fort Worth music impresario Major Bill Smith was at the center of the vortex. Smith heard vocal duo Paul and Paula (Ray Hildebrand of Joshua and Jill Jackson of Brownwood) at an audition and had them record a song they'd written called "Hey Paula." It proved regionally popular, and the Major scored them a national distribution deal with a Mercury subsidiary label, Philips.

"Hey Paula" became a number 1 smash in the States and overseas, selling over a million units in the United States alone. But popularity was short-lived, and though Paul and Paula released several more singles and a few albums, only their second single, "Young Lovers" (1963), charted anywhere near their inaugural hit, peaking at number 6.

Major Bill also had minor triumphs with Grapevine's Bruce Channel ("Hey! Baby"), Fort Worth's Ray Sharp ("Linda Lu"), and a Cowtown rockabilly act, the Rondells ("If You Really Want Me to I'll Go"), whose leader was a youthful Delbert McClinton, the soon-to-be rhythm-and-blues workhorse.

Meanwhile, on February 9, 1964, every human in the USA crowded around the television for an immortal Sunday evening broadcast when the Beatles guested on *The Ed Sullivan Show*. The event proved to be the last recorded instance of family bonding in American history, and the reason was that, afterward, every kid was busy trying to form a band.

Texas kids were no exception, and some of the youngsters were pretty damned good at it, too. The first requirement was to purchase Beatle boots, then start parting your hair on the wrong side so it looked longer. If you made it that far, you might even talk your parents into buying you an electric guitar out of the Montgomery Ward catalogue. And then . . .

Of the first batch of post–Beatles invasion bands to gain notoriety from Texas, the Sir Douglas Quintet, Sam the Sham and the Pharoahs, and ? and the Mysterians stand out. Interestingly enough, given the guitar-driven pop of the British groups, a common denominator between the three Texas groups was the utilization of a south-of-the-border keyboard sound. This was accomplished through Vox and/or Farfisa organs, and the tonal quality was cheesier than the queso dip at any East Austin Tex-Mex joint. But it worked.

Vocalist/organist Domingo "Sam" Samudio, from Dallas, formed Sam the Sham and the Pharoahs (bassist David Martin, guitarist Ray Stinnet, drummer Jerry Patterson, and saxophonist Butch Gibson) in the early sixties as a quasi-novelty act. The band members were outfitted in turbans and traveled to gigs in a hearse, and had a moderate hit with "Haunted House" on the tiny Penn label.

The song attracted some interest, and the band split for Memphis when Stan Kesler agreed to finance the sessions that resulted in their signature hit, 1965's funky, exuberant, and almost incomprehensible "Wooly Bully." The single, released on Kesler's own XYZ label, went to number 2 and sold millions, and the band's contract was subsequently purchased by MGM. *Wooly Bully* was only the first of several albums for the label, and Sam and his Pharoahs continued to chart tunes over the next few years. "Juju Hand" (number 22, 1966) and another million-plus seller, "Li'l Red Riding Hood" (number 2, 1966) boosted the sales of such albums as *Li'l Red Riding Hood*, *Sam the Sham, On Tour*, and *Best of Sam the Sham and the Pharoahs*. Finally, in 1967, with the audiences waning, Samudio split from the band. He's surfaced sporadically since then, winning a Grammy for his liner notes to 1970's solo disc, *Sam, Hard and Heavy* (Atlantic), and supplying two songs to *The Border* soundtrack.

Like Sam the Sham, ? and the Mysterians was another group forced to abandon Texas in order to get attention. Though widely regarded as a Texas band, only keyboardist Frankie Rodriguez (Crystal City) and bassist Frank Lugo (Weslaco), of a group which seemed to have a revolving-door membership policy, were actually Texan. The rest of the musicians (the most noted lineup of which included vocalist ?—whose original identity remains a closely guarded secret—drummer Edward Serrato and guitarist Bobby Balderama) were all from Mexico. ? and the Mysterians actually gained notoriety in Flint, Michigan. There, in 1965, they recorded "96 Tears," another tune built around a chugging, rhythmically simple Farfisa keyboard line. The song became a Detroit radio staple for the Pa-Go-Go label, and when Cameo Records picked up the group and distributed "96 Tears" worldwide, it sold millions. A follow-up song, "I Need Somebody," hit number 22, but subsequent singles did nothing. By 1968, the band had broken up.

☆ Part 2: Rock

"96 Tears" is perhaps the only legacy for the outfit, though one of the band's final bassists was Mel Schacher, whose grooves would later fuel several million albums worth of Grand Funk Railroad.

The third and most important of the Tex-Mex rockers was Doug Sahm. A San Antonio youth who'd recorded regularly in his teens for the tiny Harlem label, Sahm was a multitalented musician and songwriter who reveled in a variety of styles. He fell under the scrutiny of noted Houston R&B producer Huey "The Crazy Cajun" Meaux, who recognized in Sahm's songs an opportunity to cash in on the Beatles craze. Meaux hastily assembled a band of like-minded Texans around Sahm, including organist Augie Meyers, Jack Barber, John Pérez, and Frank Morin, and started digging through Sahm's material for a suitable single.

One soul-flavored composition, "She's About a Mover," reminded Meaux of the Beatles' "She's a Woman." With the addition of an addictive organ riff by Meyers, Meaux released the single on his own Tribe label. He dubbed the band the Sir Douglas Quintet in a crafty attempt to cash in on the Anglophile virus overtaking AM radio. "She's About a Mover" rocketed, and though the band's faux British cover was rapidly exposed, Sahm's reputation was sufficient that he could head west to check out the incredible scene spawning in California. He landed in San Francisco and scored an impressive contract with Mercury Records. Unfortunately, though he had a small hit with the title cut from 1969's *Mendocino*, and would later release several excellent and underrated albums (including a classic early-seventies LP for ABC called *Texas Rock for the Country Rollers*), Sahm's work at the time seemed swallowed up by the sheer volume of material bubbling up out of the Bay Area.

All three of these bands have been called seminal in the punk movement, in part no doubt due to their rebellious attitude and a collective and sloppy enthusiasm, but it seems an assessment that is an exaggeration at best. Their roots were as border-flavored as they were anarchic.

Tyler's Mouse and the Traps, on the other hand, were actually closer to what would become the punk ethic. They were formed in 1964 by Ronnie "Mouse" Weiss (vocals/guitar), Bugs Henderson (lead guitar), Dave Stanley (bass), Jerry Howell (organ), and Ken "Big Nardo" Murray (drums). Produced by Robin Hood Bryans, they had two hits with "A Public Execution" and "Maid of Sugar, Made of Spice," and, all told, released thirteen 45s (one for ABC-Bell, twelve for Cincinnati's Fraternity label) and an album for RCA. Though the band was legendary in Texas, struggles to gain attention elsewhere were less than successful, and they broke up in 1969. They still convene every decade for much-anticipated reunions.

Others making names for themselves in what we like to call the pre-dope, pre–mass exodus period included Dallas's Trini Lopez, who had a 1962 hit with "If I Had a Hammer," a 1965 smash with "Lemon Tree," and several others on the Reprise label (though sage insiders prefer to remember his Olivier-like thespian take as the singing convict-soldier in the film *The Dirty*

Dozen). Baytown's Bobby Fuller recorded "I Fought the Law," which went to number 9 for Mustang in 1966 and was later covered by the Clash. He also had a top thirty hit with a Buddy Holly song (he sounded like an irritated Buddy Holly, anyway) called "Love's Made a Fool of You." Fuller's career was cut short by his "suicide," so decreed by Los Angeles police after he was found beaten in a parked car with gasoline in his stomach.

Roy Head's 1965 tune, "Treat Her Right," was a hit for Duke's Back Beat subsidiary, and B. J. Thomas, en route to a lucrative career as a MOR balladeer, scored with an arrangement of Hank Williams's "I'm So Lonesome I Could Cry" for New York's Scepter label. Dallas's Five Americans had hits in 1967–68 with "Western Union," "Zip Code," "The Sound of Love," and "I Saw the Light."

At that point in the rock movement, drug experimentation was starting to be a fun thing to get involved with. Marijuana and acid were becoming the new liberators all over America, and most self-respecting musicians wanted to see what it was all about. Given that California seemed to be the headquarters for this movement, and that Texas had a rather conservative view of such activities, a migration of Texas artists to the West Coast was wise, large, and inevitable.

One was Houston's Kenny Rogers, who jumped on the rock bandwagon in the mid-sixties by transforming the bulk of his folk act, the New Christie Minstrels, into Kenny Rogers and the First Edition. (Drummer Mickey Jones was also a Texan, and a former percussionist for Trini Lopez.) After appearing on *The Smothers Brothers Show* in 1967, the group scored a deal with Reprise Records. Their debut LP, *The First Edition*, was released in 1968 and contained the hit "Just Dropped in to See What Condition My Condition Was In"—whose ludicrous title should have been a beacon indicating the transparency of the band's pseudo-hipness. Still, the band had several more hits before the end of the decade, including "groovy" versions of "Ruby" and "Reuben James," both of which would be huge sellers when the chameleonlike Rogers yet again switched genres in the seventies and became a country icon.

One guy who had a considerably more genuine interest in rock was guitarist/singer/songwriter Stephen Stills. He was born in Dallas but spent much of his youth in New Orleans. No matter; Stills was a textbook traveling minstrel by his late teens. He settled in Los Angeles in 1965, found work as a session player, played in a few bands, and auditioned for a spot in the TV band that would be called the Monkees. (He was reportedly turned down for bad teeth; obviously, this incident predated cosmetic surgery and such innovations as the medically enhanced, gravity-defying breasts on *Baywatch*.)

Prime time's loss, though, was music's gain. Stills joined forces with Neil Young and Richie Furay to form Buffalo Springfield. Though the band lasted only nineteen months, they released three excellent Atco LPs (1967's *Buffalo Springfield* and *Again*, and 1968's *Last Time Around*) and toured with another seminal country-rocker outfit, the Byrds. Between the two groups were laid the foundations for countless terrific, ground-breaking, and frequently annoying significant rock permutations for decades to come.

In said spirit, Stills's next project was a one-shot Al Kooper album called *Super Session* (1968, Columbia), on which Stills recorded one side with Kooper, and Mike Bloomfield sat in with Kooper for the other side. Lamentably, the concept of three guitar session superheroes was more impressive in theory than in actual practice.

But Stills then hooked up with former Byrd David Crosby and ex-Hollies Brit Graham Nash in a group that was destined to be huge—and that's *before* Crosby's love affair with burgers. *Crosby, Stills and Nash*, released in 1969 on Atlantic, trumpeted the dawn of a new era in harmony-laden, frequently political, country-sparkled rock. Featuring Still's "Suite: Judy Blue Eyes," a song for then-girlfriend Judy Collins, *Crosby, Stills and Nash* went gold and paved the way for the group to add Neil Young to the lineup in mid-1969. CSNY, as they called themselves, would kick into the seventies with a lunatic variety of albums, songs, cloying vibes, tours, arguments, and media scrutiny.

While Stills had in fact blown the Monkees gig, a Houston singer/guitarist/songwriter named Mike Nesmith didn't. Nesmith grew up in Dallas, and it wasn't until he was discharged from the air force, at the age of twenty, that he got into music. He traveled around in various bands, working briefly in Memphis on sessions for Stax-Volt, and ultimately ended up in Los Angeles. In 1965, he auditioned for and secured a role on *The Monkees*—which made him wealthy and a star virtually overnight.

But Nesmith felt hollow about his success. The other Monkees (bassist Peter Tork, drummer Mickey Dolenz, and singer Davey Jones) were marginal musicians at best (though more accomplished than, say, Milli Vanilli), and in spite of the success of their records, Nesmith felt embarrassed that the public was unaware that session musicians had done everything but the vocals on the early LPs.

Still, Nesmith *was* an accomplished player and writer. A version of his tune "Different Drum" was Linda Ronstadt's first successful single, and Nesmith released his own instrumental album, *Wichita Train Whistle Sings*, in 1968 on the Dot label. Eventually—through Nesmith's efforts—the musically improving Monkees were allowed to play their own instruments and songs in the studio. The resultant albums, *Monkees Headquarters* and *Pisces, Aquarius, Capricorn and Jones, Ltd.* (1967), *The Birds, the Bees and the Monkees* and *Head* (1968), and *Instant Replay* and *The Monkees Present* (1969), all went gold. Further, several Nesmith-penned songs were hit singles, including "Tapioca Tundra," "Don't Wait for Me," and "Listen to the Band."

Though the group disbanded in 1969, Nesmith has continued a lucrative career in music, as a video pioneer, and as a producer of feature films.

One East Texan destined for Los Angeles, whose name would be forever linked with "the California Sound," was Brian Wilson. JUST KIDDING!

It was actually Don Henley, a drummer/vocalist from Gilmer whose home-town band, Shiloh, headed west in 1969 to see what all the vibes were about. By 1971, Henley would help form the Eagles, and they'd create enough sun-baked, tequila-basted vibes for the entire nation.

But while Los Angeles had always been (and would always be) an en-tertainment mecca, oblivious to all trends, San Francisco was quite another tale. As the headquarters for Owsley and his finely crafted, cutting-edge psychedelics, Haight-Ashbury, the Summer of Love, the Monterey Pop Fes-tival, *ad narcotum*, San Francisco attracted musicians during the sixties as much for the lifestyle as for the music—not that the two weren't inextri-cably connected.

Mother Earth was a mid-sixties Austin band, fronted by an ex-Wisconsin folkie named Tracy Nelson, who relocated to San Francisco and became a staple at the Fillmore West. Featuring Nelson's supercharged blues wail, Mother Earth's core R&B stylings had been sautéed by the psychedelic era simmering in Austin and San Francisco, and it's still a mystery why the band's career didn't take off in a big way.

Steve Miller's did, though. He parlayed an affluent Dallas childhood into a career as a respected blues devotee, innovative guitarist, and, ultimately, a King Ham rock star. He attended the prestigious St. Mark's preparatory school (where, along with classmate Boz Scaggs, he formed the Marksmen, a popular early Texas band) and spent evenings being entertained by his father's dinner guests. These included Les Paul, Charles Mingus, and T-Bone Walker—though probably not at the same meal.

Miller attended college in Wisconsin, played in a number of bands and, after a brief academic trip to Copenhagen, returned to the States to settle in Chicago. A nest of young white blues fans were gathering there, at the feet of older black blues masters, and Miller jammed his way through an apprenticeship with the likes of Buddy Guy, Howlin' Wolf, Muddy Waters, and Paul Butterfield.

But San Francisco sang its sweet siren's song, and Miller took his guitar and his tunes and relocated there. He formed the Steve Miller Blues Band in 1966 (original members: keyboardist Jim Peterman, bassist Lonnie Turner, drummer Tim Davis, and second guitarist Curly Cook). The band gained immediate acceptance, scored prestigious Fillmore West gigs, and eventually signed with Capitol Records—a deal in which Miller demon-strated his scholastic acumen by negotiating an unheard-of cash advance and a handsome royalty rate. Old classmate Boz Scaggs signed on, "Blues" was dropped from the band's name, and they went to England to record.

Children of the Future (1968), with its eye-warping cover art and a mé-lange of snappy song snippets segued together, was a progressive and instant classic—though the nonstop arrangements precluded a hit single. No mat-ter; there would be plenty, such as "Livin' in the USA" (1968) and "Space Cowboy," off such rapid-fire and subsequent LPs (1968's *Sailor*, 1969's *Brave New World* and *Your Saving Grace*). The band toured heavily into the early seventies, at which time Miller suffered a broken neck in an automobile accident. He would recover, though, and make a substantial if disturbing contribution to rock for several years.

His old partner Scaggs, who seemed to crop up every now and again, also landed in San Francisco. But not before he'd played in the Texas R&B group the Wigs, then split to travel Europe. He released one album over there in 1965, *Boz*, on Polygram's UK label, but eventually returned to the states where he signed on for the first two Steve Miller Band albums. Scaggs had his own musical vision, though, and signed a solo deal at the end of the decade. Like Miller, he would own significant blocks of seventies radio airtime, though with a smoother sound combining elements of disco and R&B.

And if Scaggs was making white boy soul, than Dallas's Sylvester "Sly" Stone was a black guy traveling in rock circles. His music was actually an infectious gumbo of acid rock and funk, dating back to his Texas youth when Stone soaked in a river of gospel music. His family moved to the Oakland area when Stone was still young and, by the mid-sixties, he was a Bay Area studio veteran. Stone produced a number of singles for Autumn Records artists like the Beau Brummels and the Mojo Men, many of which were Stone's own compositions.

In 1966 he formed his own band, the Stoners, which evolved a year later into Sly and the Family Stone, an outfit that featured bassist Larry Graham, Jr., Stone's cousin, who was born in Beaumont, Texas. The band traveled the United States, earning a stellar live reputation for their infectious and original music, and signed with Epic. Their first album, 1967's *A Whole New Thing*, elicited interest, and the second, *Dance to the Music* (1968), resulted in a hit single with the title track.

Throughout 1968 and 1969, it became virtually impossible to turn on the radio without hearing Sly and the Family Stone. "I Want to Take You Higher" and "Everyday People" were the biggest, and a 1969 LP, *Stand!*, floated capably on the *Billboard* charts for over eighty weeks with four hit singles. The band's momentum would last well into the next decade.

BUT THE TEXAN WHO MADE THE BRIGHTEST DAY-GLO SPLASH in San Francisco had to be Janis Joplin—perhaps not in terms of album sales, and certainly not in longevity, but as an undeniable musical force.

Joplin was born in Port Arthur to middle-class parents, but grew up lonely and introspective. She wasn't, frankly, an attractive girl—a sin in fashion-conscious Texas. Chubby, with a potato salad complexion and nondescript features, Joplin found solace in blues and folk music. She moved to Austin in 1962 and, as one-third (along with Lanny Wiggins and future Mother Earth member Powell St. John) of the Waller Creek Boys, became a regular at Threadgill's, a folk music bar which was *the* drinking spot in Austin for two generations of UT students. Her wailing, authentic vocal delivery and enthusiastic curiosity about alcohol and drugs also bought her a certain acceptance in the university fraternity set, but after she was callously nominated "the ugliest male on campus," Joplin made a wounded retreat to California.

For a couple of mostly happy years, she maneuvered between San Francisco's North Beach and New York, developing her skills as a blues singer, drinker, and voracious drug sampler. A brief return to Texas nearly resulted in her joining the legendary 13th Floor Elevators (more on them momentarily), but then she heard about a new band back in San Francisco that could benefit from her voice: Big Brother and the Holding Company (drummer Dave Getz, guitarists James Gurley and Sam Andrews, bassist Peter Albin). Joplin joined up and, after a blistering performance at the Monterey Pop Festival in 1967, major rock dude Albert Grossman decided to manage them.

They released an eponymously titled debut on Mainstream in 1967, then Columbia signed them in time for *Cheap Thrills* in 1968. On the power of a huge single, "Piece of My Heart," and an entrancing version of "Summertime" never envisioned by the Gershwin brothers, Joplin's popularity soon dwarfed the Holding Company and she went solo.

She formed the Kozmic Blues Band (retaining Big Bro's Andrews) and did whirlwind tours of the world, as well as television shows and drinking spots. A flamboyant alter ego emerged: "Pearl," a tropically feathered, bejeweled, Southern Comfort–swilling, sexually liberated voice for a generation of misfits and hipsters.

Her first solo album, 1969's *I Got Dem Ol' Kozmic Blues Again, Mama*, featured hits like "Try (Just a Little Bit Harder)" and the pain-soaked, haunting "Kozmic Blues," the latter of which underscored a desperation wrought of her increasing addiction to heroin. Still, happiness wasn't a completely alien emotion. She became engaged to Seth Morgan (whose later novel, *Homeboy*, poignantly depicted a societal underbelly in which Joplin probably felt most at home).

Her next album, *Pearl*, celebrated a new touring group, the Full Tilt Boogie Band, but unfortunately, Joplin died of a heroin overdose on October 4, 1970. *Pearl* went on to sell a massive quantity of albums, fueled as much by songs like "Me and Bobby McGee" (written by former pal and fellow Texan Kris Kristofferson) as by her untimely passing. The usual rash of "ghoul" albums and biographies, of course, appeared at top speed, though a documentary, *Janis* (1974), a feature film based on her life and starring Bette Midler, *The Rose* (1979), and *Buried Alive*, a touching and literate biography by close friend Myra Friedman, are all worth examining.

Joplin wasn't the only Texas casualty of the West Coast drug ethic. The best of the early Texas psychedelic bands, the 13th Floor Elevators, lead by Roky Erickson, a singer/guitarist/songwriter/brain traveler who looked like a Lucky Charms cereal leprechaun, were among the first to crash-land. The Elevators helped pioneer acid rock with the 1966 LP *The Psychedelic Sounds of the Thirteenth Floor Elevators,* and its hit single, "You're Gonna Miss Me" (on Houston's International Artists label). A follow-up, 1967's *Easter Everywhere,* was almost as strong.

As dedicated proponents of, well, any dope possible, the Elevators headed to San Francisco for the Summer of Love, fitting in immediately as walking, talking chemical experiments. Their music, built around Erickson's twisted pop visions, his beast-at-midnight shrieking, Stacy Sutherland's overdriven guitar histrionics, and the odd jug-percussion of Tommy Hall, earned the Elevators a niche in the Bay Area hierarchy. But Erickson's enthusiasm for the lifestyle caught up with him. After returning to Texas, the admitted veteran of over eight hundred LSD voyages was busted two different times for marijuana possession. The second resulted in a stay at the Rusk State Hospital for the Criminally Insane—as a preferred option to actual prison time—but the plan backfired. Diagnosed as a paranoid schizophrenic, Erickson was administered electroshock and various drug therapies, and by the time he was released in 1972, his fragile cocoon of brilliance had begun to unravel. Though Sutherland led the band through the motions for 1968's *Bull of the Woods* (Decal), the trip was essentially over, and all subsequent LPs would be of the collection/outtake variety.

Songwriter Tony Joe White was another Texan who eschewed California for the East Coast, though without the fanfare or longevity of Johnny Winter. A Louisiana native who spent much of his teen years in Texas developing a bluesy, folksy Cajun rock style, the singer/guitarist/songwriter eventually made his way to Nashville. He signed with Monument Records and issued several singles (one of which, "Soul Francisco," was a European hit in 1967) before releasing his debut album, *Black and White,* in 1968. In 1969, his single "Polk Salad Annie" blew into the top ten. The song would remain the genesis of a career that would extend well into the seventies.

BUT NOT EVERY TEXAS MUSICIAN POLE-VAULTED TO THE EAST Coast or California—and it probably wasn't a coincidence that not many of them made significant noise outside their home state. Still, there were many emblematic of the late-sixties attitude and inspiration who chose to fight the regional wars in the Lone Star State. These included Kenny and the Kasuals, Bubble Puppy (whose *A Gathering of Promises* LP, released on the International label in 1969, boasted the neglected classic "Hot Smoke and Sassafras"), the Southwest F.O.B., Bad Seeds, Red Crayola, Fever Tree, the Chessmen (featuring Jimmy Vaughan), Conqueroo, Blackbyrd (with Stevie Vaughan and a pre–Point Blank Kim Davis), and the Buicks.

Two bands on a collision course for fame were Dallas's American Blues and Houston's the Moving Sidewalks. The former, mainstays in the notorious Cellar clubs—a Bermuda Triangle of bacchanalian live music/strip joints in Houston, Dallas, and Fort Worth—featured drummer Frank Beard and bassist Dusty Hill. American Blues was as memorable for the members'

Guitarist Who Changed Modern Guitar
Johnny Winter

Johnny Winter was another genius whose career would be sidelined by narcotic excess—though, thankfully, only temporarily. In the meantime, the Beaumont native's slicing, moaning, stinging brand of blues guitar would make him rock 'n' roll's first bonus baby—though his choice of coasts would be East rather than West.

Winter, a skeletal albino with crossed eyes and hair the color of Liquid Paper, grew up in a musical household. He and his younger brother Edgar (also an albino, but, unlike Johnny, one who could pass as a reasonably interesting babe; check out the cover of his 1973 Epic release, *They Only Come Out at Night*) were versatile on several instruments. As teens, their band It and Them was a staple in East Texas oil and shrimper towns. That group became Johnny Winter and the Black Plague, and Johnny eventually aborted a college career to roam the backwoods and bayous of Louisiana, playing blues in any tarpaper bar where they'd let him jam. Edgar, meanwhile, was studying jazz and becoming proficient on keyboards and saxophone, skills that would soon make him rich.

In the early sixties, though, obsessed with the blues, Johnny headed to Chicago to absorb from the greats and, as Steve Miller would later, fell in with Barry Goldberg and Mike Bloomfield. He returned home and again took up the itinerant swamp circuit, and his pyrotechnic fingers and lycanthropic vocals made him an underground icon.

A *Rolling Stone* article in 1968 defining regional music scenes touted Johnny's talent and attracted the attention of East Coast scene-creator Steve Paul. He dragged Johnny to New York City, and a variety of increasingly high-profile gigs convinced Columbia Records to sign the blues wonder for an advance of several hundred thousand dollars.

In 1969, the guitarist released a raw, energized album of authentic, electrified blues called *Johnny Winter*. Simultaneously, Liberty Records put out an album of Winter's pre-Columbia demos titled *Progressive Blues Experiment* (available years later as *Austin, Texas* on United Artists). Both records ably demonstrated that the hype was justified, and Winter was on the fast track to stardom. His work in the seventies was vital in a rock context, and everything subsequent to that was particularly valuable in a blues context.

dyed indigo hair as for their music, though a 1968 album for Karma, *American Blues Is Here*, featuring a cover of Tim Hardin's "If I Were a Carpenter," resulted in a deal with California's Uni label. *American Blues Do Their Thing* was the 1969 result, which had little impact on anything musical.

Meanwhile, the Moving Sidewalks boasted a guitarist named Billy Gibbons, who'd been touted by no less than Jimi Hendrix (on a *Tonight Show* appearance) as *the* young guitarist to watch out for. Gibbons was a veteran of other legendary Texas bands like the Saints, Billy G. and the Ten Blue Flames, and the Coachmen. The Sidewalks were managed by an enterprising Houston booking agent, Bill Ham, whose marketing savvy when the band shortly metamorphosed into ZZ Top would have extraordinary results.

☆ Three: The Seventies: Ear Shredding and Frozen Yogurt Pop

T HERE ARE STILL PLENTY OF PEOPLE WHO BELIEVE THAT, CREA-
tively, as a part of rock 'n' roll history, the seventies are no more than
a sort of bloated indigestion wrought of the self-indulgent sixties. Indeed,
the decade of Watergate was musically typified by the Brothers Gibb's disco,
Frampton Comes Alive, the neo-California Big Mellow vibe (characterized
by the Eagles, Jackson Browne, and Fleetwood Mac), and the better-
anthems-through-technology histrionics of scientist/guitarist Tom Scholz of
the band Boston.

Texas musicians played significant roles in all these movements and
more—and to their credit managed, for the most part, to perform with
dignity. And on those occasions when their work wasn't necessarily the
stuff of art, it at least performed admirably in that more important arena:
album sales.

Beaumont's Johnny Winter, who'd been signed by Columbia in the late
sixties as an authentic blues artist for an advance roughly the size of NASA's
annual budget, had gradually migrated to strident rock. After his transitory
Second Winter, he cast off longtime rhythm section Tommy Shannon (bass)
and Uncle John Turner (drums) for a more streamlined, rock-conscious unit
featuring Rick Derringer (guitar), Randy Jo Hobbs (bass), and Randy Z
(drums). Called Johnny Winter And, they released two albums, the surprisingly melodic and introspective *Johnny Winter And* and a raucous in-
concert document, *Johnny Winter And Live*.

While both albums sold respectably, Winter's accelerating affection for
heroin resulted in the band's disintegration and a brief hiatus for the guitarist. When he returned, it was sans And and with the blistering *Still Alive
and Well*, which is without question one of the best rock albums in Texas
history. The guitar tone by itself peels skin at fifty yards, and Winter (with
a new rhythm section of Hobbs and drummer Richard Hughes) sounds rejuvenated and unleashed on a joyous, angry, triumphant set of raw, brutal
rock.

Winter encored *Still Alive and Well* with two solid, similarly conceived records, *Saints and Sinners* and *John Dawson Winter III* (both 1974, the latter on a new label, Blue Sky), and two live sets: a largely forgettable reunion with his brother, 1975's *With Edgar Winter: Together*, and *Captured Live!* (1976), an incendiary disc with his own band.

At that point, Winter essentially concluded his rock flirtations and returned to his first love: the blues. By the end of the decade, he'd released *Nothin' But the Blues* (1977) and *White, Hot And Blue* (1978), and had sculpted an interesting sideline producing none other than his hero, Muddy Waters.

IF A CYNIC MIGHT HAVE VIEWED WINTER'S FORAY INTO HARD rock as nothing more than a dollar-signed infatuation (marginally true), it can be said of ZZ Top that they dove into their brand of rock 'n' roll for the long haul. The members of the band, Houston guitarist Billy Gibbons (Moving Sidewalks), Dallas bassist Dusty Hill, and Irving drummer Frank Beard (both of American Blues), did share with Winter a love of the blues and R&B. But, after first Hill and then Beard were tapped to join Gibbons in the Sidewalks, and the appellation ZZ Top was selected for the new trio, their music was an instantaneous and singular barbecue sauce of hard rock and murky blues.

Manager Bill Ham scored the band a deal with London Records and put them to work on a series of grueling tours designed to create a solid grassroots audience. In rapid succession, ZZ Top released *First Album* (1970), *Rio Grande Mud* (1972), and *Tres Hombres* (1973). These three signature records were almost olfactorily redolent of beer, lowriders, Mexican food, and tequila-soaked border-town chicanery. Listening to *First Album*'s "(Somebody Else Been) Shakin' Your Tree" or *Rio Grande Mud*'s "Chevrolet" or "Francine," it was simply not possible to imagine that ZZ Top came from anywhere *but* Texas.

And, in 1973, when "La Grange" was released as a single off *Tres Hombres*, ZZ Top began to vault tax brackets like Olympic hurdlers. They started headlining arenas across Texas and the South, and when they followed "La Grange" with the addictive jackhammer strains of "Tush," off 1975's partially live *Fandango!*, ZZ Top became authentic superstars.

And if their core fans (a kooky mix of blue-collar laborers, fraternity boys, bikers, and hippies) were content with the band's songwriting formula—three chords and what-rhymes-with-ass? couplets—well, ZZ managed to throw in enough supplemental innovations to keep it all interesting.

They set out on a year-long, Worldwide Texas Tour in 1976, a huge-grossing spectacle which included such Lone Star–motifed props as Nudie suits for the band and living stage detritus like a buffalo, snakes, vultures, tarantulas, cacti, and longhorns. It was also during this time that Gibbons and Hill began to cultivate their now-famous beards. Ironically, only drummer Beard avoided the do-I-look-more-like-Tolstoy-or-Dostoevski? concept, sporting at most a neat moustache.

Then, as Ham sought to get them out of their ho-hum London contract, the boys issued the indifferent *Tejas* and *Best of ZZ Top*, both in 1977, before taking some time off. They closed out the decade with a final London release, *Degüello*, which featured the hit single "Cheap Sunglasses."

If Ham's success with ZZ Top was the stuff of managerial dreams, his work with subsequent artists wasn't quite as lucrative. Point Blank, a prototypical Texas boogie band built around vocalist John O'Daniel and the guitars of Rusty Burns and Kim Davis, was one such act. They recorded three albums for Arista in the late seventies, 1976's *Point Blank*, 1978's *Second Season* (with a terrific tune called "Stars and Scars"), and 1979's *Airplay*. But though the band would jump to MCA at the start of the next decade, album sales would stay minimal.

Another Ham signee, Eric Johnson, was destined for huge stardom and a reputation as one of the world's finest guitar players—but not under Ham's tutelage and not until he sat out Ham's time-stealing contract in a legal imbroglio that took years. In the meantime, a self-titled album he recorded with his fusion band, the Electromagnets (1975, EGM), quickly hit the cutout bins and has subsequently been among the most sought-after out-of-print records on earth, and a solo record called *The Seven Worlds* got sucked into the black hole of showbiz kookery and as such has become, along with Hendrix's *First Rays of the New Rising Sun*, the Beach Boys' *Smile*, Prince's *The Black Album*, and the Doors' *Celebration of the Lizard*, one of those legendary albums that never saw the light of day.

Meanwhile, sixties hotshot Steve Miller, still recording for Capitol, continued his ascendency toward radio deification. Though Miller was the only constant while personnel in his Steve Miller Band shifted in kaleidoscopic fashion, his ability to craft catchy guitar pop kept albums like *Number 5* (1970), *Rock Love* (1971), *Recall the Beginning . . . A Journey to Eden*, and *Anthology* (both 1972) on the national charts.

But Miller's commercial success became staggering with 1973's *The Joker*—not coincidentally the album that marked a shift in Miller's writing to the spectacularly dumb and, therefore, lucrative. The song "The Joker" became a number 1 single, and the subsequent demand for live shows kept the band on the road for three years. Miller finally returned to the studio and spawned *Fly Like an Eagle* in 1976. No less than three smash singles came off the album ("Rock 'n' Me"—notable for a zany artistic coincidence in which Miller's main guitar riff bore remarkable resemblance to Free's "Alright Now"—the lyrically embarrassing "Take the Money and Run," and "Fly Like an Eagle"), and established Miller as a radio force to be feared, inasmuch as anyone who runs a radio could be subjected *at any time* to his music.

Miller encored with *Book of Dreams* in 1978. The LP sold even more units than its predecessors, and churned out FM radio irritants like "Jungle Love," "Swingtown," and "Jet Airliner," all of which further illustrated Miller's penchant for damnably hummable choruses and couplets pulled from the trash bins in an eighth-grade creative writing class.

These successes paved the way for his seventies swansong, *Greatest Hits 1974–78*, a comprehensive package that effectively detailed precisely how, in the space of only five years, Steve Miller became the Crown Prince of Velveeta Rock.

Elsewhere on the arena-rock spectrum, Johnny Winter's little brother, Edgar, had become a most unlikely star. A multi-instrumentalist proficient at keyboards and saxophone, and sporting an amazing voice, Edgar signed with Epic and made his solo debut in 1970 with a jazzy concept album called *Entrance*. Though critically praised, it didn't sell well, and Edgar moved in an R&B direction by organizing the horn-driven White Trash.

Featuring another East Texas native, Jerry LaCroix, a vocalist with a five-octave range, White Trash put out two records, 1971's *White Trash* and 1972's *Road Work*. But though the band became a concert attraction (they were on the Fillmore East's closing night bill), Winter broke it up to form a mainstream rock band called the Edgar Winter Group with guitarist Ronnie Montrose, bassist Dan Hartman, and drummer Chuck Ruff.

Their first LP, *They Only Come Out at Night*, sporting a cover photo of Winter in drag, boasted an unlikely hit in the instrumental "Frankenstein." The song rocketed to number 1, and both the single and the album went platinum. "Hangin' Around" and "Free Ride" also became hits, and by the time Rick Derringer replaced Montrose for 1974's *Shock Treatment*, the Edgar Winter Group was a substantial worldwide draw.

The success was short-lived, however. Winter released several more albums before the end of the decade (including the solo *Jasmine Nightdreams*, a group effort called *With Rick Derringer*, the *Together Captured Live* reunion album with his brother, and *Recycled* and the *Edgar Winter Album*), but never again duplicated his "Frankenstein"-era popularity.

Meanwhile, Doug Sahm continued to eek out a musical living. After returning from his San Francisco experimentations, Sahm grooved into the exploding Austin music scene and soaked up an incredible variety of sounds and influences. He recorded a variety of records over the course of the decade, most notably *Groover's Paradise* (Warner Brothers, 1972) and *Texas Rock for Country Rollers* (ABC, 1974). While he was only just surviving, financially, the rest of us began to take comfort in the fact that there would always be a Doug Sahm—and that he would always make valuable music.

Up in Fort Worth, a hard-rock band called Bloodrock was turning some heads—some in adulation and others in horror. Formed in 1969 and comprised of vocalist Jim Rutledge, lead guitarist Lee Pickens, drummer Rick Cobb, bassist Eddie Grundy, organist Steve Hill, and rhythm guitarist Nick

Taylor, Bloodrock hooked up with producer Terry Knight, whose similar efforts on behalf of Grand Funk Railroad had generated *mucho* cash and the vitriol of critics across the solar system.

These sentiments bothered Knight and his new charges very little, and the record-buying public even less. Between February 1970 and March 1971, Bloodrock had sledgehammered three albums into the stores, the self-titled debut, *Bloodrock 2*, and *Bloodrock 3*—all of which went gold. A single from the second album, "D.O.A.," a siren-drenched dirge about a guy dying in an auto accident, became a huge hit and further agitated naysayers.

Knight and Bloodrock parted ways after the third album, but the group continued to do well with subsequent records like *U.S.A.* (1973) and *Live* (1974). Pickens and Rutledge left before the band's final two records, 1975's *Passage* and *Whirlwind Tongues*, were released, and Pickens put out his own Capitol LP, *The Lee Pickens Group* (1977), which, though boasting the catchy "2° South," failed to generate much excitement.

Many of Bloodrock's finer songs were penned by a friend of the group, another Fort Worth guitarist/vocalist named John Nitzinger. Though he couldn't claim "D.O.A.," Nitzinger wrote enough solid tunes for the band (among them "Double Cross" and "Sable and Pearl") that he, too, was signed to Capitol.

Billed simply as Nitzinger, the songwriter, a renowned live performer whose lyrics were surely Texas rock's answer to Dylan Thomas—as was his fondness for drink—was a staple in clubs such as the Cellar and Mother Blues. Supported by drummer Linda Waring and bassist Curly Benton, he recorded *Nitzinger* in 1972, had a regional hit with "Louisiana Cockfight," and toured internationally with Leon Russell.

For his sophomore effort, *One Foot in History* (1973), Nitzinger added the services of his old pal Bugs Henderson, a speed-fingered guitar alumnus from Tyler's legendary Mouse and the Traps.

Though the record featured several literate, catchy, and energized songs like "Motherlode," "Earth Eater," and "Driftwood," *One Foot in History* sold in less-than-platinum fashion, and Nitzinger returned to Dallas–Fort Worth to regroup. Though 1978's *Live Better Electrically*, on 20th Century, contained fine tunes like "Control" and "Are You with Me?," the album did nothing and Nitzinger was once again relegated to local hero status. He resurfaced in Europe on a little-heard import album by the band PM (which featured Emerson, Lake and Palmer drummer Carl Palmer), and later did a lengthy stint as Alice Cooper's bassist. Finally after a rehab stint in the Betty Ford Center, Nitzinger bounced back in 1997 with a solid, bluesy indie CD called *Didja Miss Me?*

Speaking of ELP's tenuous Texas connections, in 1974 bassist/vocalist Greg Lake produced a hard-rock trio called Stray Dog, releasing their eponymous first album on the Manticore label. The band featured Snuffy Walden, a Texas guitarist who later gained Hollywood notoriety as the musical director for the hit television show "The Wonder Years." The Stray Dog era wasn't as fruitful, despite the album's interesting cover of ZZ Top's "Chevrolet" and far above average songs like "Speak of the Devil" and the overlooked classic "Rocky Mountain Suite (Bad Road)."

There were several other Texas rock bands attracting attention as "sure-thing" acts throughout the seventies, including Fools, Blackhorse, Lo Della, Eeze (later Automatic), Southern Cross, St. Elmo's Fire, Lynx, the Bee's Knees, Freda and the Firedogs, Krackerjack, Salt, U.S. Kids, and Genessee. Most notable were Dallas's Lightning and Austin's Too Smooth. Both were world-class rock bands and, frankly, better than many of their more successful peers. But while both acts received substantial attention from major labels, it wasn't meant to be.

At roughly the same time, up in Dallas, a depressingly similar thing was happening to an amazing hard-rock group called Lightning, whose strength was in their lead guitarist, an Oak Cliff kid named Rocky Athas. (see box, next page)

Without question the oddest—but one of the greatest—of Texas's late seventies rock bands was Dallas's the Werewolves. A roots-clustered, Stonesy outfit with plenty of sparkle in their androgynous, New York Dolls–head–south stage personas, the "Wolves" (bassist Bucky Ballard, guitarist Seab Meador, vocalist Brian Papageorge, and drummer John Brame) signed with London in the last hours of the decade. Indeed, none other than noted Rolling Stones producer Andrew Loog Oldham oversaw their two albums, the wonderful and sadly neglected *The Werewolves* and *Ship of Fools*.

Though nobody in their home state seemed to get them, the Werewolves were just gaining momentum when Meador took ill. His death a few years later effectively derailed their odd, beautiful musical passage, but the records are terrific and collectors items.

WHILE THE BIG-CITY GUITAR SOUND WAS RAGING IN DALLAS and Houston, a different kind of rock was twisting in West Texas, crafted in the plains tradition of Buddy Holly and Roy Orbison. The music of Lubbock natives Joe Ely, Butch Hancock, and Jimmie Dale Gilmore boasted the same vigor as the hard-rock outfits, yet seized on the dusty, primal energy of country, folk, and rockabilly in the same fashion as ZZ Top or Johnny Winter had utilized blues.

With a variety of other Lubbock musicians, the three were in and out of rock bands in the sixties, then formed the Flatlanders, considered one of *the* significant bands in Texas history. It was a heavenly melding of three unique singer/songwriters, and that they only released one record, 1972's *The Flatlanders—More a Legend Than a Band* (Sun Records, rereleased in 1990 by Rounder), has been widely considered an artistic travesty.

While Hancock and Gilmore have gone on to success as singer/songwriters of a folkie flavor, Ely continued to rock. His work after the Flatlanders is an essential textbook in Texas music. The Joe Ely Band has been

CRIMINALLY OVERLOOKED ARTIST
Jeff Clark/Too Smooth
☆

Nowadays, Jeff Clark holds court in a North Austin insurance office and, with his neat gray hair and three-piece suit, bears little resemblance to the Jeff Clark whose waist-length, firecracker mane and trademark Flying V guitar were once staples at the Armadillo World Headquarters and music ports across Texas.

As the main voice/songwriter/guitarist behind Too Smooth (not to mention the only original member to last the duration of the band), Clark's journey through Texas rock in the seventies and eighties is a remarkable testament to skill, recalcitrance, faith—and unbelievably bad luck.

Too Smooth was a blueprint example of progressive guitar rock: twin leads, bombastic and startlingly difficult arrangements, dense three- and four-part harmonies, and songs with more hooks than you'd find on the bottom of Possum Kingdom Lake. At a time when Boston and Wishbone Ash were seen as rock visionaries, Too Smooth was every bit as terrific and creative.

The band was formed in Austin by Clark and Brian Wooten (guitar/vocals), Danny Swinney (vocals/bass), and Tom Holden (drums/vocals) in 1972, and endured a variety of personnel changes over the course of its ten-year run. Clark, the only original member remaining at the end, had recorded albums on both coasts that never came out, signed three major record deals with labels that either folded or were sucked into larger conglomerates and forgotten, and watched *Billboard* choose the one Too Smooth single that *did* come out as a "Pick of the Week"—even as the record company collapsed and was unable to distribute the song to the radio stations requesting it.

Though Clark continued to perform in 14K after the dissolution of Too Smooth, and the band was a perennial Austin poll winner, he ultimately (and happily) opted for family life and security.

a training school for wonder guitarists (no less than Jesse Taylor, Charlie Sexton, Ian Moore, and David Grissom have all served apprenticeships therein), as well as an ever-evolving, ever-ass-kicking unit energetically capable of translating Ely's muse.

A consummate road dog, Ely's records reflect a scholar's fascination with Texas music in all its forms, and a wizard's ability to boil them down to their rocking and introspective best. MCA released three LPs in 1977, 1978, and 1979, respectively: *Joe Ely, Honky Tonk Masquerade,* and *Down on the*

CRIMINALLY IGNORED GUITARIST

Rocky Athas

In the early to mid-seventies, during an astonishingly fruitful time of virtuosity, the Holy Trinity of Lone Star guitarists were Eric Johnson, Stevie Ray Vaughan, and Rocky Athas—and of the three, it was Athas that was the best known in the state and the one most likely to become a star.

With a comic, Robin Williams sense of stage banter, crafty and oddly structured hard-rock songs, and a blinding and witty guitar style (those in the know testify that his hammer-on techniques predated Eddie Van Halen), Dallas's Athas and his band, Lightning, held court in clubs across the South.

When Lighting finally broke up for good in frustration after several recording contracts fell through, Athas joined up with Black Oak Arkansas, who in 1998 inked a major deal with Cleopatra Records, and *The Wild Bunch*, featuring several Athas compositions, was due the following autumn. He also writes and tours with ex-Trapeze/Deep Purple vocalist/bassist Glenn Hughes.

Texas music fans were finally sated, though, when Athas released a solo instrumental guitar CD called *That's What I Know*. A witty, adventuresome schoolbook of clever, quick riffing and poignant emotion, the album was long overdue.

Drag—and while they're all excellent, they were merely precursors to a fabulous library to follow.

Several Texans who'd headed west during the magical sixties were also finding success. One was Dallas's Marvin Lee Aday, aka Meat Loaf, a fleshy belter who played in vaguely promising California bands like Meat Loaf Soul and Popcorn Blizzard before establishing a history in musical theater. After traveling in *Hair*, he hooked up with a Detroit vocalist named Stoney. They released *Stoney and Meat Loaf* (Rare Earth, rereleased in 1979, after the Loaf Man was rich, as *Meat Loaf Featuring Stoney* on Prodigal/Motown).

In 1974, Meat Loaf contributed vocals to Ted Nugent's *Free for All* LP, then headed to New York, where he met songwriter Jim Steinman. The two hit it off, appearing in a national touring production for *National Lampoon* and, afterward, started work on songs from a musical Steinman had composed called *Never Land*. The bulk of that material was to become Meat Loaf's *Bat Out of Hell*. Produced by Todd Rundgren (and released in 1977 on Cleveland International), the record sold slowly at first, but singles like "Paradise by the Dashboard Light," "Two Out of Three Ain't Bad," and

"You Took the Words Right Out of My Mouth" all became Top 40 hits, and *Bat Out of Hell* became one of the biggest-selling albums in rock history. To date, it's sold more than twenty-four million copies—one, presumably, for each piece of pizza consumed by the vocalist in the last decade.

Other Texans who'd migrated to California chose to work in a less bombastic genre than Meat Loaf. The country rock movement, mellow of vibe and lushly melodic, was starting to flourish and provided a gentle but effective counterpunch to the ear-shredding guitar bands.

Steve Miller's old partner and Dallas schoolmate, Boz Scaggs, living in the Bay Area, made inroads on the national charts with a smooth fusion of white boy soul and disco. His unique, San-Francisco-fog-at-midnight voice and able songcraft produced frequent hits in the period, most notably "Lido Shuffle" and "Lowdown." Scaggs released several Columbia LPs during the seventies, including *Moments* (1971), *Boz Scaggs and Band* (1971), *My Time* (1972), *Slow Dancer* (1974), *Silk Degrees* (1976), and *Down Two Then Left* (1977), with *Silk Degrees* selling over five million copies.

Also doing that R&B-flavored rock thang, though with a decidedly more energetic groove, was Sly Stone. He started 1970 with *Greatest Hits*, which included two previously unreleased songs that became, well, great hits: "Hot Fun in the Summertime" and "Thank You (Falettinme Be Mice Elf Again)."

It was two years before *There's a Riot Goin' On*, and everything from the title to the music indicated that there *was* a riot going on—only it was as much in Stone's own brain as on the streets of America. By then, Sly's occasional cocaine prankstering had become a full-blown addiction, and his own stage fright was so great that it often took handlers longer to get him onstage than he would perform. While *Riot* songs like "Family Affair" and "Running Away" were the pleasant radio tunes fans had come to expect, Sly was a confused guy.

With 1973's *Fresh*, Stone had his last major chart success with the single "If You Want Me to Stay." By that point, the star rarely performed, and when bassist Larry Graham abandoned ship to form Graham Central Station, the Family Stone's recording heyday was over.

Stephen Stills, who spent the sixties establishing an impressive personal scrapbook, settled in California with Crosby, Stills, Nash and Young. Their 1970 Atlantic album, *Déjà-vu*, is still a staple on classic rock radio and for those perpetually enamored of the tie-dye and patchouli lifestyle. Granted, almost every song is a harmony-clustered FM staple (including Stills's "Carry On"), but the record's disturbing legacy is that it has encouraged the principals to reunite in one configuration or another, every year or so, to make new albums of songs largely void of insipiration or originality—and they show no sign of ever stopping!

Nevertheless, the remainder of their seventies output included some fine work. The live *Four Way Street* (1971, reissued in an expanded format in 1992) and 1974's greatest hits package, *So Far*, contained listenable if regurgitative moments, and one of the surprise albums of the decade was their excellent 1977 release, CSN (all three LPs on Atlantic), which featured two superb Stills songs, "Dark Star" and "I Dig You Dig Blind."

The prodigious Stills was rarely idle outside of the various CSNY projects, either. He released *ten* solo albums before 1980 (including two with his band Manassas, *Manassas* and *Manassas Live*, 1972 and 1973, Atlantic). The first two, though, 1970's *Stephen Stills* and 1971's *Stephen Stills 2*, were the best, and offered respective hit singles in "Love the One You're With" and "Change Partners." Other titles include *Down the Road* (1973, Atlantic), *Stills* (1975, Columbia), *Illegal Stills* (1976, Columbia), *Long May You Run* (with Neil Young, 1976, Reprise), *The Best of Stephen Stills* (1977, Atlantic), *Thoroughfare Gap* (1978, Columbia), and *Live* (1979, Atlantic). Though his solo stuff tended to rock harder than the material with Crosby et al., Stills's reputation as a member of that melodic aggregation will deservedly outlast his status as a guitar hero.

Another soft-rock act (though far softer than CSN) was a duo called Seals and Crofts, which mellowed its way to platinum status. South Texans Jim Seals (from Sidney) and Dash Crofts (of Cisco), formerly with the Champs and the Dawnbreakers, featured acoustic guitar, mandolin, and gentle, infectious vocal harmonies. Their debut album, *Seals and Crofts*, came out in 1970 on the TA label, as did their second LP, *Down Home*. They then moved to Warner Brothers for 1972's *Year of Sunday*, and broke big the following year with *Summer Breeze*. The title song was a huge hit, only the first of several over the course of several smooth-as-school-lunchroom-pudding albums. "Diamond Girl," "We May Never Pass This Way Again," "Unborn Child," "I'll Play for You," and "Get Closer" were all big singles, and the eight LPs they'd machine-gunned into stores by 1978 were consistently big sellers.

Jim Seals's brother, Dan, meanwhile, was part of another pleasing-to-housewives duo, England Dan and John Ford Coley. They sprinkled several saccharine hits throughout the seventies, such as "I'd Really Like to See You Tonight" (number 2), "Nights Are Forever Without You" number 10), "We'll Never Have to Say Goodbye Again" (number 9), and "Love Is the Answer" (number 10).

But without question, the Eagles wore the mitre in the hierarchy of California's frozen yogurt rock—because their country-flavored harmonies and peaceful, easy song structures went beyond the aural confection stage and devilishly masked lyrical portraits of the decadent City of Angels that would've made Jim Morrison proud.

It should be pointed out that none of this would have come about without the help of two Texans: Amarillo's J. D. Souther and Gilmer's Don Henley.

Souther played drums and sang in an early-sixties Panhandle band called the Cinders before heading west to form Longbranch Pennywhistle with future Eagle Glenn Frey. But while their one album was largely forgotten, it did introduce Souther into a circle of cronies that included Jackson Browne, Linda Ronstadt, and several soon-to-be Eaglets.

After that band was formed, Souther contributed to hits like "Best of My Love," "New Kid in Town," and "James Dean." He then started and had moderate luck with the Souther-Hillman-Furay Band (with ex-Byrd Chris Hillman and ex-Poco dude Richie Furay), releasing a few interesting records before heading into the eighties with a dignified solo career.

But Don Henley was actually *in* the Eagles—and in no small way. He wasn't just "the drummer," a time-keeping afterthought relegated to Ringo-esque buffoonery. Henley's songwriting acumen and high, aching voice were perfect for the band's sound and vision. Their first hit, "Take It Easy," came out in 1972, and kicked off a long run in which the Eagles steamrollered SoCal anthem after SoCal anthem, including such Henley-cowritten songs as "Hotel California," "Lyin' Eyes," "Take It to the Limit," "Tequila Sunrise," and "Desperado."

Their classic albums include *The Eagles* (1972), *Desperado* (1973), *On the Border* (1974), *One of These Nights* (1975), *Their Greatest Hits (1971–1975)* (1976), *Hotel California* (1976), and *The Long Run* (1979, all on Asylum), and remain, for the most part, essential parts of the thinking person's rock 'n' roll experience.

☆Four: Rock Will Never Die (No Matter What)

TWO THINGS TO REMEMBER ABOUT ROCK 'N' ROLL: IT WILL INdeed never die inasmuch as its appeal to youth is a built-in protection clause to ensure that it won't. Artists who were hot during any one generation's high school years, for example, will retain a certain nostalgic popularity *with those people,* probably until the long, steep, creepy hill of Social Security has been successfully negotiated, because the songs will always remind them of when they were young.

And 2. There really *isn't* anything new in rock anymore—and that's okay. Changes in technical gadgetry and fashion might dress it up a bit, but the lyrical themes of teen alienation, rebellion, young love, and wild times only grow back into themselves and, if they seem different, it's only because of the context of the times in which the artists live.

In the end, it's still three chords and a cloud of angst. Which is to say that, although Texas music would certainly feel the imprint, from the late seventies on, of such movements as punk, new wave, and alternative music, mainstream rock was there the whole time—same as it ever was—either in the guise of older folks like ZZ Top, or in younger mutations like Pantera and Kings X.

It was also a time when the Texas reputation for guitar genius hit a point of absolute white heat. The Vaughan brothers were coming into the spotlight in the blues arena and, also in Austin, an elfin whiz with fireworks for fingers and a background in jazz-rock fusion was starting to make a marquee name for himself. (See box, page 117.)

Fate has, thus far, been less kind to another guitar hero named Charlie Sexton, one of a batch of Stevie Ray—era Austin guitarists of astonishing talent. Born in 1969, he was a textbook prodigy, a literal child star who was famous on Austin blues and rock stages while most kids his age were still pondering the mysteries of breakfast cereal. By the time he was thirteen, Sexton was touring as the lead guitarist in Joe Ely's band, and was signed to a solo deal with MCA by his sixteenth birthday.

Unfortunately, Sexton, who was blessed (cursed?) with James Dean's cheekbones and Matt Dillon's pout, was envisioned by MCA as a fashion-statement rock star, the sort tailor-made for MTV. After high-profile sessions with the likes of Keith Richards, Ron Wood, and Don Henley, Sexton recorded *Pictures for Pleasure*, which came out in 1986 and featured the driving-yet-brooding hit single "Beat's So Lonely."

The tune's hiccuping Elvis vocals and hard-rock instrumentation, bolstered by a hot video in which Sexton came off like the model in an Obsession commercial, was a number 17 hit—and represented pretty much nothing of what Sexton was really about.

It was four years before *Charlie Sexton* followed up, but it barely dented the charts before dropping into obscurity. Happy to spend some time free of MCA's ludicrous marketing constraints, Sexton next surfaced in an Austin supergroup called Arc Angels, which also featured guitarist Doyle Bramhall, Jr., and the rhythm section of drummer Chris Layton and bassist Tommy Shannon (ex- of Double Trouble, who were bandless after Stevie Ray Vaughan's death in August 1990).

Named for the Austin Rehearsal Complex (ARC) in which they practiced, the Arc Angels were signed by DGC and seemed a good bet at the time despite their bigenerational age differences (Sexton and Bramhall being the straining-at-the-leash pups and Shannon and Layton representing the seasoned, wary road dogs).

Their one album, *Arc Angels* (1992), though speckled with moments of blues/rock intensity and some kicking tunes, failed to sustain the group through what were, in fact, the decidedly different worldviews betwixt youth and wisdom, and they broke up shortly thereafter.

Sexton's most ambitious and satisfying project, the Charlie Sexton Sextet, recorded *Under the Wishing Tree*, which was released by MCA in 1995. A surprisingly varied record of moody introspection and haunting acoustic sensibilities, *Under the Wishing Tree* came off sounding a bit like what Los Lobos might do if they lived in South Austin. Of course, the CD was far too creative and inspired to do anything in terms of sales, and MCA dropped Sexton. In 1999, Sexton surfaced for a while playing lead guitar for Bob Dylan's band.

Sexton's guitar-mate in Arc Angels, Doyle Bramhall, Jr., surfaced in 1996 from drug problems (one of the major reasons the Arc Angels short-circuited) with a fine set of bluesy/Tom Pettyish rock for Geffen. Called *Doyle Bramhall II*, the CD shows remarkable promise, and 1999's *Jellycream* is a faithful extrapolation.

Ian Moore, another shimmering example of Austin boy wonder guitar royalty, appears destined for better luck than either Van Wilks (see box, next page) or Sexton. He grew up in a Bohemian family environment and studied violin before deciding to try guitar so as to better follow the paths of early heroes like Sly and the Family Stone, Stevie Wonder, Curtis Mayfield, the Beatles, and the usual regiment of Austin musical giants.

Moore's incredible voice (with an Aaron Neville—like falsetto) and lit-

GUITARIST WHO CHANGED MODERN MUSIC
Eric Johnson

A baffling, wonderful artist of infinite taste and celestial talent, Eric Johnson periodically rewards his fans with an album or concert tour—both of which are merely by-products of his Zen-like pursuit of the ultimate tone.

Born in Austin in 1954, Johnson first studied piano, an instrument on which he is rumored to be nearly as proficient as guitar. He took up guitar at eleven and, by fifteen, was staggering Austin audiences. His early days in the seminal fusion band the Electromagnets (with bassist Kyle Brock, drummer Bill Maddox, and keyboardist Steve Barber) resulted in one near-mythic and impossible-to-find album, *The Electromagnets* (1975, EGM), before Johnson embarked on a solo odyssey.

He recorded *The Seven Worlds*, an unreleased album much whispered about by the cognoscenti, and lost years in a management imbroglio with ZZ Top honcho Bill Ham before signing with Reprise and releasing the aptly named *Tones* in 1986. The record, on which Johnson decorates his tuneful popscapes with a blistering stylistic jambalaya recalling Wes Montgomery, Jeff Beck, Jimi Hendrix, and Jerry Reed, blew the guitar world into a fresh galaxy.

Stardom followed, and the angelic-looking Johnson worked for years before releasing *Ah Via Musicom* on Capitol in 1990. It was even bigger than *Tones*, and no end of adoration followed: gold records, successive years atop various guitar magazine polls, a Grammy award for the song "Cliffs of Dover," prominent tours and session dates . . .

But the elusive hunt for the Tone continued. After six cryptic years recording in an anonymous strip-center studio in North Austin, Johnson finally finished his third album, *Venus Isle*, which came out on Capitol in September 1996. Another wizard's brew of gorgeous pop songs, jazz seasonings, blistering rock, and stretched-out, neo-orchestral pieces, *Venus Isle* is like some Joycean soundtrack to a volcanic incident in Johnson's Mensan brain.

Of late, Johnson has been playing with his blues/rock trio Alien Love Child, and *The Seven Worlds* and various Electromagnets CDs are finally landing in the marketplace.

erate songwriting acumen match his blues-from-Saturn guitar modes, and he quickly hammered out a unique reputation in the vastly competitive Austin club scene. In 1992, he was selected by that one-man finishing school of Texas guitarists, Joe Ely, for a coveted slot in his road band. A year later, Moore was signed to the resurgent Capricorn label and released

CRIMINALLY OVERLOOKED GUITARIST

Van Wilks

Another Austin gunslinger is Van Wilks, located somewhere in the stylistic gap between Eric Johnson and Johnny Winter, who writes intelligent, melodic, and progressive blues-seasoned rock tunes, spinning out Jeff Beck Drinks Lone Star Beer guitar magic.

Wilks was born in 1951 in Galveston and took up guitar as a youthful refuge while his family moved first to Lubbock and then to Brownwood. Like many of his peers, Wilks learned American musical heritage via the British invasion, and by his late teens had mastered a variety of styles by the usual array of UK guitar gods.

He migrated to Austin in the early seventies, formed the popular band Fools in 1974, and soon attracted the attention of ZZ Top manager Bill Ham. In 1979, the band signed with Mercury Records and, after legal problems over the name, became simply "Van Wilks." The subsequent debut, 1980's *Bombay Tears*, is a neglected artwork—quite simply one of the finest examples of pure Texas rock ever recorded.

Despite fine reviews and tours with Heart and Van Halen, the label gave little support to the project, and plans for a called-for second record were mutually scrapped. Wilks released an indie EP, *Boystown*, in 1982, which went nowhere, and shortly thereafter his management contract with Ham ended.

Though he surfaced with pal Eric Johnson on a goosebump-inducing arrangement of "Greensleeves" for an Amazing Records *Austin Christmas Collection* in 1983, it would be the last Van Wilks recording for a decade. In 1996, Wilks released *Soul of a Man* in Europe, where he's the star he should be over here, and followed up in 1999 with a stateside CD, the estimable *Koko's Hideaway*.

Ian Moore, which contained FM radio staples like "Blue Sky," "How Does It Feel," and "Harlem."

A live EP followed, then, in 1995, Moore recorded the critically embraced *Modernday Folklore* CD. Moore, whose idea of offstage debauchery includes bicycling, fly fishing, and reading Dostoevski and Toni Morrison, has subsequently released *Green Grass* on his own Hablador Records and, in 1999, signed with Koch Records.

But one didn't necessarily have to be a guitar hero to break out of Austin in the early eighties. A San Antonio native called Christopher Cross (born Christopher Geppert in 1951) was leading popular Austin copy bands by his late teens and spending his off-time writing original material. Cross is a genial, bear-sized guy with an incongruously breezy tenor voice whose MOR balladry seemed consciously designed to blare out of supermarket speakers and into the ears of housewives everywhere—which made him a bit of a curiosity in Austin musical circles.

Yet his tunes caught the ear of Warner Brothers executives in 1978, and by 1980 he'd released *Christopher Cross*, which of course became one of those "Where did *this* guy come from and how did everyone on earth decide to buy his record on the same day?" phenomena. Featuring song after song of infectious, smooth-as-cocoa pop, the album sported four top twenty hits: "Sailing" (number 1), "Ride Like the Wind" (number 2), "Never Be the Same" (number 15), and "Say You'll Be Mine" (number 20).

When Grammy time came around, Cross hooked up a trailer to the limo and carted off *five* of the little buggers, including Album of the Year and Record and Song of the Year (both for "Sailing"); the massive haul eclipsed the previous *in toto* record held by a blue-eyed slacker named Sinatra—no, not Nancy.

He followed up in big fashion with a hit single and an Academy Award for Best Original Song with "Arthur's Theme (The Best That You Can Do)," which Cross performed and cowrote with Peter Allen, Burt Bacharach, and Carole Bayer Sager.

Given all the hoopla and confetti, it was three years before Cross released his sophomore effort, *Another Page*. While not a carbon copy of the first record, it understandably attempted to mine that same melodic, hand-crafted, very pleasant sound. While pretty much guaranteed gold status on sheer momentum, *Another Page* did score two top twenty singles ("All Right" and "No Time for Talk"), and went top ten with "Think of Laura," a song that received a sales boost when it began appearing on the soap opera *General Hospital*.bj   And then, for no particular reason, it was turn-out-the-lights time. By the time Cross released 1985's *Every Turn of the Word*, his salability had mysteriously vanished. The album didn't work, and 1988's *Back of My Mind* fared no better. It had to be maddening to Cross; the poor fellow wasn't doing anything "wrong," or even different.

In any event, a *Greatest Hits* package and *Rendezvous*, a later album released in Europe on the Ariola label, have kept Cross's work in the marketplace, though a return to prominence is admittedly unlikely. He recently surfaced singing backup on old friend Eric Johnson's *Venus Isle* album. (Johnson was a featured soloist on Cross's first LP.)

There haven't been too many lite-pop types in Austin since Cross, though several other acts steeped in traditional rock have made inroads on the international music scene. The LeRoi Brothers should certainly be mentioned, who formed in the early eighties and whose in-and-out lineup has included ex-T-birds Mike Buck and Keith Ferguson. A premier and tireless roots-rock outfit, the band's last two CDs for Rounder, *Check This Action* and *Crowne Royal*, are properly representative.

The most interesting of these acts is Storyville, the brainchild of one Malford Milligan, who owns perhaps the finest voice in Texas rock history.

An artist with an operatic range and stylistic nods to Sam Cooke, Nat King Cole, and all four Neville Brothers at one time, Milligan belts out timeless soul/rock with an all-star band comprising That Rhythm Section Again, Tommy Shannon and Chris Layton, and guitarists Dave Holt and David Grissom, both veterans of—yes—Joe Ely's band, as well as Carlene Carter and the Mavericks (Holt) and John Mellencamp (Grissom).

Originally a solo project with various sidemen built around Milligan's songs and make-the-angels-sigh voice, he entered the studio with producer Stephen Bruton to record 1994's wonderful *Bluest Eyes* for November Records. From the array of studio musicians involved, Milligan was able to cull the above band, and Storyville took to the road. The band moved up to Atlantic/Code Blue for two tasty follow-ups, *A Piece of Your Soul* and *Dog Years*. Unfortunately, the band just didn't catch on in the deserved Big Way and eventually broke up.

Speaking of out-of-the-bonds-of-earth singers, Roy Orbison (remember him?) resurfaced in the eighties in a massive way. After the death of his wife in 1966, Orbison sort of vanished in a professional sense. Though he remarried three years later, and triumphantly returned to Europe for a series of ecstatically received shows, his recorded work throughout the seventies was sporadic and indifferent.

In 1980, though, after a tour opening for the Eagles, he won a Grammy for a duet he did with Emmylou Harris on "That Lovin' You Feelin' Again," and Orbison was back in the spotlight. Van Halen covered "Oh, Pretty Woman," and director David Lynch used "In Dreams" in the film *Blue Velvet*. The next year, more justice was meted out when Orbison was inducted into the Rock 'n' Roll Hall of Fame.

But it wasn't until 1987, after he'd charted (number 42, country) with k.d. lang on "Crying," that Orbison ran into some unlikely compatriots in George Harrison, Tom Petty, Bob Dylan, and Jeff Lynne. As everyone now knows, the quintet became the Traveling Wilburys, and their enormously successful first LP (*Traveling Wilburys, Volume One*, Wilbury/Warner Bros.) went to number 3.

Though it wasn't the "hit," Orbison's "You're Not Alone Anymore" was a highlight—a soaring, brilliant, goosebump-inducing ballad that ranks with the finest of his material.

He also scored a hit with "You Got It" on his 1989 solo CD *Mystery Girl*. Unfortunately, Orbison died only a month after the release of the Wilburys album, and his first major hits in a quarter-century were destined to be posthumous.

As maybe the best singer Texas ever produced, a terrific and underrated songwriter, and a marvelous gentleman, Roy Orbison tossed substantial honor into a frequently sordid profession.

Despite the winds of musical change, Joe Ely continues to practice timeless rock of the roadhouse variety, which he artfully sculpts from rich country, R&B, rockabilly, and Tex-Mex traditions. A consummate professional and craftsman whose work has always found favor among his peers and critics—anywhere, it would seem, except in record stores—Ely's across-all-barriers appeal was perhaps best defined by two back-to-back tours he did: a 1979 jag with Merle Haggard and a 1980 jaunt with the Clash.

As if a directional indicator, Ely's 1980 MCA release, *Live Shots*, recorded while out with the Clash, previewed a decade in which the songwriter's prodigious output rocked hardest and most experimentally. His next record, 1981's amusingly titled *Musta Notta Gotta Lotta*, effortlessly roared from benzedrine-a-billy to honky-tonk rock in sweaty glee.

Ely chose next to make *Hi-Res*, a heavily synthesized Panhandle New Wave album which is widely acknowledged as his one recorded mistake. Probably not coincidentally, Ely was dropped from MCA shortly thereafter, and wouldn't surface again until the latter part of the decade, when HighTone released *Lord of the Highway* (1987) and *Dig All Night* (1988), two records which immediately reestablished the man's intrinsic greatness.

After an obscure but sturdy effort for the Sunstorm label, 1988's *Milk-shakes and Malts*, Ely once again signed with MCA. In 1990, Ely put out yet another live CD, *Live at Liberty Lunch*, which was particularly valuable as documentation for what a kick-ass rock band his group had become, then was further lionized when Rounder Records actually rereleased *More a Legend Than a Band*, the always marveled over but rarely heard album Ely had made over a decade before as part of the Flatlanders (along with Butch Hancock and Jimmie Dale Gilmore).

In 1992, Ely came out with the masterful *Love and Danger*, a record that made wandering and loneliness sound like fine states to be in. It might well have been the album that cemented his reputation as the preeminent musical sculptor of all things Texas—until 1995, anyway, when *Letter to Laredo* came out.

On this CD, the ever-curious Ely, whose proclivity for stylistic exploration and assimilation is only part of his genius, dipped heavily into Gypsy, Spanish, and border music. The results are breathtaking. Ely skillfully mixed his West Texas rock with Marty Robbins narratives and the romantic instrumental melodicism of the Mexican night to create his finest record. The flamenco guitar work Netherlands-to-Austin transplant Teye sets an irresistibly haunting mood.

Two subsequent projects, 1998's *Twistin' in the Wind* and Ely's participation on *Los Super Seven*, have only cemented his position as the true spokesperson for Texas rock.

Not to be sexist about it, but Carla Olson might be described as a reasonable female facsimile of Ely. A roots-rock stylist whose gritty songs, impassioned barroom voice, and angelic features were a strong Austin draw, Olson's first important group, the Textones, signed a 1984 deal with A&M and released *Midnight Mission* before the band broke up and Olson decided to base out of Los Angeles and forge a solo career.

To that end, she's been marginally successful, with a string of solo albums

(*Within an Ace, Reap the Whirlwind, Wave the Hand,* and, with ex–Rolling Stone Mick Taylor, *Too Hot for Snakes*).

Houston's Chris Whitley is a strange and often brilliant songwriter. After traveling extensively while growing up, Whitley developed an intriguing worldview and a captivating and original slide guitar style on National steel guitar.

His records have been a bit of a stylish hopscotch. *Living with the Law* is the most consistent, though *Din of Ecstasy, Terra Incognita,* and *Dirt Floor* all have interesting moments.

T-BONE BURNETT AND STEPHEN BRUTON ARE TWO OTHER prominent Texans whose records are stylistic pasticcios of all that we hold dear in rock—and both are perhaps more noted for their roles as record producers than as actual artists.

Burnett, born John Henry Burnett in St. Louis in 1948, grew up in Fort Worth and spent his youth as a sort of musical quicksand pit, sucking up any and all of the area's rich melodic textures. He spent his formative years writing songs and producing local blues records, then headed to L.A. in the early seventies, where he produced albums for Delbert McClinton and former Byrd Gene Clark.

Over the next several years, he recorded his own record, 1972's *The B-52 Band and the Fabulous Skylarks* (UNI), played guitar on Bob Dylan's Rolling Thunder Review tour, cofounded the Alpha Band (with whom he recorded three albums), then, after a songwriting hiatus in Montana, seriously embarked on a solo career.

A devout Christian whose clever lyrics and profound sentiments should shame many an evangelist, Burnett has produced an eclectic and prodigious catalogue of rootsy material, highlights of which include 1980's *Truth Decay* (Takoma), a 1982 EP for Warner Brothers, *Trap Door, T-Bone Burnett* (1986, Dot), and the spectacularly far-reaching *The Criminal Under My Own Hat* (1992, Columbia).

As remarkable as his solo work is, his production on records by Elvis Costello, Counting Crows, Bruce Cockburn, Jackopierce, Los Lobos, and Marshall Crenshaw is world-class and completely innovative. But from his own personal standpoint, the work which may stand out most in his mind was when he produced Sam Phillips (the female Christian singer turned secular artist, not the Sun Studios guy): He ended up marrying her.

Stephen Bruton, another Fort Worth kid, toured the world as a hired axster before settling into his own solo career. After rockin' hometown nightclubs with a crack white boy R&B outfit called Little Whisper and the Rumors, Bruton spent several years on the international road as lead guitarist for the likes of Kris Kristofferson and Bonnie Raitt.

Finally, he decided to try his own muse, moved to Austin and signed a

Mary Cutrufello

Like any New England-born, ex-Yalie honky-tonk singer who plays guitar like Jeff Beck and happens to be an African-American female, Mary Cutrufello didn't have an easy time attracting the suits in Nashville. Charley Pride only *thought* he had an uphill climb.

Cutrufello was reading and writing music by the age of nine, played in rock bands throughout her teens; then had a life-changing experience when she heard Dwight Yoakam's *Buenas Noches from a Lonely Room*. Instantly, Cutrufello went country—and in order to do so properly relocated to Austin. She immersed herself in the omnipresent music community and began to absorb as much lore and tradition as possible.

She was an immediate attraction. The attractive, petite Cutrufello has a voice like Joan Armatrading doing Tanya Trucker, she writes great tunes like "All the Millers in Milwaukee" and "Just the Whiskey Talkin'," and in performance leaps all over the stage like Pete Townshend on moonshine.

For too long, the only available recording of Cutrufello was an independently released and eponymously titled cassette. In 1996, after touring as lead guitarist for Jimmie Dale Gilmore's *Braver New World* tour, Cutrufello released an indie CD, *Who to Love . . . and When to Leave*. Crossing her Pete Anderson–meets–Jeff Beck guitar with more Mellencamp/Springsteen–flavored songwriting, the CD resulted in a deal with Polygram. In August of 1998 she put out *When the Night Is Through*, perhaps not the album longtime fans expected—it's almost all arena-styled rock—but nonetheless an intriguing work.

deal with dos, the subsidiary of Antone's Records. In 1994, Bruton put out *What It Is,* a carnival of blues/jazz/rock songs which displayed his guitar skills as well as a witty and worldly-wise way with a song. His next two CDs, *Right on Time* and *Nothing but the Truth,* are similarly excellent.

As with Burnett, the only thing threatening Bruton's solo career is his own talent as a producer. His work with Storyville and Alejandro Escovedo, among others, is routinely honored in *Austin Chronicle* music polls, and Bruton has become a senior mover in hill country music.

Perhaps the oddest guy to be called a traditional rocker is Jimmy LaFave. His coterie of fans would probably call him a singer/songwriter, but the fact is that, however introspective and well conceived his tunes are, he *rocks*. LaFave was born in Wills Point, Texas, raised in Oklahoma, and gravitated to Austin like twelve million other musicians looking for a nirvanic gigging community.

With his beautiful, pure-as-new-snow voice, fine tunes, and a crackerjack band, Night Tribe, LaFave built an incredible reputation around Austin—then waited for years on a promised recording contract that ultimately fell through.

He finally found a home on Bohemia Beat Records—a label created specifically for LaFave, now distributed by Rounder—and finally got some product into the marketplace with a superb live record, 1992's *Austin Skyline*. The word began to spread and LaFave's since pulled off three brilliant records: *Highway Trance, Buffalo Return to the Plains,* and *Trail.* Overseas sales are skyrocketing, national media is a-gushin', and LaFave stands to break in a big way. He should; if Johnny Cash, Roy Orbison, and Elvis Costello formed a band in the Big Thicket, it would sound like Jimmy LaFave. And a lot of people would pay to listen to that.

Other not-easy-to-classify performers are Mason Ruffner, Rick Broussard, and Robin Syler. Ruffner grew up in Fort Worth, fascinated by the guitar prowess of Jimi Hendrix, the lyrical acumen of Bob Dylan, and blues stalwarts like Jimmy Reed and Muddy Waters.

After learning guitar, he served an R&B apprenticeship with Robert Ealey's Five Careless Lovers, traveled both coasts, then settled in New Orleans for a postdoctoral residency. With his band the Blues Rockers, Ruffner honed his multifaceted style in Trojan fashion at a Bourbon Street club called the 544 Club.

In 1985, Ruffner signed with CBS and released his self-titled first album late that year. A triumph of roots rock in all its hormonal simplicity, Ruffner began to tour like a one-man bus line. His second LP, *Gypsy Blood,* drew more terrific reviews, and he continued to tour tirelessly in support of such acts as U2, Jimmy Page, and Crosby, Stills, and Nash.

Though *Gypsy Blood* sold over two hundred thousand copies, and Ruffner's magical guitar prowess was sought after by everyone from Dylan to Carlos Santana and Daniel Lanois, CBS wasn't really happy with Ruffner's single-minded muse, and he decided not to record for the label anymore.

Instead, he relocated to Wimberly, Texas, just outside of Austin, and in 1992 released the searing *Evolution* on the Archer label. A bit of a recluse, Ruffner's working on an all-instrumental record. His genius is a victim of the industry.

Rick Broussard is a similar-minded rocker who's reputation, sadly, is confined to Texas and Louisiana. As the fire-breathing leader of roots-pop legends Two Hoots and a Holler, Broussard has a new band, Shadow Man, and his solo CDs include 1990's *No Man's Land* (on the French New Rose label) and 1992's *Rick Broussard* (Austin's Dynamic Records). As a musical bartender mixing Cajun, honky-punk, and pure rock forms, Broussard serves up an eye-blearing sonic cocktail—as evidenced by his numerous Austin Music Awards trophies for Best Roots Rock Band.

Guitarist Robin Syler, meanwhile, a former early bandmate of Stevie Ray Vaughan, is the state's finest purveyor of the sort of surf music made famous by Dick Dale and the Ventures. Syler, though, being from Texas, has his own rocking twists on the genre, creating a form he calls "surfabilly." While there are no recordings of Syler's material as yet, someone will be smart enough to get it out.

BUT ENOUGH OF THOSE WHO "ROCK" ON THE PERIPHERY. THERE'S been no shortage of those Texans who continue to ply a harder brand of what might be called "dinosaur rock" (it might not be called that, either, depending on who you talk to), but the following bands were influenced a lot more by Ted Nugent, the Beatles, and Guns 'n' Roses than anything remotely connected to, say, Haircut 100 or Spandau Ballet.

Arlington's Pantera is by far the most successful of the younger trad-rockers. Formed in their early teen years by bassist Rex Rocker (who's since dropped the buffoonish surname) and the guitar/drum brother tandem of "Dime Bag" Darrell and Vinnie Paul Abbott (respectively), Pantera got their start as Van Halen/Def Leppard wannabes in classic metroplex rock rooms like Cardi's, Joe's Garage, and Savvy's, opening for popular Texan hard-rock club acts like Lightning, Saavy, and Rage.

In 1988, they shifted into the shred-metal direction pioneered by Metallica, and added a New Orleans–born vocalist named Harry Connick, Jr. JUST KIDDING! They *did* add a Crescent City singer, but it was Phil Anselmo, whose surf-Nazi demeanor, bleeding angst, and blistering societal observations are such as to cause fellow tortured dudes like Morrissey, Bono, and Michael Stipe to sit in a circle mainlining each other with hornet repellent.

After a dubious album for Metal Magic (1988) called *Power Metal*, Pantera signed with East/West and released 1990's *Cowboys from Hell*. Utilizing incredibly fast and arcane licks, wearing their Texas heritage like biker tattoos, and sounding like 33 rpm recordings of cougars thrown into a tree shredder played at 78 rpm, Pantera had definitely come up with something that was, if not new, at least refreshingly different.

And if any moron thought Pantera wasn't setting up a grassroots following, 1992's *Vulgar Display of Power* changed all that. The album, against which *Cowboys from Hell* came across like Art Garfunkel, broke into the *Billboard* Top 50, and 1994's *Far Beyond Driven*, bursting with more ear-melting, heart-pulverizing rhetoric, debuted on the album charts at number 1. By then, the boys were headlining arenas and festivals worldwide on two-year, party-intensive tours, buying a strip club when they did go home, and generally having the prototypical large time.

In spring of 1996, *The Great Southern Roadkill* became the latest CD to add to Pantera's Bill Gates–size bank accounts. In lunatic fashion, the Pan-terists actually injected some melody and harmony into their latest album, though it hardly sounds like a Vienna Boys Choir recording. Still, it shows a bit of growth. And though the old Texas adage warns that if it ain't broke, don't fix it, in Pantera's case, they'd probably taken their brand of crazoid rock as far as it could go.

Dallas's Lord Tracy was not totally dissimilar to Pantera—their over-the-top speed and chops were absolutely the stuff of true virtuosity—but their irreverent and neocomic approach to subject matter was far more asinine and fun.

Formed from the ashes of the legendary Lightning, and comprised of bassist Kinley Wolf, drummer Chris Craig, guitarist Jimmy "R" Rusidoff, and vocalist Terrence Lee Glaze, Lord Tracy's *Attitude du Sophomore* was instrumental in getting them a deal with MCA. Originally called Tracy Lords after the group's favorite porn star, they were forced to change the name when the sultry actress threatened legal action.

The maneuver didn't alter their spirit, though, and the showcase that clinched their deal was supposedly, er, climaxed when Glaze masturbated an open, full beer bottle, hopped off the stage, and spewed an ejaculatory jet of foam all over the coed contingency of MCA A&R reps.

Deaf Godz of Babylon came out in 1989 and scored massive critical approval and MTV airplay, though sales weren't as encouraging. Protracted label squabbles eventually precluded a second album, and Lord Tracy passed into legend as a great band that deserved better. (Of passing interest is the fact that bassist Wolf, a sublime player, subsequently spent further time in the global spotlight as a member of The Cult's road band.)

Two Houston-based groups, King's X and Galactic Cowboys, created small but sturdy niches in the major label marketplace, both relying on dense vocal harmonies and complex, neometallic chord structures.

King's X (guitarist/vocalist Ty Tabor, bassist/vocalist Doug Pinnick, and drummer/vocalist Jerry Gaskill) came together in 1980 through various Christian rock associations, toured the Midwest rock circuit, then headed to Houston where they hooked up with Sam Taylor, a manager who'd worked in the ZZ Top hierarchy.

With long, complex songs and fantastical, vaguely spiritual lyrics topped by pop melodies and sugary harmonies, King's X signed with Megaforce Records and released *Out of the Silent Planet* in 1988. They developed a small but devoted following, and recorded *Gretchen Goes to Nebraska* the next year. The changes in American rock music (particularly the rise of grunge) made King's X perhaps a bit passé, but their fervent fan base continued to grow.

They broke through with 1990's *Faith, Hope and Love*, which featured heavy airplay for the single "It's Love" and a top sixty charting for the CD. The band jumped to Atlantic for their next record, 1994's *King's X*, which had another hit in "Black Flag," then shifted to a slightly simpler, tougher sound for *Dogman*, which was released later that year.

In the latter part of the nineties the band came out with *Ear Candy* and

Tape Head, while both Pinnick and Tabor have placed solo projects in the marketplace.

Galactic Cowboys—guitarist/vocalist Dane Sonnier, vocalist Ben Huggins, bassist/vocalist Monte Colvin, and drummer/vocalist Alan Doss—are similar in most respects to King's X. They shared the same management, the harmonies are definitely there, and so are the faux-McCartney melodies. But where the X-men lean toward progressive rock form, the Cowboys have tossed elements of jazz, psychedelia, punk, and grunge into their étouffée.

They've released two albums for Geffen, the eponymously titled debut (1991), which drew as much confusion as affection, and 1993's *Space in Your Face*, which seemed to focus their Faith No More Jams on *Queen II* sound, and the result has been encouraging record sales.

A move to the Metal Blade label seemed to affect the band's output not at all: starting in 1996, *Machine Fish*, *Feel the Rage*, *The Horse That Bud Bought*, and *At the End of the Day* have appeared successively.

And while the subject concerns neo-progressive rock in South Texas, Pat Mastelotto (drums) and Trey Gunn (bass/Chapman stick) should be mentioned. These hyper-talented players are members of the latest incarnation of King Crimson, arguably the best progressive band ever. How their Lone Star states of mind meld with band leader and arch-weirdo/genius Robert Fripp is anybody's guess, but the music—as on *Thrak* (Virgin, 1995)—is unbelievable.

Austin's premiere entry in the hair-rock sweepstakes was Dangerous Toys. Original members were Mark Geary on drums, guitarists Scott Dalhover and Paul Lidel, bassist Mike Watson, and vocalist Jason McMaster, and the band quickly became a huge club draw in a town that, admittedly, looks down on such music.

The Toys were probably hugely amused, then, when they signed with Columbia Records in 1990 and sold eight hundred thousand copies of their first two records, *Dangerous Toys* and *Hellacious Acres*. When foolish label execs (is that redundant?) attempted to push the DTs in a southern rock direction, they jumped ship and signed with Austin's dos/DMZ label. *Pissed*, from 1994, sounded like it, and the 1995 follow-up, *The R-tist 4-merly Known as Dangerous Toys*, with Michael Hannan replacing Watson on bass, rocked just as hard while throwing in an interesting nod to industrial bands.

A terrific San Antonio/Austin hard-rock band whose end was beset by tragedy was Pariah. Formed at SA's Clark High School in 1986 by brothers Sims and Kyle Ellison (bass and guitar, respectively), drummer Shandon "Son o' Doug" Sahm, vocalist Dave Derrick, and, later, guitarist Jared Tuten, Pariah was basically like any other bunch of teensters who wanted to be rock stars—except they could play their asses off and they wrote great songs.

They signed a multialbum deal with Geffen and, in 1991, just at the dawn of the Seattle explosion, released *To Mock a Killingbird*. With a

CRIMINALLY OVERLOOKED GUITARIST

Andy Timmons

In Dallas, an arena rock veteran from his days as a member of MTV puff-hair faves Danger Danger, Timmons is probably the brightest hope for good ol' guitar-based rock 'n' roll in Texas.

He's a classically trained jazz buff, blues fan, and Beatles freak from Evansville, Indiana, via the University of Miami music department (Pat Metheny, Jaco Pastorius), where he spent his nights earning tuition money playing in Top 40 bands. After college, Timmons moved to Dallas and played in various rock bands before joining Danger Danger, with whom he recorded two albums and toured the world with such acts as Kiss, Warrant, and Extreme.

When Danger Danger broke up, Timmons returned to Dallas to pursue his own aims. An articulate, Will Rogers–style altruist with surfer boy good looks and an affection for his cats and wife that charmingly recalls a *Donna Reed Show* mentality, Timmons released an indie CD, the all-instrumental *ear X-tacy* in 1994. The album, reminiscent of Joe Satriani/Steve Vai material, is a wonder work, stunning in its variety, sense of melody, and sheer technique, and only served to cement his reputation as a guitar mag hero. The record sold well enough that it was picked up by Oo/Sony-Japan in 1996 for distribution in the Far East, where Timmons is something of a cultural hero.

An in-demand session whiz, Timmons also tours and records with fusion drummer Simon Phillips, tours with the *Ear X-tacy* trio, and heads up a blues band called The Pawn Kings (who've released two CDs).

The ever-prolific guitarist has released another fretboard-happy CD, *Ear X-tacy 2*, and is readying a third stylistically similar effort, *The Spoken and the Unspoken*. Too, he recorded a harmony-laced CD of captivating pop-rock tunes demonstrating his love of Brian Wilson, John Lennon, and Elvis Costello. Called *Orange Swirl*, the record is irresistible.

global chilling toward hard rock, though, the second Pariah album never materialized and, after the band parted ways with Geffen in early 1995, then decided to break up, bassist Sims Ellison committed suicide. Perhaps the best result of that unfortunate incident was the establishment, by Ellison's family and the Austin Rehearsal Complex, of SIMS (Services Invested in Musician Support), a nonprofit outreach hotline that connects troubled Austin musicians with counseling services.

Though hard rock did in fact undergo a popularity crisis for a time, as with all things musical, it's again picking up momentum. In any event, it's always had its Texan practitioners, and among those deserving mention from the eighties are Solinger, Bellicose, Agony Column, Dead Horse, Petting Zoo, Obscene Jester, Minstral Gravy, and Absu, a band from the Dallas suburb of Plano that is almost completely unknown in their home state but sell thousands and thousands of records on the European black/death metal circuit.

Perhaps the most nefarious of all the hard rock/metal bands is the dichotomous King Diamond, the complex singer/songwriter who fronts not only the band King Diamond but also Mercyful Fate.

The Danish-born King, who settled in Dallas in 1991, launched his profitable and prodigiously creative career in the mid-eighties on the European metal circuit. His greasepainted visage is reminiscent of Kiss and Alice Cooper, but where the former are cartoonlike and the latter is almost vaudevillian, King Diamond's gothic/horror concepts are decidedly darker. It doesn't hurt, of course, that he's a practicing Satanist, though he's quick to point out that he's a disciple of Anton LaVey's Church of Satan (which, as he indicates, preaches absolute religious freedom for each individual), and *not* the horns-on-the-head, *Rosemary's Baby* sort that sacrifices babies and animals to the Crimson Imp.

In any case, sporting a voice of amazingly diverse expression and range, Der Kingle has made several records that are much-copied landmarks of metal. His first album, Mercyful Fate's 1983 Megaforce release, *Melissa,* crossed Black Sabbath riffing with far more intriguing lyrics and melodies, and was followed in rapid succession by several LPs, most notably 1984's *Don't Break the Oath,* 1992's *Return of the Vampire* (on Roadrunner), and the recent *Into the Unknown* (Metal Blade).

The King Diamond output is just as staggering, in terms of quantity as well as quality. The 1986 debut, *Fatal Portrait* (Roadrunner), set the stage for 1987's conceptual *Abigail,* which many fans regard as the *Sgt. Pepper's* of dark metal.

Again, King Diamond has released almost an album a year for the past decade, and while all have their chilling highlights, 1990's *The Eye* (Roadrunner) is particularly creepy and 1996's *The Graveyard* (Metal Blade) is a narrative and retro-metal work of genius. King Diamond is that rare metal guy who understands that the genre doesn't have to be structurally dumb and melodically dead to rock. In fact, his emphasis on interesting chord changes, dynamics, operatic vocal lines, and clustered harmonies is rather delicious in the context of his visceral lyrics. (The King's story lines, it should be pointed out, drag the listener into the pit with him, rather than to simply point at it from a few football fields away, which is the case with many so-called dark metallurgists.)

In 1998, perhaps in a nod to his new southern roots, the King came out with a new concept album called *Voodoo.*

Another foreign import to Texas's sunny climes—in 1980—was England's

Arthur Brown, the honcho behind 1968's Crazy World of Arthur Brown, which boasted a number 2 U.S. hit that year called "Fire."

Though he never nearly achieved that original success, he worked in the early seventies with Arthur Brown's Kingdom Come, with whom he released such LPs as 1972's *Galactic Zoo Dossier* (Polydor) and 1973's *Kingdom Come* (Track U.K.). In Austin, he surfaces periodically with a combo called the Even Crazier World of Arthur Brown.

THE FACT THAT WE'RE APPROACHING THE MILLENNIUM HAS not kept a small band of prototypical Texas rockers, who started years ago when the world was young, from carrying on—with varying degrees of success.

ZZ Top shows no signs of ever stopping—unless Billy Gibbons should be dragged to death when his magic carpet–length beard gets intertwined in the wheels of a passing truck. In any case, the band kicked off the eighties with the marginal *El Loco*, then was revitalized by the possibilities of MTV.

They incorporated a droning synthesizer beat, made a variety of videos featuring vintage cars and scantily clad, breast-enhancement test-case babes and, surprisingly, their efforts to grow with the times paid off hugely. *Eliminator* (1983) sold enough records to give one to every human in China, with major hits like "Sharp-Dressed Man" (number 56), "Gimme All Your Lovin'" (number 37), and "Legs" (number 8) charting impressively.

The follow-up, which many argue is exactly the same record with different cover art, was 1985's *Afterburner*, which clocked in with four hits: "Sleeping Bag" (number 8), "Stages" (number 21), "Rough Boy" (number 22), and "Velcro Fly" (number 35). Apparently, the MTV kids thought the kooky old dudes with the cough-drop-box beards and the Playmate videos were something new, not realizing how hollow the material was after earlier efforts like *Rio Grande Mud*.

On 1990's *Recycler*, ZZ Top did just that—recycled the past few records painfully.

And then, just when one hoped King Diamond would sacrifice all three Toppers to some dark god, they signed a new deal with RCA and released 1994's *Antenna*. It's not a great ZZ Top record, but it showed signs of blues-rock life and set the stage for 1996's *Rhythmeen*, a rejuvenating and raw return to the deep past—without the criminality of photocopying the material.

The Eagles broke up in 1982, a sad situation since none of the members was worth over five trillion dollars. As such, Don Henley, the Texas lad who played drums, wrote, and sang for the band, decided to get right to work, and came out with a 1982 Asylum record called *I Can't Stand Still*. Featuring a brainy pop style that moved away from the country-flavored inflection of the Eagles, the album contained a number 3 hit in "Dirty Laundry" and went gold effortlessly.

He followed up with 1984's *Building the Perfect Beast* (Geffen), on which Henley nearly built the perfect pop record. With gorgeous, thoughtful ruminations on age and the decline of the California dream ("Sunset Grill" and "The Boys of Summer") and an irritating radio staple in "All She Wants to Do Is Dance," *Building the Perfect Beast* stayed on the album charts for over a year.

After several months off in which he got married to a woman who played high school tennis with the author's wife (so, who's prouder at the reunions?) and devoted himself to the ecological pursuit of saving Walden Pond, Henley returned to the solo wars with 1989's *The End of Innocence*, his biggest success yet. Boasting a tender but strong ballad in "The Heart of the Matter," the CD further explored the themes of the previous album and, in a fashion, those originally brought up on the Eagles' *Hotel California*.

In fact, the Eagles actually reunited shortly thereafter, recording two albums, *MTV Unplugged* and *Hell Freezes Over*, the latter a sardonically titled tribute to the nonlikelihood that the reunion would ever have happened in the first place. It did, though, and they are all richer for it.

Boz Scaggs, whose output has always been sporadic, actually recorded and toured a little in the eighties, producing two respectable albums, 1980's *Middle Man* and 1988's *Other Roads* (both Columbia). He waited until 1994, though, to release what is maybe his greatest record, *Some Change* (Virgin). Shifting easily from R&B to roadhouse rock to Cajun to Northern California balladry, Scaggs crafted an infinitely pleasing winner. The heartbreakingly lovely "Sierra" is alone enough to justify the cost of the CD.

Stephen Stills, who will continue to record with pals Crosby and Nash as long as even one buckskin-fringed freakster shows up at a gig, recorded two solo efforts after his seventies heydays: *Right by You* (1984, Atlantic) and *Stills Alone* (1991, Vision), both of which are better *left* alone.

On the other hand, in the CSN bins, one can find occasional rewarding moments on almost any of the albums they released since 1977's triumphant *CSN*. Of the six records subsequent to that, 1982's *Daylight Again* is a nice bit of work, but one is encouraged to ignore the rest and invest in the 1991 *Crosby, Stills and Nash Boxed Set* (Atlantic). It reminds the snide among us just how great they could be.

Meanwhile, Steve Miller snored into the eighties with the mediocre *Circle of Love* (1981, Capitol), then hit another jackpot with next year's *Abracadabra*. The title cut zoomed straight to number 1 on the strength of an idiotic, ascending/descending guitar figure and the Bertrand Russell–inspired chorus which began "Abra, abra-cadabra/I wanna reach out an' grab ya." Painfully stupid—but then, why can't any of us get the damned thing out of our heads?

There followed several more pedestrian efforts, with the interesting 1988 *Born 2B Blue* tossed in to see if we were paying attention. His latest, though, 1993's *Wide River*, (Polyram) is a mostly soporific effort. Miller continues to tour annually, drawing hordes of fervent fans in the not-really-understandable fashion of Jimmy Buffett.

Oh yes: Meat Loaf. He spent most of the eighties trying lamely to replicate the astonishing success of 1978's *Bat Out of Hell*, then decided, well, to *hell* with it—literally. In 1993, he recorded *Bat Out of Hell II: Back into Hell*. Whatever.

In a coda to this chapter, one musician who won't rest—for which we are grateful—is Doug Sahm. While he continues to be a driving force in the Tex-Mex supergroup Texas Tornados, he hasn't forgotten his rock roots.

He signed with Takoma Records for 1980's *Hell of a Spell*, then reunited with the Sir Douglas Quintet—whose *queso* organ fills were simultaneously inspiring a new generation of wavers by then anyhow—for 1981's infectious *Border Wave*. He continued to record throughout the decade (with 1988's Antone's release, *Jukebox Music*, particularly memorable).

In the nineties, when not involved with the Tornados, Sahm periodically rejuvenates the Quintet, as per the spectacular 1994 release, *Daydreaming at Midnight* (Elektra), which featured his sons Shawn and Shandon—the latter ex- of Pariah—as well as Augie Meyers and former Creedence Clearwater drummer Doug Clifford.

And, since he just can't keep still, Sahm formed the Last Real Texas Blues Band for a self-titled Antone's Records release in 1995—a giddy, stompin' set of archetypical Lone Star rock 'n' blues.

Sahm stayed happily busy with travel and a variety of recording projects, including a 1998 solo release for Watermelon called *Get a Life*, until his sudden death in November 1999. The loss is significant.

☆ Five: Punk, the Wave They Called "New," and Various Alternatives

S URE, BY NOW, PHRASES LIKE "NEW WAVE" AND "ALTERNATIVE" are completely archaic and utilized only by potbellied middle-aged men wearing bleeding madras shorts with black socks who are still trying to be "with it" (like your dad—or, for that matter, potbellied middle-aged men wearing Spandex who are also still trying to be "with it," like REO Speedwagon).

But, back at the end of the seventies, when punk music was fresh and new and would metastasize from the Ramones and the Sex Pistols (the latter's infamous U.S. tour in 1977 actually included two Texas dates, in Dallas's Longhorn Ballroom and in San Antonio's Randy's Radio) to full-blown scenes of musical anarchy and, in turn, "new wave," well, it was all cool. Similarly, by the time new wave spawned "alternative," *those* labels were hip. And now they're as outdated as, well, Jerry Lee Lewis or the Rolling Stones or REO Speedwagon or A Flock of Seagulls—all of whom are just representative examples of acts spanning all four generations of rock that continue to tour without any considerations of decency or good taste. And it will always be that way.

This principle cannot be more garishly illustrated than in the manner represented by the Sex Pistols' 1996 Reunion Tour, when they blatantly destroyed any meaning or integrity they'd ever had in a feeble crusade for bucks.

But in 1977, what the Sex Pistols represented was diametrically opposite: They hated everything that rock had become and stood for, and sought to rip it apart and infuse into the genre the spirit of honesty and raw rebellion that had made rock 'n' roll necessary to begin with.

Texas was certainly not immune to that spirit and, though only a few bands actually made substantial commercial inroads on any national or international scenes, the energy and backwash of the Texas movement had a terrifically cleansing effect on the state's rock scene.

Healthy clusters of punk bands and clubs sprang up in Austin, Dallas, and Houston, with a handful of visionary groups becoming notorious overnight. Among the earliest of the punk bands (and those tangential groups that would not have been formed were it not for punk) that made other musicians want to actually explore the movement were Dallas's Nervebreakers, Telefones, Stick Men with Ray Guns, Quad Pi, Tex and the Saddletramps, Ralphs, the Doo, (featuring now-famous cartoonist Dan Pirarro of "Bizarro" fame), Moving Products, and the Hugh Beaumont Experience, who found places to play in the Hot Club, Charlie's Twilight Room, DJ's, Magnolia's, and Ground Zero.

In Austin, the Skunks, Violators, the Huns, the Next, Big Boys, Not for Sale, the Dicks, the Re*Cords, Meat Joy, and Standing Waves held court at Raul's, Club Foot, and various apartment complex clubhouses.

Other notable bands from around the state included Houston's the Judys (who opened all the Texas dates for the first B-52s tour and who had a song called "Will Somebody Please Kill Marlo Thomas", Fort Worth's Ejectors and the Fort Worth Cats, and El Paso's Sweetie Pie.

Several of these bands caused national ripples: The Telefones were so popular that REM opened for *them* on their first trip through Dallas, and the 'Fones are still listed in the *Trouser Press Guide to New Wave*; the Nervebreakers actually played with both the Ramones *and* the Sex Pistols on their inaugural tours through Texas, and had popular singles in towns like Boston and San Francisco; Hugh Beaumont Experience drummer King Coffey would become the drummer for the Butthole Surfers; Standing Waves won Best New Wave Band in the *Austin Chronicle* poll two consecutive years; and Moving Products was one of the first Texas bands to appear on MTV's *Basement Tapes*.

But probably the first of the quasi-punk acts to achieve a big national breakthrough was Joe "King" Carrasco and the Crowns. Carrasco, from Dumas, grew up fascinated with the *con queso* sound of the Farfisa organ, Tex-Mex rhythms, beer-swilling Saturday nights, and the fresh energies and attitude of punk.

Carrasco, Austin-based by 1973, streamlined his sound with a horn-driven punk/polka band called El Molino (a rerelease of an early cassette, *Tex-Mex Rock-Roll*, is out on the ROIR label; the record was popular in England and lauded by none other than Elvis Costello), then formed the Crowns in 1979. Quickly garnering a reputation as a most significant party band, and sounding a bit like ? and the Mysterians as if they had gone on a mescal binge, they signed with England's archetypical punk label, Stiff, and released two records (*Joe "King" Carrasco and the Crowns* and *Party Safari*, both distributed by Hannibal in the United States) before getting a deal with MCA.

Synapse Gap (Mundo Total) came out in 1983, but the momentum inexplicably began to wane. Though His Highness continues to draw wherever college kids can purchase liquor, and has released CDs sporadically over the years (including a fine representation on One Way Records, 1995's *Anthol-*

ogy), his status is probably locked in that party entertainment mode for as long as he continues to wear the crown.

Not long after Carrasco had settled in Austin, a seriocomic punk outfit was being brainstormed at Trinity University in San Antonio: the Butthole Surfers. Vocalist Gibby Haynes and guitarist Paul Leary, after deciding their business studies represented a quick route to chaos, formed the Surfers in 1981 with a now-forgotten rhythm section and headed to California to avoid real work. There, they opened a gig for the Dead Kennedys, whose vocalist, Jello Biafra, was so jazzed by the Texas boys' irritating but hysterical musical anarchy that he promptly signed them to his Alternative Tentacles label.

Haynes and Leary blasted through a variety of bassists and drummers before adding ex–Hugh Beaumont Experience drummer King Coffey, all the while cranking out albums and EPs at roughly the same speed and quality of Haynes's bowel movements—which was basically the whole idea. With their ludicrous, abrasive, and always entertaining material, and a nothing's-too-offensive approach to live performances, the Buttholers gradually developed a cult-type zealotry among their fans—even as they expanded their base-level punk in psychedelic and experimental musical and theatrical directions.

In 1985, they signed with Touch and Go, and while many would argue that the titles of their records are the artistic high points of that period (1985's *Psychic . . . Powerless . . . Another Man's Sac*, 1986's *Rembrandt Pussyhorse*, 1988's *Hairway to Steven*, for example), the band has always claimed that their songs and antics weren't conscious efforts to offend, anyway. Rather, their work is merely an artistic reflection of a creepy and vile society that, by necessity, created Butthole Surfers to begin with.

Philosophy aside, after years of mid-level buffoonery, the band inked a deal with Capitol and became major label artists. The 1993 debut for Capitol, *Independent Worm Saloon*, produced by genuine rock legend John Paul Jones (former bassist/jack-of-all-musical-trades for Led Zeppelin), was, not surprisingly, their most commercial effort. An actual alternative hit, "Who Was in My Room Last Night," was a far cry from earlier tunes like "The Shah Sleeps in Lee Harvey's Grave," but it wasn't exactly Split Enz, either.

A 1996 CD, *Electriclarryland*, combines spacier material with mainstream alterna-punk, while 1998's *After the Astronaut* is depressingly tame.

Band members also have multiple side projects. Leary has produced the Meat Puppets (existing members of which have relocated to Austin) and Daniel Johnston; Haynes plays with a band called P, marginally notable because Johnny Depp is a member; and Coffey is the wizard behind the respected Trance Syndicate label. Along with such Texas acts as Paul Newman, the Fuzzy Things, and intriguing punkers And You Will Know Us by the Trail of Dead (whose name has one more letter than the author's one-time group, Last One Dead Has the Paws of a Cheetah).

The late, lamented Bedhead was also a Trance Syndicate band. A less-is-more (unless you go to sleep) act out of Dallas, Bedhead was a perpetual critics-favorite-nephew sort of act. Songwriter brothers Matt and Bubba Kadane orchestrated a musical sort of undersea guitar world where Morpheus comes off a dezoxyn-fueled biker. Drop Spacemen 3 and codeine (the pharmaceutical, not the band) into a rainy-day blender, mix with interwoven bass and guitar lines, and break out the mushrooms. *Beheaded* and *What-FunLifeWas* entertained college boys for most of a decade—despite which there was some true brilliance going on.

Another Austin band, sleepy-fi popsters American Analog Set, have released several nice works for Trance subsidiary Emperor Jones, including *The Fun of Watching Fireworks* and *The Golden Band*.

Another Austin band that might be thought of as the collective afterbirth of that first punk explosion is one whose name—Scratch Acid—exemplified all that is onomatopoeic. Pioneers in the attempt to fuse punk and metal, Scratch Acid was conceived in 1982 and released their first self-titled EP in 1984 on the Rabid Cat label. Following a credo of Louder, More Obnoxious, Faster and Patently Offensive, Scratch Acid expanded on that concept through *Just Keep Eating* (1986) and *Berserker* (1987, Touch and Go Records), touring extensively before disbanding in late 1987. Their influence on what would be grunge far exceeds their record sales, though they continue to wreak musical havoc as Jesus Lizard, as highlighted on 1992's ear-scraping *Liar*.

AS THE POPULARITY OF PUNK GREW, IT WAS INEVITABLE THAT certain players and songwriters would ruin it by interjecting such things as melody, song structures requiring more than three chords, and—a most egregious development—keyboards, and, more specifically, synthesizers. This music would be called new wave and, following the lead once again of the Brits, its funhouse-mirror distortion of the punk ethic was peculiar indeed.

At first, new wave was simply punk crossed with traditional pop songs, but the resultant expansion of musical styles and the attendant fashion statements were undeniably panoramic. Again, Dallas and Austin seemed to foster the greatest experimenters in the field.

One such pioneer was a Dallas guitarist/songwriter/singer named Gary Myrick. Along with bass-playing pal David Dennard, the two quietly processed the essence of seventies rock into a stripped-down new wave format and, by 1979, had signed with Epic Records as Gary Myrick and the Figures. Their first album included the hit "She Talks in Stereo," and was quickly followed up with 1982's *Livin' in a Movie* and a 1983 EP called *Language*. Material from all three recordings was utilized on the soundtrack to the film *Valley Girl*, at which point Myrick went solo. A record for Geffen stiffed, and Myrick hooked up with ex-Clash member Paul Simonon to form Havana 3 A.M., which signed with IRS for a self-titled 1985 album (which featured the quasi-hit "Reached the Rock").

After Havana 3 A.M. broke up, Myrick joined established rocker John Waite, with whom he toured and cowrote several hits. Rumors of a new incarnation of Havana 3 A.M. are currently circulating.

Despite Myrick's major label activity, the big haps in Dallas, though, were taking place in the Deep Ellum neighborhood, a trashed-out warehouse district that was home to countless winos and street persons (and, ironically, the same area that had been a fertile ground for blues back in the twenties), which would rapidly become a national focal point for the new music scene.

By the mid-eighties, bands like Feet First, End Over End, the Trees, Three on a Hill, About Nine Times, T42, the Fact, Four Reasons Unknown, Watusi, Fever in the Funkhouse, Ten Hands, and Shallow Reign—covering an astonishing variety of offshoot styles from reggae and ska to hardcore to the collective pops: synth-pop, power pop, punk pop, and pop rock—played on a nightly basis not only in Deep Ellum clubs like 500 Cafe, Theatre Gallery, the Prophet Bar (whose house sound man was a future star named the Reverend Horton Heat), Club Clearview, and Club Dada, but in spin-off rooms like Tango, Suds, Bar of Soap, and Sparxx.

But the group that really took Deep Ellum national was the New Bohemians. The band formed in 1985 and mixed improvisation and elements of jazz, rock, and folk with danceable song structures; they were impressive but a bit aimless until one night when Edie Brickell, an SMU art student emboldened by Jack Daniel's, sat in. She immediately captivated the band and the crowd with her waifish, breathy soprano, spontaneous melodies, and poetic lyrical abstractions, and within two weeks bid adieu to her studies to give music a shot.

The band's ever-shifting lineup solidified quickly after that, with Brickell, bass player Brad Houser, guitarist Kenny Withrow, percussionist John Bush, and drummer Brandon Ally. The New Bo's, as they were referred to by the terminally hip, rapidly became Godlike, drawing massive crowds throughout Dallas—even if they'd played three or four nights in a row.

The inevitable big label frenzy ensued, and the band eventually signed with Geffen. They recorded their first LP, *Shooting Rubber Bands at the Stars* (during the course of which the band name became Edie Brickell and New Bohemians, and drummer Ally was replaced with Matt Chamberlain). The LP came out in 1988 and the first single, a bouncy, infectious, philoso-babble tune called "What I Am," became a radio mainstay and peaked at number 7. The album itself climbed to number 4 and, at top speed, the band members found themselves touring with acts like the Grateful Dead, appearing on *Saturday Night Live*, and generally living well.

A follow-up, 1990's *Ghost of a Dog*, charted at number 32, largely on the momentum of the first album, and quickly faded away, as did the band. Brickell married Paul Simon (whom she'd met during a *Saturday Night Live* taping), in a pairing that must've astonished Deep Ellum denizens who surely classified Simon as completely outdated at best and, at worst, sentenced him to death for writing stuff like "For Emily Whenever I May Find Her."

In any case, Brickell released a solo album in 1994, *Picture Perfect Morning*, a likable collection of pleasant and clever songs that bear little resemblance to "What I Am." Which is fine; it would be too easy to moan about Mrs. Simon's lifestyle—complete with Robin Leach voice-over—but why? She married a genius, she's happy, and, as evidenced by her work with the New Bo's *and* her solo album, she's a not inconsiderable talent in her own right.

As for the rest of the band, well, it's not as though they stopped living. Bassist Houser tours with John Doe and performed in a Seattle group called Critters Buggin with Chamberlain and Bush, and Withrow and Bush get together occasionally in a band called the Slip—which features a singer named Edie Brickell.

To say that the Bohemians' success drew attention to Deep Ellum would be an understatement. Island Records came to town and released an entire compilation called *The Sounds of Deep Ellum*, then signed a young band called the Buck Pets to a contract on the strength of their compilation performance.

The Pets were made up of guitarist Andy Thompson, guitarist/vocalist Chris Savage, bassist Ian Beach, and drummer Tony Alba, and found themselves recording their major label debut whilst each of them was barely eighteen. A loud, sloppy, aggressive postpunk unit that seemed to cross the Buzzcocks with Crazy Horse, the Buck Pets were painfully honest and surprisingly literate in their musical treatment of angst and babes.

The Buck Pets came out in 1989, and the band hit the road for a year of heavy touring. A second album, 1990's *Mercurotones*, seemed weary, and despite a tour with and kind words from Neil Young, the band was dropped from Island when Polygram bought the label.

Back in Dallas, Alba quit and was replaced by Ricky Pearson, and the band signed a new deal with Restless Records. They released *To the Quick* in 1993, but despite an economy of songwriting and new energy, it just wasn't working. In a case of perhaps too much too soon, the Buck Pets finally sputtered to a halt. After much casual jamming and personnel shifts, the band renamed itself Atlas Throat in late 1995, though rumors the following spring indicated yet another incarnation of Buck Pets might surface.

Meanwhile, in the Dallas suburb of Irving, Rigor Mortis was gaining popularity as one of the new crop of postpunk metal acts that came to be called thrash bands (which added White Kids on Amphetamines tempos and even grislier lyrical concepts in an attempt to freshen outdated metal philosophies). Comprised of vocalist Bruce Corbett, guitarist Mike Scaccia, bassist Casey Orr, and drummer Harding Harrison, Rigor Mortis's particular hook was that all of their material was written about their favorite splatter movies. They caught the eye of a Capitol Records A&R person who was in town to check out a pop band—and Rigor Mortis became the first thrash band anywhere to be signed to a major label.

They released one album for Capitol, *Rigor Mortis*, before hopping to Restless Records for *Freaks* and, in turn, Triple X Records for a swan-song CD, *Rigor Mortis vs. the Earth*. Indeed, it must've seemed that the entire planet was against the band; they couldn't generate any momentum and eventually imploded when some of the members hopped ship for more lucrative opportunities. (Scaccia joined Ministry and Orr hooked up with GWAR.)

FOR ALL OF THE POSTPUNK AND TRASH AGGRESSION OF THE Deep Ellum scene, there was also a plethora of melodic pop and synthesizer bands that were popular. T42, a synth dance duo comprised of Will Lonconto and Jay Gillian, was one of the pioneering acts that preprogrammed backing tracks onto various tape machines, then performed with banks of keyboards in the fashion that was becoming popular with artists like Howard Jones, ABC, the Thompson Twins, and New Order. They built a fervent local following, worked the business angle with the tenacity of Bill Graham, and eventually scored a contract with Columbia. They released a catchy but lightweight record called *Intruder* in 1992, which had some success on the disco and dance club circuit, but a second record never materialized.

Another band with the numeral 4 in their name was 4 Reasons Unknown, a Dallas pop band comprised of, well, four guys (vocalist/keyboardist Paul Nugent, vocalist/bassist Morgan Ferguson, guitarist Mike Clements, and drummer Edward Harvey). They looked like GQ cover models and dressed as though MTV cameras might be lurking around every corner—and, as a matter of fact, the band scored a recording contract after winning an MTV *Basement Tapes* competition. They released one self-titled album for Epic before it became clear the contract was more of a contest publicity gimmick for the label and MTV than any commitment to the band, and efforts to release a second album failed.

Though generally despised by their peers, 4 Reasons Unknown was nevertheless extremely popular with virtually any human qualifying as female, and in fact their songs were probably better than similar radio ilk by bands like Kajacoogoo or Modern English. Nugent and Ferguson resurfaced in Voodoo Cowboys, which went nowhere, and Nugent eventually found success in artist management (Deep Blue Something, Soak).

In fact, Dallas had several quality pop bands that followed in the melodic footsteps of Squeeze and Crowded House, among them the Mystics, Fever in the Funkhouse, the Trees, Safety in Numbers, Secret Cinema, and Schwantz Lefanz. Lubbock's the Nelsons frequently performed their West Texas new music in the area, too. But perhaps the best of the lot never got the break they deserved.

Down in Austin, a similar pop ethic produced what was perhaps Travis

CRIMINALLY UNDERRATED BAND
The Elements/All the Tea in China
☆

Fueled by the intricate and bizarre instrumentation of Gentle Giant, King Crimson, and Yes, but captivated by the melodies of the Police and the simplistic energy of postpunk, the Elements became the most astonishing pop band in Texas during the eighties.

Originally called Hands, the group was formed in the Dallas suburb of Carrollton by school pals Ernie Myers (vocals/guitar), Steve Parker (vocals/ bass), drummer John Rousseau, and keyboardist Michael Clay. After years performing maddeningly complex Zappa-flavored originals, Hands disintegrated at the dawn of new wave.

They reformed as the Elements (with John Fiveash replacing Rousseau) and began to write compact, danceable pop songs. The Elements carved a sizable reputation from the burgeoning Deep Ellum pie, earning *BUDDY Magazine*'s 1983 Best Unsigned Texas Band Award, and began to draw some national curiosity.

A fledgling label, New Plateau, offered the band a single deal for their amazing arrangement of the Beatles' "Please Please Me," and Passport Records offered them a pressing and distribution deal for a full album.

But the band held out for an offer from Dutch rock czar Freddie Haayen, who was starting up his own label, 21 Records, a subsidiary of Polygram. After months of negotiations, the deal fell through.

The band continued to draw steadily in Texas clubs, but finally tired of waiting and splintered like shell-shocked war veterans. A recent offshoot, All the Tea in China, featuring Myers, Fiveash, Parker, and ex-Fact/Safety in Numbers bassist Steve Powell, has resurfaced in pleasing fashion in Dallas clubs, and in 1999 released *Steep* on Dallas's upstart Ridgeback Records label. An otherworldly collection of acousto-pop, art-rock *lagniappes*, *Steep* sounds like, oh, Martin Barre and Dave Matthews joining up with Neil Finn and Elvis Costello on a musical exploration of the diaries of William Blake.

County's finest band, a group called Zeitgeist. As the leaders of what hardcore punkers had come to facetiously call the "new sincerity" movement, Zeitgeist featured the melodic, intelligent songs of guitarist/vocalist John Croslin. After the band (permanent lineup: Croslin, guitarist/vocalist Kim Longacre, bassist Cindy Toff, and drummer Garrett Williams) released 1985's *Translate Slowly* on DB, they became hometown heroes with a 1987 Capitol recording contract. When a legal dispute over the name arose, Zeitgeist became the Reivers, and came out with *End of the Day*, a treasure chest of pop gems that elicited much critical favor, as did 1987's *Saturday*.

Capitol, though, didn't quite seem to know what to do with a group that wrote great, smart pop songs and dropped the act. The Reivers returned to Austin oddly buoyed, but though a subsequent album for DB, 1991's *Pop Beloved,* was just as charming as its predecessors, the group's collective energy dissipated.

Croslin has since gone into record production and worked with a number of younger Austin bands, including major label acts Spoon (*Telephono,* Matador) and Sixteen Deluxe (*Emits Showers of Sparks,* Warner Bros.).

Timbuk 3, a husband/wife duo (guitarist/vocalist/harmonica huffer Pat McDonald and even more multi-instrumentalist/vocalist Barbara K) from Wisconsin, moved to Austin and developed a following on the fringe of the eighties Austin music scene. They relied on surface gimmickry like two acoustic guitars and an amplified beat box booming recorded backing tracks, but their songs were diverse, catchy, and witty barbs against a society gone insane.

They surprised the entire Austin music community by signing with IRS in 1986, and then shocked the rest of the United States with their first single, the massively popular and sardonic "The Future's So Bright (I Gotta Wear Shades)," a delightful musical dung fork twisted into the stomach of the American Dream.

Unfortunately, though the song went to number 19 and the album hit number 50, the innate cleverness of "Shades" established Timbuk 3 with a novelty tag they never really lived down. Seven intelligent albums later (including *Edge of Allegiance* and *Shot in the Dark*), they still hadn't eclipsed the yuppie-anthem popularity of "Shades," and they parted ways. In 1997, Pat released *Pat McDonald Sleeps with His Guitar* on Ark 21.

Another Austin group that released major label albums without really breaking through to mainstream acceptance was Poi Dog Pondering. An eclectic outfit whose United Nations of styles embraced Hawaiian, folk, pop, Celtic, and African music without prejudice and with wit and invention, Poi Dog was the brainchild of songster/guitarist/vocalist Frank Orrall.

They scored a contract with Columbia, which probably stunned their more conventional peers, and in 1987 came out with an eponymously titled debut that puzzled most reviewers and intrigued the rest.

Though too clever for the bulk of Wal-Mart Nation, they've persisted over the years with several interesting records, including *Thinking Like the Sea* and *Pomegranate.*

A founding member of the band, Abra Moore, opted for a solo career and set about crafting strange and mostly wonderful pop/folk records. Graceful of lyric, keen (and often angry) of mind, and always melodic, Moore recorded an indie album, *Sing,* which garnered delighted reviews and led the way to a deal with Arista/Austin. In 1997, she came out with *Strangest Places,* a seriously great record.

Other Austin acts meriting mention from the postpunk arena included the Coffee Sergeants, the Andy Van Dyke Band, Bad Mutha Goose, the

Wild Seeds, Doctor's Mob, the Dharma Bums, the Rhythm Rats, and an eccentric songwriter named Daniel Johnston, whose material was painfully engaging when he did it, and absolutely brilliant when covered by a singer named Kathy McCarty.

Another genius is Austin's Alejandro Escovedo, whose participation in San Francisco's the Nuns was a pioneering maneuver in the West Coast punk scene, just as his involvement in Rank and File was groundbreaking in the country punk movement.

But it wasn't until Escovedo settled in Austin and formed the True Believers (with his brother Javier) that he started a songwriting career that has held the hearts and ears of Texas music fans captive ever since. The Believers envisioned the rock 'n' roll sound of Iggy Pop in a Nudie suit, and recorded a first album that was picked up by Rounder/EMI and critically lionized.

A second, finished album was shelved when EMI underwent a corporate shakeup, and though the corpse twitched on for a while, the True Believers were essentially dead. After the suicide of his girlfriend and a grueling series of subsequent hardships, Escovedo gradually picked up the artistic pieces. He started to write seriously great songs—everything from introspective folk ballads to brutal rock—and began appearing in clubs with the loosely defined Alejandro Escovedo Orchestra.

He signed with Watermelon Records and, from 1992 to 1994, recorded two brilliant, haunting, and, ultimately, healing studio records, *Gravity* and *Thirteen Years*. After winning every possible Austin poll except the governor's race (he didn't run), Escovedo hooked up with Rykodisc for *Hard Road*, a one-package rerelease of the True Believers records, and an estimable solo effort titled *With These Hands*. Moving to Bloodshot, Escovedo aimed toward the end of the decade with two more nice CDs, *More Miles Than Money Live 1994–1996* and the oft-lovely but ultimately spotty *Bourbonistis Blues*.

Escovedo's metamorphosis from punk visionary to wizened poet is an appropriate symbol for the change that gradually took place in Texas modern rock as the decade shifted into the nineties. New wave was suddenly passé, and all that came after subsequently fell under the all-encompassing labels of *alternative*—as typified by any new twists on the pop/rock/new wave ethic, and *grunge*—which was essentially defined by what was happening with Seattle and Pacific Northwest acts like Nirvana, Mudhoney, Pearl Jam, Soundgarden, Tad, the Posies, and Alice in Chains.

And so the newest tide of Texas bands took their cues and began to develop accordingly—which is to say that they wrote and performed pop, rock, punk, and metal in ways that were a lot more traditional than the practitioners ever dared.

The Toadies, for example, who are most often compared to the Pixies, ooze material like centipedes from the intriguingly disturbed brain of vocalist/guitarist/songwriter Todd Lewis. They are, musically speaking, a com-

CRIMINALLY OVERLOOKED ARTISTS
Daniel Johnston and Kathy McCarty

From 1983 to 1993, McCarty was the ingenue behind Austin's Glass Eye: an odd, twisted, catchy art wave band that seemed destined to pull Texas rock into areas where it could be enjoyed by thinking persons.

Frequently described as a hill country Talking Heads trying to write like mid-period King Crimson, Glass Eye consisted of a core duo of McCarty (vocals, guitar, and bass) and Brian Beattie (vocals/bass/guitar/lap steel), with various interchangeable musicians of both sexes filling out quartet requirements.

The band was a frequently amusing and engagingly weird unit, but the strength of Glass Eye was always in McCarty's voice and vision. But after a decade of trying to make the high jump from critical darlings to major label income-generators (including three interesting LPs: *Christine, Bent by Nature*, and *Hello Young Lovers*, all on Bar None Records), Glass Eye succumbed to frustration and McCarty ventured forth as a solo force.

Though her writing has always been melodic and thought-provoking, and her voice as soaring or folkie as she wantsta be, the fuel for her first project came from a most unlikely source. Daniel Johnston, a manic depressive former carnival corndog salesman and stream-of-consciousness/speed-of-light song sorcerer, had once presented McCarty with a cassette crammed with crudely recorded songs that, to her surprise, McCarty found to be the stuff of genius. But while his tunes had a certain homemade charm, their intrinsic rawness needed someone with McCarty's gifts to bring them to fruition.

Dead Dog's Eyeball, her first solo record (1994, Bar None), was comprised of eighteen Johnston tunes and became a surprise critical hit. The material ranges from pure, Cole Porter–on-mescaline pop to raucous but melodic journeys into the glittering cobwebs in Johnston's brain.

The record actually ended up at number 36 on *The Village Voice*'s annual Best Album poll, and McCarty released a follow-up EP of Johnston's stuff, 1995's *Sorry Entertainer*. Finally, after touring Europe, she's readying a CD of her own songs—which were, after all, the heartbeat of Glass Eye to begin with.

In the meantime, Johnston, of whom it can be said that he has claimed the Austin Eccentric Genius crown once worn by Roky Erickson, signed with Atlantic Records and entered the studio under the production guidance of Butthole Surfer guitarist Paul Leary. The resultant LP, 1994's *Fun*, didn't sell particularly well, but among wise people established the artist with a national reputation for skewed melodicism and an engaging if twisted worldview. More recently, the interesting *Frankenstein Love: Daniel Johnston Live at the Houston Room 1992* came out.

puter geek gone amok with an automatic weapon on Easter morning in a crowded church—though it sounds pretty great.

Lewis formed the Toadies in the early nineties with bass player Lisa Umbarger and, after a 1992 indie cassette called *Velvet* and a 1993 CD, *Pleather*, on the Grass label, rounded out the quartet with guitarist Darrel Herbert and drummer Mark Reznicek. That summer, the group signed with Interscope and, a year later, released *Rubberneck*. For a while, it looked as though the record was dead in the water. But constant touring and a wide-spread groundswell of support from kids who *knew* Lewis's raw anguish and, perhaps, shared his nightmares of religious disillusionment and the Poe-like homicidal and necrophiliac impulses vented in songs like "Backslider" and "Possum Kingdom" turned things around.

Those tunes became hits, and with the band making subsequent appearances on the soundtrack albums for motion pictures like *Escape from L.A.*, *The Crow: City of Angels*, and *Basquiat*, *Rubberneck* has gone platinum. The Toadies might well make neuroses as hip in the nineties as dating the homecoming queen was in the fifties—if they ever finish the follow-up to *Rubberneck*.

Tripping Daisy, employing pure-sixties liquid light shows and a whining, melodic, guitar-driven pop sludge, signed with Dallas indie label Dragon Street after they began filling concert-sized halls in their hometown.

Formed by vocalist/guitarist Tim DeLaughter, guitarist Wes Berggren, bassist Mark Pirro, and drummer Bryan Wakeland, the group's 1992 debut, *Bill*, boasted a regional hit in "Blown Away" which so propelled CD sales that a bidding war developed among majors—and the company that flew them to the Super Bowl and wined and dined them in a luxury box lost. Caligula would shudder to imagine what it took for Island to get the band, but they did. After remastering and rereleasing *Bill*, the band toured extensively and, in 1995, finished the kookily titled second record, *i am an ELAS-TIC FIRECRACKER*, which sported a huge hit in "I Gotta Girl." After personnel shifts, TD finally gelled to produce their masterpiece—*Jesus Hits Like the Atom Bomb* (and, no, the gospel song of the same name doesn't appear on the record)—only to be dropped by Island. The future of the band appeared in jeopardy in late 1999 after Berggren died of a drug overdose.

Course of Empire has had similar luck. The industrial-goth band turned soundtrack-to-mental-ward guitar-mongers released worlds-different CDs in *Carpe Diem* and *Initiation* (the latter on Zoo) before settling on a sound for *Telepathic Last Words*—which was turned in to Zoo just in time for the label to go bust. TVT eventually distributed the politically active, conspiratorially paranoiac, metallically interesting disc.

On the poppier side of things, Dallas has hit several major label home runs. Lisa Loeb, known fairly or unfairly as the Edie Brickell of the new generation, somehow twisted a prep school/Ivy League education into music stardom. Toughing it out as a club musician in New York City, she caught the ear of her neighbor, actor Ethan Hawke, who helped get one of Loeb's songs, "Stay (I Missed You)" slotted as the closing-credits tune for the soundtrack to the Ben Stiller film *Reality Bites* (the obvious question is, If Loeb was such a struggling artist, how could she afford to live next door to a movie star?).

In any case, the damnably catchy single sold over eight hundred thousand copies and became the first nonlabel single ever to reach number 1. Not surprisingly, Loeb wasn't without a deal for long. With her band, Nine Stories, she inked a lucrative contract with Geffen. Her 1995 debut, *Tails*, shipped gold, but its staying power on the charts wasn't particularly long. *Firecracker* followed up two years later and scored a hit with "I Do."

Similarly, Deep Blue Something parlayed a sappy regional hit single, "Breakfast at Tiffany's," into national status as a sort of Hootie and the Blowfish starter kit. Formed during their college days as the University of North Texas, DBS (bassist/vocalist Todd Pipes, guitarist/vocalist Todd Pipes, drummer John Kirtland, and guitarist Clay Bergus) earned a following on fraternity/sorority row through their earnest, clean-cut strum pop.

They signed with Dallas indie label RainMaker Records and released *Home* in 1994, and "Breakfast at Tiffany's," a fortune cookie of a song with the endurance of a Kenyan distance runner and an industrial-strength hook, drew the attention of Interscope Records, which rereleased the CD in 1995 and sat back as the song took over the world. While Deep Blue Something has been critically crucified in a manner not seen since, well, Hootie, and the big money says they'll fall on their faces with the next album, the critics have been wrong before.

The third of the North Texas popsters who've pissed their peers off by beating them to record contracts are Jackopierce, which, like Deep Blue Something, found early favor among gentried Greeks while students at Southern Methodist University. Originally just guitarist/vocalists Cary Pierce and Jack O'Neill, the duo thumbed their noses at Deep Ellum and quietly went about releasing a series of CDs on their own label—which sold thousands and thousands of copies.

A&M Records, which, like most majors, could care less *how* an indie band moves all those units or what the critics say, signed the band and released a 1994 album produced by T-Bone Burnett called *Couldn't Stand the Weather*. Though the follow-up, 1996's *Finest Hour*, sported an excellently promising song in "Get It Together," the band broke up not long after the disc's release.

A New Braunfels–conceived band called Sixpence None the Richer, gentle of tune and sporting front-babeness in vocalist Leigh Nash, is steadily approaching superstar status. A vaguely Christian outfit that quietly built a following touring for years with acts like the Smithereens, Abra Moore, and 10,000 Maniacs, the band was cofounded by Nash and fellow Texan Matt Slocum (guitar). An indie CD, *The Fatherless and the Widow*, attracted a great deal of industry attention.

Sixpence then relocated to Nashville and hooked up with Squirt Entertainment—a company formed exclusively to handle the band. The first single of the subsequent, self-titled CD was an infectious little ditty called "Kiss Me," which is now tattooed onto the brain of every human who ever turned on a radio. A Grammy nomination, countless late-night and morning-show TV appearances, soundtrack tunes, and millions of units-moved later, the band has incredible momentum. A second single, a remake of the la's "There She Goes," shows every sign of exploding.

Austin's Flowerhead is another pop-flavored rock act with incredible promise. Formed at the top of the decade by guitarists Eric Schmitz and Buzz Zoller, vocalist/bassist Eric Faust and drummer Pete Levine, their punchy brand of snot-slingin' pop first came to surface on 1992's indie release, *Ka-Bloom!*, which resulted in a major deal with Zoo Entertainment. While that debut, 1995's *The People's Fuzz*, hasn't been out long enough to indicate how things are going to go, it's a general consensus that the band's too fun to fail.

Two bands that straddle the fence between pop melody and more driving guitar rock are Dallas's Spot and Austin's Soul Hat. Spot (bassist/vocalist Reggie Rueffer, guitarist/vocalist Chad Rueffer, drummer Davis Bickston), born of a late, much-loved Deep Ellum progressive band called Mildred, stripped down, wrote some more concise tunes and quickly signed with Memphis's prestigious indie label, Ardent. Built around a recipe mixing brainy pop-craft with strident, exuberant guitar rock; wry poetry with snide disillusionment; and soaring melodies with the howling harmonies of drunken choirboys, their 1995 debut, *Spot,* scored a national hit with "Moon June Spoon," then hopped to Interscope. Unfortunately, the deal fell through and the band imploded.

Soul Hat is a curious amalgamation of Allman Brothers–style twin-guitar jams and brutal aggressive rock. Conceived at Southwest Texas State University in Georgetown, just twenty-five miles north of Austin, Soul Hat is Kevin McKinney (vocals/guitar), Brian Walsh (bass), Bill Cassis (vocals/guitar), and Frosty Smith (drums).

They quickly became a phenomenon in Austin, won a 1992 Album of the Year Award for their indie *Live at the Black Cat* cassette, and followed up with a Spindletop release called *Outdebox.* That album, featuring infectious, rolling tunes like "Things Aren't Like That Anymore" and the guitar tornado of "Build It Up/Tear It Down," earned them a major deal with Epic.

The Epic album, *Good to Be Gone,* was a departure into hard rock and featured a regional hit in "Bone Crusher," but the band has since been an on-again, off-again proposition with Cassis having bailed permanently.

Perhaps the most astounding success story is that of Greenville's Radish, a post-Nirvana trio under the songwriting guidance of singer/guitarist Ben Kweller—who was all of fifteen when the band signed a mega-dollars deal with Elektra. With bandmates John David Kent (drums) and Bryan Blur (bass), Kweller's been the subject of analysis in no less than *The New Yorker.* While Kweller's tender age and the band's advance makes them likely targets, it can't be denied that the "sugar metal" (Kweller's term) of *Bolt,* their debut CD, is catchy—in particular the song "Little Pink Stars." Critical response was fairly cruel, though. With the addition of new bassist/songwriter Joe Butcher (ex-UFOFU), Radish's sophomore effort might work better with critics and fans alike.

Not all breakout Texas acts worry about melody. Several represent neoindustrial and metal concerns, as interpreted through the alternative revolution. Dallas's Brutal Juice spewed forth from Denton like blood-flecked bile out of a French Quarter drunk—which is precisely their ambition. In that moonscape of rock where progress and one-upsmanship between bands are calculated with volume, speed, and lyrics designed to make Cannibal Corpse come off like Elizabeth Barrett Browning, Brutal Juice was doing its job well.

A well-received indie record, *How Tasty Was My Little Timmy?*, earned them a deal with Interscope. But after one CD, *Mutilation Makes Identification Difficult*, the band disintegrated.

Hagfish (vocalist George Reagan, bassist Doni Blair, guitarist Zach Blair, and drummer Tony Barotti) is the unfortunate Dallas band to have been doing Green Day– and Offspring-style retro punk before those bands were— only their record came out after the other two. As such, even though Hagfish has an excellent album out on London Records, *Rocks Your Lame Ass*, they've thus far been lost in the new punk shuffle. The London deal fell through, and though the band carried on with indie releases *Hagfish* and *Caught Live*, the momentum, unfortunately, seems to have run out.

In the past year, so many Texas bands have signed major recording contracts that, as we approach the millennium, Texas qualifies as *the* fertile music garden in America. Texas modern rock acts continue to sign with major and significant indie labels at an overwhelming pace. The most successful has been Austin's Fastball, a Cheap Trick–style trio whose Robin Yount–like work ethic paid off when "The Way," the utterly addictive hit from their second Hollywood Records CD, *All the Pain Money Can Buy*, went platinum and turned millions on to their infectious rock (which includes the first Hollywood disc, *Make Your Mama Proud*, though it sold only about six hundred copies before *Pain* came out).

By now, every human who has ever been awake has heard "The Way," a hooky fairy tale which sounds like Badfinger wrote *On Golden Pond*. In a world of Limp Bizkits and Cakes, it's frankly refreshing that bands like Fastball can still be successful.

Composed of bassist/vocalist/songwriter Tony Scalzo, drummer Joey Shuffield, and guitarist/vocalist/songwriter Miles Zuniga, Fastball has scored two Grammy nominations, topped *Billboard*'s Modern Rock chart for seven weeks, appeared on virtually every late-night network television show you've ever watched, and toured the world with all manner of even bigger rock stars. More power to them.

Occasional tourmate Davíd Garza, also an Austinite, is enjoying critical and commercial success. *This Euphoria*, out on Lava/Atlantic, is an exhilarating pastiche of millennial rock songwriting—and that the lead track, "Kinder," has already been used in a hip clothing chain ad is indicative of his engaging hipness.

Other recent major label activity: Austin's wonderful Trish Murphy, long an independent success story in any case, signed with Dolittle/Mercury for *Rubies on the Lawn*; sugar-punk quintet Sincola's *What the Nothinghead Said* (Caroline); Prescott Curlywolf's volume-friendly *Six Ways to Sunday* (Mercury); industrial-metal irritatos Skrew have released three CDs for Metal Blade, including the amusing *Angel Seed XXIII*; Ugly Americans, born early in the decade of such acts as Cracker and Poi Dog Pondering, have several jam-happy CDs out, including two for Capricorn. *Stereophonic Spanish Fly* and *Boom Boom Baby*; Houston's David Rice commingles Peter Gabrielisms with odd, pastoral 12-string folk musings on *greenelectric* for Columbia; Sister 7 (*This the Trip* for Arista/Austin).

Also: cottonmouth, tx (which is more or less spoken-word artist Jeff Liles) issued *Anti-Social Butterfly* for Virgin; a subsequent release on his own Heiress-Aesthetic label, *The Right to Remain Silent*, is a more provocative if less amusing effort); and hand-gleefully-stuck-in-the-blender rockers Soak recorded *Flywatch* for Sire.

Other bands of note include: Amarillo's Blue Johnnies; Houston's Pain Teens and the Hadden Sayers Band; San Antonio's Dead Crickets, SunDay, Bouffant Jellyfish, and Stretford; Austin's Blue Cartoon (two great pop CDs on their own Aardvark label: *Blue Cartoon* and *Downtown Shangri La*), Kacy Crowley, Peglegasus; the Metroplex's Sugarbomb (amazing Rainmaker release called *Tastes Like Sugar*), Moon Festival, spaceoids Mazinga Phaser, Caulk, Slow Roosevelt, Dooms UK, Buck Jones, Kim Lenz and Her Jaguars, and Centro-matic.

Three musicians have made significant names for themselves in alternarock land, though with decidedly non-Texas bands. Dave Abbruzzese, who now resides outside Denton, was behind the kit for Pearl Jam's rise-to-the-top-and-get-incredibly-rich period, and is now the mastermind behind the Green Romance Orchestra.

Aaron Comess, a former student at Dallas's Arts Magnet High School, moved to New York after graduation and was a founding member of the Spin Doctors. And Dallas bassist Larry Tagg was a cofounder and songwriter in the too-short life of later-eighties brain-popsters Bourgeois-Tagg. (If you can find either of their Island albums, *Bourgeois Tagg*—with the best suicide song ever. "Dying to be Free"—or *Yoyo* jump on it.)

But not all the triumphs of the alternative years are of the expected variety. Perhaps two of the greatest "alternative" heroes come from the most unlikely source: the age-old form called rockabilly.

And speaking of rockabilly artists qualifying as "alternative" rock stars, the Reverend Horton Heat, a bizarre half-rockabilly/half-punk guitar creature, blew out of a new wave chautauqua tent in the primordial ooze that spawned Deep Ellum.

CRIMINALLY UNDERRATED ARTIST
Ronnie Dawson

Ronnie Dawson is an ageless phenomenon, a fire-fingered genius who helped create rockabilly and then resurrected it forty years later—all without seeming to move in time.

A mid-fifties Oak Cliff kid with a blond flattop and a Little Leaguer's smile, Dawson was playing the Big D Jamboree by the time he was sixteen. He was signed to Columbia as Commonwealth Jones in 1961, released a few sides, was dropped, then re-signed to the label for another stint eight years later. In the meantime he made a living as a multi-instrumental session guy (he played drums on Paul and Paula's "Hey Paula") and appeared on shows like *American Bandstand* and *Hootenanny*.

From 1970 through the early eighties, he led a country rock outfit called Steel Rail, but in 1986, a call from English record collector Barney Kouris convinced Dawson that rockabilly was still thriving in Europe. A collection of Dawson's earliest hits was released on the No Hit label as *Rockin' Bones*, and subsequent overseas tours reestablished Dawson as a dimension-defying phenomenon: a fifties hero whose star is more luminescent *now*.

Still a Lot of Rhythm came out in 1988 and *Rockinitis* in 1989, with the former tacked on to a 1994 American release, *Monkey Beat!* His status in the States now rivals his European fame, and in early 1996 a rerelease of *Rockinitis* has revealed to domestic audiences the high-energy, clean rhythm style that has made Dawson a rockin' god to a generation of guitarists—from Sid King to the Reverend Horton Heat. All this was only highlighted with a summer 1996 album of blistering new material, *Just Rockin' and Rollin'*, out on the Upstart label.

In 1999—the year he turned sixty—Dawson released *More Bad Habits*, his first American studio recording in decades. A flamethrower of a record fueled by the primal energy of rock 'n' roll, *More Bad Habits* is just another priceless addition to his nonpareil and ongoing legacy.

He was born Jim Heath in Corpus Christi, picked up a guitar and assimilated the diverse Texas musical traditions represented by Jimmie Vaughan, Billy King, and Freddie King. Before his self-ordination, Heath played throughout the seventies with Teddy and the Talltops, a straight rockabilly band working an all-but-forgotten genre in the netherworld of punk clubs and R&B dives—the only places that would book them.

Heath then found himself living in Deep Ellum, where his revivalist persona began to emerge, and by 1987 he became the Reverend Horton Heat and blew rockabilly into the space age.

Within the pro-forma trio structure (with drummer Jimbo Wallace and stand-up bassist Tasz Bentley), the Rev earned a hysterical following with a stage show that might have been choreographed by several bikers on a crystal meth–and-gin warpath, amusing but energized tunes that melt walls, and his ever-surprising flurries of guitar heroics. They signed with super indie Sub Pop and released *Smoke 'em if You Got 'em* in 1992, a riff-happy debut which began to clue in our planet as to the Reverend's magic.

The sophomore LP was a frenzied dose of speedway rock, *The Full Custom Gospel Sounds* (1993), after which the band jumped to Interscope for 1994's *Liquor in the Front (Poker in the Back)*. In rapid succession, the Rev came out with *Martini Time*, *Space Heater*, and *Holy Roller*, and though his liver has taken a beating, he remains an ass-ripping example of the future of Texas guitar.

And from the "there but for the grace of God go I" department is the saga of Houston protorocker and girl/booze enthusiast Herschel Berry, a decades-enduring club fiend whose many bands (chiefly the Natives) deserved better.

Finally, it should be noted that two of the guiding lights of posteighties rock, Bob Mould (ex of Hüsker Dü and Sugar; currently solo and possibly retired) and Al Jourgensen (Ministry) spent time as residents of Austin, though it appears neither move to the Lone Star State was permanent.

Jourgensen's work in the Hill Country was to guide Ministry through a series of industrial metal excursions (*A Mind Is a Terrible Thing to Taste*, the in-concert *In Case You Didn't Feel Like Showing Up . . .*, and *Psalm 69: The Way to Succeed and the Way to Suck Eggs*). On *A Mind*, ex–Rigor Mortis guitarist Mike Scaccia was a member of the band.

Mould did some nice work in Austin before he relocated to New York City, recording three CDs with Sugar (*Copper Blue*, *Beaster*, and *File Under: Easy Listening*) before heading east.

CRIMINALLY UNDERRATED MUSICIAN
John Thomas Griffith
☆

As the lead guitarist for New Orleans' mighty Cowboy Mouth—inarguably one of the world's greatest rock 'n' roll bands—Lubbock-born John Thomas Griffith spent his formative years in Houston and still considers Texas his home.

But it was in Louisiana, after he'd studied classical piano and garage guitar, that he flunked out of L.S.U., formed seminal punk band Red Rockers, and migrated to California. Dividing their time between L.A. and San Francisco, the Red Rockers signed a major-label deal and became one of the first MTV star bands on the strength of "China," a song cowritten by Griff.

After several years of a gradually changing musical aesthetic, Griff returned to New Orleans and hooked up with the then-burgeoning Cowboy Mouth—a band that absolutely rules the South with their fiery live shows and a succession of indie and major-label records (including *Are You with Me?*, *Mercyland*, and the soon-to-be-released *Hurricane Party*). Though a multi-instrumentalist/singer/songwriter of great creative strength (he's venturing into film scoring and composing music for computer games), Griff's guitar playing is clearly a singular gift.

Equally adept at Townshendesque rhythm and laugh-out-loud-at-how-cool-they-are leads (which infuse his classically trained structures with an almost Jimmy Vaughan–like sense of space and simplicity), JTG is a true musical prince.

☆ Part 3: Blues

☆ One: The Southern Oral Tradition and Country Blues

▼

I T WOULD BE TOO EASY TO MAKE A GRANDIOSE GENERALIZATION like "art is born of pain." For one thing, art is just as frequently born of joy. And to further compound the concept, anyone who's ever listened to Billy Ray Cyrus will tell you that pain can also be born of art (most frequently in the form of a headache).

But it would be wrong to say that the blues is anything *but* the direct result of human misery—which is easily enough traced to the advent of slavery in the New World. And, as the South became comfortably established as an agrarian society built on the labor and suffering of black slaves, the blues spontaneously generated in the sweltering fields as a form of therapy as much as for entertainment as to pass never-ending hours. Evolving from traditional African chants and rhythms, and incorporated into "call and response" field hollers, early spirituals, and dance music, the blues soon enough became an identifiable and separate artistic entity unto itself.

And though Emancipation did not end the suffering that had necessitated the blues, it did allow the music to spread. Blacks were free to travel—and frequently did so in the generally futile hope of escaping racism—but the work they found was not appreciably different from that of before the Civil War. Thousands of migratory laborers, following the harvest trail or lumber camps across the South, spread into Texas and established sharecropper communities. As such, prison laments, tales of barroom heartbreak and the perpetuation of crushing poverty were all elements that further wove their way into the orally preserved blues tradition.

And when a boll weevil plague decimated cotton fields in the early 1890s, starving and desperate workers flooded cities like Houston and Dallas, congregating in whatever part of town would have them. These urban substructures each evolved their own blues communities—and it thus became possible for someone like Blind Lemon Jefferson to become the first authentic Texas blues star.

Huddie Ledbetter, known of course as Leadbelly, was a remarkable artist

GUITARIST WHO CHANGED MUSIC
Blind Lemon Jefferson

Jefferson was born in Wortham, Texas, in 1897 and, literally blind, did perhaps the only thing he could: He learned to play the guitar. He was a veritable sponge of various blues permutations, and when he moved to Dallas's Deep Ellum district at twenty, Jefferson quickly polished his awkward country-boy technique, melded his influences into a unique style, and developed a rabid following. His unorthodox guitar voicings and diverse narrative song structures perfectly mirrored the singularity of the black experience, and song subjects ranged from the deeply spiritual to the transparently ribald.

By the early 1920s, "race records" were becoming popular across the country, and labels catering to these artists became lucrative ventures. Victor, Black Swan, Columbia, Paramount, Vocalion, and Okeh were probably the biggest of these labels, and when a Paramount executive heard Jefferson playing on a Dallas sidewalk, he invited the guitarist to Chicago to record. The first single, "That Black Snake Moan," was hugely successful, and Jefferson went on to make over eighty recordings for Paramount (he also released two records for another prominent race label, Okeh, and a variety of religious tunes under the pseudonym Deacon L. J. Bates). Other Blind Lemon Jefferson hits included "Penitentiary Blues," "Jack O'Diamond Blues," "Matchbox Blues," "Booger Rooger Blues" (from which the phrase "boogie woogie," meaning debauched fun, evolved), and perhaps his best song, "See That My Grave Is Kept Clean."

Jefferson was the largest-selling race artist in the country from 1926 to 1929, at which time he was found frozen to death in Chicago under suspicious circumstances. (Interestingly, you *can* see that his grave is kept clean; it's at the far end of the Wortham Cemetery on Highway 14—but ask directions, it's not easy to find.)

Blind Lemon Jefferson's songs and innovations had a terrific effect on generations of performers in a variety of ways, and his reputation as an absolute blues giant is inviolate. But his influence during his lifetime was similarly impressive. No less than Huddie Ledbetter, T-Bone Walker, Lightnin' Hopkins, and Robert Johnson were indebted to Jefferson—of which Ledbetter and Johnson could be considered country blues artists.

of almost schizophrenic temperament. He could be kind and considerate—and then again he could kill or maim you.

Versatile on several instruments, Leadbelly became known as "the King of Twelve String Guitar," though his proficiency as an instrumentalist was actually inferior to his songwriting. He was born on the Louisiana side of Caddo Lake in 1889 and, after honing his musical skills and boisterous inclinations in Shreveport, moved west to Dallas. He met Blind Lemon Jefferson, and the two played together (frequently in whorehouses) from 1912 to 1917.

Leadbelly then murdered a man and was sentenced to do time in Huntsville Penitentiary. After six years of hard labor, Leadbelly improvised a freedom song in front of Governor Pat Neff, who happened to be visiting the prison. Neff was so impressed that he pardoned Leadbelly, and this Clarence Darrow of song was soon back in Louisiana, playing the blues.

In 1930, he was convicted again, this time for assaulting a woman, and sent to Angola. In 1934, noted blues folklorist John Lomax, traveling the South taping authentic chain-gang songs, field hollers, and rural blues, came across Leadbelly in Angola. Lomax was astounded at Leadbelly's repertoire, and in the material he collected was another plea for clemency, this one aimed at Louisiana governor O. K. Alan. Lomax personally delivered the tune to the governor, who, astonishingly enough, released Leadbelly again.

At that point, Leadbelly secured the services of Lomax as a manager, and in return, Leadbelly reportedly became Lomax's chauffeur, a hierarchical maneuver of dubious ethics. (It's difficult today to imagine a similar situation in which, say, Ken Griffey, Jr., performed as his agent's chef in addition to his duties as the greatest baseball player in the world.) In any case, the new agreement required that Leadbelly relocate to New York, where he piloted Lomax around as well as performed with the likes of Woodie Guthrie and Burl Ives. Between 1937 and 1942, Leadbelly recorded a voluminous three-record set for the Library of Congress. Though unavailable for years, all three volumes were released by Rounder in 1991 (titled, respectively, *Midnight Special*, *Gwine Dig a Hole to Put the Devil In*, and *Let It Shine on Me*), which remains the definitive Leadbelly collection. The musician passed away in 1949, and is credited with such timeless songs as "Irene," "You Don't Know My Mind," and "The Midnight Special."

FOR A VARIETY OF REASONS, ROBERT JOHNSON WAS PERHAPS the world's most renowned practitioner of country blues. There is, of course, the matter of his having sold his soul to the devil in return for his talent—an obviously apocryphal tale which is nevertheless intriguing. It's true that Johnson was a player of modest ability when he mysteriously disappeared and returned only a year later, blazing with talent. Where did it come from? His own tune, "Crossroads Blues," details a midnight meeting at a crossroads between a desperate musician and the Great Crimson Imp at which a pact was negotiated. What remains is that he stuffed a wealth of genius in a very short time—and would die in an appropriately sinister fashion.

If the whole demon thing is true, and Johnson's art came at the forfeiture of his soul, one wishes Kenny Rogers had struck a similar bargain. And if it's not true, then Johnson's incredible work is even more astonishing.

But the fact of the matter is that Johnson wasn't from Texas and never lived here. He's included here because his entire recorded legacy—a precious little twenty-nine songs—was recorded in Texas.

During the course of Johnson's meandering and mysterious travels, he'd met Ernie Oertle of the American Recording Company's Vocalion label, who took the musician to San Antonio to record. During the afternoon of November 23, 1936, in a hotel room, Johnson recorded the bulk of his material, including the blatantly sexual "Terraplane Blues." The song would be the only hit in Johnson's lifetime, though several more ("Dead Shrimp Blues," "From Four Until Late," "Believe I'll Dust My Broom," "Stones in My Passway," and "Love in Vain") would become immortal in years to come. Another tune from that session is the aforementioned "Crossroad Blues," which describes his putative Faustian encounter with Beelzebub.

Fueling that myth were songs of a similar ilk, recorded in a second Texas session, in a Dallas warehouse in June 1937. "Hellhound on My Trail" and "Me and the Devil Blues" were taped then, and though a third date a few days later managed to get down for posterity a few of the songs Johnson had learned growing up, these dates marked the end of Johnson's woefully inadequate body of recorded work. He would die in August of 1938, according to one version, poisoned at a house party (where he was the entertainment) by the jealous host after waxing seductively to the lady of the house.

Johnson's entire persona and the undeniable brilliance of his recordings have inspired thousands of blues and rock artists (and fans) to study his phrasing, timekeeping, single string runs, melodies, and chord structures. And while Johnson's recorded body of work is indeed brief, the sheer volume of (generally inferior) renditions of his songs by other artists is strong testimony to his timelessness. CBS's boxed set, The Complete Recordings, is probably the finest way to hear the material.

A similar stylist to Mance Lipscomb was Henry "Ragtime Texas" Thomas, probably the oldest of the original Texas blues kings. Thomas was a versatile performer whose virtuosity on the panpipes (or quills) did not inspire generations of youngsters to take up the instrument. He was born near Big Sandy in 1874, and it was his chronological proximity to the actual slave generations that probably accounts for his "folk" style. It should be added that, in addition to the pipes, Thomas was also proficient on guitar and harmonica, and by his mid-teens he had left home to hobo about as a singer/musician/dancer.

CRIMINALLY OVERLOOKED GUITARIST
Mance Lipscomb

Many of the Texas country blues musicians toiled in obscurity, only to be discovered late in their lives. Mance Lipscomb is probably the best example of these artists. He was born in 1895 in the Navasota River bottoms and spent his life as a sharecropper. An intuitive and cunning guitarist who'd originally learned fiddle from his father, Lipscomb entertained at parties and barn dances. But, though he made trips to Dallas to pick cotton during the harvest, and would anonymously watch Blind Lemon Jefferson play, he never made the trek to any of the urban blues centers with the idea of performing himself.

Lipscomb "turned pro" when he was sixty-five—which seems, interestingly enough, the median age of the members of the Rolling Stones. In 1960, Chris Strachwitz of Arhoolie Records, an archival label in San Francisco, was led by Houston disc jockey Mack McCormick to Navasota, where Lipscomb could generally be found playing on his porch.

A guitarist whose staggering technique underscored a lifetime spent writing and cataloguing a spectacular range of material (from country blues to ballads to jazz and folk) by all accounts Lipscomb was a devout, friendly, gentle man, and it must have been astonishing to him when the records he recorded for Arhoolie brought him a bit of fame.

He crisscrossed the United States, appearing before adoring fans and bedazzled musicians at various clubs and blues and folk festivals, but he found a spiritual home in Austin. For almost ten years, Lipscomb was a kind godfather to a city-wide family of players, preaching his gospel of Texas music in "churches" like the Armadillo World Headquarters and the Vulcan Gas Company. He passed away in 1976, but scores of modern guitarists— from Jimmie Vaughan to Ian Moore—are quick to point to Lipscomb as a genuine Texas musical force. Arhoolie's *Texas Sharecropper and Songster* and *You Got to Reap What You Sow* are recommended.

Though his early travels are ill recorded, "sightings" of Thomas were reported at the Columbian Exposition in Chicago in 1893 and at the 1904 St. Louis World's Fair, and it is fairly certain that he worked virtually any-place where there was a chance someone might throw him a tip or offer him a meal or drink for his services. As such, that his audiences consisted of church parishioners as often as brothel aficionados was fairly typical of the times. And, as with Mance Lipscomb, his virtuosity was so all-encompassing and his material so eclectic that he could entertain in vir-tually any situation.

He eventually wound up in Chicago, where he was signed by the Vocalion label, and from 1927 to 1929 released twenty-three songs, most of which were of the nineteenth-century "dance hall" variety and included straight blues as well as reels, ballads, and one spiritual. Thomas's singular guitar style—in which he capoed well up the neck for a trebly, banjo/ukelele sound—was instantly memorable in conjunction with his panpipes.

Thomas misted into obscurity after the Vocalion years, and though reports of his working in East Texas surfaced as late as 1950, his fate remains unknown. A complete collection of Thomas's recordings, called *Texas Worried Blues*, is available from Yazoo.

Another of the early country blues guitarists who should be remembered is Alger "Texas" Alexander, whose blues legacy rests not only with his music but with the fact that he was Lightnin' Hopkins's cousin and also, like Leadbelly, he served time for murder.

Too, at one time or another, Alexander, who was born in Jewett in 1900, played street and/or house party gigs with the likes of Blind Lemon Jefferson and Hopkins, did sessions with King Oliver, and toured with Howlin' Wolf and Lowell Fulson. He recorded sixty-seven tunes for the Vocalion label, many with Lonnie Johnson in support, and his influence was probably more as a singer and interpreter of prison tunes and field hollers than as a guitarist. He is perhaps best remembered for his tune "Penitentiary Moan," and the bulk of his best material is available on the Matchbox label.

John "Funny Papa" Smith belongs with this group, but it's uncertain whether he was, as rumored, actually born in Texas (supposedly in 1890). What is known is that Smith spent substantial time in the state, and that his playing and melodic compositional skills were very influential in the "Texas songster" style (though he had a tendency, later emulated by many Seattle alternative rock acts, to play out of tune).

He recorded for the Vocalion label in 1930–31 and assumed the nickname "Howlin' Wolf" after the title of one of his own songs, though there are no other connections to the more famous Chester "Howlin' Wolf" Burnett. In fact, one wonders why, with a nickname as cool as "Funny Papa," Smith would opt for the wolfen moniker. ("Funny Papa," incidentally, is thought to have been in tribute to Smith's habit of appearing in a stovepipe hat.) While serving the early bluesman's seemingly requisite sentence for murder, Smith continued after parole to record sides for Vocalion and was to have toured frequently with Texas Alexander until Smith disappeared sometime after 1939. A collection of his material, *The Howling Wolf*, has been issued on Yazoo.

Blind Willie Johnson deserves inclusion here, not only because he was a fluid stylist, but also because he was not convicted of homicide. Indeed, a mellifluous slide player who used a pocketknife instead of a bottleneck, his repertoire consisted entirely of religious material (almost to the point of zealotry). Which was okay; the Marlin-born (1890) Johnson was a Baptist preacher.

In any case, he recorded several successful sides for the Columbia label, including "Jesus Make Up My Dying Bed" and "Motherless Children," and his guttural, chautauqua-tent moans over continual, melodic, single-note guitar solos were absolutely unique and captivating. He voluntarily aborted his recording career in 1930 (though that's probably not the word he would've chosen) and played as a street musician in central Texas until his death in 1947. Yazoo has issued the complete work in two volumes: *Praise God, I'm Satisfied* and *Sweeter as the Years Go By.*

Finally, Black Ace (Babe Kyro Turner) and Jesse Thomas should be mentioned. Ace (born in either 1905 or 1907 in Hughes Springs) was a medicine bottle slide virtuoso of the "Hawaiian" style—which is to say he played with the guitar flat on his knees. A partner of Oscar Woods, an influence on Smokey Hogg, a radio raconteur and recording artist for Decca, Black Ace was a fine purveyor of East Texas country blues, as is evidenced on the Arhoolie *Black Ace* album.

Thomas, a guitarist born in Logansport, Louisiana, in 1911, played Deep Ellum with pals Blind Lemon Jefferson and Leadbelly, recorded for the Victor label, and would eventually relocate to California and play with the likes of T-Bone Walker and Nat King Cole. TopCat Records recorded Thomas for *Blue Goose Blues* more than seventy years after his first session. He passed away at the age of eighty-four.

IT WAS ONLY NATURAL THAT THE BLUES WOULD SURFACE ON as evocative an instrument as the piano, and Texas had a modest share of early greats. "Whistlin'" Alex Moore (born in Dallas in 1899) was the most renowned of these "barrelhouse" pianists. His reputation extended east and throughout the Midwest, and he began recording for Columbia in 1929. His predilection for mixing an early ragtime style into his blues would later influence a variety of jazz, boogie woogie, western swing, and Dixieland pianists. Though Moore jumped to the Decca label in 1937, later recorded for Arhoolie, RPM, and Kent, and left a substantial "songbook" legacy, he actually preferred to improvise new material every time he sat down at the piano. He claimed that to have done otherwise would have taken away from his time playing dominoes, but one can't argue with success. And anyone who ever saw him play (he continued to perform regularly at Dallas's Lakewood Yacht Club until his death in 1989) knows his work embodied success—artistically if not financially. Rounder's *Wiggle Tail* is a selection of Moore's latter recordings that can yet be found today.

Other pianists contributing to the genre's stylistic growth in the early 1900s and into the Prohibition years were Curtis Jones, Robert Shaw (aka "Fud"), and Jesse "Tiny" Crump (who was also versatile on organ and clarinet).

Jones was a native of Naples, Texas, born in 1906, and patterned his style very much after Alex Moore. After working the bar circuit throughout the country, in 1937 he recorded a big hit for Vocalion, "Lonesome Bed-room Blues." Jones subsequently released over a hundred sides over the next three years, for Bluebird and Okeh as well as Vocalion, but never matched his initial success. He eventually relocated to Chicago and slid slowly out of sight—until a French blues critic found him living in a slum and booked Jones on several tours of Europe and Morocco (where he lived for several years). Jones was able to record for several more labels in the latter part of his life, with moderate popularity, and passed away in Germany in 1973. *Curtis Jones Live in London*, available as an import from Limelight, is a compelling work from his later years.

Robert Shaw was born in Stafford in 1908 and taught himself to play piano while working on his father's cattle ranch. While his actual recorded body of work was extremely limited, most notably on the Almanac label in the early sixties, Shaw's itinerant career as a barrelhouse pianist had him playing continually in a variety of bars throughout Texas and the Midwest, and his reputation as a terrific stylist was well earned and widespread.

Though he eventually opened his own grocery, private gigs and radio appearances led to well-received European tours late in his life. He died in Austin in 1985, and an Arhoolie collection, *The Ma Grinder*, is a reasonable primer.

Crump was born in Paris, Texas, in 1906, and recorded in support of vocalist Ida Cox and with Billy McKenzie (as "Billy and Jessie") for the Paramount label. It's difficult to find any of his recordings and, when one does, the material is often more vaudevillian than straight blues, but that his muscular style was an influence is indisputable.

Of greater significance to the early blues were the contributions of female singer/pianists Victoria Spivey and Sippie Wallace. Both were classic blues singers of the Bessie Smith variety—an idiom that many would argue has long since been obsolete—and, like Crump, frequently worked in vaude-villian road shows, but the two were nevertheless sensationally gifted.

Beulah "Sippie" Wallace was born in Houston in 1898, and throughout her youth sang and learned piano and organ in the choirs of the Shiloh Baptist Church, where her father was a deacon. A terrific songwriter with a soaring voice of great strength and a honeyed richness, Wallace toured with local tent shows in her late teens, moved to Chicago, and by 1923 had signed with the Okeh label. An early tune, "George, George," became a hit (the first of dozens), and Wallace had effectively started an incredibly prolific career.

Though she toured and recorded with her younger brother, Hersal, and the likes of King Oliver and Louis Armstrong, Wallace was never far from church. Many of her tunes were born of spiritual concerns, wrapped in bluesy melodic packages, and despite a heavy and international tour sched-ule, she managed to find time to serve as the director of the National Convention of Gospel Choirs and Choruses.

Over the years, she recorded for such labels as Bango, Storyville, Reprise, and Spivey (a label started by her contemporary, Victoria Spivey), and influenced artists from Satchmo to Bonnie Raitt. She continued to perform until her death in 1986, including gigs with such modernists as Raitt and the Jim Kweskin Jug Band and on such programs as *The Today Show* and David Letterman's. Alligator Records has released *1923–29*, a collection of her early recordings, which is perhaps the finest introduction to her work.

Spivey's career was equally enduring. She was born in Houston in 1906 and, like Wallace, was proficient on piano and organ (and, for that matter, ukulele—an additional talent which begs the question: *why?*). Spivey learned piano as a child, and by her teens she was the pianist at the Lincoln Theatre in Dallas, and by her early twenties was reputed to have graduated to accompanying Blind Lemon Jefferson in various gambling and prostitutional establishments in the Houston/Galveston area (by which we mean she was performing music). With a moaning and seductive voice of great power, Spivey scored a recording contract with Okeh shortly thereafter, working as a solo artist as well as in support of many of the same artists as Wallace.

From 1926 to 1929 Spivey was a staff writer for the St. Louis Publishing Company, for whom she penned such tunes as "Black Cat Blues," "Dirty Woman Blues," and "Dope Head Blues," displaying a perhaps less lofty (but far more intriguing) muse than Wallace—which is interesting inasmuch as she was arguably as spiritual as Wallace.

In any case, it is not known whether the two ever got together to discuss theology but, after Spivey spent the next several decades working a variety of tours and road shows across the States and in Europe, writing magazine articles and recording (solo, instructional tapes, and in support of artists like Sonny Boy Williamson), Spivey eventually started her own eponymously named label, for whom Wallace eventually recorded.

Spivey also devoted much of her time to the discovery and nurturing of young artists and continued to perform and record until her death in 1976. Discovery's *1926–31* is a representative album.

Of the other women blues singers from Texas in the early part of the century, a few stand out. Hillsboro's Maggie Jones, reportedly born in 1900, was particularly active in the twenties, working a heavy club date schedule and recording for the Black Swan/Victor/Pathé labels as well as Paramount and Columbia. Despite her early popularity, though, she was last heard of in Fort Worth in 1934.

And Hociel Thomas, another Houston native (born 1904), also made a mark as a singer/pianist. While her voice wasn't as expressive as either Wallace's or Spivey's, and her range not as impressive, she was nevertheless a solid blues singer and a convincing stylist. Thomas in fact worked with Spivey in some of the finer houses in New Orleans's Storyville district— again, as a *singer*—and recorded at various times over the years for the

Okeh, Gennett, Circle, and Riverside labels. She relocated to the West Coast in 1942 and worked with Kid Ory until she lost her eyesight in a brouhaha with her sister.

On the other hand, her sibling *died*, so one supposes Hociel got the better end of the fight—and what more poetic way to conclude this chapter than to report that, yes, in the finest tradition of early Texas blues, Thomas was indicted for manslaughter. (It should be added that, though she was acquitted, she made no more musical contributions and died of heart failure a few years later.)

☆ Two: Early Electricity and the California Exodus

▼

IF ONE WERE PREDISPOSED TO THINK OF MUSIC IN CULINARY terms—and we frequently read about an artist's style as being, for example, a "gumbo" of this and that or a "stew" of varied influences—then Aaron "T-Bone" Walker must surely be anointed as a gourmet chef (and not because his nickname has anything to do with a particularly enticing cut of beef).

No, Walker is a gourmet because he added his own outrageous instrumental prowess and songcraft to a stock of solid blues, then roasted the whole dish to perfection with high-voltage doses of electric guitar and amplification, and thus made blues an exotic and infinitely more complex meal.

Indeed, with the invention of the electric guitar, microphones, and amplifiers, music became not just louder, but far more textural inasmuch as shifting dynamics—subtle (and not so subtle) alterations in tone, feel, volume, and emphasis—were suddenly discernible to entire audiences, and not just those who happened to be sitting in the first few rows.

With volume came power, and with power came possibilities. T-Bone Walker was a genius *and* an opportunist, and exploding like star shells under his innovation and experimentation were myriad Texas blues musicians who would blast through the new open door in ways never imagined by Leadbelly or Blind Lemon Jefferson.

But it was an also contradictory growth: Over the years, through Prohibition, World War II, and the postwar era, into the fifties and until the Beatles; with improvements in radio, the expanding awareness of blues, and the emergence of jazz and R&B; the establishment of a nightclub circuit and a West Coast scene to nurture existing activity in the Delta, Texas/ Louisiana, Chicago, and the Northeast, blues music fostered an explosion of creativity and growth—while at the same time turning back into itself, entrenching the music in a steadfast form and a tradition that seemed to defy progress even as it gave birth to it.

* * *

BUT AARON THIBEAUX WALKER SURELY HAD NO SUCH PRETEN-tious visions when, as a nineteen-year-old country blues artist called Oak Cliff T-Bone, he recorded his debut tunes for Columbia Records in 1929, "Trinity River Blues" and "Wichita Falls Blues." In fact, that he got to record at all must've seemed a miracle to the kid. If someone had told him then that he would shortly lead an exodus of Texas musicians to California to create West Coast jump/blues and change the course of blues and R&B forever, he might well, at that point, have simply asked, "What's California?"

Walker was born in 1910 in Linden, and his family moved to the South Dallas suburb of Oak Cliff when T-Bone (as his mom called him in punning approximation of his middle name) was two. Though he began strumming a homemade guitar while quite young, and was exposed to the fervent, bluesy gospel of the Holy Ghost Church in his neighborhood, Walker became a serious student when he began to hang around the Deep Ellum street musicians and medicine show performers.

One in particular, a family friend named Blind Lemon Jefferson, took a liking to the kid, and Walker scored a gig of sorts leading Jefferson around from saloon to saloon, passing a tin cup while the great bluesman sang. Walker supplemented his lead-boy job for Jefferson by practicing guitar and as a tap dancer/comic/singer/musician in regional touring medicine shows such as Ida Cox's.

But, though he became an adept player and got to record the two Columbia sides in 1929, they didn't sell, and T-Bone spent the next five years playing jazz with the likes of Cab Calloway, the Coley Jones Dallas String Band, Count Biloski, Milt Larkin, and Ma Rainey.

Through such associations, Walker met jazz guitar great Charlie Christian and began to fool around with a new contraption called the electric guitar. Shortly thereafter, around 1935, as part of a massive Texas musical migration, T-Bone moved to the West Coast. His instinctive mastery of the electric guitar's bubbling possibilities, coupled with a madcap stage presence and a wonderfully evocative singing voice, made Walker an immediately sought-after commodity and a wildly popular performer. He dazzled audiences across the country in a variety of jazz bands, most notably the Les Hite Cotton Club Orchestra, recording with them for the Varsity label in New York City in 1940.

But T-Bone had his own concepts, and formed a blues-flavored band—surely one of the first to utilize an electric guitar on point—to augment his jazz sideman status. He returned to the West Coast, where his individual celebrity was particularly great, and it was at that point that a crop of record labels began to get seriously curious about the new, electrified blues/R&B.

In the early forties Walker released a number of sides for Capitol's Black and White label, including "T-Bone Blues," "Mean Old World," and "I Gotta Break, Baby." Through such songs, and through his increasingly outlandish stage shows (in which he did the splits, played guitar with his teeth and behind his back, and gyrated in several seductive pre-Elvis gyrations), Walker accomplished a significant one-two punch in making the world aware of the electric guitar as well as the palatable union of amplification and blues.

With an increasingly prolific recording output, by 1947 Walker was able to forgo "featured sideman" status and concentrate on fronting his own combo (which included piano, bass, drums, and a small brass section). It was seminal West Coast blues music: electrified country blues at the core with Nat King Cole–style balladry for smooth sophistication and a jazz swing feel for arcane considerations. Embodying the sound that year was the issuance of Walker's most successful single, "Call It Stormy Monday," which, to put it in moronic terms, many consider to be the "Stairway to Heaven" of blues music.

And, showmanship aside, Walker's playing was continually fresh and innovative. He incorporated Charlie Christian's single-note runs concept into the chordal density of the traditional blues solo, weaving tight spirals of notes into his leads. Essentially, he rammed a bottle rocket of innovation into the staid ass of the blues.

For the next thirty years, Walker recorded for over twenty labels (including Imperial, Decca, Atlantic, and Reprise) and toured the United States and Europe, appearing at prestigious festivals and on the big-time television shows of the day. In 1970, he won a Grammy for Best Ethnic/ Traditional Recording for "Good Feelin'."

By 1974, however, Walker's various infirmities had forced him to become inactive, and a bout with bronchial pneumonia finally killed him in 1975. There are plenty of surviving T-Bone Walker albums, and *The Complete T-Bone Walker, 1940–54* (Mosaic), Atlantic's *T-Bone Blues*, and a three-CD set called *The Complete Capitol/Black and White Recordings* (Capitol) are primo.

AROUND THE SAME TIME WALKER HEADED TO L.A., ONE OF HIS disciples, Connie "Pee Wee" Crayton, left Texas (where he was born in Rockdale in 1914) to become part of the migration of Lone Star musicians testing the fertile artistic grounds of the Golden West.

Crayton waxed ironic on his evolution as a blues singer/guitarist. He once told *Living Blues* magazine that he found it amusing that, invariably, singing in gospel quartets and/or church choirs led Texas singers to the blues—and that, though he'd done both, they had zero influence on his blues career.

Maybe not, but Crayton's talent was nothing if not celestial. He did the "built a guitar out of a cigar box" gig as a kid—which makes one wonder about the evolution of music had cigars not been invented—and later learned trumpet and ukulele in high school. At twenty-one, he opted to move to Los Angeles, where he worked for years in nonmusical capacities. Still, he fell under the influence of Charlie Christian and T-Bone Walker, and his playing improved dramatically. By 1945, he'd moved to the Bay Area and formed his own trio. His reputation as a guitarist began to grow, and though his style at that point was little more than an amalgamation of Walker and Lowell Fulsom, it was at least a damn good amalgamation.

He soon recorded in support of popular Oakland acts like Ivory Joe Hunter, Jimmy Witherspoon, and Turner Willis, and by 1948 was able to release a few of his own sides for Los Angeles's Modern Records: "Texas Hop" and "Blues After Hours." The latter was one of the first instrumental electric guitar number 1 hits, and though both were base-level blues tunes, Pee Wee's style as a player had started to carve out its own singularity. Along with the bluesy single-note runs and rhythms of T-Bone and Fulsom, and a new mastery of Christian's jazzy chord clusters, Crayton's solos combined bubbling waterfalls of notes and complex, melodic arpeggios. With a husky voice at once aggressive and gentle, Crayton was becoming quite a commodity.

He incorporated within his bands that mellow California blues approach to melody, sprinkling his slicing, rocking blues with subtly stated brass and an occasional velvety love song. Into the fifties, Crayton worked with Gatemouth Brown, Dinah Washington, Ray Charles, and others, recording along the way for the Aladdin, Hollywood, Imperial, and VeeJay labels, among others.

By the end of the decade, though, Crayton had fallen on hard times. He lived in Detroit, impoverished, for a while, then met and became friends with jazz guitar great Kenny Burrell. He managed to regain some confidence and returned to Los Angeles, where he worked as a truck driver, and played guitar on weekend gigs.

Finally, through another new friendship, with pianist Johnny Otis, who was resurrecting the careers of a number of the California blues artists, Crayton managed to appear at several festivals and recorded new material for the Vanguard label. He subsequently played with Big Joe Turner, Sarah Vaughan, and Roy Brown, and though his popularity never matched the early Modern Records years, Crayton was happy and creatively fulfilled by the time a heart attack claimed him in 1985. Crown's *Pee Wee Crayton* is an ideal collection, as is Imperial's *Blues Before Dawn* and the *Rocking Down on Central Avenue* set from ACE.

If Walker was the king of California blues, and Crayton was his prince, then Lowell Fulson surely belongs in the court somewhere. But as the genre developed, it too began to subdivide. The blues in Los Angeles was of the "midnight sophistication" variety, with heavy influences from stylists like Nat King Cole. Blues in the Oakland/San Francisco area also had jazz influences, but there was a hint of the rural, old-line blues missing from its Southern California counterpart.

Fulson represented the latter. As compassionate and prolific as any of the practitioners of California "swing blues," as the genre came to be called (a reference to an overall mellowness in tone, with the music borrowing from jazz and emphasizing balladry), Fulson had a remarkable and enduring career. He was born on an Indian reservation in Oklahoma in 1921. With his father and uncles prolific on guitars, fiddles, and mandolins, he became a proficient instrumentalist early on.

Fulson immediately and instinctively dug blues music—in particular Texas blues, for its organic spirituality—and, at the age of eighteen, he scored an opportunity to replace the aging Funny Papa Smith as accompanist to country blues great Texas Alexander. He immediately began to contribute as a writer and singer as well as guitarist, and after playing with Alexander for a few years, moved to Gainesville, Texas, where he worked as a fry cook and played Saturday night fish fries. After a stint in the navy (during which he entertained at USO shows in Guam), Fulson returned to the States and moved to the Oakland area.

Winding down his days in the service, he saw T-Bone Walker play and was fascinated by the Bone's electric guitar blues, and it wasn't long before Fulson (with his brother Martin on rhythm guitar) began working Bay Area clubs performing Texas country blues. In the mid-to-late forties, Fulson recorded for a variety of California labels, including Aladdin, Big Town/ Swingtime and Downtown/Trilon.

But Walker's (literal) electricity was too compelling, and gradually Fulson moved in that direction. In 1950, he added the great pianist Lloyd Glenn to his band, and their recordings of "Blue Shadows," "Everyday I Have the Blues," and "Low Society" became big hits. Fulson's butterscotch voice and lean guitar phrasings were tastefully augmented by Glenn's jazzy piano stylings, and it was a difficult aural package to ignore.

In 1954, Fulson signed with Chess Records and had an immediate hit with "Reconsider Baby" on their Checker label. For ten years (though there were no "smash" hits) Fulson enjoyed consistent success, adding a brass section to his band and churning out a variety of eminently pleasing songs, including "Tollin' Bells," "Hung Down Head," and "I Want to Know."

In the mid-sixties, Fulson hopped to the Kent label and churned out such hits as "Tramp," "Make a Little Love," and "Black Nights." By 1969, however, with psychedelic rock and the Woodstock Nation in full glory and the soul charts peppered with Sly and the Family Stone, Fulson's slick, suave sound was deemed dated by the record-buying masses.

Still, his talent and commitment have kept Fulson working, and a variety of festival dates and consistent albums have been recognized. A 1978 LP, *Lovemaker* (Big Town), and Rounder's 1988 release, *It's a Good Day*, were both among the finest of Fulson's career. Fortunately, a new generation's curiosity and appreciation of the blues has included Fulson. In addition to the two later albums, any of the Chess albums are good, as are Black Lion's *San Francisco Blues* and Capitol's *Tramp/Soul*.

* * *

TWO OTHER INTERESTING TEXAS GUITARISTS WHO MADE IM-
pressions in the West Coast blues community are Smokey Hogg and Sonny
Rhodes.

Hogg, whose propensity for drink surely impeded his career (hey, with a
name like Smokey Hogg, I'd drink, too—or at least go into porn), nonetheless experienced some success melding electric guitar with the rural sentiments and traditions of Blind Lemon Jefferson. Hogg was born in 1914 in
Westconnie but by thirteen had run away to work minstrel and tent shows
across the United States. As his playing developed, he worked in support
of a variety of blues musicians (none of any particular note) through the
twenties and thirties.

As a result of his extensive travels, he was able to incorporate influences
like Peetie Wheatstraw and Big Bill Broonzy to his country blues, and
when T-Bone went electric, Hogg added his own slant to the new concept.
Traveling (and drinking) extensively between Texas and Los Angeles,
Hogg managed to develop a following for his percussive style and melding
of the new and traditional, and from 1947 to 1954 he recorded hundreds of
tunes for several labels. He managed to chart twice, with "Long Tall
Mama" and "Little School Girl," both on Modern Records, but alcohol
abuse took its toll and he died in 1960. Specialty's *Angels in Harlem* is a
good introduction.

Sonny Rhodes, an aggressive self-promoter who wears a turban and calls
himself the "Disciple of the Blues," justifies his own hype. Born in Smithville, Texas, in 1940, Rhodes is a multi-instrumentalist/singer/songwriter
whose abilities on guitar, slide guitar, and pedal steel are equally fluent.

Heavily influenced by Elmore James, Rhodes learned guitar and headed
to Austin where he worked as a chauffeur for Junior Parker (a major educational experience). Then, thinking the opportunities for a young player
were brighter in California, Rhodes gradually established himself in the
Oakland scene. He managed to record a number of sides for Galaxy.

But it wasn't until the late seventies that Rhodes's skills were sufficiently
rewarded. His melancholy hit, "Cigarette Blues," drew attention, and he
now has several highly respected albums to his credit—as well as a full-time
career. Advent's *I Don't Want My Blues Colored Bright* and Ichiban's *Disciple
of the Blues* are his best records.

L. C. Robinson (whose lap-steel histrionics and fusion of raw blues and
western swing were particularly unique), Cal Green, Roy Gaines, Pete
Mayes, Phillip Walker, and Johnny "Guitar" Watson are other fine Texas
guitarists who made a splash on the West Coast scene. (Watson will be
discussed with all attendant minutiae in the Soul/R&B/Disco section.)

BUT GUITAR WAS BY NO MEANS THE ONLY INSTRUMENT REPRE-
sented in the California migration. Several great Texas pianists stamped

their brands by the ocean and, of those, Charles Brown's contributions were more than significant.

Not that that was his concept. Brown, a teacher/chemist who was born in Texas City in 1922, followed T-Bone Walker to California but, though he was a terrific piano player and singer, his reasons for relocating had everything to do with chemistry and little or nothing to do with music.

To say it worked out differently from what Brown had imagined is a rather titanic understatement.

Though he displayed immense musical talent at a tender age, and studied classical piano throughout high school (picking up beachfront or church gigs with the help of his physics/chemistry teacher), Brown matriculated to Prairie View State College aiming for a career in academia or the sciences. He performed in the college band, heavily influenced by Nat King Cole, Pha Terrell, and the Ink Spots, meanwhile majoring in chemistry and minoring in math and education—which, as we all know, is the route followed by most successful musicians.

After college, Brown taught awhile, then became a chemist. The war was on, and with Brown's asthma prohibiting his service, he decided to move to California. A job at a research facility fell through, and Brown discovered he could make a pretty good living playing the piano. After a variety of gigs and talent contests, Brown was called by guitarist Johnny Moore, whose Three Blazers was a popular black act in the Los Angeles area. An immediate club sensation, the Blazers began to back the likes of Frankie Laine on various recording dates, and it wasn't long before Moore was able to secure some sessions for his own band.

From 1945 to 1947, Johnny Moore's Three Blazers recorded a variety of tunes for the Aladdin, Modern Music, and Exclusive labels, and "Driftin' Blues," featuring Brown on vocals, became a huge hit. A subsequent awareness of Brown as a pianist, singer, and songwriter was beginning to percolate; his dramatic, soulful crooning and sensual, tinkling piano sounds were particularly seductive to hordes of young babes.

By 1948, Moore was extremely ill and Brown started his own band. They signed with Aladdin, and the first single, "Get Yourself Another Fool," became a hit—which, Brown theorized, happened because fans incorrectly thought he was aiming the tune at Moore over some intra-Blazer ill feelings.

In any case, from that point until 1953, Charles Brown became a huge force in West Coast blues; "Black Nights," "Merry Christmas," "All Is Forgiven," "Trouble Blues," and "My Heart Is Mended" were all big sellers. Brown's blues were actually an early form of what would be R&B balladry. He relied on smooth, melancholic, almost pop melodies over gentle, jazz-tinged blues progressions.

Though Brown's blues balladry remained popular for years, and he was able to tour and record (in addition to Aladdin, Imperial, King, Mainstream, Bluesway, and Reprise also released Brown material), his popularity, in competition with the rise of rock 'n' roll, had clearly waned by the mid-sixties. Still, a firm believer in his music, Brown persevered and—astonishingly and appropriately enough—a 1990 release for the Bullseye Blues label, *All My Life*, so terrifically captured the essence of the artist that no less a fan than Bonnie Raitt called on Brown to open a three-month string of tour dates for her. As such, thousands of youngsters, who probably believed the blues started with the Vaughan Brothers or perhaps B. B. King, were treated to a rare slice of genius.

Besides *All My Life*, EMI's *Driftin' Blues: The Best of Charles Brown*, and Route 66's *Sunny Blues* are prime samplings.

Marshall, Texas's Floyd Dixon (born 1929) will probably always be remembered as the guy who wrote "Hey Bartender," which was of course a huge hit when covered by John Belushi in *The Blues Brothers*.

But his career was far more substantial than that; he was a superb jump blues pianist whose style was similar to that of Charles Brown. Dixon's family moved to California in 1942, where the self-taught kid began immediately winning talent shows and contests in front of artists like Johnny Moore and Johnny Otis, and eventually he got to cut a tune called "Dallas Blues" for Modern Records. The tune shot to number 2 on the *Billboard* charts and, in 1949, he followed up with the hit "Broken Hearted" (cowritten, incidentally, by Smokey Hogg) for the Supreme label.

Dixon's bubbling piano, his sleepy, three A.M. baritone voice, and a warm, whimsical way with a song would be responsible for dozens of fine recordings over the next few decades, as he worked for several labels including Aladdin and Jewell. Though he's continued to record and appear at clubs and festivals, and experienced a brief career resurgence in the seventies, Dixon's heyday was during the peak of the postwar jump-blues era: the late forties and early fifties.

He remains a legend of Southern California blues piano, and records such as Route 66's *Opportunity Blues* and Specialty's *Marshall Texas Is My Home* are encompassing examples of his work.

Other Texas pianists who should be remembered as important pieces in the Texas-California connection include Little Willie Littlefield (who wrote "Kansas City"), Lloyd Glenn (the terrific player and songwriter who backed T-Bone Walker and, later, B. B. King), and Dave Alexander.

☆ Three: Postwar Blues and the Chitlin Circuit

NOT ALL OF THE TEXAS NEW ELECTRIC BLUES GODS FOLLOWED T-Bone Walker into the Golden West. And the ones who stayed behind would help evolve over the years what became known as the "chitlin circuit," a KKK-flavored tag describing the network of tarpaper-and-clapboard bars and shotgun-shack juke joints that dotted the Dallas and Houston ghettos and popped up on rural highways and in tiny black communities along the Texas-Louisiana border—and constituted the prime performance spots for blues artists for forty years.

Like anything else predominantly associated with black culture during the decades from Prohibition to the slow dawn of the civil rights movement, blues music, in a strictly societal sense, was pretty much a go-to-the-back-of-the-bus phenomenon. And although a few perspicacious whites actually enjoyed the music (an even more select group *performed* it, though none had a sufficient impact to be included here), blues continued to *be* blues because of what the music signified to its practitioners and fans. It was *not* the music of the country club rich, and Lightnin' Hopkins did not go yachting with F. Scott Fitzgerald when relaxing after concert tours.

Instead, the likes of Hopkins worked where and when they could, updating Texas's relaxed, rural songster sound even as they refined the single-string guitar solo aspect. And while the jazzier piano riffs of their West Coast brethren were generally eschewed, it was not unusual to find Texas blues bands eventually augmenting their basic guitar/bass/drum/harmonica format to include horn sections. Similarly, while the West Coast artists weren't above a bit of stylish soul, the stay-at-home Texans could get funky, too, with a sweaty brand of roadhouse rhythm and blues evolving from the basic forms.

OF THE UNDENIABLE TITANS OF THE ERA, SAM "LIGHTNIN'" Hopkins (born in Centerville, 1912), a contemporary of T-Bone Walker's, is frequently mentioned as perhaps the most significant of the Lone Star bluesmen who stayed home. Like Walker, Hopkins was another guitarist who grew up a novitiate of Blind Lemon Jefferson, but where Walker's instrumental virtuosity was a strong point, Hopkins is probably best remembered for his prolific and narrative compositional skills. He learned guitar while barely qualifying as a postinfant, taught by his older brother John Henry, and when young Sam saw Jefferson perform at a church social in 1920, he was hooked. The story has it that Hopkins was in fact so moved by Jefferson's performance that the precocious youngster hopped onstage in an attempt to jam with the legend. Unfortunately, the sightless Great One didn't like what he heard, and trumpeted, "Boy, you got to play it right!"

The rebuke only served to strengthen Hopkins's resolve, and over the years he was able to develop an increasingly singular guitar sound—equal parts Jefferson, Lonnie Johnson, Alger "Texas" Thomas (who was Hopkins's cousin), and his own syncopated, emotive technique. But as impressive as his playing was, it served a greater purpose: to support Hopkins's songs.

For the early part of his career, Hopkins performed as the prototypical country blues guys did—just him and his acoustic guitar—though he could be found touring as a partner to Alexander and, for periodic bursts, as an inmate road gang member. Hopkins, it seems, liked to drink and brawl a bit, and there was a decided menacing aspect to his personality.

By the late thirties, though, Hopkins worked principally outside the penitentiary and outside music, living comfortably in Houston's Third Ward ghetto and performing only at occasional garden or house parties as they might come up throughout the South, or doing street corner gigs with Alexander. He didn't record until 1946, when Aladdin records' Lola Cullen discovered him in Houston playing with pianist Wilson "Thunder" Smith. They went to Los Angeles and laid down a few tracks (during which Hopkins was pinned with the Lightnin' moniker), but things really began to take off a year later when Hopkins returned to Houston and began recording for Bill Quinn's Gold Star label. The first single, which featured just Hopkins and his guitar, was "Short Haired Woman" b/w "Big Mama Jump," which sold a respectable forty thousand copies. The next release doubled that amount and, over the next two years, Hopkins's reputation grew as he recorded a wealth of terrific and unusual material—not a small amount of which was improvised on the spot, which seems, in retrospect, an almost therapeutic technique. Indeed, listening to Hopkins, one hears naked emotion in every mood (and he covers them all: alternately playful, suggestive, wounded, petulant, or melancholic), with yet an omnipresent and faintly malefic tone throughout all of his songs.

After 1946, Hopkins began to record with an electric guitar, and while detractors point to those recordings as sloppy and inferior to his "authentic" acoustic stuff, enthusiasts rave about Hopkins's incredibly greasy tone—a raw and creosote sound which would fuel the imaginations of generations of rock guitar heroes. Too, his volatile and frequently amusing material, such as "Tim Moore's Farm," "Coffee Blues," and "Don't Embarrass Me, Baby," were rallying points for his black audiences.

Over the next several years, Hopkins recorded for virtually any label that would pay him cash to do so—thereby sidestepping a corrupt royalty system that had screwed black artists since the first reel of tape had been spooled onto a recorder for the purpose of preserving music. But a backlash from Hopkins's shrewd system of restitution is that it is now virtually impossible to catalogue his massively prolific output.

By 1959, Hopkins's popularity had begun to wane. Though Chris Strachwitz, founder of Arhoolie Records, managed to record several nice sides, and a subsequent new awareness of Hopkins by a younger audience resulted in a flurry of festival appearances as well as recordings for a variety of folk labels, Hopkins was essentially content to cruise the streets of Houston in his Coupe de Ville.

All in all, his massive legacy is long on quality and output and includes precious little repeated material—a true rarity in blues history. Considering that he worked solo and with a band, recorded electric and acoustic, wrote turn-of-the-century blues and ad-libbed stuff off the evening news, Hopkins, who was felled in 1982 by cancer, could do it all.

Countless recordings by Lightnin' still exist, but the curious may want to consider *Gold Star Sessions* and *L.A. Burning* (both on Arhoolie), Rhino's *Mojo Hand Anthology*, and *Blue Lightnin'* (on Jewel).

BIGOTRY DOES NOT ALWAYS PRECLUDE THE POSSIBILITY OF IN-telligence or cunning, and whoever it was that called Clarence "Gate-mouth" Brown "the Mozart of the Catfish Set" was right on target—however ill advised his phraseology may have been.

Brown, born in 1924 in Vinton, Louisiana, is absolutely one of the greatest of the Texas bluesman, but it would be an injustice to simply label him as such. In fact, his mastery over a variety of instruments (guitar, fiddle, mandolin, drums, bass, and harmonica) and styles (blues, R&B, country and western, zydeco, jazz) serves to qualify him as a genius of Texas music—period.

His family grew up in Orange, Texas, and under the tutelage of his father, a multi-instrumentalist and zydeco/blues songster who performed at fish fries and house parties, Brown began to learn fiddle at the age of ten. By his early teens, he was a drummer, and played in a succession of bands in the South and up the Mid-Atlantic Seaboard until the outbreak of World War II.

After the war (in which Gatemouth served), he became entranced by the guitar virtuosity of T-Bone Walker, and in his prodigal fashion, shortly developed a fluid, stinging style that rivaled the master's. A chance meeting with Walker at Don Robey's Bronze Peacock Club in Houston, in which

Brown supposedly picked up Walker's guitar when the performer abruptly left the stage ill, then blew the house away with an improvised tune, irritated Walker to the extent that he overcame his malady at top speed. Walker came back onstage to wrest his guitar away from the smokin' upstart, but Robey was sufficiently impressed by Gatemouth's ability that he signed him to a management contract, and, in 1947, flew Brown to L.A. to record four sides for Aladdin.

Robey was dissatisfied with the sessions, however, and brought Brown back to Houston and started his own record label, the notorious Peacock Records—renowned as one of the great record labels in the history of American music, and just as notorious for its owner's alleged willingness to sign his clueless artists to contracts that made Robey a lot of money and frequently left his charges without deserved royalties, publishing, or residuals.

At the time, though, it was a huge break for Brown, and it required very few recordings to demonstrate that he was much more than a T-Bone Walker knockoff. Beginning with 1949's "Mary Is Fine" and continuing for the next decade, Brown recorded a dazzling array of sides for Peacock, including "Okie Dokie Stomp" (which blues great Sumter Bruton describes as the "proper state song of Texas"), "Gate's Salty Blues," "Boogie Uproar," "Dirty Work at the Crossroads," "Sad Hour," "Boogie Rambler," "Mercy on Me," and "Rock My Blues Away."

The material ranged from driving blues shuffles to pain-wrenched ballads, sizzling, jazz-flavored instrumentals, and country- or zydeco-influenced party tunes, and it was a truism that younger club bands simply couldn't pull off covers of Brown's intricate and complex songs. Though he rarely charted songs, Brown was an incendiary live draw and his albums sold consistently. After a stint as house bandleader on the R&B variety show *The Beat*, Brown enjoyed time as featured performer at European festivals, then returned to the States at the end of the seventies to experiment with country music.

He recorded several such albums, including *Makin' Music* (MCA), the memorable duet LP with C&W guitar wizard Roy Clark, but returned to the blues at the end of the decade. He signed with Rounder and recorded three essential records: *One More Mile*, *Real Life*, and *Alright Again* (the latter of which won a Grammy in 1981). Lest he again get typecast as a strict blues guy, Brown once more shifted directions with his debut disc for Alligator, *Pressure Cooker*, which owes as much to jazz as to blues. Blasting toward the millennium, the multifaceted Gatemouth shows no signs of slowing down. A favorite performer at the New Orleans Jazz and Heritage Festival and prestigious clubs across the country, it's possible Brown will never die.

In addition to the aforementioned albums, Rounder's *The Original Peacock Recordings* is highly recommended.

Another giant of the postrural years—literally and figuratively—was Willie Mae "Big Mama" Thornton, one of the few women blues stars of the forties and fifties. A lion-voiced singer of healthy physique and voracious narcotic and alcoholic appetite, Thornton was born to a religious family in Montgomery, Alabama, in 1926, and her first stage was a choir loft. Still, she was working the Southern juke-joint circuit with the Hot Harlem Review by the time she was fourteen, and early on selected Houston as her base of operations. A self-taught drummer and harmonica player with an already singular vocal style, Thornton caught the ear of Don Robey, the nightclub entrepreneur and founder of the prestigious Duke/Peacock label, who immediately signed her to a contract.

In 1951, she recorded her first sides, fronting Joe Scott's band on "Mischievous Boogie" and "Partnership Blues," and followed them up with "Let Your Tears Fall, Baby," which was sufficiently popular that Thornton began to develop a national reputation. Over the years, in fact, she was able to tour with popular Southwest and West Coast acts like Johnny Otis, Roy Ligon, Gatemouth Brown, and Joe Liggons, or in Deep South packages with other Peacock artists (Johnny Ace, Junior Parker, Bobby "Blue" Bland). Though her raucous and powerful delivery was the antithesis of the Nat King Cole–style subtlety that marked much of the blues of the period, it was a nonetheless popular voice, and in conjunction with a highly visual onstage persona, Thornton was a valuable commodity in any band.

It was the records she made with Otis's band, from 1952 to 1957, though, that were arguably the highlights of her career. She had a big hit with 1953's "Rock a Bye Baby," and went to number 1 well before Elvis with "Hound Dog."

She toured the West Coast throughout the late fifties and early sixties, recording for such labels as Galaxy, Kent, Movin, and Baytone. And when the Great Blues Revival hit in the mid-sixties, Thornton was temporarily deified, touring Europe, appearing at a variety of festivals and recording, among other songs, "Ball 'n' Chain," which would later become more associated with one of Thornton's most fervent admirers, Janis Joplin. As with many blues artists of the period, Thornton hopped labels with frequency, recording for Vanguard, Irma, Bay-Tone, and Kent, but it was with Mercury and the artist-friendly Arhoolie that she recorded her last great work.

But in the same manner that drink and pharmaceuticals eroded her once mammoth physique to a Popsicle-stick frailty, so did her once warm personality become embittered by injustices in the music business. Ironically, though she died sick and angry in 1984, Thornton was still the Queen of the Blues.

Of her recorded legacy, *Hound Dog: The Peacock Recordings* (MCA) and Arhoolie's *Ball 'n' Chain* are representative essentials.

Z. Z. Hill, whose actual body of work would most accurately be described as soul or R&B, will nevertheless go down as one of the most important of Texas blues artists, for one simple reason: the astonishing success of the single "Down Home Blues" and the basic blues album from whence it sprang, *Down Home*, on the Malaco label.

Hill, who was born in Naples, Texas, in 1935, grew up singing in church choirs. He moved to Dallas after high school, and though he continued to join a gospel group, the Spiritual Five, he also worshipped at the altar of soulsters Otis Redding and Sam Cooke.

As such, it wasn't long before Hill was wailing in a number of South Dallas nightclubs, and in 1963, he relocated to Los Angeles to record for his brother's MHR label. An inaugural release, *Tumbleweed*, attracted the attention of more high-profile labels like Kent, and he spent the next two decades issuing a variety of soul-based records for several companies (including United Artists and CBS). He experienced moderate success with songs like "You Were Wrong," "I Need Someone to Love," and, in particular, "Don't Make Me Pay for His Mistake," coasting along comfortably until 1980, when he made the fortuitous decision to sign with Malaco.

His second album for that label was *Down Home*, a more traditional and straight-ahead blues effort than his R&B fans were used to, and no one, Hill included, could have foretold the amazing success of the first single, "Down Home Blues." Overnight, Hill went from chitlin circuit soul man to absolute blues star; the song hit the *Billboard*'s charts and settled in for an incredible ninety-two-week run. *Down Home* became one of the top-selling blues LPs of all time, and Z. Z. Hill's tune was suddenly and irrevocably a "standard" on blues jukeboxes everywhere.

Unfortunately, the only thing that could have short-circuited Hill's newly rejuvenated career happened: In April of 1984, Hill died suddenly from complications after an auto accident. Of course, it's not too late to enjoy his catchy synthesis of blues and soul and his woodsmoke-at-midnight vocals. The curious should check out Malaco's *In Memorium (1935–84)*.

Another major singer from the postwar Texas period was Herman "Little Junior" Parker, who was at heart a true blues original even as his liquid-fire voice set myriad female hearts a-flutter when he crooned soul ballads. He was born in 1932 in Mississippi and raised in Memphis, and in his formative years hung out with James Cotton and Sonny Boy Williamson and sang gritty roadhouse blues with Howlin' Wolf and B. B. King.

That his jewel of a voice often overwhelmed his talent as a harpist was surely frustrating, but that his singing was almost "too pretty" for blues was possibly even more troubling to Parker. The voice certainly didn't bother the record labels, however, who by 1947 were clamoring for him to record R&B material. Parker scored two hits with "Feelin' Good" and "Mystery Train" for the legendary Sun label (the latter was yet another tune that would substantially add to Elvis Presley's bank account when the King covered it a few years down the road), and did well with a straight-ahead blues tune called "Boogie Chillen."

He moved to Houston in 1954 to record for that city's Duke label, where the curious dichotomy of his musical personality became even more subdivided as producers had him recording primordial rock 'n' roll songs. "Driving Wheel," "Riding in the Moonlight (Pretty Baby Blues)," and "Next Time You See" were typically diverse hits, though Parker was persistently

Gene Autry

Bob Wills and His Texas Playboys

Alvin Crow

Ray Benson

George Jones

Willie Nelson

SCOTT NEWTON/AUSTIN CITY LIMITS

RON MCKEOWN

RON MCKEOWN

SCOTT NEWTON

Waylon Jennings

Roger Miller

Jerry Jeff Walker

Kris Kristofferson and Rita Coolidge

RON MCKEOWN

Ray Wylie Hubbard

RON MCKEOWN

Bill Simmonson and Kinky Friedman

Billie Joe Shaver

Rusty Wier

Michael Murphey and son Ryan

Willis Alan Ramsey

Gary P. Nunn

Tanya Tucker

Ricky Lynn Gregg

Mark Chesnutt

Lyle Lovett

Junior Brown

SCOTT NEWTON/AUSTIN CITY LIMITS

Killbilly

JAMES BLAND

Craig Taylor & Alan Woole

Stephen Stills

Roy Orbison

SCOTT NEWTON/AUSTIN CITY LIMITS

RON McKEOWN

Boz Scaggs

Steve Miller

Edgar Winter

Johnny Winter

ROBERT GREESON

RON MCKEOWN

Joe Ely

ZZ Top

SCOTT NEWTON

JAMES BLAND

Charlie Sexton

Van Wilks

Ian Moore

Stephen Bruton

Jimmy LaFave

SCOTT NEWTON

Lord Tracy

JAMES BLAND

The Buck Pets

JAMES BLAND

JAMES BLAND

Edie Brickell

CLOCKWISE FROM TOP LEFT: Mike Scaccia of Ministry, T42, Rigor Mortis, Dime Bag Darrell of Pantera, Kathy McCarty

Deep Blue Something

Al Escovedo
of True Believers

LESLIE MOSIER-TEMPLETON

Tripping Daisy

The Toadies

JAMES BLAND

Jackopierce

Hagfish

Reverend Horton Heat

Pump'n Ethyl

CLOCKWISE FROM TOP LEFT: Freddie King,
W. C. Clark, Robert Ealey,
Jim Suhler, Stevie Ray Vaughan

CLOCKWISE FROM TOP LEFT: Jimmie Dale Gilmore, Selena, Nanci Griffith, Guy Clark, Josh Alan

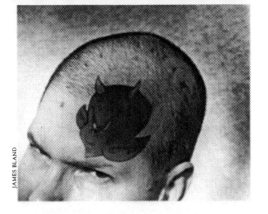

JAMES BLAND

RON MCKEOWN

SCOTT NEWTON

RON MCKEOWN

RON MCKEOWN

CLOCKWISE FROM TOP LEFT: MC 900
Foot Jesus, Brave Combo,
Bugs Henderson, Delbert
McClinton, Texas Tornados

led further and further from authentic blues as his career progressed. This was due as much to the popularity of his soul ballad material as to his propensity for touring with Bobby "Blue" Bland, another blues belter whose R&B leanings grew more substantial in the evolution of his career.

But in the final analysis, it could be argued that Parker was so distinctive in his treatment of all these musical forms that, in a sense, he made them his own—and in doing so crafted his own distinctive brand of blues.

And, in any event, as his career evened out into the seventies and Parker maneuvered from label to label (among them Merchant, United Artists, and Capitol), he was able to return to his hardcore blues roots for a series of albums. Though erratic in quality, there were flashes of harmonica brilliance and Parker's singing was as remarkable as ever. In 1971, he was felled by a brain tumor.

MCA's *Junior's Blues/the Duke Recordings, Vol. 1*, and a Rounder compilation of the Sun years, *Mystery Train*, are recommended.

HE COULD JUST AS EASILY HAVE BEEN CALLED LICORICE STICK or Ginger Snap, and his considerable starshine will probably lack the longevity of the really famous guys, but it is nevertheless true that Peppermint Harris should be remembered as a bona fide, one-of-a-kind biggie of Texas blues.

Born Harrison Nelson (reportedly in Texarkana) in 1925, little is known about his musical upbringing other than that, during the service, he bought his first guitar aboard a ship in the South Pacific. After the military he entered the University of Texas, got a degree in speech, and indulged in lengthy weekend forays into the Houston ghetto, where he'd stay up all night listening to Lightnin' Hopkins and Gatemouth Brown.

His interest in music gradually overtook any interest in careers his degree might have afforded him, and young Harrison relocated to Houston and began playing and singing his own tunes at the Eldorado Ballroom. After being selected by the Sittin' in With label at an en masse audition (where he was tagged with the Peppermint Harris moniker), the young guitarist had his first hit with 1950's "Raining in My Heart."

The soggy motif of that first title was certainly appropriate, inasmuch as Harris's subsequent string of popular tunes invariably celebrated the myriad joys of liquor. Though it's not certain whether Harris was even drinking at the time, his 1951 smash for Aladdin, "Let's Get Loaded," certainly curried favor among those who did. (Harris himself said the tune could just as easily have been about marijuana; it just wasn't acceptable to sing about herb at the time.) In any case, the song's popularity led to a whole series of drinking songs, among them the call-to-party anthem "Have Another Drink."

Harris should be remembered for his sensuous voice and clean, lean guitar stylings, but the sheer volume of quality material he cranked out is the stuff of legend. By his own estimation, from 1947 to 1984, he wrote over a thousand tunes, recording for over fifteen labels (including RCA, Checker, Duke, Gold Star, and Jewel) and selling dozens of songs (and all attendant publishing and royalty rights) directly to artists like Johnny Ace, B. B. King, and Bobby Blue Bland.

Harris was perhaps *too* versatile. Crafting everything from slow blues to precisely and imaginatively arranged soul and pop tunes, utilizing a wacky sense of humor and (for the genre) particularly literate lyrics, Harris frequently confused his fans *and* record labels—neither of whom knew quite what to do with him.

By the twilight of his career, when he preferred to stay around Houston and in the Gulf Coast blues clubs rather than head to Europe and take advantage of the blues revival festivals and tours, Harris probably cemented his place in the mid-level of Texas blues lore.

But that's not to say he doesn't deserve better. *Sittin' in with Peppermint Harris* (Mainstream), *I Got Loaded* (Route 66), and *Being Black Twice* (Collectibles) adequately represent his amazingly varied and ongoing career.

Several other influential and talented artists worked the circuit over the years, paving the way for the explosion that was to come in the seventies.

Frankie Lee "I'm the Only Blues Guy on Earth Without a Kooky Nickname" Sims, a nephew of Alger "Texas" Alexander and compatriot of Smokey Hogg and T-Bone Walker, was born in New Orleans in 1917. He ran away from home at an early age, learned guitar from "Little Hat" Jones, taught elementary school, served in the marines and, after the war, settled in Dallas to helped sculpt the North Texas blues and burgeoning R&B scene.

While his compositions were steeped in traditional blues structures, the kindly Sims was lyrically inventive and his electric guitar work was a potpourri of percussive rhythm and searing, staccato solos. His singing style had a faintly sneering tone, as though Peter Lorre had taught him phrasing, but a warm sense of humor was evident throughout Sims's presentations. His use of the newly electric combo concept was a precursor to rock 'n' roll itself, and his guitar innovations became de rigueur influences on virtually every fifties and sixties blues player who grew up in Texas.

Sims died of pneumonia in 1969—just before he was set to record material for Arhoolie. Though he'd released sides for a variety of labels, Specialty's *Lucy Mae Blues* is, regrettably, one of the few records to document Sims's vastly underrated talent.

Melvin "Lil Son" Jackson, who for a brief span in the late forties and early fifties was as popular a blues guitarist as one could find in Texas, grew up a Blind Lemon Jefferson fan in Barry, Texas, where he was born in 1915.

After the war, his odd juxtaposition of bass-heavy rural riffing and electric guitar sensibilities drew the attention of producer Bill Quinn, who signed Jackson to the Gold Star label. Jackson's spacey, I'll-wake-up-in-a-minute vocal delivery often masked a curious fury.

The Gold Star recordings did sufficiently well that he signed on with

New Orleans' Imperial Records. The label released over fifty sides through 1954, including a Jackson tune called "Rockin' and Rollin'," which was the precursor to B. B. King's "Rock Me Baby."

Jackson grew disgruntled with the music biz in the mid-fifties and retired to become a mechanic and, though he resurfaced briefly in the early sixties to record for Arhoolie and Decca, he proved no competition for John, Paul, George, and Ringo. Jackson died of cancer in 1976, and of his recorded body of work, Arhoolie's *Lil' Son Jackson* is the definitive choice.

There will always be a certain musical repetitiveness to the blues; many say it's the form's inherent structure which gives it its therapeutic properties. But within those structures are many, often subtle differences—the ones that set the players apart from one another. Weldon "Juke Boy" Bonner (born in Bellville, Texas, in 1932) stood out in particular because of his lyrical contributions.

Though it's been said that his guitar style was overly reliant on Jimmy Reed mannerisms and his harmonica honkings percussive at best, his lyrics were astute and poetic. Bonner's acute, "Percy Shelley of the Fifth Ward" observations on the world of the Houston ghetto or on his own alcohol-plagued health rendered his country-tinged, one-man-band performances ever so much more than the down-home ramblings of a street corner drunkard.

Though he played all over the country, recorded sporadically for a variety of labels and participated in a series of European festival tours after a series of later albums for Arhoolie, Bonner's home turf was always inner-city Houston. His peak period was probably between 1968 and 1974, but by that point he was in the throes of alcoholism and unable to realize the full potential afforded him by his late celebrity. He died in 1978, and of his recordings, Flyright's *Juke Boy Bonner, 1960–1967*, and Arhoolie's *Going Back to the Country* are excellent examples of his blues-as-poetry creations.

Clarence "Bon Ton" Garlow was another woefully underappreciated guitarist. He was born in Welsh, Louisiana in 1911, and grew up in Beaumont, Texas. And though his fame scarcely extended beyond southeast Texas throughout his life, Garlow will, if nothing else, be remembered as a huge influence on Johnny Winter—and as the guy who immortalized on record the phrase *bon ton roula* ("let the good times roll").

Garlow's father was heavily into zydeco, and Clarence early on learned fiddle, guitar, and accordion. But hearing T-Bone Walker detailed the youngster's zydeco inclinations and turned him instead to blues. He hung around the elder Walker as much as possible, holding down a postal gig to pay the bills while he worked his way into the club circuit. In 1949, he was signed to Houston's Macy's label. Among those first tunes was "Bon Ton Roula," which became Garlow's only national hit (and, even then, in a minor capacity).

He subsequently recorded for a variety of regional Louisiana and Texas labels over the years, as well as briefly for Aladdin, but his status pretty

much remained as a regional performer until his death in 1986. His guitar playing, slashing and frenetic, is echoed in Winter's work, and can be heard on source material like Flyright's *New Bon Ton Roula*. A series of East Austinite guitarists should also be mentioned: Hosea Hargrove, Calvin Thompson, and Matthew Robinson.

THERE WERE A FEW PARTICULARLY NOTABLE PIANISTS DURING this period, as well, and one with Cajun seasonings similar to Garlow was Katie "200 Pounds of Joy" Webster, a terrific pianist adept at blues, boogie-woogie, pop, R&B, country and western, jazz, and gospel. Growing up in Houston (born 1939) under the tutelage of her pianist/minister father, Webster knew over seven hundred songs by the time she was fifteen—most of which were deeply rooted in gospel tradition.

She majored in music in college, was influenced by family friends like Amos Milburn and Little Willie Littlefield and through exposure to heroes like Dinah Washington, Sarah Vaughan, and Ella Fitzgerald, and began to work clubs throughout Houston and up and down the Louisiana border. She became an in-demand session player, in particular for producer J. D. Miller, architect of the Louisiana "swamp blues" sound, and also formed her own band. Between her own gigs, doing sessions for Juke Boy Bonner, Lazy Lester, Clifton Chenier, and Slim Harpo, and touring with Sam and Dave, Otis Redding, and James Brown, Webster's piano was as indelible as ink on virtually any Deep South blues or soul record throughout the fifties and sixties.

But her personal heyday didn't come until the eighties, when, newly discovered by a wiser youth, Webster began to tour Europe as much as nine months a year. *The Swamp Boogie Queen* (Alligator) and Paula 13's *Katie Webster* are essential slices of her work.

Sammy Price was also a pianist of exceptional talent. A Honey Grove, Texas native who was born in 1908, Price was one of the last great barrel-house keyboardists. He spent years as a singer and dancer in various swing bands before landing in New York in the late thirties to take a gig as the house piano player for the Decca label. Though rarely surfacing as a featured performer, his blues-flavored jazz and R&B riffs were in constant demand on a variety of sessions for years, and can be heard on recordings by Trixie Smith, Eddie Durham, King Curtis, and Sister Rosetta Tharpe. He stayed active until his death in 1992, and Savoy's *Rib Joint/Roots of Rock 'n' Roll* is a fine example of Price's work.

The Grey Ghost—Roosevelt Thomas Williams—born in Bastrop in 1903, a pianist of inimitable style who worked clubs along the Dallas to El Paso rail line in the years before World War II. Afterwards, he was pretty much a phenomenon exclusive to the Austin area, where he happily performed his barrelhouse blues on a weekly basis for forty years. Though his recorded legacy is small, two albums for Catfish survive, *The Grey Ghost*

and *Texas Piano Professors* (recorded with two other notable players, Erbie Bowser and Lavada Durst).

There are numerous other noteworthy Texas blues artists who worked the chitlin circuit and played anyplace they could score a gig. Among them are guitarists Joe Hughes, Goree Carter, Pete Mayes, L. C. Williams, Oscar "TV Slim" Wills, Harding "Hop" Wilson, Nelson Carson, and Lester Williams. Pianists of note include Monette Moore, Teddy Reynolds, Big Walter "Thunderbird" Price, Doug Finnell, and Buster Pickens.

And though they weren't blues musicians per se, Don Robey and Joe Scott were substantially influential figures in the development of Texas blues. Robey, of course, founded the Peacock label, an outstanding and archetypical blues record company. He was a fine discoverer of talent, a shrewd businessman of whom it could arguably be said did not always give his artists their financial due—just as it could be said that, without his vision and industry, countless blues artists would never have recorded at all. And a great part of the success of Peacock was due to musical director Joe Scott, whose trademark arrangement and production were a part of the development of the Texas sound that cannot be overemphasized.

IT IS ALSO TRUE THAT, AT THE HEIGHT OF AWARENESS OF THE wellspring of Texas blues, the Beatles and rock 'n' roll would take over the nation's musical consciousness and effectively destroy any momentum made by blues artists throughout the forties and fifties. Instead, blues artists reluctantly found a new permanence to the "chitlin circuit" mentality—a return to the back-alley venues from which they'd only just begun to rise.

But the setback was temporary, and it wouldn't be long before the scorching work of younger black guitarists like Albert Collins and Freddie King—neither of whom, incidentally, was a stranger to Saturday night "free beer" gigs in tarpaper shacks—would begin to influence white rock players like Eric Clapton.

And that, in turn, would set the stage for two brothers, Jimmie and Stevie Ray Vaughan, to actively seek out the artists responsible for the blues—and subsequently blow the doors open for such musicians all over the world.

☆Four: Stevie Ray Vaughan and the New Respectability

▼

I T SHOULD BE OBVIOUS, BY NOW, THAT IN TEXAS, BLUES MUSI-
cians sprout like wildflowers. It is, after all, the only state in the union
where mastery of a I-IV-V chord progression is a prerequisite for obtaining
a driver's license. And *that*, ultimately, is because of Stevie Ray Vaughan,
who is responsible for making blues palatable to the record-buying masses
in this solar system.

On the surface that's a ludicrous statement, but it's a point that has been
made numerous times by the likes of Buddy Guy, Muddy Waters, B. B. King,
and other blues luminaries. Yet the fact remains that, in order for there to
have been a Stevie Ray Vaughan, it was necessary for there to have been
his older brother, Jimmie Lee Vaughan. And, spinning backwards in turn,
for Jimmie to have led the way for Stevie, it was necessary for there to have
been cool blues guys to begin with.

Otherwise, in the mid-sixties, during the ubiquitous explosion of the free-
love generation, there would not have been a plethora of young rock musicians who were fascinated by authentic bluesmen. Artists like the Rolling
Stones, Cream (and later the solo Eric Clapton), early Fleetwood Mac, Ten
Years After, Canned Heat, Jimi Hendrix, and Johnny Winter were students
of the old masters and were able to open the collective eyes of a younger
generation of white, rock-bred players to the intricacies, discipline, and
Zen wonders of the blues—and among those kids would be the Vaughan
Brothers.

But to go back further: Two black Texas blues guitarists, young but not
exactly newcomers to the chitlin circuit themselves, somehow broke
through the color barrier to the white rock artists in a serious way during
the years immediately after the Beatles hit America. They were Albert Collins and Freddie King, and it was this pair that started the movement that
bridged blues past with blues future.

* * *

COLLINS WAS BORN IN 1932 IN LEONA, TEXAS, A COUSIN OF LIGHT-nin' Hopkins, and his family moved to Houston a few years later. He grew up in the same Third Ward neighborhood as pals Johnny Copeland and Johnny "Guitar" Watson but, though musically inclined, Collins actually studied organ until high school. When a thief purloined his keyboard, however, the youngster switched to guitar.

He was exposed early to the likes of cuz Hopkins, Guitar Slim, Lowell Fulson, and Gatemouth Brown, but was perhaps more influenced by piano players and organists than by guitarists (a fact that had a definite influence on his chordal and structural development). Another cousin, Willow Young, played guitar in the Hawaiian lap style, utilizing a bizarre minor-key tuning, and Collins incorporated that, along with a self-taught thumb and two-finger picking technique, into what would become a decidedly unique sound.

Eventually, he settled on an F-minor triad tuning (or a D-minor-7-flat-5 without a root, for all the laypeople out there), using a capo well up the neck for an amazing tone—at once stinging, brittle, and sharp as a scalpel. Collins began playing around, formed his own band, the Rhythm Rockers, and also served apprenticeships with Gatemouth Brown, Piney Brown, Johnny "Guitar" Watson, and even Little Richard.

By the late fifties, Collins was well known on the Gulf Coast and in the Beaumont–Port Arthur area (where he frequently hung out with Johnny Winter and Janis Joplin), and had begun recording obscure singles for small labels like Kangaroo, Great Scott, and Hall. One such tune, a 1958 instrumental called "The Freeze," drew significant regional response. It was the first of a series of instrumental 45's including "Sno-Cone," "Frostbite," "Thaw-Out," "Hot 'n' Cold," and, in 1962, "Frosty." Lest ye glean a recurring boreal motif therein, well, a friend of Collins's early on had commented that the very sound of "The Freeze" suggested something cold and that perhaps the concept could serve Collins well as his trademark; the guitarist ran with it.

And when "Frosty" became an actual hit, cementing Collins's reputation as a craftsman of bad-ass, cookin' instrumental blues, folks beyond southeast Texas began to take note. In fact, out in California, a prototypical blues-groove psychedelic-jam band called Canned Heat, comprised of young white hippies, were huge fans and brought Collins to the attention of various rock stars and management and booking agent wizards.

Before long, Collins (known alternately as "Jazzbeau" and "the Master of the Telecaster") was appearing on rock bills at prominent ballrooms like the Fillmore West and at pop festivals like Newport and Seattle. He signed with the Imperial label and released three spotty albums which nonetheless featured a number of strong tunes of funk-based, howling blues—instrumental as well as vocal.

For the next decade, Collins recorded sporadically for other labels like

Blue Thumb and Tumbleweed and performed for racially mixed and sonically hip audiences in showcase clubs throughout the United States and Europe. In 1978, Collins signed with Alligator Records and, on the advice of his bassist, named his backing band the Icebreakers.

Collins released several excellent records for the label, including *Ice Pickin'*, *Frostbite*, *Frozen Alive*, *Cold Snap*, *Don't Lose Your Cool*, and 1978's *Showdown*, a collaboration with Johnny Copeland and Robert Cray that won a Grammy award. His unorthodox technique had reached the amazing stage, and songs like "Too Many Dirty Dishes" (in which Collins conjures up a variety of appropriate dishwashing sounds: plate scraping, scrubbing, and rinsing noises with his ax) and "Dyin' Flu" are astounding examples.

He further expanded his audience with a prominent role as—what else?—a curmudgeonly blues guitarist with a beneficent heart in the hit film *Adventures in Babysitting*, and was the featured artist in a PBS documentary called *Ain't Nothin' But the Blues*.

Over the years, with increased recording budgets in high-quality studios, Collins revealed a playful, gravelly vocal style which sounded fine in counterpart to his piercing, glacial guitar. His popularity continued to spread exponentially, and he was a revered entertainer with a multidimensional audience until his unfortunate death of lung cancer on Thanksgiving Day, 1993.

MCA's *Truckin' with Albert Collins* represents his early recordings admirably, while any of the Alligator LPs are noteworthy.

AS A SMOKIN' PURVEYOR OF BLUES INSTRUMENTALS, FREDDIE "The Texas Cannonball" King was in many ways similar to Collins, as is his lasting legacy as a player who broke the color line between black blues artists and white rock bands. King was born in Gilmer, Texas, in 1934, received guitar lessons from an uncle at an early age, listened heavily to B. B. King (no relation) and T-Bone Walker, then moved to Chicago with his family. He continued to learn guitar into his teens, worked in a mill job to pay the bills, and played in a variety of South Side juke joints by night. In 1960, he signed with the King/Federal label, and went to Cincinnati to record.

He laid down over a hundred sides for the label, and an instrumental from those years, King's own "Hideaway," became a smash of surprising and ultimately staggering popularity. At first, blues and R&B units covered the tune, then it became a staple on the rock 'n' roll Top 40 circuit, until megacool guys like Eric Clapton would utilize the tune as high points in their own concert repertoires. (Clapton also recorded another King hit, "Have You Ever Loved a Woman" on the immortal *Layla* LP, and numerous bands have covered King's versions of "The Stumble" and "Goin' Down".)

In the meantime, though, King's own career took off. A bear of a man whose smiling, sweaty visage and three-piece suits lent a familiar dignity to his raucous, sinewy solo work, King moved to Dallas in 1963 and began to work the chitlin circuit in earnest. In 1966 he signed with the prestigious Atlantic label and recorded two (King Curtis–produced) LPs for their Cotillion subsidiary, including 1970's *My Feeling for the Blues*.

He then released three albums for Leon Russell's brand-new Shelter Records (*Getting Ready*, *Texas Cannonball*, and *Woman Across the River*) before label hopping to RSO—which was not coincidentally Clapton's post–Derek and the Dominoes label—for the *Burglar* and *Larger Than Life* albums. Though his material occasionally strayed off course over the years in various pop and rock directions, his odd, two-fingerpick style and blazing, barbed-wire tone stayed consistent to the end—which, unfortunately, came all too soon.

On December 28, 1976, the Texas Cannonball, who'd become a familiar and revered face in the lily-white world of rock royalty, died of heart failure and internal bleeding in Dallas's Presbyterian Hospital. Rhino's *Hide Away: The Best of Freddie King* and TopCat's live *This Is the Blues!* are recommended.

A frequent side guitarist in King's band was Dallas-bred Andrew "Junior Boy" Jones, who has gone on to sculpt quite a nice solo career. Frequently ill as a child, Jones utilized convalescent time to learn guitar and, at a tender age, set off on the professional trail. In addition to King, Jones backed such varied artists as Bobby Patterson, Katie Webster, Johnnie Taylor, and Charlie Musselwhite.

Returning to Dallas, Jones hooked up with the sensational Hal Harris & the Lowlifers (R. L. Griffin's backup band), and in 1996 released his first solo CD, *I Need Time*. He encored two years later with *Watch What You Say*. Both records are typical blues fare, but his guitar playing is inarguably astounding.

WITH THE BLUES THUS INTEGRATED, AND THROUGH THE MASSIVE breakthrough achieved by Johnny Winter (despite record company manipulations that would turn him into a rock artist for most of the seventies), it became possible, too, for white guys to actually plays blues music. Granted, it generally required the artist to creep "across the tracks" and to willingly twist the time-honored perception of "outsider" back onto himself, but it happened.

Two young Texas guitarists who were particularly interested in just those maneuverings were brothers Jimmie and Stevie Ray Vaughan, who grew up in Oak Cliff, the same Dallas suburb that produced T-Bone Walker.

And if in the big picture one subscribes to the generally acknowledged theory that Stevie Ray Vaughan ripped through this cross-cultural crack and blasted blues into the realm of hip for the great white buying public everywhere, then credit his older brother Jimmie with making guitar hip for Stevie Ray.

That alone is an accomplishment to be grateful for, but the musical contributions wrought of Jimmie's own calloused fingertips are damned significant, too. An incredibly versatile player of much taste and imagination, Jimmie was born in 1951 and, from postinfancy on, was a determined, self-taught guitarist fascinated with vintage R&B radio and "forbidden" black artists like Howlin' Wolf, Li'l Son Jackson, Little Walter, Slim Harpo, and Buddy Guy. His reputation as a pint-sized virtuoso grew quickly throughout South Dallas in bands like the Chessmen but, by 1970, Vaughan shrewdly noted that Dallas had little going on in the way of a nurturing blues scene, and he migrated down I-35 to the more liberal and open arms of Austin with like-minded musicians including Doyle Bramhall, Paul Ray, and Denny Freeman—all of whom would play important roles in the development of a white blues scene.

By the time Stevie followed him a few year later, Jimmie was the talk of South Austin. He was a retro visionary with his Ed "Kooky" Burns haircut, vintage wardrobe and whiskey 'n' Ray•Bans persona; a primo guitarist of the gunfighter persuasion, and as wild and incendiary as his younger brother would someday be. (In fact, until his death, Stevie would modestly react to compliments on his Hendrixian virtuosity by saying, "You oughtta see *Jimmie* play.")

Stevie was right: Jimmie *could* do it all. With Texas Storm (later just the Storm), Jimmie and various bandmates rendered blues cool for an entire city of college kids. But at some point Vaughan stopped the guitar histrionics and went simple. And that was coolest of all, because Jimmie had discovered the *real* secret: the space between. By placing a premium on tone and utilizing an absolute minimum of notes required, Jimmie was able to capture the soundtrack to his own heart and soul—as much by what he *didn't* play as by what he did. Jimmie Vaughan's blues were lean and astringently clean, seasoned with dollops of R&B, wherein every note was essential. In an age of "more is better" guitar heroes, Jimmie Vaughan had learned what the old masters knew all along: simpler is better.

And when he met up with a transplanted Minnesotan harp-player/vocalist named Kim Wilson, the Fabulous Thunderbirds were born. After a few roster shuffles, Vaughan and Wilson settled on bassist Keith Ferguson and drummer Mike Buck, and the T-Birds worked Texas and the Southeast with a greasy, economical brand of blues and R&B which was, frankly, anathema to white musicians at the time.

They released *The Fabulous Thunderbirds* on the Takoma label in 1979, scored a European tour opening for supergroup Rockpile, then signed a major label deal with Chrysalis that would result in fame and riches. Over the next decade the band churned out a succession of increasingly successful albums: *What's the Word* (1980), *Butt Rockin'* (1981), *T-Bird Rhythm* (1982),

Tuff Enuff (1986), *Portfolio* (1987), and, after switching labels to Epic, 1987's *Hot Number* and 1989's *Powerful Stuff*. Hit singles like "Tuff Enuff," "Wrap It Up," "Stand Back," and "Powerful Stuff" kept the Thunderbirds on the radio and in the financial gravy, but Vaughan eventually grew tired of the T-Birds' direction and left the band in 1990.

His subsequent work has been defining. He recorded an album with Stevie, *Family Style* (1990, Epic), and two fine solo CDs, *Strange Pleasure* (1994, Epic) and *Out There* (1998, Sony/Columbia), all of which reinforce the stylistic idea that Jimmie is the yin to his brother's yang.

AMONG BLUES PLAYERS THROUGHOUT AMERICA, THERE IS A decided lack of bitterness over the following cultural incongruity: that it took one white kid to do what countless talented black men had not been able to do with regularity since the Civil War—take blues out of backwoods shacks and ghetto nightclubs and put the music in the biggest arenas and festivals in the world.

They're not bitter because, for one thing, no matter how it happened, the influence and popularity of blues music *is* now far-reaching for *all* blues purveyors. And for another, Stevie Ray was as wonderful and reverent toward the musicians who passed before him and shaped the art as he was a supremely bad-ass guitar player.

He grew up emulating brother Jimmie, dropping out of high school to play in Blackbird (with future Point Blank guitarist Kim Davis) before following his elder sibling to Austin. There he paid excruciating dues, heavy on poverty, and lived with the burden of trying to play a style of music few people gave a shit about. Along with the two Jims (his brother and Hendrix) he painstakingly worked on the secret techniques of Lonnie Mack, Buddy Guy, and the three Kings—B. B., Albert, and Freddie.

Along the way, through brutal practice and jamming with any blues artist who'd let him onstage, Stevie tapped into his own genius and became special. With bands like Krackerjack, then in Paul Ray and the Cobras, and ultimately with his own Triple Threat Revue and Double Trouble, Stevie was at the center as the Austin blues scene literally grew up around him. Bassist Tommy Shannon and drummer Chris "Whipper" Layton became the foundation of Double Trouble (later augmented by keyboardist Reece Wynanas); in said unit, before long, Stevie superseded Jimmie as the guitar monarch of Austin.

His name became an "I've *heard* of that guy" legend across the country—even as Stevie was still crashing on people's couches in cheap rented homes in South Austin. Gradually, though, breaks started to happen for him, and after a playing for a Rolling Stones private party and at the Montreaux Jazz Festival, Stevie Ray and Double Trouble signed with Epic Records and became massively successful. The band's popularity increased arithmetically over the course of albums like *Texas Flood* (1983), *Couldn't Stand the Weather* (1984), *Soul to Soul* (1985), *Live Alive* (1986), and 1989's *In Step*.

Interestingly enough, as these recordings testify, Stevie Ray cannot be classified as a pure blues artist. Though he recorded many blues songs and performed a variety of blues classics onstage, the bulk of his original material added doses of rock and R&B to a blues stock. Still, his heartfelt worship of the blues and its creators was a driving force in Vaughan's music, and whatever direction he spun off in retained blues flavorings.

As a stylist, Vaughan was a showboatin' genie; a chops-saturated trickster. In his trademark black gaucho he could cross-pollinate Hendrix's Chinese New Year explosiveness with gut-wrenching emotion and reverent nods to the bluesters of yore.

But even as he became a household name, Vaughan was descending into a quagmire of cocaine and alcohol. It's true that many of his most triumphant moments were blurry fragments in his memory, and the situation reached a virtual Code Blue when he collapsed onstage during a European tour in 1986. Fortunately, he got help. In a recovery he described as miraculous, Vaughan pulled out of his sicknesses and, for the rest of his life, was clean, healthy, positive, and, in some circles, as much an inspiration for his sobriety as for his music.

The 1989 LP *In Step* recorded after his recovery had solidified, featured a wealth of material cowritten with old friend Doyle Bramhall (himself recovering from drug problems), and gave promise of a terrific and productive future (as typified by the songs "Wall of Denial," "Caught in the Crossfire," and "Riviera Paradise," the latter of which was recorded in one magical take that Vaughan later described as "praying through his guitar").

He also got to record a long-anticipated album with brother Jimmie, *Family Style*, which they finished shortly before an outdoor concert at Alpine Valley, Wisconsin, in August 1990 featuring Eric Clapton, Double Trouble, Jimmie Vaughan, and Robert Cray.

Directly after the show, Stevie Ray grabbed a seat on a helicopter bound for Chicago. The craft took off into a shroud of fog and moments later crashed into the side of a hill, killing all aboard. Stevie Ray Vaughan was thirty-five years old.

His legacy as a guitar hero supreme is, of course, eternal, and aspiring teen guitarists will no doubt be wearing Spanish hats into guitar shops and record stores far into the next century. Perhaps, though, Stevie might wish as well to be remembered as a guy who was winning a battle with addiction—and who was able to open a window of opportunity for the musicians he loved and who had inspired him.

The expected postdeath deluge of product in the marketplace is a full-throttle gig and includes *The Sky Is Crying*, *In the Beginning*, several greatest-hits and remastered packages, a live recording of a show with Albert King, and, surely, at some point, a collection of SRV's telephone answering machine messages.

*   *   *

OF COURSE, THE VAUGHAN BROTHERS HARDLY CONSTITUTED
the entire blues scene in Texas in the seventies. (Austin was, realistically,
the blues scene in Texas, though Fort Worth had some interesting things
going on.) All over South Austin, several bands popped up and disintegrated, only to pop up again with a new name and slightly altered personnel,
and the list of players shifting in and out of various musical configurations
was as convoluted and incestuous as possible. Bands like the Storm, Krackerjack, Southern Feeling, and the Nightcrawlers would eventually dissolve
and, one way or another, become Paul Ray and the Cobras, the Fabulous
Thunderbirds, or the Triple Threat Revue.

Several players and singers should be noted from this period, including
guys who were already famous for other things, like Doug Sahm and Marc
Benno.

Sahm, of course, was well known from his sixties rock days in the Sir
Douglas Quintet and various national solo projects. But while his perspicacious amalgam of musical styles—Tex-Mex/rock/country/soul—was always creative and interesting, Sahm was also an inveterate blues freak who
frequently showed up in various Austin clubs to sit in with the young blues
hounds, lending an aura of legitimacy to the early rumblings. And though
he's mostly been associated with the in-state, cross-musical supergroup the
Texas Tornadoes, Sahm has been signed to the Antone's label, the house
record company for Austin's venerable blues club. The first album, called
The Last Real Texas Blues Band Featuring Doug Sahm, was released in early
1996.

Benno, too, had experienced fame as a rocker, most notably through his
association with Leon Russell and through their Shelter albums, *Asylum
Choir* and, particularly, *Asylum Choir II*. A native of Dallas, Benno was
more of a songwriter than an instrumental virtuoso, though he is more than
adept at guitar and piano.

For several wild years in California, Benno lived in Leon Russell's closet,
played with the likes of the Doors, Rita Coolidge, Eric Clapton, and Jose
Feliciano, and released four critically lauded solo albums for A&M (*Marc
Benno*, *Minnows*, *Ambush*, and *Lost in Austin*).

He then returned to Texas, met and studied under Mance Lipscomb
for several months, then toured with Lightnin' Hopkins for a year and a
half. Obviously, by that point, he was completely into the blues. Benno
scored another contract with A&M and assembled a cast of Austin superstars called the Nightcrawlers, which included Stevie Ray Vaughan
and Doyle Bramhall, to record the album. Unfortunately, the label hated
the record and it was never released. Though Benno has subsequently
won a Grammy award for his songwriting, his days as a Hollywood big
shot are probably over. He lives in the Texas hill country and makes music, and two recent European releases, Parisian Sky Ranch's *Take It Back*

to *Texas* and Provogue's *Snake Charmer*, are fine examples of Benno's postmodern blues.

In a more traditional sense, the number of Austin blues guitarists that cropped up in the wake of Collins, King, and the Brothers Vaughan is staggering. Of their contemporaries, players such as Derek O'Brien, Bill Campbell, T. D. Bell, Omar Dykes, Denny Freeman, and W. C. Clark were all notable—particularly the latter two.

OF COURSE, NOT ALL THE NEW AUSTIN BLUES MAESTROS WERE guitar players. A trio of female singers comprised an awesome well of talent: Marcia Ball, Lou Ann Barton, and Angela Strehli.

Of the three, Barton is the most notorious, as well as the one possessed of the most intriguing set of pipes. She grew up in Fort Worth, frequently sitting in as a teenager at the New Blue Bird with R&B mainstays like Robert Ealey. A slinky ingenue who exudes sexuality like cigarette smoke, Barton relocated to Austin and garnered a quick reputation as a bawdy, power-throated white chick who could wail and moan in the finest lascivious tradition of Big Mama Thornton and Janis Joplin.

She sang for both the Fabulous Thunderbirds and the Triple Threat Revue before striking out as a solo artist. In 1982, she recorded her major label debut, *Old Enough*, on Asylum. Despite strong reviews, Barton's propensity for drink and all things bacchanalian frightened the record company, and she soon found herself back in Austin. When Antone's formed their label, Barton was one of the first acts signed.

They rereleased *Old Enough*, and she's since recorded *Read My Lips* (1989) for the label, both of which are gin-marinated roadhouse *tours de force*. Barton also teamed up with Strehli and Ball for 1991's *Dreams Come True*. Though her career has definitely been affected by her well-publicized troubles with drink, Barton has reportedly dried up and remains a breathtaking talent.

Angela Strehli was born in Lubbock in 1947 and grew up in a heartland of country music, sneaking late-night hits of raw blues out of Louisiana radio stations. After soaking up a bit of music-biz reality in Chicago and L.A., she returned to Texas to finish college and found herself in Austin as the first lady of the new blues vortex.

She formed the group Southern Feeling (with W. C. Clark and Denny Freeman) and, with her intelligent good looks and a warm, emotive voice, Strehli became the leading female presence in Austin R&B. When Clifford Antone opened his club, she immediately offered her services in a variety of capacities from stage manager to heading up the company record label.

With her acclaimed Angela Strehli Band she released the seductive *Soul Shake* in 1987, followed a few years later by the collaboration with Barton and Ball. Seeking fresh inspiration, Strehli moved to San Francisco, and has since released two sturdy albums, *Blonde and Blue* (Rounder, 1993) and *Deja Blue* (A&M, 1998).

W. C. Clark and Denny Freeman

A native of East Austin, Clark grew up in a musical family and naturally gravitated to the black blues scene flourishing in the neighborhood.

Clark played bass and then guitar with artists like T. D. Bell, Erbie Bowser, Grey Ghost, and L. P. Pierson in landmark joints like the Victory Grill and Charley's Playhouse. When thrill-seeking UT kids began heading into East Austin on weekends to hear the blues, a tiny crack in Austin's segregated musical wall began to open.

By the time Clark had served a stint on the road as guitarist for Joe Tex and returned to Texas, white guitarist Bill Campbell had become somewhat of a fixture in the East Side blues bars. And when Jimmie Vaughan showed up, bringing the likes of Angela Strehli, Denny Freeman, and brother Stevie, a variety of biracial precedents were established.

The multifaceted Clark, whose R&B, soul, and straight blues machinations were blueprint prototypes of style, played first with Strehli and Freeman in Southern Feeling, then joined up with the older Vaughan in Storm. But Storm wasn't exactly a blizzard of income and Clark took a gig as a mechanic, a job at which he was happy and is particularly adept.

But Stevie Vaughan felt a spiritual kinship with Clark—and the feeling was mutual—so the younger Vaughan kept hanging around the garage and bugging Clark while he was trying to work. Eventually, when Clark couldn't get rid of the kid, the two formed Stevie Vaughan's Triple Threat Revue with Lou Ann Barton, traveled Texas and the Southeast, and were particularly significant in fanning the flames of Blues Awareness at Antone's.

But when Stevie's substance abuse problems began to increase, Clark peeled off and formed the W. C. Clark Blues Revue, an act with which he still tours. Clark's inimitable solo work is best found on two later CDs, 1994's *Heart of Gold* and 1996's *Texas Soul* (both on Black Top). Despite recent familial tragedy, Clark stays strong musically. A new CD, *Lover's Plea*, is a wise and reflective project.

Though blues guitarist Denny Freeman claims he was "cheated out of being born on Texas soil," it was merely a scheduling misunderstanding. His parents had him in Hillsboro soon enough, and he grew up in Dallas playing teen surf tunes in garage bands.

He shifted focus to blues and, as part of the musical exodus from Dallas to Austin that included the Vaughan brothers, Freeman found the simmering scene invigorating. He played with Stevie Ray in Paul Ray and the Cobras, then in Angela Strehli's band and, by the early eighties, found himself heading up Antone's house band. It was a dream gig in which Freeman found himself backing up an encyclopedic variety of blues pioneers: Ted Taylor, Jimmy Reed, Lazy Lester, Albert Collins, Fathead Newman, Little Johnny Taylor . . .

Freeman's own brand of exotic and well-seasoned blues worked particularly well, and his reputation grew exponentially as a player who could flesh out sound as much as support artists. And though being the lead player in Antone's house band was a position drooled over by guitarists across the solar system, by 1985 Freeman wanted to record his own material.

He released *Blues Cruise* in 1986 and *Out of the Blue* in 1987, both instrumental records on the Amazing label (both are now out of print). While blues-based, Freeman laid down a warm and technically amazing smorgasbord of shuffles, slow blues, jazz, rock, and soul tunes.

After relocating to L.A., Freeman's toured and recorded with Jimmie Vaughan, toured Australia with his own band, and just finished recording a new album (for which he's actively searching for a new label).

If Barton was the bad girl of the Austin blues scene and Strehli its home-coming queen, then Marcia Ball was surely its student council president and head cheerleader. A piano-pounding explosion of talent from Orange, Texas, who grew up in the backwoods of Louisiana, Ball moved to Austin in 1970 and quickly blew the walls of skepticism down as a progressive country artist in Freda and the Firedogs. But drawn to the sound of New Orleans blues and amazed by the blues scene developing in Austin, Ball began to carve out a niche as a singular stylist.

A willowy, pretty woman with the soul of Irma Thomas, legs like Tina Turner, and the piano chops of Professor Longhair, Ball's Cajun-soaked R&B is at once simmering, joyous, adventurous, and reverent. After years haunting clubs like Antone's as well as New Orleans' JazzFest, Ball signed with Rounder Records and, in 1978, released *Circuit Queen*, an ill-advised attempt by Capitol Records to fuse her R&B propensities with progressive country.

She then hooked up with Rounder in 1983, and has subsequently released a chain of smokin' albums sandwiched around *Dreams Come True* (1983's *Soulful Dress*, 1986's *Hot Tamale Baby*, 1989's, *Gatorhythms*, 1994's winning *Blue House*, and 1997's *Let Me Play with Your Poodle*). Ball has since relocated to Houston, but continues to frequent Antone's, both with her own band and to reunite with old pals Strehli and Barton. In a reunion of even greater significance, Ball teamed up with some other old friends, Tracy Nelson and New Orleans R&B vodoun Thomas, for a magical 1998 CD for Rounder called *Sing It!* Also that year, Ball won the W. C. Handy Contemporary Blues Female Artist of the year. She's a national treasure.

A fourth Austin blues diva is noteworthy. Toni Price, whose Tuesday night "Hippie Hour" shows at the Continental Club are perhaps the coolest things in Austin, is a legitimate blues-rock force. As prolific as she is good, Price's catalogue (*Low Down and Up, Sol Power, Hey,* and *Swim Away*) are worth investigating.

Other stalwarts from those heady days in Austin were, of course, the Fabulous Thunderbirds, who've carried on successfully even after Jimmie Vaughan jumped ship. Harmonica king Kim Wilson, who also served as the group's singer and main songwriter, was born in Detroit and grew up in California. A lifelong disciple of R&B and blues, and in particular harpist Little Walter, Wilson was working in Minnesota when he was brought down to record an all-star project with various Austin blues stars.

Wilson shortly hooked up with Stevie Vaughan and Doyle Bramhall, and was subsequently introduced to Jimmie Vaughan, who was still in the Storm. Though Wilson returned to Minnesota, the Storm eventually broke up and Jimmie Vaughan persuaded Wilson to move to Austin permanently, and to help him form a new band he'd envisioned to play at a new blues club that was opening as a sort of musical shelter for Austin's bluesy homeless: Antone's.

With the addition of an eccentric but truly excellent Houston bassist named Keith Ferguson, and Vaughan's old compadre Mike Buck on drums, the Fabulous Thunderbirds, as Jimmie's dream act was called (and as has been discussed earlier in this chapter), took off. Though Ferguson exited after the *T-Bird Rhythm* album and was replaced by Preston Hubbard, and Fran Christina eventually replaced Buck, the band carried on with Wilson and Vaughan at the helm until 1990, when even Vaughan became disenchanted and split.

Wilson thought the band still had momentum; it was, after all, his virtuoso harp, sinewy, low-rider vocals, and skewed, greasy take on R&B (as much as Jimmie's guitar) that gave the T-Birds their distinctive sound. Two New England guitarists, Roomful of Blues founder Duke Robillard and Doug "the Kid" Bangham, replaced Vaughan for 1991's *Walk That Walk, Talk That Talk*.

As the group's momentum waned, Wilson signed as a solo artist with Antone's, and has released two CDs, 1993's *Tigerman* and 1994's *That's Life*. Wilson remains the glue behind the T-Birds, who've continued to shuffle record labels and personnel through water-treading CDs like *Different Tacos* (Country Town) and *High Water* (High Street).

NO DESCRIPTION OF THAT MAGICAL TIME PERIOD WOULD BE complete without mention of the guys who were most important in helping Stevie Ray Vaughan become the ultrastud he became. The essential Double Trouble rhythm section of Tommy Shannon on bass and Chris Layton on drums were metronomic cohorts to SRV's success (though the original Double Trouble consisted of vocalist Barton, sax man Johnny Reno, bassist Jackie Newhouse, and drummer Freddie Pharoah); they were also stalwart companions and remain active and monster musicians. Shannon had played with Johnny Winter in his early CBS days, and Layton, who'd come to Austin to play in the progressive country act Greezy Wheels, came aboard after the usual six or seven dozen personnel changes, and after their arrivals, SRV never looked back. In later years, B3 organ wizard Reece Wynans, a veteran of Texas music for years, was hired on to thicken the band's sound.

But still, without the compositional skills of Fort Worth drummer/vocalist Doyle Bramhall, Stevie Vaughan and Double Trouble would not have been the same. Bramhall, who grew up in another Dallas suburb, Irving, was one of Stevie's oldest friends and had been part of that first contingency to move to Austin. A ruggedly handsome man with a killer voice most blues fans would swear couldn't come out of a white boy's throat, Bramhall was a highly sought-after talent. His drums chops were impeccable, and his way with a melody and lyrics was far more clever than that of the average blues songwriter.

He'd first recruited Jimmie Vaughan to play in the Chessmen, then bounced around with the Nightcrawlers, Al "TNT" Braggs, Texas Storm, and a variety of plum gigs until drug problems curtailed much of his professional activity.

In an effort to clean up, Bramhall moved back to Dallas–Fort Worth and for the next several years worked with Freddie King and Johnny Reno before starting his own band. Every Double Trouble album featured at least one Bramhall song, and when Stevie joined Bramhall in sobriety, the songs they wrote together were particularly sparkling ("Caught in the Crossfire," "Wall of Denial," and "Tightrope," for example).

Bramhall, who continues to head up his own band, now lives in Wimberley in the Texas hill country, and records for the Antone's label.

Other significant players from that era include drummers George Rains, Rodney Craig, and Uncle John Turner, keyboardist Mike Kindred, guitarists Bill Campbell, Derek O'Brien, Lubbock's Jesse "Guitar" Taylor, Matthew Robinson, and Mark Pollack (whose forays into rockabilly didn't obscure his blues guitar acumen), vocalist Paul Ray, and, though he's not a musician, Clifford Antone, without whose namesake club and subsequent record label the entire scene would not have existed or prospered.

Austin continues to be a hotbed of blues activity, and in that kooky way of time, a new generation of devotees has carried on the tradition. Vocalist Kari Leigh (who also authored a biography of Stevie Ray Vaughan), Toni Price, writer/harpist/singer Gary Primich, and organist Eric Scortia are all talented, as are the Holy Moellers, a twin-guitar blues machine out of Denton that frequents the state's hallowed blues halls. Omar and the Howlers is the band that probably best exemplifies the transitional musical unit between the two generations.

Guitarist Kent "Omar" Dykes, whose gargling-with-powdered-glass voice is as distinctive as his beef stew blues/rock and his linebacker physique, grew up in Mississippi playing in black juke joints despite his status as a white schoolboy.

He honed a Jimmy Reed and Bo Diddley sing Creedence sound, and in the mid-seventies moved to Austin with the first of an ever-changing set of backing Howlers. After a few indie label releases, the band scored a major label deal with Columbia/CBS and released two respectfully received albums, 1987's *Hard Times in the Land of Plenty* and the following year's *Wall of Pride*.

Though Dykes couldn't sustain the sales required by a major label, he's managed to keep recording with respectable outfits such as Rounder (*Courts of Lulu*), Black Top (*Swingland*), and Watermelon (*Muddy Springs Road* and *World Wide Open*).

Guitarist/vocalist Sue Foley, a transplanted Canadian whose testicular style belies her petite, Rickie Lee Jonesesque appearance, is one of the finest of the younger blues fiends. Clifford Antone saw her playing in Memphis, was astounded at the her skills, and lured her to Austin. She slid smoothly into the live music scene, signed with the Antone's label and, in 1992, released her debut album, *Young Girl Blues*.

The twenty-six-year-old subsequently toured with Buddy Guy, George Thorogood, Koko Taylor, and John Mayall, and continues to build a sturdy career with such CDs as *10 Days in November*, *Walk in the Sun*, and *Without a Warning*.

Chris Duarte is the latest heir-apparent of the Stevie Ray Vaughan crown—and if there's a criticism of his work, it's that Duarte is a bit *too* derivative of SRV's sound. He was born in San Antonio, got into jazz and rock guitar, and quit school to head to Austin and sharpen his guitar skills. It was there that he immersed himself in blues—and heroin.

Duarte had the good sense to get away from bad habits, and spent two years in New England refining his technique and regaining his health. Having exhausted the blues possibilities of the Northeast, he returned to Austin, formed the Chris Duarte Band, and signed a contract with Silvertone Records. As *Texas Sugar/Strat Magik*, his 1994 debut, demonstrates, there are plenty of volcanic and rhythmic surprises to go along with his Vaughan-flavored music.

The CD sold over one hundred thousand units, and Duarte, now in his early thirties, started popping up on major tours and in readers' polls in various guitar magazines. As his style continues to evolve and Duarte develops his own identity, his future as a Texas guitar legend is virtually assured.

One more Austin guitarist should be mentioned. Alan Haynes, who left his hometown of Houston to glean the Austin vibe, is a remarkably fleet stylist with a keen slide style reminiscent of early Johnny Winter. He made his mark in Austin with his first group, Alan Haynes and His Stepchildren, then progressed to solo act status. His debut album, 1995's *Wishing Well*, released on Austin's Focus label, is a treat.

Two young Austin blues guitarists to keep an eye on are Jake Andrews, a massively hyped talent whose *Time to Burn* CD shows prowess, and Mike Keller.

Three Dallas-based guitarists are particularly fine: Lucky Peterson, Anson Funderburgh, and Smokin' Joe Kubek. Peterson is a Buffalo, NY–born multi-instrumentalist who is as good on keyboards as he is on guitar—and that's damned good. A child prodigy (Willie Dixon produced Peterson's first single when the kid was *five*), he was leading Little Milton's band at seventeen and moved soon thereafter to Bobby Blue Bland's group.

A stunningly fast player with appropriate nods to space and a stinging mournful tone, Peterson was destined to branch into a solo career. Thus far, two CDs, *Lucky Strikes* and *Triple Play*, indicate he's a giant in the making.

Funderburgh looks like a soda jerk out of an "Archie" comic book, but his clean, quicksilver guitar has been, with his backing group the Rockets, a staple of Texas blues for fifteen years. The band has recorded for Black Top Records for years, and when older Mississippi blues legend Sam Myers (whose drum work, vocals, and harmonica are the stuff of Delta Blues legend) signed on, the dichotomous relationship became one of the most fruitful relationships in Texas blues.

My Love Is Here to Stay (1986), *Tell Me What I Want to Hear* (1991), and a greatest hits package, *Thru the Years: A Retrospective (1981–92)* are recommended samplings.

Smokin' Joe Kubek, who was playing chitlin circuit gigs by the time he was fourteen (and stopped just long enough for a brief flirtation with Top 40 rock in the seventies), is a brooding, hulking stage master with corn-colored hair and a penetrating, Freddie King style. In the same biracial format favored by Funderburgh and Myers, Kubek's band features black vocalist/rhythm guitarist B'nois King, a Monroe, Louisiana native with a soulful, searing set of vocal chords.

The band signed with the Bullseye Blues/Rounder label in 1991, and *Steppin' Out Texas Style* (1991) and *Texas Cadillac* are strident, capable examples of fiery Texas blues/rock.

Other Dallas blues acts of note include Mike Morgan and the Crawl, Pat Boyack and the Prowlers, Cold Blue Steel, the Pawn Kings, drummer/singer Mercy Baby, and guitarists Mark Pollack, Hash Brown, David Brown, and Henry Qualls, an Elmo native whose country blues are a throwback to the days of Blind Lemon Jefferson.

Qualls is typical of a small group of blues stylists who represent the old school, and somehow its members have essentially escaped the fame and respect they deserve. Dallas pianist/vocalist Big Al Dupree is a wonderful and talented man who spent years in elegant supper clubs playing Gershwin and Cole Porter tunes for diners more concerned with their crème brûlée than with the musical genius in their midst.

Now in his seventies, the Dallas native has played with a scrapbook collection of spectacular blues artists, ranging from T-Bone Walker to Ike Turner, and has developed over the years a warm and magical vocal style to complement his extremely wicked swing, jazz, and barrelhouse piano

More Criminally Overlooked Guitarists

John Campbell

☆

Not surprisingly, Texas blues guitar is not strictly an Austin phenomenon. John Campbell, who was born in Shreveport and reared in East Texas, was a white guitarist of vibrant and compelling ability with a tortured, haunting body of work.

Campbell's legacy will probably be the closest thing the young blues dudes have to a Robert Johnson/Satan legend. An intense artist whose lyrics, stage setting, and CD covers were rife with the paraphernalia of voodoo, Campbell's driven guitar and mouthful-of-graveyard-dirt vocals were positively creepy but absolutely riveting.

His first album, *A Man and His Blues,* was released on the German Crosscut label and nominated for a 1989 W. C. Handy Award. This led to an American major label deal with Elektra. *One Believer* (1991) was a strident and much-lauded record, and the encore, 1993's *Howlin' Mercy,* is simply one of the best modern blues albums ever made. A disturbing, wailing, driven record obsessed with images of *gris-gris,* High John the Conqueror, evil and decay, the record would have come off like a sort of blues version of death metal if it weren't so vibrant and authentic.

Howlin' Mercy was incredibly promising, but the forty-one-year-old Campbell suffered an unexpected and fatal heart attack—and rumors that the artist was deeply involved with voodoo and drugs can only nurture his eerie legend.

Jim Suhler

☆

Dallas's dry-witted Suhler was not a normal kid. He immersed himself in the music of Charlie Patton, Robert Johnson, Magic Sam, Freddie King, T-Bone Walker, and Tampa Red. At twelve, he realized his chances at being a number 1 draft pick in the National Football League were remote and began studying guitar in earnest. After a brief flirtation with southern rock (in which he played in a Lynyrd Skynyrd copy band), Suhler began following his own muse. He backed blues greats Zuzu Bollin and Son Thomas, then formed his own R&B-tinged rock bands, the Road Hogs and then the Home Wreckers.

When the Home Wreckers self-destructed, Suhler assembled a new trio, Monkey Beat, whose demo drew the attention of producer/engineer Terry Manning (George Thorogood, ZZ Top, Led Zeppelin, Johnny Winter). Man-

(continued)

ning loved Suhler's songs, his madcap stage presence, utterly raw style and demon slide playing, and signed Monkey Beat to his Lucky 7/Rounder label. The band put out *Radio Mojo* (1993) and *Shake* (1995), and have toured the United States and Europe twice. Suhler is working on a third album and has toured as the lead guitarist for George Thoroughgood.

Bugs Henderson

If the music industry is indeed a battlefield, then the major label fruitcakes who have passed on Bugs Henderson in favor of far less talented guitarists are guilty of war crimes. Because Henderson, a gnomic fellow with a flare for expensive stage wear (tank top, gym shorts, barefoot), is guitardom's Unknown Soldier.

Born in California, the guitarist moved to East Texas in the fifties and hooked up with the archetypical Texas puck outfit, Mouse and the Traps. But his super-twister approach to rock, surf, R&B, rockabilly, and country— all trussed in a vintage blues wrapping—made him a valuable commodity. He played briefly in Nitzinger (appearing on 1973's Capitol release *One Foot in History*) before taking the advice of poker buddy Freddie King and branching out on his own.

Since then, as an SRO draw in clubs across the United States, Henderson has released several successful indie albums, including *Have Blues...Must Rock, Daredevils of the Red Guitar*, and *That's the Truth*.

It was *Guitar Player* that called Henderson "a national treasure," and it remains a critical assessment absolutely devoid of hyperbole.

maneuverings. Though he's played professionally since he was thirteen, it was only in 1995 that Dallas Blues Society Records signed Dupree, and *Swings the Blues* is an affectionate and spirited voyage through a sea of jump blues of the Les Hite, Eddie "Cleanhead" Vinson, Louis Jordan variety. Though it was sixty-some-odd years coming, *Swings the Blues* will hopefully be only the first of a substantial body of work for Big Al Dupree.

Long John Hunter is another journeyman blues musician whose remarkable talent was all but ignored for decades. The guitarist, who was born in Louisiana in 1931 and learned guitar while working in a Beaumont factory, signed a deal early on with Don Robey's Duke Records—a deal Hunter claims was nothing more than an effort by the mogul to keep the guitarist from competing with his more established artists.

Understandably bitter, Hunter played in a variety of road bands and ended up in self-exile in El Paso. He played for thirteen years in Juárez's Lobby Bar, gradually developing a style so uniquely . . . *Hunter*, that his blues could never be mistaken for anyone else's. He finally relocated to the oil town of Midland—not exactly a blues mecca—and after a few recording efforts turned out to be dry holes, he finally secured a deal with Alligator Records.

Border Town Blues (1995) is a boogie-drenched autobiography of Hunter's peculiar and somehow excellent life as a bluesman. In 1999, Hunter reunited with guitarist Ervin Charles (in the fifties, the two played together in a Port Arthur band called the Hollywood Bearcats) and two other PA blues veterans, Lonnie Brooks and Phillip Walker, for a pumped-up session of refinery-country soul-blues called *Lone Star Shootout* (Alligator).

Fort Worth's Robert Ealey is Cowtown's lord-on-high of Texas blues. Born in 1924 in Texarkana, Ealey sang gospel as a kid even as he studied Frankie Lee Sims, Lightnin' Hopkins, and T-Bone Walker. He moved to Dallas and began singing and dancing in R&B-style shows, then moved to Fort Worth to form the Boogie Chillen Boys.

When he bought the Bluebird nightclub, a legendary juke joint sautéed in barbecue smoke, draft beer, and serious soul music, he rechristened it the New Bluebird and formed one of Texas's first and greatest of the multiracial classic R&B bands: Robert Ealey and the Five Careless Lovers. In addition to their hometown gig, they began to hit Austin, competing admirably with their Austin brethren, though they were happy to hang in Fort Worth, just to let the rest of the state know how bad-ass they were. The club also regularly hosted a new crop of hot musicians including Gerald Dailey, Freddie "Little Junior One-Hand" Cisneros and the Blasting Caps, Joe Jonas, the Bruton Brothers (Sumter and Stephen), and several of the soon-to-be Austin heroes like Lou Ann Barton, Mike Buck, and Johnny Reno.

Ealey, in addition to his own gigs, also did time with the Juke Jumpers, a band formed by Sumter Bruton, Jim Colgrove, Mike Buck, and Jack Newhouse (the latter two of whom would shortly head for success with Jimmie and Stevie Vaughan, respectively). Ealey has recorded sporadically, and his recent Black Top release, *Turn Out the Lights*, is certainly recommended.

Sumter Bruton, with Ealey a grand ambassador of Texas music, is a middle-aged white guy, one of the preeminent practitioners of swing blues guitar playing in the world today. He grew up fascinated with T-Bone Walker and ultimately developed and mastered a buttery, jazz-flavored guitar style that is nothing short of awe-inducing.

Bruton and the Juke Jumpers—which was essentially the Fabulous Thunderbirds before there was a Fabulous Thunderbirds—ruled the Fort Worth blues scene for years, but their sedentary ways precluded much growth in the fan base department. When the Juke Jumpers eventually petered out, Bruton decided to pursue a different dream.

Along with movie critic/fellow T-Bone nut/piano madman Michael Price, Bruton began in 1993 to record a genuine, steeped-in-the-forties blues classic, *Swingmasters Revue*. Finally released in 1995 on their own label, *Swingmasters Revue* is a loving and authentic tribute to the time of T-Bone—and a small and too easily overlooked bit of Texas blues.

CRIMINALLY OVERLOOKED GUITARIST
Jesse "Guitar" Taylor

Consider the rich musical legacy of Lubbock—and then remember that Jesse "Guitar" Taylor probably played lead guitar on just about any rock or blues band that's come out of the plains city for the past quarter-decade.

A friendly bear of a guy with a lifelong pompadour and a love for Texas music in all of its forms, Taylor is a wonderful stylist whose rock excitability is tempered by a melancholic sense of loneliness whenever he attacks more blues-based material. As a session player who's worked with Terry Allen, Marcia Ball, Jimmie Dale Gilmore, and Kimmie Rhodes, to name a select few, Taylor is probably best known as the off and on lead guitarist in Joe Ely's road band. His live work in that group's latest incarnation is effectively gritty and contrapuntal to fellow axman Teye's flamenco lines, and provides an appropriate Lone Star blues underpinning to Ely's quilt-work tunes.

Taylor is gradually establishing a solo reputation, too. A 1999 release, *Texas Tattoo*, follows a terrific and greasy roadhouse disc called *Last Night*.

Much of the Ely band, including Donald Lindley and Glenn Fukunaga, backed up Taylor on *Texas Tattoo*, and the Hancock-penned "Naked Light of Day" featured background vocals from Gilmore, Hancock, and Ely.

Other Fort Worth–area legends who rose to local prominence in the seventies and on include Ray "Linda Lu" Sharpe, Big Bo and the Arrows, Curly "Barefoot" Miller, and U. P. Wilson, whose immense popularity in Europe centers around the fact that, on a good night, he's one of the best pure blues guitarists around.

Finally, if it seems the Houston area has been ignored, it's more that, despite its prodigious quantity of juke-joint heroes before the Vaughan Era, the scene since that time has not been particularly fruitful.

Rocky "Yeah, for the Last Time, I'm the Guy in ZZ Top's Brother" Hill is a sparkling if reclusive blues guitarist of note, while Joey Long, a half-Mexican/half-white legend, was a major influence on Johnny Winter. Pete Mayes, who was born between Houston and Beaumont, is a gifted stylist, and younger Turks Mark May (Allman Brothers) and Texas Johnny Brown are pretty nice players.

☆ Part 4: Folksingers and Songwriters

☆ One: Early Folksters and the Seventies Archivists

THE EASIEST THING IN THE WORLD TO BE BAD AT IS FOLK-singing. This is not the fault of folk music, per se, though it is the "solo performer" aspect of it that makes it accessible to any kook with a guitar, a rhyming dictionary, and a cause.

In fact, it is the "message" aspect of the folk song which is the part that's easy to screw up. And for every Woody Guthrie, Phil Ochs, or Pete Seeger who stirred the downtrodden or abused with their plaintive songs and simple acoustic accompaniment, there are hundreds more who remind us of the guy in *Animal House,* the simpering fellow strumming his guitar on the staircase of the Delta house. And when Bluto, the John Belushi character, shatters the folkie's instrument, it's the most celebrated destruction of a guitar since Hendrix first set fire to his Strat at Finsbury Park in March of 1967.

But while we exult *with* Hendrix, we sympathize with Bluto *against* the folkie. And the reason for that is our natural inclination to shudder at the thought of another folk song telling us to spare whales or citrus-field workers. Whales and citrus-field workers *should* be spared—at least most of them—but we know that. We don't need any more beret-clad people in coffeehouses whose knowledge of the guitar does not extend beyond D, C, and G chords telling us.

But folk music doesn't have to be preachy. And it wasn't back at the beginning, unless one counts the noted pro-labor anthem "Turkey in the Straw."

Like many of our musical forms, folk was what happened when a variety of cultures collided. The music of these cultures documented their travails and celebrated their passions, but, inevitably, it was the music of the uprooted and the migratory.

In the early days of Texas, there was a strong Mexican ballad and *corrido* tradition melding Spanish and Indian romanticism with the plight of those flowing across the Rio Grande, desperate for opportunity. Several communities of European immigrants formed in central Texas—chiefly German or

Czech, but Cajun, Scandinavian, and Italian as well—and the hill country rang with the centuries-old, keyboard-rich songs of the Homeland(s). The bulk of the Anglo settlers in Texas, though, came from other southern states, bringing with them early hillbilly music and their ancestors' traditional songs from the British Isles. Also from the Deep South came the varied and heartfelt blues of the freed slaves, sharecroppers, and indentured servants settled throughout Texas, not to mention the trail songs of the migratory cowboys and buffalo hunters.

This was all the music of people struggling to build new lives in the Texas terrain, and in the music's diversity were the common threads of subjugation, freedom, oppression, and hope. It was inescapable, then, that, despite differences among people, their music would mix together and result in a new, universal hybrid: folk music as we know it.

Like a lot of the prototypical country-and-western music, the early Texas folk songs were simply older songs—sea chanties or working tunes, with the lyrics changed to reflect situations indigenous to the new Texas experience. "The Eyes of Texas," for example, is nothing more than "I've Been Working on the Railroad."

Eventually, though, songsmiths began penning their own material. It is pretty much accepted that the first folk song written in Texas was Mary Holley's "The Brazos Boat Song," written in 1831, and the first Texas folk song to gain national popularity was "The Yellow Rose of Texas." Emerging from the great body of slave songs, "The Yellow Rose of Texas" is about Emily Morgan, the black girl who supposedly distracted General Santa Anna at the Battle of San Jacinto.

The popularity of folk music began to grow and a body of independent work evolved to supplement the existing traditional material. By the early twentieth century, when an actual phonograph industry had taken root, and people bought actual records, Texas folk musicians began to draw national attention. San Antonio's Oscar Fox was the first Texas folk songwriter to score a big-time reputation (not to mention a deal with a New York music publisher). Among the hundreds of songs Fox composed were "Corn Silks and Cotton Blossoms" and "The Hills of Home."

The most prolific of the early folkies, though, was Ballinger's David Guion. He had enormous success not only with his own compositions ("What Shall We Do with a Drunken Sailor," "Ol' Paint," "Ride Cowboy Ride") but as a surgeon on preexisting stuff. It was Guion's take on "The Yellow Rose of Texas" that became a huge seller in the 1930s, and his new lyrics and/or arrangements on familiar tunes like "Home on the Range" and "Arkansas Traveler" further cemented his reputation as a folk innovator and archivist.

Still, folk didn't become a musical force in Texas until about the time of the Cuban missile crisis. With the emergence of country music and its subdivision into genres like honky-tonk and western swing, those musicians who might've been inclined to create "folk" music were probably sucked into the C&W tornado. Besides, there were no coffeehouses to speak of during those World War II and postwar years, only taverns—which, until the last twenty years or so, seemed anathema to the "John Henry was a steel-drivin' man" mentality.

By the early sixties, after the Kennedy assassination and when it became apparent that the Vietnam War was going to be something in excess of a small military exercise in Indochina, the country began to ripple with unrest. Folk activists like Pete Seeger, Lee Hays, and Peter, Paul and Mary began rejuvenating the mostly forgotten folk concept and sang songs that fired the imaginations of various bohemians and distraught college kids. And when Bob Dylan took folk out of the coffeehouses and into the rock clubs (when he went electric at Newport in 1965), the lines of demarcation between rock and folk blurred considerably. Suddenly, folk music was not only popular again, it was marginally hip.

Carolyn Hester, who was born in Waco in 1937, was Texas's first major folksinger. A student of the Old Folk style whose early repertoire emphasized treasured and archival folk material, Hester started playing in Austin clubs and quickly graduated to headline status working the national folk circuit in the sixties. Signed to Dot Records on the basis of her rich, where-eagles-dare-to-fly voice and genuine commitment to tradition, Hester released *That's My Song* (1964) to national critical adulation. She encored with a set of live albums in 1965 (which are available from Bear Family on one set called *At Town Hall*).

By that point, Hester had begun to write a bit of her own material and to cover more contemporary folkies like Bob Dylan. She remained a mainstay in folk clubs and became the traditional headliner at the Kerrville Folk Festival upon its inception twenty-five years ago. Though Hester grew a bit reclusive in later years, she'll occasionally venture forth to remind the youngsters what real folk is all about.

El Paso's Phil Ochs (born in 1940), who grew up in Queens and had stints in military school and journalism school to ignite his antiwar sensibilities, moved to Greenwich Village in 1961 and became a folksinger. His anger and delivery matched Dylan's (though he lacked the latter's talent), and through the sheer militancy of his material he carved out a significant niche in the folksinger-as-protester arena. He wrote two antiwar classics, "I Ain't Marching" and "Draft Dodger Rag" (both from the 1965 A&M album *I Ain't Marching Anymore*).

His artistic peak was probably on 1967's *Pleasures of the Harbor* LP (A&M), but despite a few more successes with increasingly tired antiwar rhetoric, Ochs became more and more disillusioned with his own role as a rebel. He traveled extensively, and on one excursion in Africa his vocal chords were severely damaged in an obscurely detailed assault. For that and many other reasons, his depression deepened and, in 1975, he hanged himself.

Several other Texan folk artists achieved varying degrees of notoriety and success in the sixties. John Deutschendorf, aka John Denver, a Roswell, New Mexico native who grew up in Fort Worth and who attended Texas Tech in Lubbock, served a musical apprenticeship in the Chad Mitchell Trio, which was a big early-sixties draw on the hootenanny circuit. (The late Denver later became an easy-listening supernova; see the "Music My Parents Like" chapter.)

Similarly, country-schmaltz king Kenny Rogers spent a year-and-a-half as a folkie in the New Christy Minstrels (long enough to appear on their ludicrous, time-warped *New Kick! The New Christy Minstrels Sing the Hits of Today and Tomorrow*, a 1967 Columbia release) before forming his rock band, the First Edition.

Another country music hero, Floydada's Don Williams, presaged his stardom by moving to Corpus Christi and forming a folk trio called the Pozo Seco Singers (along with Susan Taylor and Lofton Kline). They recorded three hit singles for Columbia Records, 1965's "Time" and, the following year, "I Can Make It with You" and "Look What You've Done." The group stayed together until 1971, but no further chart successes were forthcoming.

Trini Lopez, the Dallas singer/actor who would score big with the Top 40 song "Lemon Tree," also had a smash hit with his 1963 rendition of the folk standard "If I Had a Hammer" before he segued his career into the adult contemporary arena.

One Texan who played a significant role in making "folk" legitimately "groovy" was Shawn Phillips. Born in Fort Worth in 1943 of creative and traveling parentage (by the age of thirteen, it was easier to list places in our world young Shawn *hadn't* lived than places he had), Phillips grew up with myriad experiences and influences radically outside the norm.

He naturally gravitated to the guitar and, landing in England in 1963, made his first folk record for Capitol, *First Impressions*. It sold poorly, and although he was dropped from the label, he spent the next six years in a variety of activities which, in hindsight, are of rather scrapbook quality: taught Joni Mitchell the nuances of twelve-string guitar, cowrote Donovan's "Sunshine Superman," roomed with Tim Hardin, hung out with the Beatles and Moody Blues and became the original lead singer for the Broadway production of *Jesus Christ Superstar*.

Finally, in 1969, Phillips caught the ear of A&M Records chief Jerry Moss, who was intrigued by Phillips's ability to inject jazz, rock, and orchestral elements into the folk form. With his low, intense voice, waist-length hair, and quasi-mystical lyrical forays, Phillips would become a rather unique commodity for the post-Woodstock marketplace.

Over the next decade, Phillips released several LPs for A&M on a roughly annual basis, including *Contribution*, *Second Contribution*, *Collaboration*, *Faces*, *Bright White*, *Furthermore*, *Do You Wonder*, *Rumplestiltskin's Resolve*, and *Spaced*—which included charted singles in "Woman," "Bright White," "We," and the theme song for the film *Lost Horizon*.

Phillips, substantially woven into the hallucinatory fringe of the vast drug tapestry of the time, also wandered the vague, incense-cloaked corridors of Eastern mysticism. As such, his commercial appeal, as the seventies begat the Disco Age in the music business, was barely quantifiable.

Phillips now lives in Austin and, though he continues to write music and tour overseas to substantially appreciative crowds, he remains bitter and all but neglected in his homeland. His biggest crime lay in the fact that his music was always too challenging and creative. Think of him as the gentle giant of folk music.

BY THE EARLY SEVENTIES, WHEN AUSTIN GAVE BIRTH TO THE progressive country movement which would alter the face of both country and western and rock, folksingers began the subtle evolution that would result in the tag "singer/songwriter."

Austin was quickly establishing itself as the heart of all things musical at that point, a reputation that certainly included the singer/songerwriter movement. An enterprising bar owner/folk enthusiast named Ken Threadgill was influential. His gas station–turned–beer bar would be a home-away-from-dorm for two generations of UT music lovers. Threadgill and his own new-folk outfit, the Hootenanny Hoots, made noise on the national scene, and Threadgill's is of course famous for giving Janis Joplin her first real club exposure. Joplin frequently appeared with Lanny Wiggins and Powell St. John (who were soon to be semifamous as members of a rock/soul outfit called Mother Earth with another ex-folkie, Tracy Nelson).

Too, Austin was beginning to fill up with singer/songwriters like Jerry Jeff Walker and B. W. Stevenson—most of whom would evolve into "progressive country artists." One of that bunch, though, Bobby Bridger, stayed most true to his folkie roots. Born in East Texas and raised in Louisiana, Bridger was a folk ballad researcher, high school teacher, and amateur guitarist/songwriter when he decided that being a professional musician sounded a lot more interesting than being a career educator. Armed with an innocuously pretty voice and a committed way with a folk narrative, Bridger relocated to the Austin music community he'd heard so much about and released two erudite RCA albums, 1970's *Merging of Our Minds* and the 1972 encore, *I Just Wanted to Sing for the People*. Even with the reefer-swayed country movement unfolding around him, Bridger remained fervent in his folkist beliefs. A conceptual LP called *Jim Bridger and the Seekers of the Fleece*, based on an obscure Old West true story involving Indians, beaver trappers, a Calvinist minister, and grizzly bears, was deemed too arcane by RCA, though, and Bridger was left without a major label deal— which, in the long run, he probably preferred.

Austin's folk scene was terrifically enhanced by Walt Hyatt, whose Uncle Walt's Band was a comforting, everybody's-big-brother presence on the whole musical scene. The band was comprised of Hyatt, Champ Hood, and David Ball, a triumvirate of engaging personalities whose effervescent songs mixed happy-hour jazz, blues, and country. Their collective acoustic instrumental prowess was the stuff of music school faculties, and when they sang, their blended harmonies were weep-inducing. Uncle Walt's Band was spawned of the same genesis that brought on the whole Armadillo prog-country community.

They recorded several long out-of-print albums during the seventies, moved to Nashville in 1978 for a fruitful five-year tenure, then finally broke up for the inevitable solo pursuits. A fan of the group, Lyle Lovett (for whom UWB sang background on the song "Once Is Enough" from *Lyle Lovett and His Large Band*), subsequently produced Hyatt's solo *King Tears* CD for MCA—Hyatt was the first vocalist selected as part of MCA's Master Series—and the record of course utilized the support of Hood and Ball.

A second Hyatt solo record, 1993's *Music Town*, was issued on Sugar Hill, again featuring his old pals and sporting a singular batch of cleverly structured, harmony-kissed tunes. The guys would occasionally reunite for benefits and side projects, and there was always hope in Austin of a permanent reunion. Unfortunately, Hyatt perished in a plane crash in 1996. Two Sugar Hill compilations of early Uncle Walt's Band material are *An American in Texas Revisited* and *The Girl on the Sunny Shore*.

Other prominent artists working the shadowy peripheries of the folk network at that time include Lisa Gilkyson, Dee Moeller, Traci Lamar, Kurt Van Sickle, and Tim Anderson.

Stalwart members of the Texas folk community for a quarter-century, husband and wife duo Bill and Bonnie Hearne sculpted an impeccable reputation for country-rain harmonies and a rich and original country-folk style. For too many years they were noted more for their influence on other folkies (and for their seeing problems; Bonnie's completely blind and Bill nearly so) than their own work—fortunately, a deal with Warner Western has at long last resulted in a triumphant major label debut: *Diamonds in the Rough*.

FORT WORTH NATIVE HUGH MOFFATT, AFTER GRADUATING from Rice University in the early seventies, headed immediately to Austin to try his hand at its fruitful folk scene. In 1973, he ended up in Nashville to try songwriting—and met with immediate success. He penned tunes for Ronnie Milsap, Dolly Parton, Merle Haggard, Kathy Mattea, Lacy J. Dalton, Jerry Lee Lewis, Johnny Rodriguez, Alabama, and probably anyone else with a country recording contract.

An accomplished singer as well, it was inevitable that Moffatt would record his own albums, as he did with reasonable success throughout the next several years for a variety of American and European labels (including Mercury). In the late eighties, Moffatt signed with Rounder/Philo and released two particularly strong country/folk opuses, 1987's *Loving You* and

1989's *Troubadour*. He hooked up with his sister, Katy Moffatt, an accomplished roots rock singer in her own right, for *Dance Me Outside*, a harmony-laced, country-flavored foray that came out in 1992.

Hugh recently signed with Austin's Watermelon label, for whom he recorded 1996's *The Life of a Minor Poet*. The album is an accomplished *tour de force* by a songwriter whose sensitivity is poetic without ever being too saccharine. The lovely-voiced Katy has also continued to make records, and her 1993 Philo release, *The Evangeline Hotel*, is a stark, beautiful effort.

As inundated as Austin was (and has always been) with songwriters, West Texas was, in the early seventies, still the spiritual birth canal for the singer/songwriter. Three Panhandle pals named Joe Ely, Jimmie Dale Gilmore, and Butch Hancock were at the forefront of the movement. The trio had grown up in Lubbock, wallowing in the rock 'n' roll of Buddy Holly and the West Texas sagas of Bob Wills. Under the guise of the Hub City Movers, the three moved to Austin as a rock band, became the legendary Flatlanders (along with Steve Wesson and Tony Pearson), and infused into the rock scene a new folk sensibility.

Not surprisingly, when the Flatlanders split up, Ely, Gilmore, and Hancock would each gain reputations as world-class songwriters. But though they all continued to mine the storytelling traditions in their tunes, each of the singer/songwriters would probably describe his work as something other than "folk." Ely, admittedly, if one must fit into a niche, is a rocker (and, as such, is discussed in other chapters).

Hancock and Gilmore, on the other hand, do work that singer/songwriter vein, though they are significantly different from each other. Hancock embodies the workingman-as-artist ethic, in more ways than one. In a literal sense, he's done time driving tractors and working construction, but in the more artistic sense, he's a song machine. He's written hundreds of songs over the years, and though he's released over a dozen albums since 1978, he's only now becoming known as an interpreter of his own material. Until recently, he was most renowned for the versions other people had of his songs. (Ely, Gilmore, Emmy Lou Harris, Jerry Jeff Walker, the Texas Tornadoes, and Alvin Crow are just a sampling of the artists who've covered Hancock's tunes.)

One reason for that is that Hancock's voice, to put it politely, is on the raspy side—which has been a problem for similar tunesmiths like Dylan, Guy Clark, and Townes Van Zandt as well. But though covers of Hancock's songs by those with the voices of angels serve to emphasize just what a lovely and thoughtful writer he is, there is a certain intimate poignancy to hearing Hancock sing his own songs. For while he's a superb melodist, his sense of imagery and wordplay are most sympathetically interpreted by Hancock himself. "She Never Spoke Spanish to Me," "Bluebird," "Eats Away the Night," "Eileen," and "Pumpkineater" are all triumphs of craft, and the *Eats Away the Night* album (Sugar Hill, 1994) is a sterling example of Hancock at his estimable best.

In 1999, Rainlight Records came out with several Hancock reissues, including *You Coulda Walked around the World* and *Diamond Hill*.

Possessing an odd spirituality and a voice reminiscent of Roy Orbison if he'd had the delivery of Jimmy Stewart, Jimmie Dale Gilmore is perhaps the strangest of Lubbock's divine trio of song. After the Flatlanders broke up, Gilmore moved to Colorado and spent several years on a variety of philosophical, religious, and artistic pursuits. Eventually, in the early eighties, he surfaced in Austin recommitted to music, and set out to develop a following.

He scored a deal with HighTone Records and released *Fair and Square* in 1988 and *Jimmie Dale Gilmore* in 1989. The following year, he recorded *Two Roads: Live in Australia* with Butch Hancock, then signed with Elektra for 1991's *After Awhile*. The album was so successful that *Rolling Stone* named him Country Artist of the Year for the ensuing three years.

But what Gilmore does is far closer to folk tradition than C&W—at least by the standards of the times. And if marketing insists on further labeling his folk, call it space-a-billy or Zen-country folk. Whatever; though Gilmore's songs are traditionally structured, he has a knack for a gorgeous melody. Too, though his subject matter is often familiar, he has a mystical side that causes the characters in his material to head off into uncharted territories. Which is to say that, for all his predictability, Gilmore is pretty damned unpredictable—and the results are generally rewarding.

Gilmore's next musical search for meaning, 1993's *Spinning Around the Sun*, while not remotely approaching Bono or the Moody Blues for spiritual pomposity, managed to expound on Larger Concerns in a captivating manner, and his trait for tossing disparate elements together in a big, mostly tasty musical salad was essentially triumphant.

He combined covers of Hank Williams and Elvis Presley with his own songs (which turned away from traditional folk and onto the access ramp of pop). The album received critical raves from really big publications, including nonmusical heavyweights like *Esquire*, and it's basically acknowledged that, as long as Gilmore keeps searching for answers, his work continually evolves. A 1996 CD, *Braver New World*, produced by T-Bone Burnett, is even better—a sheer sonic treat.

ANOTHER FOLKIE IN THE LUBBOCK TRADITION IS TERRY ALLEN. His is a sporadic but endearing body of work, and he also falls into the My Voice Ain't That Great but I Sure Do Have a Way with a Couplet school of singer/songwriters. Unlike his Lubbock compatriots, Allen opted for L.A. instead of Austin and a career as a visual artist and teacher as well as a musician.

It's the subsequent, distanced perspective about Texas that has developed his dichotomous style. He combines a world-weary sarcasm and belligerence with his West Texas roots, and the results are almost always insightful, witty, and curiously affectionate. Of his rare album releases, 1977's *Lubbock (on Everything)*, 1983's *Bloodlines*, 1995's *Human Remains*, and 1999's *Salivation* (all available on Sugar Hill) stand out. Allen has also been an active playwright and a force in musical theater.

Guy Clark is another of the West Texas writers whose work stands among the best in the country. From Monahans, Clark is a gruff-voiced songster who's always believed that a good song's lyrics work on paper, independent of the music and melody that will eventually fuse them into song.

Like Robert Earl Keen, Clark has a background saturated in poetry and literature, and his reputation as a writer whose work is coveted by other artists is significant. Among his well-known tunes, covered by the likes of Jerry Jeff Walker, Vince Gill, Ricky Scaggs, and the Highwaymen, are "Desperadoes Waiting for a Train," "The Last Gunfighter Ballad," "She's Crazy for Leavin'," and "Heartbroke."

But Clark has slowly prospered as a solo artist as well. Another of the singer/songwriters whose evocative narratives would fit comfortably as the soundtrack to a Cormac McCarthy novel, Clark has released eight albums over his career, the most recent two, *Boats to Build* (1992) and *Dublin Blues* (1995), being major label efforts for Asylum.

If Jo Carol Pierce came to songwriting late in life, it wasn't for lack of a muse. The ex-wife (and still friend) of Jimmie Dale Gilmore, Pierce was born in the Panhandle town of Wellington and grew up surrounded by Gilmore, Hancock, Ely, and Terry Allen. She moved to Austin with the rest of the free world in the seventies, and spent years writing plays, screenplays, musicals, and a novel. But it wasn't until the mid-eighties that musician pals convinced her to start writing songs.

Her tunes drew immediate approval, and when a variety of Austin musicians recorded an album of her songs, *Across the Great Divide: Songs of Jo Carol Pierce* (DejaDisc, 1993), her reputation as a songwriter was cemented among the cognoscenti. The album kicked ass at the 1993 Austin Music Awards, and 1995's *Bad Girls Upset by the Truth* (Monkey Hill), based around her musical theater piece of the same name and featuring many of the songs from *Divide*, furthers not only her songwriting promise but the notion that it's fun to hear her sing her own compositions.

But Lubbock isn't the only fertile ground for singer/songwriters; the whole vast expanse of the state is liberally peppered with giants in the field—some appropriately rewarded and some still ignored.

Even Dallas had a folk scene centered around the Rubaiyat Club, from whence sprang future redneck rockers like B. W. Stevenson and Michael Martin Murphey. Later, clubs like Poor David's Pub and artists like Shake Russell and Dana Cooper would incorporate folk flavorings into the city's self-inflated sense of cosmopolitan importance.

In the case of Seguin's Nanci Griffith, though, justice has triumphed.

Townes Van Zandt

☆

It's possible that Townes Van Zandt is known as the singer/*songwriter* of the entire crew—as opposed to the *singer*/songwriter (which incidentally would probably be Griffith, Lucinda Williams, Tish Hinojosa, or Gilmore). For, in a genre full of marginal vocalists, Van Zandt tops the poll of those least likely to make a Christmas album with Pavarotti and Carreras.

On the other hand, Van Zandt *was* undeniably brilliant, the Dylan Thomas of popular music. He was born in Fort Worth in 1944, was inspired by Elvis to start playing guitar, worked the Southwest folk circuit, and long ago opted for the songwriter-friendly zip code of Nashville. Starting in 1967, Van Zandt released a series of "small gem" albums for the Tomato label on a roughly annual basis (including *First Album, For the Sake of Song, Our Mother the Mountain, Townes Van Zandt, Delta Mama Blues, High, Low and Inbetween, The Late, Great Townes Van Zandt, Live at the Old Quarter,* and *Flying Shoes*).

He then grew tired of a mainstream Nashville attitude in which he'd had no interest anyway, and headed to Austin for a while. It was a mellow period for Van Zandt, who seemed to spend the bulk of his time playing small club dates, drinking, and reaping the royalties from the catalogue of his songs, which were being covered with increasing frequency by major country stars like Don Williams, Merle Haggard, Willie Nelson, and Emmylou Harris. (In fact, it's easiest to say that Van Zandt has written several songs that routinely show up on "Best Texas Songs Ever" lists: "Tecumseh Valley," "Katie Belle Blue," "A Song For," "The Hole," "Buckskin Stallion," "Mr. Mudd and Mr. Gold," "Pancho and Lefty," and "Marie," for example.)

He ended his self-imposed recording hiatus in 1986 after returning to Tennessee, where he signed with Sugar Hill Records and put out the brooding but excellent *At My Window*. There followed a series of national tours and live records, then, in 1994, he recorded *No Deeper Blue*, a creepy but beautiful record steeped in ghost stories and despair.

It's no secret that Van Zandt was a bit of a melancholic loner who sought solace in the company of, well, a beer or two—or thirty. Perhaps it was his privileged and gentried ancestry—which he eschewed for years—or maybe it was just his melancholy poet's vulnerability. But there was a gentle and twisted pessimism to Van Zandt's work that effortlessly brings out the beauty in the bleak; a sorcery in which he made loneliness and sadness somehow sound like his poker buddies.

It's discouragingly possible that Van Zandt, who passed away on New Year's Day '97, had no hope for himself; it's inspiring that he may well have harbored some hope for the rest of us. In 1999, *A Far Cry from Dead*, his

major label debut for Arista, came out. Though short on new material, the
CD is interesting because of the concept: to broaden solo recordings of
Van Zandt by augmenting them with accompaniment from a studio band.
Maybe not a great idea in spite of the spirit.

Kinda. While Michael Jackson need not fear a publishing takeover by Griffith, the spectacularly talented, self-described folk-a-billy artist has released
twelve albums (three of which have gone gold, two platinum) and recieved
five Grammy nominations.

A former schoolteacher, Griffith began working Austin clubs as a sideline. In 1978, she released her first album, *There's a Light Beyond These
Woods*, on her own B. F. Deal album. (Can teachers cuss? Even if it's im-
plied?) With her clear, lovely voice and a poetic songwriting quality, Griffith's next two records were distributed by the folk-friendly Philo label. The
second of these, *The Last of the True Believers*, featured stellar songcraft and
bluegrass-flavored backup.

By then, Griffith's reputation as a writer and performer had begun to
circulate throughout Nashville. Other artists (among them Kathy Mattea
and Lynn Anderson) had started to record her songs, and in 1987 MCA
released the classic *Lone Star State of Mind*.

Several other albums followed, including the curiously melancholy *Late
Night Grande Hotel*, a gentle, bluegrassy masterpiece called *The Last of the
True Believers*, and two separate tribute CDs, *Other Voices, Other Rooms*,
and *Other Voices, Too* (*A Trip Back to Bountiful*).

☆ Two: The Emergence of the Singer/Songwriter

A T THE DAWN OF THE EIGHTIES, AS THE CONCEPT OF THE "FOLK-singer" swung back into general public disfavor—Robert Earl Keen says he consciously calls his music "country" simply because, apart from certain Ivy League types in the Northeast, no self-respecting music fan in America today would be caught dead browsing through the Folk section of a record store—it became necessary to evolve a new stylistic tag for those who practice folkcraft. Presto: Enter the phrase "singer/songwriter."

Therefore, though today's "singer/songwriters" aren't doing anything remarkably different from what Joan Baez or Arlo Guthrie did in terms of song structure, instrumentation, and content, it is no longer politically correct to call them "folkies." So much so that, should one ever be confronted by a new neighbor or a just-hired coworker and invited to "go see some folk music or maybe catch a hootenanny sometime," one knows to race off at top speed with the cheesiest excuse possible, in the hopes that the kook will never again attempt to engage one in social congress.

Perhaps the highest-profiled of the young Texas singer/songwriters would be Michelle Shocked, who was born in Dallas in 1962 and, upon reaching an age at which she could properly assess the town's qualities, has spent as little time there as possible.

An army kid who hopscotched from base to base until her early teens, Shocked then ran away from various relatives until she found safe harbor, first, with her biological father, a folk musician and aficionado named "Dollar" Bill Johnson, and later in young anarchist hotbeds like San Francisco, New York, and Amsterdam. Having assimilated a bit of musical education from her dad and at various bluegrass and folk festivals in her itinerant youth, Shocked channeled her talent into a variety of punk rock and activist movements—which proved fortuitous when, in 1986, she found herself at the Kerrville Folk Festival. She sang an impromptu set of her strident, catchy-yet-distilling political folk at one of the many "campfire sessions" at the urging of a British producer named Pete Lawrence, who recorded the performance on a Sony Walkman.

He released the *au naturel* material in England as *The Texas Campfire Tapes,* and all stood by in gape-mouthed astonishment as the record went to number 1.

Shocked suddenly found herself with a huge Mercury contract, and after a bit of (sincere) revolutionary maneuvering, she recorded *short sharp Shocked* in 1988. The album was a solid success and, in finest folk fashion, *short sharp Shocked* managed to convey a variety of political sentiments in a daring and winning musical package. She followed a year later with the bluesy *Captain Swing,* which was another creatively divergent package, then went stylistically lunatic on 1992's *Arkansas Traveler.* A true throwback exercise, digging deeply into bluegrass, gospel, and hillbilly music, *Arkansas Traveler* managed in its vast ambition to confuse everyone—including Shocked's record company.

When she followed up with a series of eccentric public appearances and statements, Shocked received a release from the label (which she claims to have wanted all along). *Kind-Hearted Woman* followed in 1994 and, more recently, Shocked released *Artists Make Lousy Slaves* (presumably based on the author's job history) and *Good News.*

Another of the high-profile youngsters is James "Yes, My Dad Is Larry" McMurtry. A Fort Worth native born in 1962, James grew up with his father in Houston and toted a guitar to Virginia boarding schools and throughout bartending and housepainting gigs from Alaska to Tucson. In 1987, McMurtry won the New Folk Competition at the Kerrville Folk Festival and, after his dad passed James's demo cassette to John Mellencamp during a film project, was signed at Mellencamp's urging to Columbia Records.

Utilizing his scholarly good looks and sandstorm voice, McMurtry strives to link short story narrative with folk balladry, and his brushfire-dry tunes are three-minute bursts of Flannery O'Connor by way of Bob Dylan. All four of his albums, 1989's *Too Long in the Wasteland* (coproduced by Mellencamp), 1992's *Candyland,* 1995's *Where'd You Hide the Body,* 1997's *It Had to Happen* and *Walk Between Raindrops* (the latter two on Sugar Hill) are consistently fine works, and he probably lacks only a "hit" to enter mainstream radio consciousness in a big way.

Katy Moffatt, whose older brother Hugh was profiled in the previous chapter, has established a peripheral spot in the singer/songwriter caravan, though her myriad and fairly pronounced influences categorize her folk as of the tossed salad variety. She grew up in Fort Worth, a child of the Beatles (not biologically) who also dug Motown and Broadway show tunes. In high school she discovered Tom Rush, Leonard Cohen, and Judy Collins.

She learned a few guitar chords and hazarded a try at singing. Moffatt found out she could do both quite well—and performed blues and show tunes through her college years. Postschool stints in Austin and Denver folk clubs brought her to the attention of Columbia Records, for whom she recorded two superb records, 1976's *Katy* and 1978's *Kissin' in the California*

CRIMINALLY OVERLOOKED ARTIST

Vince Bell

☆

Vince Bell is lucky to be singing his own compositions—or anyone's, for that matter. He's an undeniably perspicacious and tender writer, born in Dallas in 1952, whose place on the Hancock/Van Zandt/Gilmore/ Keen/ Clark mantel was a certainty—until he literally died in 1982. Driving back from a recording session for Eric Johnson and Stevie Ray Vaughan, Bell was hit by a drunk driver. Declared dead at the scene, Bell was somehow resuscitated.

He spent weeks in a coma and emerged from it a physical and mental ruin, faced with years of intensive therapy and blackly depressive self-doubt and frustration. But Bell persevered and, after *twelve* years of indomitable will and effort, he is finally realizing the artistic potential he's shown all along.

His 1995 Watermelon release, *Phoenix*, produced by Bob Neuwirth, is a heartbreakingly triumphant examination of time lost, of life torn away, and of Raggedy Andy redemption. His arrangement of Gary Burgess's "Frankenstein" is breathtakingly evocative and eerily autobiographical, and original compositions like "Sun and Moon and Stars" and "Woman of the Phoenix" are vibrant and poignant, reminiscent of work by San Francisco's brilliant Mark Eitzel (ex-of American Music Club).

With his raspy, bewildered delivery and penchant for aching melodies, and after stirring performances at 1996's South-by-Southwest music conference, it's now time for Bell's *artistic* resurrection. His moving autobiography, *One Man's Music*, came out in 1998, and the consistently terrific and witty *Texas Plates* CD followed in 1999 on the Paladin label. A ballet, *Bermuda Triangle*, has also been made of Bell's work.

Sun. Both showcased her Broadway-style freight train of a voice and a clever and eclectic songwriting style that, in fact, scared Columbia off.

She moved to California and worked with young outlaw country artists like Rosie Flores and Dwight Yoakam, but despite such activity and a 1985 Academy of Country Music nomination for Best New Female Vocalist, Moffatt was having a difficult time finding anyone to do anything about her talent besides say how great it was.

Finally, she released two albums for European labels which stirred some domestic interest (*Child Bride* and *The Greatest Show on Earth*—both of which later came out in the States on the Philo label, the latter retitled *The Evangeline Hotel*). In 1980, she recorded *Walkin' on the Moon* for Rounder, another sterling set of fresh, constantly challenging songs that continually rewarded the listener.

She had one more Rounder record, *Sleepless Nights*, then hopped to Watermelon for *Midnight Radio*, and two years later came out with *Angel Town*. Moffatt continues to pull wonderful songs from the broad and vividly colored palette in her brain, and it's too bad most of the world is too stupid to appreciate her skill and ambition.

TWO OUT-OF-STATE ARTISTS WHO WERE FAMOUS BEFORE THEY decided to move to the "heaven on earth" setting of Austin are Iain Matthews and Shawn Colvin. Matthews, born in Lincolnshire, England, in 1946, was a founding member of Fairport Convention, the Celtic/rock group whose mid-sixties fame was substantial. A smooth-tenored singer/guitarist/songwriter whose material and influence were substantial on Fairport's first two records (1968's *Fairport Convention* and 1969's *What We Did on Our Holidays*, both on Polygram), he then formed Matthews Southern Comfort, which had a hit single with Joni Mitchell's "Woodstock."

He eventually started a solo career, moved to the States, and throughout the seventies, in California and Seattle, released, oh, six or seven thousand solo albums of folk/pop and tinkered in groups like Hi-Fi and Plainsong. In the early nineties, after solo efforts for Elektra and Mesa Blue Moon, Matthews moved to Austin and signed with Watermelon Records. He released a winsome LP called *The Dark Ride* in 1994 and, as a member of a NutraSweet pop/folk trio called Hamilton's Pool, recorded a second Watermelon CD, 1995's *Return to Zero*.

South Dakota native Shawn Colvin (born in 1958), a gorgeous-voiced, master-of-craft folk-popster, echoed Matthews's wanderings before settling in Austin. She taught herself guitar in the folk tradition, but traveled around in a variety of musical guises (including a brief, mid-seventies stint in the Dixie Diesels, a Texas western swing act) before hitting the folk circuit in Illinois and San Francisco. She finally ended up in New York, fronting the Shawn Colvin band, where her shake-the-cathedral-ceiling soprano earned Colvin a regular slot on the northeastern folk circuit—and where she drew the attention of Suzanne Vega and her management.

She sang backup for Vega and toured with her; then, in 1988, Colvin signed with Columbia. Her debut, the sweet but acerbic *Steady On*, won Colvin a Grammy for Best Contemporary Folk Recording. *Fat City* (1992) was another critical success, and in 1993 the newly married Colvin moved back to Austin. Her 1994 release, *Cover Girl*, did nothing but further her reputation as a fave of the cognoscenti, and she basically became a superstar when 1996's *A Few Small Repairs* exploded behind the insanely catchy hit single "Sunny Came Home." The entire CD was top-to-bottom great. ("Get Out of This House" and "Wichita Skyline" could've just as easily have been as big—and the European import was even better thanks to a collaborative effort between Colvin and Neil Finn called "What You Get Paid For.") Colvin was suddenly the toast of the music

CRIMINALLY OVERLOOKED GUITARIST

Josh Alan

A most peculiar guitar hero, Alan, born in New York in 1956, is most often typed a folkie. But to watch the former editor and writer for *Screw* magazine play is to witness, an often breathtaking fireworks display of country blues, folk, rock, jazz, and musical theater.

After publishing a critically acclaimed study of the various denizens of the Manhattan night in a book called *Tales of Times Square*, Alan relocated to Dallas. He put his journalistic career on semipermanent hiatus while he pursued an older dream of playing guitar, one which he'd harbored since watching the Beatles on *The Ed Sullivan Show* in 1964.

An exceptionally gifted student, Alan cites Johnny Winter, Leslie West, and Stephen Sondheim as principal musical influences, and boasts an instrumental prowess that brings to mind Mississippi John Hurt and Michael Hedges. Alan's percussive fingerpicking, Rory Gallagher-style slide, and high-speed fretwork is at once respectfully derivative and engagingly original.

And while the bulk of his performances are of the solo acoustic variety, they are but part of a much broader and intriguing artistic spectrum that includes the Josh Alan Orchestra, a high-energy blues-rock trio, and *The Worst!*, his original soundtrack to his proposed musical about B-movie director Ed Wood (the libretto and score to which he'd finished before he ever heard of *Ed Wood*, Tim Burton's film of the same subject. Still, Alan's CD, released in 1994 on his own Black Cracker label, premiered in conjunction with Burton's film in Britain and Europe, where it has been far more popular than in the States).

To date, besides *The Worst!*, Alan's recorded output consists of *Famous and Poor* (cassette only, Four Dots, 1990), a more traditional folk exercise, and 1997's *Blacks and Jews*, a staggering acoustic plea for racial harmony consisting of staggering instrumental and vocal acoustic performances—particularly on the evocative cut "Harlem Time."

solar system, and few are the awards she didn't win or magazines she wasn't featured in.

Shortly after becoming a mother, Colvin released an album of seasonal and children's music called *Holiday Song and Lullabies*.

A mentor of Josh Alan's is Sara Hickman, whose precious demeanor would be really irritating if she wasn't (*a*) completely genuine and a wonderful human and (*b*) a substantially talented singer/songwriter/entertainer whose career has been heartbreaking and frustrating.

Hickman started playing guitar and writing songs at seven, and was playing in bars while still an Arts Magnet High School student in Houston. She graduated from North Texas State University with a painting degree, then moved to Dallas and began to garner a reputation as a cute, earnest, smart vixen who could project an SPCA volunteer image while simultaneously tossing off the F-word with naughty aplomb at performances (in a song title, no less).

With a toothy, Carly Simon smile, porn star lips, and soar-to-the-sky voice, Hickman would attract attention in any case. Because her clever, melodic tunes *work*, covering as they do every possible topic from women's rights to romance to familial relationships to the plight of the universally downtrodden to skewed, wonderful, and somehow hopeful observations on a creepy and degenerating world.

Her first record, *Equal Scary People*, was released on Denton's Four Dots label to such giddy response that Elektra signed Hickman and rereleased the record in 1989. A followup, *Shortstop*, came out in 1991, though acrimony between Hickman and the staid corporate mentality holding court at the label was intensifying and was evident on the record itself.

After a third album was completed, Elektra declined to release it, wanting more smooth, commercial pop material than Hickman's more intelligent, challenging, folk-based stuff. Hickman declined; Elektra dropped her. She called on her fans to help her and, astonishingly, she was able to raise $50,000 to buy the master tapes from the label. The CD, now called *Necessary Angels* (so named for her benefactors), was indeed angelic in execution and ambition, and was eventually released in 1994 by Discovery.

A side project, Domestic Science Club, in which Hickman is joined by the breathtaking talents of bluegrass vocalist Patty Mitchell Lege and former Dixie Chicks singer Robin Macy, also released a self-titled and interesting record on Discovery in 1994.

Hickman has appeared on numerous collections and benefit CDs, and has in the past few years released two new albums of original material: *Newborn* and *Two Kinds of Laughter*.

DARDEN SMITH IS ANOTHER ALUMNUS OF THE AUSTIN "SINGER/ songwriter" scene who's experienced international acclaim. Born in Brenham, Texas, and raised on AM radio, Smith moved with his family to Houston when he was fourteen, immersing himself in a dazzling array of musical influences from rock to western swing. He knew, instantly, that he wanted to be part of it all. He attended UT, began working the bars, and released *Native Soil* in 1986. Featuring an original, storyteller's perspective, a way with a hook, and a tenor voice liberally dosed with sincerity—and with "guest appearances" from Lyle Lovett and Nanci Griffith—*Native Soil* scored two country hits: "Little Maggie" and "Day After Tomorrow." The 1988 big label debut, *Darden Smith* (Epic), recycled some of the *Native Soil* cuts, interspersing them with newer, stronger material, and Smith's reputation for effortlessly catchy choruses began to spread.

He then met Boo Hewerdine, a British folk/pop star from the Bible (the band, not the religious tome), and the two collaborated on 1989's *Evidence* (Ensign Records), a thoughtful, harmony-crusted LP that had the critics gushing even as the masses stayed away in droves; still, Smith and Hewerdine remain close pals and collaborators, and Hewerdine's Brit-pop influences give an interesting twist to Smith's Lone Star folk.

Smith continued to hone his Hill Country Jackson Browne persona with several fine records, including *Trouble No More*, *Little Victories*, *Evidence*, and *Deep Fantastic Blue*.

WITH A POET FATHER AND A MUSIC-TEACHER MOM, IT WAS probably a genetic impossibility that Lucinda Williams could've been anything *but* a singer/songwriter. Born in Louisiana and raised in Austin, Williams began taking guitar lessons at twelve. She spent her teen years locked in her room, obsessed with Bob Dylan, Judy Collins, Van Morrison, and Buffalo Springfield, then headed to college and club performances.

She gradually began working her own material into cover sets, and soon her songs were more raptly listened to than the Famous People tunes. Williams signed with the Folkways/Smithsonian label, released two albums, *Ramblin'* and *Happy Woman Blues*, then signed with Chameleon in 1988. *Lucinda Williams*, the debut, kicked the doors in a little bit. With her sensual, slightly hoarse voice and bittersweet songs, Williams began to gain a following—including artists like Mary Chapin Carpenter and Linda Thompson, both of whom recorded Williams songs.

Passionate Kisses was next, a more confident, playful, but middle-of-the-road record, and a newer CD, *Sweet Old World*, shows a willingness to explore more mature (read: somber) themes. But it's a ruminative style that suits Williams well; her melodic reflections and worldview are the cautious stuff of greatness. Her 1998 release, *Car Wheels on a Gravel Road* although not as commercially successful as Shawn Colvin's *A Few Small Repairs*, caused even more of a firework display in the minds of the cognoscenti. An erudite, witty, and supremely melodic record, *Wheels* is arguably the work of a lifetime—though with Williams one can never be sure.

Eric Taylor is a Texas folk—er, singer/songwriter—tradition; it's just that, for years, no one *knew* he was a tradition. A twenty-year-old Georgia guitarist who was passing through Houston in 1970, Taylor saw Lightnin' Hopkins and Townes Van Zandt on successive nights and decided to stay.

He was rapidly swallowed into the city's then-thriving music scene, working regularly alongside Nanci Griffith (to whom Taylor was married briefly),

Tish Hinojosa

The recordings of Tish Hinojosa, the San Antonio artist whose heritage and interests have metamorphosed into a body of work that is, in her field, perhaps most emblematic of Texas's multicultural heritage, should be on every human's required listening list.

She grew up in a large Mexican-American family held together by love, faith, hard work, and music, and after assimilating everything from border balladry and *conjunto* music to the Beatles and rock 'n' roll radio, Hinojosa learned guitar. She was playing San Antonio folk clubs by her early teens and, possessed of a heart-melting soprano voice, found work recording jingles and Spanish language pop tunes.

She moved to Taos in the late seventies, honing her songwriting skills with doses of progressive country, then made her way to Nashville in 1983, where she worked as a songwriter for four years (releasing one single on Curb, "I'll Pull You Through") before deciding the cleansing New Mexican air was far more therapeutic. In 1987, she released her own indie cassette, *Taos to Tennessee*, then pulled up again upon hearing of the open musical vistas of Austin.

There, Hinojosa quickly made a splash on the local club scene as well as in the migrant workers' rights movement, then scored a contract with A&M, for whom she recorded a 1989 debut, *Homeland* (produced by Steve Berlin of Los Lobos). A stunning album replete with wonderful melodies and insightful, touching narratives, it made Hinojosa an instant success on public radio and overseas.

She moved to Rounder for 1992's *Culture Swing*, a poignant, witty album for which Hinojosa wrote all the material and for which she won the National Association of Independent Record Distributors' Folk Album of the Year award. Her next two records, 1991's all-Spanish *Aquella Noche* and a 1992 rerelease of *Taos to Tennessee*, came out on the Watermelon label. Hinojosa's final records for Watermelon were a well-received children's album, *Cada Niño/Every Child*, and 1993's *Frontejas*, which more thoroughly explores her Mexican-American roots.

Destiny's Gate, her 1994 CD for Warner Brothers, represented a conscious bid for commercial acceptance, with the material almost too poppy, but it was a listening pleasure nonetheless and it set the stage for 1996's *Dreaming from the Labyrinth* (also on Warner Brothers). A haunting, literate, spiritual, bilingual masterpiece, influenced heavily by the writings of Octavio Paz, an epic neofeminist poem by a seventeenth-century nun, a fifteenth-century poem, "We Only Come to Dream" by the Aztec writer Coyolchiuhqui—as well as Hinojosa's own past—*Dreaming from the*

> *Labyrinth* is a marvelous, dreamy rumination on solitude and the comfort of the past. Easily one of the best-conceived and executed "singer/songwriter" albums ever recorded in Texas, and featuring the gorgeous "Whisper Goodbye," *Dreaming from the Labyrinth* confirms that Tish Hinojosa is, in fact, a landmark Texas composer and singer.

Lyle Lovett (who cites Taylor as a major influence), Van Zandt, Steve Earle, Vince Bell, and Guy Clark.

Though Griffith and Lovett both recorded his material, and Taylor himself released a 1979 indie album called *Shameless Love*, it took Taylor a decade to iron out drug and alcohol problems. Which he did—to the extent that he became a counselor. He then married and started a family. But all along, Taylor kept writing and singing. His vivid, singer-as-novelist narrative style is positively cinematic, and his language is lush and stirring.

Finally, some twenty-five years after he landed in Houston and became a legend, Taylor released *Eric Taylor* on Watermelon Records. The album not only confirms his legendary status, it expands it and a follow-up CD, *Resurrect*, featuring a bounty of wondrously poetic and thoughtfully hummable songs such as "Louis Armstrong's Broken Heart" and the heartbreaking "Strong Enough for Two."

The Amazing Redhead, Patty Griffin, is another artist splashing the singer/songwriter stereotype with doses of almost roadhouse rock 'n' roll. In fact, her major label debut, 1996's haunting *Living with Ghosts*, is a stark and acoustically revealing set of work; two years later she rocks it up in an almost schizophrenic turnaround on *Flaming Red*. Perhaps it's all due to the fact that Griffin, a native New Englander who traveled around extensively, ultimately settled in the musical melting tub we call Texas. Whatever guise she chooses is compelling.

Two quirky bands toiling in the eccentric wing of the folk mines that need to be mentioned are Trout Fishing in America and the Austin Lounge Lizards. Trout Fishing in America, a Mutt-and-Jeff duo comprised of former college basketball star Ezra Idlet (guitar and vocals) and Really Short Guy Keith Grimwood (bass and vocals), are bright, funny, accomplished songwriters and performers whose hysterical stage show often overwhelms their thoughtful material. Originally from Houston, Trout Fishing has carved out a totally respectable living working a national circuit and recording both adult and children's records on their own label. Of the several LPs available nationwide, 1994's *Who Are These People?* and 1992's *Over the Limit* are perhaps their finest CDs and indicate that they are far more than a novelty act.

Likewise with the Austin Lounge Lizards, whose bluegrass stylings are firmly anchored in a whimsical (nay, even comic) folk narrative tradition. Formed in the early eighties in Austin, the Lounge Lizards are currently comprised of rhythm guitarist/vocalist Hank Card, lead guitarist/vocalist Conrad Deisler, multi-instrumentalists Richard Bowden and Tom Pittman, and bassist/vocalist Boo Resnick—who is not to be confused with Darden Smith compatriot Boo Hewerdine; only in Singer/Songwriter Land are there overlapping "Boos."

Over the course of their twisted and brilliant career, the Austin Lounge Lizards have forged an enduring reputation as crack instrumentalists whose erudite and satirical ravings come off as though Frank Zappa, Butch Hancock, and Jonathan Swift all formed a bluegrass band together. They've won Best Band honors at the Kerrville Folk Festival, appear with monotonous regularity in the *Austin Chronicle* music polls, and have released several albums as well: 1991's *Lizard Vision*, 1993's *Paint Me on Black Velvet* (both on Flying Fish), 1984's *Creatures from the Black Saloon*, 1988's *Highway Cafe of the Damned*, 1995's *Small Minds*, and a 1996 EP called *Live Bait* (all on Watermelon).

Several other promising singer/songwriters are sturdily crafting quality reputations. Tim Keller, who grew up in California and spent years in New Mexico honing a sound born of Robert Johnson, the Carter Family, and Woodie Guthrie, landed in Dallas and has quietly become a staple amongst North Texas songsters of note. With a style reminiscent of a rustic Don Henley, Keller has three albums out, 1987's *No Stranger to Wishes*, 1989's *Live at Uncle Calvin's* (both on his own indie label), and 1995's *Little Miracles* (on Chamisa Records).

With deep roots in the old style folkie mythology, Michael Fracasso of Austin has one of those King Romance tenors and a traveler's sense of visual storytelling. He graduated from Ohio State and spent several years on the brutal New York City coffeehouse scene before hitching his wagon to Austin's musical star. He was quickly accepted by peers and audiences alike, and in 1992 released *love and trust* (DejaDisc), a record packed with easy melodies and captivating images.

Fracasso toured the United States and Europe, released *When I Lived in the Wild* in 1995 on the Bohemia Beat label, and is currently a member of the Austin supergroup Hamilton's Pool along with Iain Matthews and Mark Hallman.

Michelle Solberg's kaleidoscopic voice and airy, intelligent songs have staggered Austin since she started singing there in her late teens. As a UT freshperson, she began releasing homemade cassettes like *Skin* and *Shrill* and packing clubs all over town. A 1994 self-titled CD on the Chocolate label quickly won virtually every award the town has to offer, and Solberg's only flaw—an understandable and youthful desire to try to do too much—is already evening out as she matriculates past the college years. Essentially, she has it all.

Sarah Elizabeth Campbell is another Austinite whose work has been performed by the likes of Rick Danko, Levon Helm, and Jim Messina. Campbell has also released two excellent and stylistically singular records. The first, *Little Tenderness* (1986, Kaleidoscope), is a simmering set of old-style balladry that borrows as much from country blues as it does from folk, and remains in print today. In 1993, Campbell released *Running with You* on the DejaDisc label, a thematically similar LP to *Little Tenderness*, though the production is a bit more crisp and focused than the earlier album's. Both are sterling and unique examples of contemporary folk.

Dallas's Colin Boyd, a quasi-protégé of Sara Hickman, is also regarded as a sensitive-without-being-too-gooey singer/songwriter for the romantically impaired. In fact, as is evidenced on his 1994 CD, *Romeo*, Boyd's tunes come off as a musical game of burnout between Michael Martin Murphey and Marshall Crenshaw.

Like Boyd, Austin's Slaid Cleaves has great potential. The winner of the 1992 Best New Folk competition at Kerrville, Cleaves has released three solid records of folky-tonk: 1990's *Promise* (Rock Bottom Records), 1992's *Life's Other Side* (Play Hard Records), and 1993's indie *For the Brave and Free*. Though traveling some of the tired thematic highways common to most singer/songwriters (longing, wandering, social misfits), Cleaves usually manages to throw in a twist.

Dallas's Tom Faulkner, a noted jingles writer, has created his own singular folk vision on a wonderful CD called *Lost in the Land of Texico*. With bluesy bottleneck slide and a gravelly but delicate voice, Faulkner's song-cycle of tunes—mutating Cajun, pop, blues, and folk in a roux of Texan, new and old Mexican, and Louisianan influences—is scarily good.

Ana Egge is an Austin singer/songwriter with an old-school musical sensibility and a remarkably insightful and clever sense of storytelling. Her debut indie album, *River under the Road*, betokens great things.

Other young singer/songwriters who bear watching include Meredith Louise Miller, Kris McKay, Elizabeth Wills, Kim Miller, Seela, Kimberly M'Carver, the Therapy Sisters, Michael Elwood, Abra Moore, and Latvian transplant Ingrid Karklins.

Indeed, with the wealth of talent now plying the singer/songwriter trade, it's entirely possible that it will one day be okay to call someone a folksinger again without it sounding like an obscenity.

☆ Part 5: The Flavors of Ethnicity

☆One: North of the Border— The Age of *Conjunto*

▼

I T WOULD BE TOO EASY TO SAY THAT, IF THERE IS ANY AWARE-
ness throughout the world of Mexican music at all, other than that of
the faceless mariachis which are as de rigueur as margaritas when eating in
Mexican restaurants, it is because some kook murdered Tejano singing star
Selena.

Admittedly, to be crass about it, Selena's death didn't hurt her album
sales any—at least in a short-term view of such things. But, as we've seen
with Jim Morrison and Jimi Hendrix and John Lennon, death has always
translated well in that all-important Units Moved category because people
are ghouls and bandwagon hoppers (or, more accurately, hearse-hoppers).
It will always be that way.

The fact is, though, to ascribe Selena's stardom to her premature demise
would be a major injustice to her life and her work because she was well
on her way to becoming the first Tejano recording artist to break through
the language barrier and achieve international stardom—and she wouldn't
have needed martyrdom to push her to that level. She had the voice, personality, charm—the *magic,* if you will—that we associate with big stars,
and it went beyond the limitations of the Spanish-language entertainment
industry; Selena had achieved legitimate gold record status even *before* she
started work on English-language recordings (which was, of course, the direction she was headed when she died).

Yet, just as it would be an injustice to Selena to say she was popular
simply because of her tragedy, it would be grossly unfair to the Mexican
heritage and music in general to suggest that Selena was the only important
purveyor of Mexican music ever. In fact, that's laughable; the history of
Mexican artists and song is particularly rich, and their place in the annals
of Texas music is significant.

WHILE IT'S TRUE THAT THE PRECISE INSTRUMENTATION OF MEX-
ican folk music prior to the twentieth century is uncertain, it's accepted

229

that obvious cultural links with Spain resulted in a string band tradition. As well, through various European influences, Italian opera made a significant melodic contribution to the evolving styles in Mexico.

As the music grew, differences between religious and secular songs, as well as the rift between social classes and their respective entertainment and musical needs, begat a variety of musical forms, many of which found their way into Texan border towns in the late 1800s and early twentieth century. Migratory workers heading into Texas looking for jobs brought Mexican folk music with them, as did the early touring entertainment groups that ventured north.

By the 1920s, two typical ensembles existed in the Mexican-Texan communities. One was the *orquesta típica*, a string group that typically included violins, guitars, contrabass, mandolins, and the always popular psaltery (a plucked string instrument dating back to the Middle Ages). The string tradition is pretty much history, though it should be noted that a fine fiddler/mandolinist from the Rio Grande Valley named Jose Moreno was recently signed to the Arhoolie label. The other type of ensemble was the accordion-based dance band, which ranged in personnel from the solo accordionist to slightly larger units (with, perhaps, guitar, contrabass, and *tambora de rancho*, a sort of parade-ground percussion instrument which looks a bit like over-sized bongos, hangs from the waist and is played with mallets), whose functions were primarily for working-class celebrations and, as such, were smaller groups by financial necessity.

It is from the accordion tradition that *conjunto* music evolved; though its practitioners tend to call the music "Tex-Mex," we'll stick with *conjunto* (because the italics look cool). By the 1920s, the traditional Mexican folk music of the *norteños* (as the immigrants came to be called) had mixed with elements of early American folk and country, plus ethnic music from the German, Polish, and Czech communities in south and central Texas, and *conjunto* came into being. It indeed centered around the accordion, but the *bajo sexto* (a twelve-string bass guitar) replaced the *tambora de rancho* as the percussive foundation over which the accordion soared. And, unlike the larger *orquestas* which might employ wind instruments and several strings, *conjunto* typically relied on a guitar and violin for supplemental instrumentation.

The music is generally bouncy, rendered in an irresistible 2/4 polka beat, and songs, boasting either heartbreaking choruses or buoyant, raucous melodies, center around the experiences of the working class (frequently, as with country music, the foibles that one might reasonably expect to ensue when one spends all of one's paycheck in a bar over the course of a relatively compact period of time). There are, of course, many compositional styles within *conjunto*, including *boleros* (dervish-style dance numbers introduced in the forties and generally played only by the *Orquestras*), *corridos* (ballads), *cumbias* (heavily rhythmic and syncopated pieces that originated in Colombia and didn't actually make an appearance in Tex-Mex until the late sixties), *rancheras* (which are sort of the Mexican equivalent of country music), and purely original forms, including *valses* (*vals alto, vals bajtto, vals ranchera*), *redova, mazurka, huapango,* and the *corrido.*

The earliest giants of Texan *conjunto* are undeniably Narciso Martínez and Santiago "Don Santiago" Jimenez, Sr., though the accordion maestros who probably inspired them were Bruno Villarreal, José Rodríguez, and Jesús Casiano, all three of whom performed in an earlier, more traditional style which predated *conjunto* as we know it—the *conjunto* of Martínez and Jimenez.

Martínez was born in Reynosa, Mexico, just south of McAllen, Texas, but spent his youth as a migrant farmer in the citrus groves of the Rio Grande Valley. Acknowledged as the Father of Conjunto, Martínez and *bajo sexto* virtuoso Santiago Almeida were the two who established the instrumental link that so characterizes *conjunto.*

Furthermore, Martinez was a pioneer of the two-row button accordion, utilizing a choppier style in which he abandoned the old-school technique that called for the accordion to provide bottom-end and chordal support from the player's left hand; Martínez figured he had Almeida for that, and the new sound caught on.

In 1935, after an insightful furniture salesman heard the two and arranged a recording session—the result of which was the successful single "La Chicharronera" b/w "El Tronconal"—Martínez and Almeida recorded prolifically for San Antonio's Bluebird label for the next five years.

Thereafter his popularity accelerated dramatically, and Martínez was a much-in-demand performer at any function of importance throughout the Valley and up to San Antonio.

He recorded dozens of tunes, mostly instrumental polkas, for labels like Ideal and San Benito as well as Bluebird, and was also the accompanist of choice for popular singers like Carmen and Laura and Lydia Mendoza. At that point in the recording industry, in *conjunto* music, Martínez was paid by the session and saw nothing in royalties or performance mechanicals, and was by no means able to support himself and his family through his wages as a musician.

Still, his popularity remained strong for decades and he eventually played throughout most of the Southwest. In 1983, his musical legacy earned Martínez a National Heritage Fellowship Award, and he continued to play until his death in 1992.

Don Santiago Jimenez, Sr., also known as "El Flaco" (the Skinny One), is just as important to *conjunto* history. Born in San Antonio's La Piedrera barrio in 1913, Santiago learned accordion from his own father, who performed at neighborhood dances and parties in the early 1900s and who would take young Santiago into any of several German settlements near San Antonio and as far away as New Braunfels to soak up the nuances of their European-flavored polka.

They were lessons well learned; by the time Santiago was performing at parties and community gatherings in his mid-teens, his Tex-Mex material was interwoven with the German style, creating a freshly festive sound. Too, as he got older and developed his style, Jimenez relied on a less frenetic, more melodic solo style than Martínez (which Jimenez himself joked was because he couldn't play as fast as his contemporary).

Still, Jimenez's skill on the standard two-row accordion was virtuoso stuff. He was also the musician who introduced the string bass—*el tololoche*—into *conjunto*, an innovation he came up with during his first recording sessions in the mid-thirties—and which predated said incorporation by other *conjunto* groups by at least ten years.

He first recorded in 1936 for Decca, then quickly switched to the Mexican Victor label because their fee per session was substantially higher. Jimenez is probably most famous for his recordings of two polkas, "A Piedrera" and "Viva Seguín," but was certainly well known for all of his recordings. He also had a San Antonio radio show in the late thirties and recorded briefly for San Antonio's Ideal label. (The work was later reissued on the Imperial or Globe labels.)

He continued to perform actively through the sixties, when he pulled back for a few years, but after two of his seven sons, Santiago Junior and Leonardo "Flaco," were grown and making *conjunto* a household world, Don Santiago roared into his golden years with his accordion cranked full-blast. He passed away in 1984.

There were other important Tex-Mex figures from those days, including Pedro Ayala, Lydia Mendoza, Carmen and Laura, and in particular Valerio Longoria (a *huge* influence who continues to record and whose *El Estilo Romantico de Valerio Longoria* is a treat).

In the fifties and sixties, the metamorphosis of the music continued. Tony de la Rosa, born in Sarita, south of Corpus Christi, in 1931, was a most significant explorer, a fluent-fingered accordionist who recorded a number of exceedingly popular polkas for Ideal Records in the fifties but was important for many other reasons.

Aside from keeping *conjunto* in the public eye, he'll also go down in history as the artist who integrated drums into conjunto groups—an innovation which, for volume purposes, necessitated amplification for the *bajo sexto* and brought electric bass into the format. He was also the first to stand upright on stage (as did his band) and actually move around. De la Rosa recorded over seventy-five albums in the course of a long, popular career.

Along with de la Rosa, Paulino Bernal was one of the greatest of the mid-period conjunto accordionists. Formed with his brother Eloy in 1952, their group El Conjunto Bernal was responsible for the most experimental movements within traditional *conjunto*. El Conjunto Bernal was the first group to emphasize the importance of all the instruments in the band; considerations such as varying solo possibilities, three-part harmonies (a true first), dueling accordion (as well as chromatic accordion) dynamics, phrasing, and representative mixes came to the fore. The Bernals later converted to Christianity and led *gospel conjuntos* for years.

Bernal and de la Rosa typified the "Valley sound," called *Taquachito*, which, like modern hip-hop, is its own culture. (Smithsonian just released a comprehensive CD of the *Taquachito* sound well worth buying.)

Esteban Jordán should also be mentioned, since he is what might be thought of as the Miles Davis of the accordion—at least in the Anglo community. While he worked from the sixties through the eighties within the stylistic parentheses of conjunto, his stuff gradually got wilder and wilder. His utilization of modern technological effects like an echoplex unit and bizarre, jazz-flavored solos resulted in a reputation as not only a rebel but also as a true virtuoso.

In contemporary times, Santiago Jimenez, Junior—one of two sons of Don Santiago Jimenez, Sr., who have investigated the possibilities of *conjunto* (albeit in two significantly different directions)—is known as a fierce curator of the old ways.

Born in San Antonio in 1943, Santiago Junior views *conjunto* as a very sacred, traditional musical form and, as such, seems to be devoting his career and estimable talent to safeguarding the music of his father.

Inasmuch as the whole Jimenez family was what might be referred to as the Kennedy family of *conjunto* (minus the various deviant aberrations), Santiago Junior grew up playing guitar, accordion, and *bajo sexto*, and made his first record with his brother while he was only seventeen. From that point on, he has seriously followed his own devoted journey into the past.

He recorded several albums for archival labels like Arhoolie and Rounder and, after his father's death in 1984, made a conscious shift from merely recording traditional music to fueling the fires of his father's legend. After several collectible cassettes on his own Chief label, Santiago Junior signed with Watermelon Records and, under the production guidance of Mark Rubin (student of Texas musical history and bassist for Bad Livers, Austin's runaway roller-coaster bluegrassers), has recorded three superb LPs mixing his own material with the work of his father.

All three albums (*Corazón de Piedra, Canciones de Mi Padre [Songs of My Father],* and *Pasados, del Presente y Futuro*) are far more than dredged-up replications of a dusty past. Because Santiago Junior can match his reverence for tradition with an autonomy of style and interpretation, the material is at once a reminder of where the music came from as much as it is an indication of the genre's innate and continual freshness.

Austin has its own style of Tex-Mex, utilizing a saxophone generally associated with *Norteño* groups. This movement was headed up by Camil Cantu and furthered by his acolyte, Johnny "the Montopolis Kid," who worked the Austin area for over forty years. Another pioneer, Manuel "Cowboy" Donley, born in 1928 and one of the first artists ever to infuse traditional sounds with rock 'n' roll, still holds court in East Austin.

* * *

MINGO SALDIVAR DESERVES SPECIAL MENTION.

Saldivar is another South Texas accordion guru who's known as the "Dancing Cowboy." He's a *conjunto* practitioner who began texturing his music in a country direction for the strangest of reasons: He spent significant military time in both Minnesota and Alaska, playing in frontier bars where the patrons had no clue about *conjunto* but definitely dug their C&W. As a survival mechanism, the magic-fingered Saldivar would fuse *conjunto* with country, though he was far from the first to mix C&W into the repertoire. He is a huge sensation in northern Mexico, and his onstage balletics have inspired a dance craze called "the Mingo." Check out his release on the Hacienda or his own Espada labels.

Los Pinkys, an Austin group comprising a variety of Anglo and Hispanic musicians who borrow heavily from Polish accordion tradition, have a few nice CDs out on Rounder, and some of the members are otherwise involved with a Cajun-flavored act called the Gulf Coast Playboys.

Also, Beto and the Fairlanes is a long-popular Austin party outfit featuring oft-splendid mixtures of jazz, salsa, rock, and tropical.

Two other accordionists worth checking out are Don Leedy (ex-guitarist for the Tailgators), whose band Los Cadillos is a fine traditional outfit, and part-time Asleep at the Wheeler Tim Alexander.

☆ Two: Selena and the Rocketing of Tejano

▼

I F PUNK MUSIC RIPPED THE TWITCHING CORPSE OF ROCK 'N' ROLL off the floor and kicked some life back into it, a younger generation of Texas Mexicans gently pulled the tired form of *conjunto* from a complacent hammock, dusted it off, and shoved an electric guitar into one hand and a synthesizer into the other.

Or so it would seem. Because while Tejano is indisputably the music of Texas Mexican youth, their respect for the form and tradition of *conjunto* bears no resemblance to Johnny Rotten's feelings for, say, Procol Harum. Tejano, in fact, utilizes many of the characteristics of *conjunto*—particularly the polka feel and accordion sound—though they are tossed into a large, enticing salad of pop, country, and rock.

The Father of Tejano Music is "Little" Joe Hernandez, a Temple, Texas, native who was born in 1941 and started playing guitar when he was sixteen. As enthralled by country and rock 'n' roll as he was by the Mexican music that was always around while he was growing up, he formed La Familia, the group with which he's recorded more than forty albums since the sixties (for a variety of indie companies, as well as on CBS, Sony, and his own Tejano Discos label).

His bilingual formula and mishmash of danceable styles has made his a household name among three generations of Tex-Mex fans, and not coincidentally earned what was the first Grammy award ever given to a Tejano artist (in 1992, for the 1991 Sony LP *Dies y Séis de Septiembre*).

In addition, Little Joe y La Familia (current lineup: Steve Silvas, keyboards; Jesse Lopez, drums; Sam Jones, congas; Clark Ellison, bass; Al Gomez, guitar) appear regularly on Farm Aid bills, at Willie Nelson Fourth of July picnics, and at various gubernatorial balls and charity benefits.

His most recent LP, *Reunion '95*, brought Joe together with his brothers Rocky and Johnny—who were early members of La Familia—for their first recording together in years.

Over the course of Little Joe's run, more and more Texas Mexican artists have begun playing Tejano, and by the end of the eighties, its force in the

Texas music industry was substantial. Major record companies like Sony, Arista, BMG, and EMI started Latin imprint labels—all of which have offices in Texas as well as in Miami, another locale with a heavy Hispanic population. Groups like Houston's La Mafia, which can charitably be thought of as a sort of Tex-Mex Bay City Rollers, and Mazz (originally Grupo Mazz) began selling astonishing numbers of albums on a regional basis.

But it wasn't until the appearance in the marketplace of a pretty young singer named Selena Quintanilla-Perez that the theretofore confining parameters and possibilities of Tejano blew outward like a foundry explosion.

Selena, as the world came to know her, was born in Corpus Christi in 1972. Her father, Abraham Quintanilla, Jr., who had sung with a popular South Texas group called Los Dinos while growing up and whose passion for music ensured that his children were surrounded by it from infancy, recognized early on that Selena had talent.

He opened his own restaurant in 1980, where Selena, then eight years old, would sing to the accompaniment of her brother Abraham III on bass and her sister Suzette on drums. When the restaurant went under in the oil collapse, the family band was forced to turn pro in order to survive. Billed as Selena y Los Dinos, and touring in a beat-up van, the group graduated over the years from playing birthday parties and weddings to honky-tonks and dances across South Texas and eventually the United States—and, along the way, a fan base slowly began to coalesce.

Selena began recording LPs for small Texas labels and it all began to click: She was beautiful, she had a terrific voice, and she was now old enough to dress in revealing and provocative outfits yet seem like a "nice girl" rather than an aspiring porn actress.

Plus, the music was undeniably good. Her breathy, playful, slightly husky voice floated airily over an intoxicating blend of dance-pop as bubbly as champagne, percolating tropical *cumbias*, and melancholy, mariachi-flavored balladry. Los Dinos, which had expanded and featured Selena's future husband, Chris Perez, as well as her brother A. B. Quintanilla on bass (and writing most of the material) and sister Suzette on drums (and with dad Abraham serving as manager), was an accomplished, energetic backing unit that sounded great, was pleasant to look at without being distracting, and came across as what they were: family.

Though Selena's native language was in fact English and she had to learn the Spanish song lyrics phonetically, there was an undeniably proud aspect to her Mexican heritage, just as there was something intriguingly (but nonintimidatingly) American about her—so that she did in fact cross over to virtually anyone who might hear or see her in Texas, Mexico, or Latin America.

In 1987, Selena won Best Female Vocalist at the Tejano Music Awards and, two years later, Abraham hit a big home run: He negotiated a six-figure deal for Selena y Los Dinos with EMI's new Latin Music subsidiary.

In 1992, the LP *Entre a Mi Mundo*, featuring the single "Como la Flor," was the album that broke her through to the mainstream, becoming the first Tejano CD to achieve massive Latin radio airplay.

A terrific live album followed in 1993 (which would ultimately sell over a million copies), then the last of her Spanish-language studio records, *Amor Prohibido*, was released in 1994. Featuring the silly but fun hit, "Bidi Bidi Bom Bom," it became the first Tejano album to go RIAA-certified gold while she was alive (which is to say it sold five-hundred thousand copies; Latin albums, because of the regional market, normally go "gold" with sales of fifty thousand and "platinum" with sales of one-hundred thousand).

Along the way, Selena chalked up more Tejano Music Awards and a 1994 Grammy for Best Spanish Language Album. Clearly, she was going to put Tejano on the global map in a big way—and compete directly with the likes of Madonna and Gloria Estefan in *their* ballparks. And people in the record business were betting she could pull it off.

Not the least of these was SBK Records, with whom Abraham negotiated a contract for Selena's first English-language record. She had completed four tracks for the project, and had appeared with Los Dinos as mariachi performers for the film *Don Juan DeMarco*, for which she'd recorded a few more English-language tunes, when, on March 31, 1995, she was assassinated by the president of her fan club—a woman who'd been befriended by Selena, entrusted with a variety of increasingly responsible jobs within the organization, and had lately come under suspicion for embezzling funds.

The immediate and collective grief was the Mexican equivalent of the death of John Lennon or Elvis Presley. It's ironic that her ultimate goal—to become a huge star and carry the entire Tejano musical community on her able back—was accomplished through her death. Millions of people who might never have known who Selena was are aware of her now, and may well have bought a record or turned on a Spanish-language radio station out of curiosity or sympathy.

A posthumous release, *Dreaming of You*, which featured a mixture of classic Selena hits and her recently completed English-language tunes, sold astronomically, of course, but it only whispers about where she might have ended up had she lived. If there has to be a good part it's that, of course, Tejano is indeed bigger because of the slaying. But, just as obviously, Selena isn't around to ensure that the Tejano leap to the major leagues can send its heaviest hitter to the plate.

Which is not to say there isn't any talent out there. Even before Selena died, Emilio Navaira (known by nicknames like "the Tejano George Strait," "the Great Brown Hope," or, presumably behind his back, "the Male Selena") was a bright star whose luminescence was intensifying rapidly. That hasn't changed.

A singer of great talent and presence who's won myriad trophies at the Tejano Music Awards over the past six years and has been nominated for two Grammys, Emilio (who is now marketed just by his first name) is attempting to become the first Tejano artist to cross over into mainstream country. There are, of course, famous Mexican-American country stars—Freddie Fender, Johnny Rodriguez, and Linda Ronstadt, and plus young country artist, Rick Tejano, who's trying to break into the Spanish-language market—but none of them started out in Tejano.

Emilio did, in a big way. Born in San Antonio in 1962, he grew up listening to the Ray Price/Willie Nelson C&W preferred by his father, and to the rock and pop tunes of his generation. He sang in school and church choirs, made all-state choir and won a college music scholarship, and was planning to study to become a music teacher when an offer came to join a popular Tejano group called David Lee Garza y Los Musicales.

The nineteen-year-old Emilio couldn't resist the chance to perform and so hit the road with Los Musicales. A few years later, Emilio made the decision to go solo, which turned out to be fortuitous indeed. Working the road tirelessly with his band Rio, forging a tight, pleasing brand of country-flavored *conjunto*, Emilio rapidly gained a following the same way Selena did—with a smattering of indie label records like *Pienso en Ti*, *Sensaciones*, and *Shoot Out* that saturated Spanish-language radio (and created the need for major-label Latin subsidiaries to begin with).

Also like Selena, Emilio signed with EMI Latin, then became a star. Over the next few years, CDs like *Unsung Highways*, *Live!*, *Shuffle Time*, *Southern Exposure*, and *Soundlife* hit the charts like mortar fire. He recorded with Selena and toured with her, and his clean-cut, clerk-in-a-western-wear-store appearance gave him the same approachable quality that his female counterpart had.

But Emilio had been tempted all along by the churning waters of contemporary, English-language country music—which, from a marketing standpoint, isn't that big a stretch.

Or so the marketing folk in Nashville believe. Capitol Nashville signed him up, and in 1995 released *Life Is Good* (which spawned a series of ads for Miller Lite beer, an Emilio endorsee, whose current slogan is "life is good"). The leadoff single, a shiver-inducing ballad called "It's Not the End of the World," chugged steadily to the top twenty, and a tour with Alan Jackson (only slightly harder to get than a Nobel Prize for Chemistry) took Emilio's triumphant blend of country, Tejano, and whatever else he and Rio feel like playing to the hordes. In 1996, Navaira's Capitol follow-up, *Emilio*, was released. So far, so good.

IT'S A SIMILAR, BUT DIAMETRICALLY OPPOSITE, THEORY AT work in the Rick Trevino camp. The blossoming country star, who was born in Austin in 1971, has experienced immediate success on the country charts—and is now attempting to backtrack and attract Spanish-language audiences.

His two popular Sony/Nashville albums, *Rick Trevino* (1994) and *Looking for the Light* (1995), both of which have gone gold, have now been rereleased in Spanish on the label's Latin imprint, Sony Discos, a maneuver that necessitated Trevino taking a hiatus in Mexico for intensive lessons in his ancestral tongue.

Trevino did grow up quite familiar with Tejano—his father had been a Tejano musician and Rick shared his love of music. He took classical piano lessons from an early age and was soon performing Debussy and Beethoven pieces in school recitals. By his teenage years, Trevino was enamored of rock bands like Van Halen and Journey, and played for a while in an Austin Top 40 group.

But eventually, a love of country music began to seep in. The Young Wizards of C&W like Keith Whitley, George Strait, Clint Black, and Garth Brooks turned Trevino's head significantly and he began playing around town as a featured country singer. He finally quit college to give music a chance and was discovered by a Sony/Nashville A&R guy who'd seen Trevino's picture in a restaurant where the young singer sometimes performed.

It wasn't long before Trevino recorded his debut LP, a boogie-laced brand of hard honky-tonk, which resulted in the hit "She Can't Say I Didn't Cry." Subsequent CDs (*El Corazon de Rick Trevino* and *Learning As You Go*) seem to be working both camps sucessfully.

One who's been into the concept from the beginning, though, is Joel (pronounced *Joe-el*) Nava. But whereas Emilio was already established as a Tejano star when he tested Nashville waters, and Rick Trevino a country biggie when he went Spanish, Nava is the first musical astronaut to head into the galaxy they now call Tejano Country. His first Arista/Texas LP, *Joel Nava*, contains an equal number of English and Spanish tracks—as opposed to simply releasing alternate versions of the same record.

Nava, who grew up in a bilingual environment in Port Lavaca, Texas, listening to the usual blend of Texas music, started as a drummer for a country cover band, then formed his own Tejano group with himself as the lead singer. Called Joel Nava and the Border, the group signed with Arista/Texas in 1993, and when the bilingual debut album came out two years later, both Tejano and country radio tentatively embraced the concept. Singles like "Para Qué?" and "Abrázame" have since dotted Tejano radio, while "Four-Letter Word" and "Mama's Boy" have done reasonably well on mainstream C&W airwaves.

But many Tejano artists are comfortable with the niche they're in, which is fine, too; the popularity of Tejano music continues to grow independently of English-language country radio. La Mafia, for instance, remains a huge act across the United States, Mexico, the Caribbean, and Latin America.

Formed in Houston in the early eighties by brothers Oscar and Leonard Gonzáles, La Mafia quickly developed a following through their Teen King good looks and an addictive blend of poppy, synthesizer-drenched Tejano.

They released a self-titled LP on CBD Discos (now Sony Discos) in 1986, and a whitewater blast of albums and international tours has made La Mafia one of the most popular Tejano bands ever. They've attained gold and platinum status here and in Mexico, won *Billboard* Band of the Year and Song of the Year honors, and their position on *Billboard*'s Latin charts is more or less eternal.

Despite the popularity of recent LPs like *Un Millión de Rosas*, *Agarron Norteño*, and *El Corazon de la Mafia*, La Mafia decided to call it a day in 1999.

A challenger to the La Mafia crown, though, comes from La Diferenzia, a Texas-based group of Latino players from divergent ports like Chicago, Lubbock, Houston, and Mexico City. Spearheaded by Richard Castillo's classic, neo-operatic show-band croon and the songwriting of keyboardist Miguel Spindola, the octet seems effortlessly great. Like La Mafia, they are constantly reshaping the molecular components of Tejano, adding diverse Latin elements such as merengue, flamenco, salsa, and norteño to timeless pop melodies.

They signed with Arista/Texas and released *La Diferenzia* in 1994, which went platinum (Latin) and had two number 1 singles (Latin). The band was a Grammy award nominee, won a Tejano Music Award for most promising new act, and their sophomore album, 1996's *Fue Mucho Más Que Amor*, featuring the single "Tú No Tienes Corazón," bolted up the charts in similar fashion.

Of late, Castillo has stepped into solo mode, issuing a "farewell" greatest-hits package for La Dif and a self-titled solo disc of new material under his own name.

There are several other young Tejano groups with talent that are being grabbed up by the new Latin major labels, including Ram Herrera, Los Palominos, Fama, Michael Salgado, Los Temeraríos, and, of particular interest, La Trope F (whose reverence for traditional *conjunto* emerges with a fresh coat of Tejano paint). Selena's widower, Chris Perez, a main creative force behind his wife's success, has formed his own Chris Perez Band, a unique, bilingual band melding classic American rock with traditional Spanish flavors. The immediate result is the CD *Resurrection*, out from Hollywood Records, which includes guest appearances by members of Cheap Trick.

But the question most frequently asked is, "Who will replace Selena?" The obvious answer is no one, but on a different level, there are several talented women singers in the Tejano marketplace. The problem for them has been that—dead or alive—Selena has so obliterated her female competition that only now is there even a chance for women Tejano singers to break out.

In a perfect world, Shelly Lares wouldn't have to compete with a popular martyr; her significant talent more than stands on its own. In fact, Lares is now the most popular Tejano female singer in the world, and Selena would have wanted it that way. (The two were pals; Selena's husband Chris Perez actually played in Lares's band first and met his future wife at a rehearsal.)

Lares, born in 1972 in San Antonio, is a longtime fan of both country and Tejano music. She joined her first band at the age of nine and by twelve had been nominated for a Tejano Music Award for Best New Artist.

In 1989, she signed with Manny Records (now a WEA-Latin subsidiary) and released *Dynamite*, the first of a string of top-selling LPs (which have included 1991's *Tejano Star*, a greatest hits package, 1993's *Apaga la Luz*, 1994's *Sabes Que Sí*, and 1995's *Quiero Ser Tu Amante*).

The single "Soy Tu Amor" from the last album went number 1, and Lares signed a new contract with Sony Discos. Thus far, Lares has worked much the same strategy as Trevino and Navaira over the course of such CDs as *Aqui Mi Encuento* and *Donde Hay Fuego*.

Nydra Rojas, a seventeen-year-old singer whose debut on Arista/Texas seems to be moving mariachi to the Tejano mainstream, is another contender for female stardom, as are Stephanie Lynn and Elsa Garcia.

In a stylistically similar vein, such Cuban-influenced musicians as Ned Sublette, Fito Olivares, and Perez Prado, and members of the new "rock en espanol" movement like Filo and Tequila Rock, are adding even more textures to the Latin music scene.

BUT THE YOUNG TEJANO STARS AREN'T THE ONLY TEXAS MEXI-cans making big news on international entertainment fronts. In fact, a couple of old-timers, Freddie Fender and Flaco Jimenez, separately—and together, in the Texas supergroup the Texas Tornados—are extremely high-profile guys as the nineties wind down.

Fender, of course, who was born Baldemar Huerta in San Benito, Texas, in 1937, has been up and down so many times in his life that he's known as the Elevator of Country Music.

After he got out of the marines, Huerta worked South Texas bars and Chicano *funciones* as a singer/guitarist, recording Spanish-language singles and American country/rockabilly tunes for small labels like Duncan and Imperial. Calling himself Freddy Fender, he had two country-flavored singles, "Holy One" and the self-penned "Wasted Days and Wasted Nights," which began to attract national attention—but unfortunately at about the same time Fender got busted in Baton Rouge for marijuana possession and ended up with a prison term in Angola.

After jail and a variety of bottom-end jobs, Fender caught the eyes and ears of Texas music mogul Huey P. Meaux. Meaux, who's responsible for more brilliant Texas music than probably any other one person, heard Fender's lightly accented, sky-high, quivering tenor, instinctively knew that the voice was meant to be lovingly wrapped around pure country songs, and signed the singer to his Crazy Cajun label. Meaux had Fender record "Before the Next Teardrop Falls," which became a number 1 hit in 1975, and then scored Fender a distribution deal with ABC Dot. Meaux and Fender followed up with a rerecording of "Wasted Days and Wasted Nights," which also went gold, as did the two subsequent singles—and Fender found himself a star.

For three years, Fender could do no wrong, and though his career stalled a bit into the eighties, he managed to stay moderately successful. By 1985, however, he'd bottomed out on drugs and drink, and spent significant down time in a rehabilitation center.

Still, when he emerged clean and sober, he bounced back yet again. With a modest film career developing (he appeared in *The Milagro Beanfield War*, *She Came to the Valley*, and *Always Roses*), he also joined forces with musical icons Augie Meyers, Doug Sahm, and Flaco Jimenez in what is arguably Texas's coolest band, the Texas Tornados. He signed a solo deal with Arista/Texas that didn't work out for mostly philosophical reasons, but he continues to tour solo as well as with the Tornados.

Flaco Jimenez, born Leonardo Jimenez in San Antonio in 1939, is the best known of the Jimenez family of accordion royalty. With his father, Don Santiago Jimenez, Sr., as a teacher and built-in connection to *conjunto* insiders, Leonardo and his brother, Santiago Junior, both took advantage of their pedigrees and worked their asses off learning accordion.

But where Santiago Junior has followed the traditional path of their father, Leonardo (who took his father's nickname, Flaco, which means "the thin one"), mastered *conjunto* and has frequently utilized the traditional form as a diving board into a variety of stylistic directions.

Still, he started off in a most conventional manner, as a member of legendary San Antonio *conjunto* groups Los Caporales and Los Caminantes, and then for much of his young adulthood played the traditional dances, weddings, bars, and parties across the state.

But there was flash and excitement to Flaco's style, too, and his reputation grew until Doug Sahm called in 1972 to ask if Flaco wanted to do a session with Bob Dylan. Jimenez's work was creative and flame-inducing, and word of his prowess spread throughout the rock world. He soon began to perform on a wet-dream circuit of famous-artist recording dates for the likes of Emmylou Harris, the Rolling Stones, Stephen Stills, Dwight Yoakam, Santana, Bryan Ferry, Los Lobos, and the Chieftains.

As his fame spread, so did Jimenez's work schedule: soundtrack gigs, television appearances, national tours as a featured side man . . .

Still, along the way, Jimenez always found time for his own music, too, which mixes traditional *conjunto* sounds with more experimental, rock-twisted material. He released his own albums for years on small labels, and won a 1986 Grammy for a recording of his father's tune, "Ay Te Dejo en San Antonio." Jimenez signed his own major label deal with Reprise in 1991 and released *Partners* the following year. The album, a refreshing concept in which Jimenez performed duets with a number of guest stars from track to track (including Dwight Yoakam, Linda Ronstadt, John Hiatt, and Ry Cooder), was a critical success.

He later jumped to Arista/Texas, and his 1995 LP, *Flaco Jimenez*, won a

Grammy for Best Mexican American Performance. His third major-label solo record, 1996's *Buena Suerte, Señorita*, is a continuation of his constantly invigorating work, remolding *conjunto* in new and different ways, with the help of pals like the Mavericks' Raul Malo, Lee Roy Parnell, and Radney Foster. More recent CDs include *One Night at Joey's (Joey's Sessions)* and *Said and Done*.

Flaco's periodic experiments with the Texas Tornados are always worthy, though the death of Doug Sahm will seriously impede any protracted future ambitions.

If the Texas Tornados comprise a band that dances around the perimeter of Tejano music, they're not a bad musical analogy for what's happening in the movement. Tejano artists are themselves the purveyors of something new, seeing as how they molded *conjunto* music to fit the technological and stylistic trends of the late twentieth century.

And now they're adapting Tejano to fit a variety of new trends: those that anticipate the future even as they glance into the rear-view mirror of the past. Selena would be proud.

One of the most sensational events in Tex-Mex music ever was the assemblage in 1998 of a group called Los Super Seven, which is comprised of Tornados Flaco Jimenez and Freddy Fender, Texas music king Joe Ely, Los Lobos heroes David Hidalgo and Cesar Rosas, Rick Trevino, and burgeoning Tejano artist Ruben Ramos. Conceived by actual industry executives after a songwriters-in-the-round event at that year's South-by-Southwest music conference, the individual members were gradually assembled under the production wing of Los Lobos' Steve Berlin to record a CD for RCA Nashville.

In addition to a variety of equally substantial guests, Los Super Seven took turns backing one another on the crosscultural, multistylistic sessions rooted in Tex-Mex, and the resultant, self-titled album was a genuine masterpiece—and a Grammy winner for Mexican-American Record of the Year. Whether it was a one-off project (the band did some touring) remains to be seen, but one remains hopeful for more.

CRIMINALLY OVERLOOKED BAND
The Texas Tornados
☆

It came together as an impromptu booking in San Francisco in 1989: old pals Doug Sahm, Augie Meyers, Freddy Fender, and Flaco Jimenez—all veterans of the Texas music scene who found themselves in the same town at the same time—billed themselves as the Tex-Mex Revue for a two-night-only deal, a kooky idea for a fun bit of jamming conceived primarily because, somehow, all four of them had escaped playing on the same stage at the same time before.

But the magic was just as palpable as the recipe, and the possibilities were too enticing: blend two archetypical gringo Tex-Mex rockers, mix in a stock of hearty *conjunto*, then add a layer of Fender's pristine, Latin Romeo vocals, and serve flaming on your CD player.

As a result, Reprise signed the band, and their 1990 Grammy-winning, self-titled debut was a confirmation that the idea was among the better of our century. A picante-laced menudo of tunes featuring Butch Hancock's "She Never Spoke Spanish to Me," and the hangover classic, "Hey Baby (Que Paso)," *The Texas Tornados* was a hall-of-fame record of good vibes, wild times, and rare musical wisdom.

Zone of Our Own, which came out the following year, was another winner, a true highway-sallin' good time, but they hit the miracle level with 1992's *Hangin' On by a Thread*. That third album—curiously the most maligned by critics—featured Sahm's ball-rocking title cut, two aching ballads, the curious but enchanting MOR tune "The One and Only," and the border-at-twilight "Adiós Mi Corazón," as well as the liquor-infused "Ando Muy Borracho."

As the various members' own careers weren't exactly idle, the band took a break for four years amidst rumors that the Tornados had blown through town for the last time. Fortunately, like kinfolk, they reupped for at the least one more record, 1996's refreshing and reenergizing *Four Aces*. Though the band is apart far more than they're together, they did enough gigs to release *Live from the Limo* early in 1999. It seemed we'd always be able to count on the Tornados, but the death in November 1999, of Sahm was probably a crippling blow to the band. Perhaps Shawn and/or Shandon Sahm can step in and carry on.

☆ Three: Sounds of the Melting Pot

WHILE THE MEXICAN INFLUENCE ON TEXAS SOCIETY IS CER-
tainly obvious in the state's culture and music today, they are
certainly not the only ethnic group to have learned how to play an accordion.

From Louisiana has come a terrific societal impact as well, particularly
in the border towns like Beaumont and Port Arthur, where many Cajuns
migrated in the late nineteenth and early twentieth centuries, And, just as
Mexican folk music danced its way into Texas, so did the Cajun folk music
called zydeco.

Another stylistic summit conference which includes Acadian, Anglo-
Saxon, French, and Creole traditional musical forms, zydeco evolved for
one purpose and one purpose only: for poor people to have something to
dance to on Saturday nights before starting another week of having the
affluent heirs of the Confederacy screw them around.

The traditional zydeco band early on utilized a diatonic accordion (generally in the key of C), a washboard, a fiddle, and a triangle, and over the
years evolved to add electric guitars, drums, and steel guitars—all to better
pump out driving, waltz-time Fais-do-do music (*Fais-do-do* being the term
for the prototypical Cajun dance). Over the course of time, zydeco has
mixed N'Awlins R&B, rock 'n' roll, and hardcore honky-tonk into its early
folk structures—all the better for anxious dance-floor feet.

There are many similarities between zydeco and *conjunto*, just as there
are with European polka music, but it's instantly identifiable as its own
wonderful art form as well. Understandably, zydeco music is principally a
Louisiana phenomenon, but owing to the influx of Cajuns into southeast
Texas, there have been zydeco stars who were born in or spent significant
time in the Lone Star State.

The biggest was a biggie indeed: Clifton Chenier, the inarguable King
of Zydeco, who was born in Opelousas, Louisiana, in 1925. Chenier was
raised at a time when zydeco was thought to be an endangered musical
species—an outdated provincial form best left to rot in the dying past.

But young Chenier *liked* zydeco. He also grew up listening to the greats
of New Orleans piano—Professor Longhair, Fats Domino, James Booker—
and, in 1947, Chenier got his hands on an accordion. He was self-taught,

and as such, as he got proficient on the instrument, he revolutionized technique and accepted accordion theory. Having moved to Port Arthur with his brother, he started playing rock in Lake Charles and Houston clubs but, tiring of it rapidly, utilized an inverted transfusion process to mix old-line zydeco into the newer rock. It was a concept that bordered on genius.

By 1954, Chenier had made his first records on the Elko label, and had scored his first hit a year later on Specialty Records, "Ay Tit Fille (Hey Little Girl)" b/w "Boppin' the Rock." In a short time, Chenier had single-handedly resurrected zydeco—albeit with a decided nod to contemporary rock—and, finally able to pursue music as a career full-time, personally delivered zydeco's dance-floor ultimatums from coast to coast. With his accordion sending Roman candles of sound and his swamp-rich voice calling out over the music, Chenier was the personification of Louisiana Saturday Night.

He moved to Houston in the early sixties and, in 1964, began to record for the archival Arhoolie label; quickly Chenier was a Gulf Coast superstar, well known for hits like "Louisiana Blues," "Black Gal," and "Zodico Stomp."

Chenier became much in demand at festivals and fairs, and his Arhoolie LPs were instant classics (including *Louisiana Blues and Zydeco, Bon Ton Roulet,* and *King of the Bayous*). With his legendary Red Hot Louisiana Band, he continued to record for a variety of labels, including Tomato and Alligator, and won a Grammy for the 1983 Alligator release *I'm Here*.

Slowed by diabetes, the King passed away in 1987. The legions of great zydeco artists who were directly called into service by Chenier are staggering in both scope and quality—not the least of which was his son, C. J.

Another Cajun who belongs in the annals of Texas zydeco, even as a human asterisk, is Harry Choates. Though Louisiana-born and bred, the remarkable fiddler—whose 1946 version of "Jolie Blon" is regarded by most as the shimmeringly definitive take—spent more than a little time in Texas. In fact, the hard-living Choates, whose fondness for drink would've frightened Hank Williams, *died* in Texas—drunk, in an Austin jail. Somehow, there's a bit of musical poetry there.

The state's all-purpose zydeco accordionist is surely Ponty Bone. Though his playing infuses Tex-Mex and Caribbean flavors, it has been put to good use on countless sessions of various musical styles.

Bone, though, is at heart a zydeco guy, and though only two of his three solo albums are still available (*Easy as Pie* and *My, My . . . Look at This*, both for Amazing Records), his session and live work continue to form a fevered backbone for the Texas music community.

There are other zydeco artists with Texas connections. Bébé Carriére, a Louisiana native, now makes his home in Port Arthur. He's a fiddler of speed and grace and, with his deceased brother Dolon, headed up the Lawtell Playboys, an act that recorded for Rounder in the midseventies. Houston's Anderson Moss is a renowned master of the piano accordion. Queen

CRIMINALLY OVERLOOKED ARTIST
C. J. Chenier
☆

Born in Port Arthur, Texas, in 1957, C. J. Chenier originally had no interest in ascending to his father's zydeco monarchy. In fact, though he knew his dad was a musician, C. J. had no concept of what zydeco sounded like.

Instead, he spent his time learning saxophone and listening to Miles Davis, Parliament/Funkadelic, James Brown, and John Coltrane. He earned spending money in high school playing in black Top 40 bands and had dreams of going to college to study for a career in jazz or funk.

Instead, at twenty-one, C. J. was invited by his father to a gig and told to bring his sax. The confused youngster did, sat in for the night, faking his way through with the guidance of band members, and fell in love with zydeco on the spot. Shortly thereafter, as Clifton's diabetes began to take its toll, he gave his son his accordion and told him to figure it out. And when the King died, C. J. inherited not only the accordion but the Red Hot Louisiana Band.

Though no one will ever be the player Clifton Chenier was, C. J.'s years listening to Miles and George Clinton weren't idle, and his approach to zydeco is as different and innovative as his father's was when he started out.

Between 1989 and 1994, C. J. led the Red Hot Louisiana Band on several LPs for a variety of labels, including two Slash releases, Hot Rod and I Ain't No Playboy, and two Arhoolie records, Let Me in Your Heart and My Baby Don't Wear No Shoes. All four were solid, party-time albums that had the gradual effect of convincing skeptics that, while Clifton was gone, C. J. was doing damned fine as a successor.

It didn't hurt that C. J. has never avoided reinterpreting his father's material, although, over time, he's concentrated more and more on his own compositions. But that's as it should be.

In 1995, C. J. signed with Alligator and released Too Much Fun, the first of two CDs on which his musical personality can genuinely be said to have blossomed into something absolutely his own. The zydeco's still ebullient and spicy, C. J.'s voice is confident, powerful, and playful, the band simmers as always, and the kid's accordion shrieks, gurgles, and moans as though possessed. The 1996 CD, Squeeze This, is another must-own album.

Ida Guillory, the famous female accordionist, lived in Beaumont for most of her childhood. Lil' Bryan & the Zydeco Travelers are from Houston and successfully meld hip-hop influences with the more traditional form.

Also memorable: L. C. Donatto, Lonnie Mitchell and Willie Green, Albert Chevalier, and Vincent Frank.

* * *

IF EAST TEXAS IS A LANDING SPOT FOR CAJUN TEXANS, MANY
communities in central Texas are home to German and Czech citizenry.
There is a rich history of polkas, "oom-pah" music, and other traditional
musical forms emanating from these towns, readily on display at any of the
seasonal and celebratory festivals that dot their social calendars.

The first American Czech band to record in America was Bacovas Ceska
Kapela (or the Baca Band) a nineteenth-century outfit from Fayetville,
Texas. They were followed by the Joe Patek Orchestra out of Shiner, who
led the way for artists like Ray Krenek, Lee Roy Matocha, and Alfred Vrazel.

Adolph Hofner, the western swing accordionist and bandleader, grew up
in a Czech household in San Antonio and, with his brother Emil, played

---

CRIMINALLY OVERLOOKED BAND

Brave Combo

Descartes said, "I think, therefore I am." Brave Combo's Carl Finch said, "I
have an accordion, therefore we dance"—and it's a toss-up which statement
is more profound.

The concept of Brave Combo dates back to the late seventies, when
multi-instrumentalist Finch grew bored with the directions of contemporary
rock, pop, and jazz, and started listening to thrift store polka records. To
his surprise, Finch found himself captivated by the melodies, tradition,
structures, and global connections to the accordion—and founded Brave
Combo as a self-described "nuclear polka" band in 1979.

At first, playing polka interpretations of Jimi Hendrix songs garnered the
group a healthy nightclub and frat party reputation. But, as they progressed,
Finch's world music explorations inevitably became intertwined in the
central core of the band's *cumbias*, tangos, polkas, waltzes, and cha-chas,
and Brave Combo ceased being a musical punchline and began to earn
critical raves.

After releasing a few albums on their own Four Dots label, Brave Combo
signed a deal with Rounder Records and have subsequently toured the
world and released several albums to unanimous approval from journalists
as well as a small but global fan base. Though the players have rotated
through the years, the quality of the work remains progressive and
interesting, and Finch's leadership and vision belong in the White House
perhaps more than on the bandstand. There are several BC albums out,
many from the fine folks at Rounder, and *Polka for a Gloomy World* is an
excellent intro.

in a variety of European polka bands in clubs throughout central Texas while growing up.

In fact, sprinkled into his discography over a long western swing career was the occasional Czech/Bohemian album, and regional acts like the Czech Harvesters, Kovanda's Czech Band, the Vrazel Band, and HOT Czechs still perform the Old Country tunes, as does the German group Alpenfest.

German music is heartily represented today by the Walburg Boys and the Brushy Creek Brass Band, heirs to a tradition started by San Antonio's Herr Louie, Schulenberg's Rhine Winkler Orchestra, and New Braunfels' Hightoppers.

There is also a small community of Texas Polish musicians originating in Washington and Bremond counties and presently thriving in the Houston area. Fiddler Brian Marshall is probably the finest purveyor of this music; search out his *Texas Polish Roots* CD on Arhoolie.

But if any one act is doing its part to carry the torch for traditional polka music—of all ethnic varieties—it's Denton's Brave Combo.

WHILE IT SEEMS THAT THE GREAT CULTURAL TIE-IN, MUSICALLY, at least, is the accordion, it should probably be pointed out that there are several buzzing scenes of ethnic musical activity in Texas that do not require an accordion.

Reggae is a popular commodity across Texas, particularly in college towns. While there is no one identifiable reggae star, as such—virtually all of those seem geographically tied to Jamaica—there are plenty of reggae bands flourishing on the club scenes. Of particular note are Leroy Shakespeare and Ship of Vibes (Shakespeare actually does hail from Jamaica), Irie Time, Kimbute and Freedom Tribe, the Grown-Ups, Watusi, Ragga Massive, and Michael Johnson and the Killer Bees.

Music from the United Kingdom—all manners of Irish, Celtic, and Scottish traditions—are bountiful, and most big cities sport at least one Irish music society. Covering all instrumental and stylistic possibilities from bagpipes, tin whistles, and hammered dulcimer to any combination of renaissance, *a capella*, folk, and jig ensembles: Dallas's Lu Mitchell and Catch 23, Ravens Killdares, and Linda Baker; San Antonio's Cliff Moses; Houston's Flying Fish Sailors, Godfrey's Rangers, and Gordian Knot; Austin's Hair of the Dog, Ptarmigan, Ed Miller, Silver Thistle Pipes and Drums; and Fort Worth's Lost Tribe and Jenny Glass are but a representative sampling. The North Texas Irish Festival, held every March, is a spectacular introduction to music from the United Kingdom.

Various amalgamous world music bands are popular, too, such as Susanna Sharpe and Samba Police, the Horsies, Beledi Ensemble, 8½Souvenirs, and Shoulders—all indicating a terrific curiosity and virtuosity among the state's musicians.

There has also been an explosion of indigenous musics in Austin, which

CRIMINALLY OVERLOOKED BAND

Café Noir

Among the awards Café Noir has won, from a variety of regional and national publications, are: best jazz group, best world beat/instrumental group, best experimental/avant-garde group, and best classical ensemble. Which effectively states that it's hard to pin down Café Noir's music.

Perhaps one could imagine a tea party in an outdoor bistro somewhere in a village in the Carpathian mountains. It is a lovely autumn afternoon, with a mellow sun shining through leaves of kaleidescopic color. And seated at one table of the bistro are Kurt Weill, the Gipsy Kings, Los Lobos, Federico Fellini, Django Reinhardt, Bob Wills, and Igor Stravinsky. Perhaps Dracula and Frankenstein will drop by. Then they will all play rugby . . .

That's what Café Noie sounds like. Kinda.

Frankly, Café Noir's talent is above and beyond the tiresome journalists' need to constantly label stuff. It's just that when a band as good as Café Noir comes along, bewitched critics want to share the good news with those cretins standing at record store check-out counters with the new Bob Seger tucked under their arms. "Listen to *this!*" the critic wants to say. "Grow ears!"

Café Noir was formed as an instrumental group in 1985 by cofounders Norbert Gerl (viola and guitar) and Gale Hess (violin, viola, clarinet, accordion). After an intriguing, self-titled debut on Carpe Diem records in 1988 and an early period when the cream of Dallas's avant-garde music scene passed in and out of the band, Gerl and Hess settled in 1990 on a permanent unit with yodeling wizard Randy Erwin (vocals, accordion, guitar), Jason Bucklin (guitar, mandolin) and Lyles West (bass).

The new lineup flexed their considerable instrumental and melodic chops on 1993's *Window to the Sea*, a witty, lovely album that served as a tantalizing hint of things to come. *The Waltz King*, released in 1995, is the further realization of that potential—an album as tender, adventuresome, virtuosic, and artistically staggering as anything released on the planet that year.

isn't surprising. Anything Latin: Brazilian, Puerto Rican, Cuban—even Vaqui—music all have their neighborhood scenes with dozens of acts working every weekend. Artists like Mambo Red, Son Yuma, Centzontle, Toqui Amaru, Con Rimba Son. Killeen's La Cave, Cubanbop, and Ta Mère hold court busily.

There are even Jewish klezmer bands in Texas, though that traditional "wedding music" form is admittedly rare in the Southwest. Nevertheless, Bill Averbach's Austin Klezmorim and Houston's Best Little Klezmer Band

CRIMINALLY UNDERRATED GUITARIST

Teye

☆

Netherlands transplant Teye has almost single-handedly brought flamenco music and flamenco guitar to Texas. A hauntingly great player who played ordinary rock before studying in London and Spain and then making his way to Texas, Teye fist came to widespread attention as the textured player on Joe Ely's wonderful *Letter to Laredo* CD.

A student of flamenco master Paco Peña, as well as Spanish Gypsy musicians, Teye immersed himself in the form and eventually ended up in the U.S. He appeared on the Ely record almost by accident, just before he was to leave the country—Ely was so taken with Teye's magical sound and input that he scrambled to secure the guitarist a green card for touring purposes.

Now set in Austin, Teye played on Ely's *Twistin' in the Wind* CD and tours in Ely's road band. But his primary concern is his own band, Viva Flamenco. Comprising two guitartists and two dancers, Viva Flamenco has been playing regularly in Austin and was scheduled to release a CD in September 1999.

in Texas hold court, and Bad Liver bassist and musicologist Mark Rubin has a dance-happy outfit called Rubinchick's Orkestyr that has done a festival tour of France and released *Flipnotics Freilachs*. A second CD is presently in the works.

In brief, Texas is a big state. But regardless of one's background or interests, it's probably possible to find the sort of music you want to hear—and find someone who's damned good at playing it.

☆ Part 6: Soul, R&B, Funk, Disco, and Rap

☆ One: Out of the Blues

T EXAS HAS A GROOVE-HAPPY TRADITION AS OLD AS SOUL AND R&B music. Barry White, Billy Preston, Little Esther Phillips, Delbert McClinton, Johnny "Guitar" Watson, and scores more were all born in the Great State and have melted dance floors across the world since, well, to since two-steppin' proved to be a decidedly white way to dance.

So it's mildly ironic, then, that probably the one line everyone remembers in the annals of Texas soul is "Hi, everybody, we're Archie Bell and the Drells from Houston, Texas." To be sure, the "Tighten Up" is an undeniably infectious bit of radio vibe, but can anyone actually *do* the Tighten Up? Are there really dance steps, as for the Frankensteinian "Freddie" dance by sixties Brit-poppers Freddie and the Dreamers? Could Mikhail Baryshnikov teach us to "Tighten Up," or could we perhaps follow some yellow "Tighten Up" footprints on the floor of an Arthur Murray dance studio?

The point is, while it would be perhaps cruel to write off Archie Bell and the Drells as "one-hit wonders" (they're in fact not), their *in toto* contributions to Texas soul and R&B legend is probably not as substantial as that of some others. In fact, at this point, the difference between soul and rhythm and blues should probably be cleared up.

In the time line of music, R&B predated soul, if only in terminology. And the origin of the term *rhythm and blues* is easy enough to figure: In the beginning, there was blues, and when some of its practitioners got tired of being bummed out all the time and decided to pep it up a bit by making the music more rhythmically danceable, well, rhythm and blues was born.

In its strictest sense, this involved the incorporation of certain jazz syncopations within blues structures (which would in turn become rock 'n' roll when adapted by white rockabilly singers, but that's another saga). In the forties, the California brand of blues that came to be called "jump blues" was probably the first movement toward R&B; eventually, in a labeling sense, R&B was simply a more politically correct term for "race records," which had been a catch-all phrase for any music performed by black artists since the days of Blind Lemon Jefferson.

Later, when the smooth sounds of gospel and elements of commercial pop entered into the mix, "soul" came into being. Labels like Detroit's Motown and Memphis's Stax/Volt made radio superstars out of early soul singers, the effects of which trickled into Texas and resulted in a small but prodigious group of operators and visionaries: Don Robey's Duke/Peacock label, a blues/gospel outfit out of Houston known primarily for establishing the careers of Bobby Blue Bland and Junior Parker; the unwieldy musical kingdom of Huey "the Crazy Cajun" Meaux, also out of Houston, who produced, recorded, and/or discovered an astonishing array of hits and artists of all styles including Freddie Fender, Doug Sahm, Lightnin' Hopkins, George Jones, Clifton Chenier, T-Bone Walker, Dr. John, and scores more, and whose own Tribe label was of the fly-by-night sort (he frequently licensed his records to other companies); Fort Worth's Major Bill Smith (whose LeCam label was operated out of the trunk of his car and who was instrumental in the early successes of Bruce Channel, Delbert McClinton, and Paul and Paula); and Houston's Lelan Rogers, who worked with his brother Kenny, Mickey Gilley, and Little Esther Phillips, among others, on his own Lenox label and through various licensing deals with other companies, as well as the Macy's, Freedom, and Gold Star labels.

By now, of course, tags like "soul" and "R&B" are frequently interchangeable, and to call Stevie Wonder a soul artist and Ray Charles a rhythm and blues guy would probably confuse the average radio consultant (most of whom aren't exactly Wittgenstein, anyway).

To return to history, though, Houston's Amos Milburn (born in 1927) was probably the first of the great Texas R&B singers. He was reportedly all of five when he wandered up to a rented piano the morning after a cousin's wedding (not having Barney the Dinosaur to watch) and instinctively pounded out a credible version of "Jingle Bells." Subsequent lessons couldn't keep up with the youngster, so he'd stand outside bars on Saturday nights, listening to jukeboxes, then return home and work up the tunes he'd memorized that night.

With such a start, it would seem inevitable that Milburn would be a blues star—and in fact that's what he became before adding his substantial spin to the advent of R&B. He dropped out of school to join the navy at fifteen and after the war returned to Houston and formed a small band. A benefactor paid for a recording of "After Midnight" as well as a train ticket to Los Angeles, where Milburn was signed to Aladdin in 1945. Thus located on the West Coast, Milburn crossed his hard-drinkin', good-timin' Texas boogie-woogie background with the more sophisticated California jazz/blues sound. Under the guidance of saxophonist/producer Maxwell Davis, Milburn recorded several hits: "Chicken Shack Boogie," "In the Middle of the Night," "Hold Me Baby," and a series of blow-the-roof-off party tunes, including such paeans to drink as "Bad Bad Whiskey," "Good Good Whiskey," "Let's Have a Party," "House Party (Tonight)," "Let Me Go Home, Whiskey," "Vicious, Vicious Vodka" and "One Scotch, One Bourbon, One Beer."

Given such a recurring motif, and the uptempo grooves of the material, it's not surprising that Milburn was a huge success in dance-happy burgs like New Orleans. What *is* surprising is that he didn't become a rock star in the fashion of Fats Domino or Little Richard, both of whom he influenced greatly. Still, over the course of several years, Milburn recorded hundreds of tunes for Aladdin as well as for labels like Ace, King, and Motown as his career moved through the fifties and into the sixties. Though it's true that he had experienced his greatest success by 1953, Milburn's contributions and joy over music were obvious to the end; unfortunately, Milburn was a dedicated believer in that which he sang about. Eventually, his liver and brain revolted and, after suffering two strokes, losing a leg to amputation and some down time spent as an invalid, he passed away in 1980.

Whether he would tell us that it was fun while it lasted is unknown, but EMI's *Down the Road Apiece: The Best of Amos Milburn* and Route 66's *Amos Milburn and His Chicken Shackers* are guaranteed to transform any dying party into an inferno of fun.

Milburn is the most famous Texas R&B singer only because Bobby "Blue" Bland, one of the greatest ever, hails from Memphis and has lived most of his life in Tennessee. But for a few wonderful years, Bland lived in Houston. And his work for the Duke/Peacock stable—and beyond—established him as pretty much the voice of Texas R&B.

Like a lot of similar artists, whether Bland was a straight blues guy or an R&B singer is open to debate. But the sheer orchestral balladry of his love songs and his reliance on grooves outside the strict I-IV-V structures dictate (here, anyway) that he fall into the rhythm and blues category.

Bland grew up singing along with the star-clustered jukebox in his mom's cafe and signed with Duke Records in 1952. After a military obligation, he returned to discover Don Robey had bought the label, and Bland relocated to the Bayou City. Over the course of several pedestrian records, Bland struggled to find his own style, but when he did—as earmarked by the delightful, weeping twitch in his voice (which he described to *Texas Monthly* as the "squall")—he embarked on several years of redefining R&B.

Throughout the fifties, ably backed by the definitive razor guitar of Clarence Holliman, Bland released such classics as "Don't Want No Woman," "I Smell Trouble," "Loan a Helping Hand," and "Teach Me How (to Love You)."

Into and through the sixties, he melded gospel soul with gritty roadhouse blues and funk—"Farther Up the Road," "I'll Take Care of You," "Pity the Fool," "Turn On Your Love Light," "Poverty," dozens more. When Robey sold his labels to ABS in the early seventies, the "major label" machinations smoothed out Bland's edge (though *His California Album* is nice work), and while some duet LPs with B. B. King were nice, he slowly drifted towards the easy-listening arena.

Finally, after health problems, Bland ended up on Mississippi's small-but-sincere Malaco. His voice ain't what it was, but he's still capable of soaring moments, as on 1995's *Sad Street*, 1998's *Live on Beale Street*, and 1999's *Blues and Ballads*.

Ivory Joe Hunter was another of the earliest of what might be called

Texan R&B stars, and of whom it can be said that he never met a musical style he didn't like. Born in Kirbyville in 1914, Hunter was, like Milburn, a pianist. He started playing by ear at thirteen, quit school in the eighth grade to be a musician, and was a renowned gospel performer and regional church draw as well as hosting his own Beaumont radio program—all in his early teens.

"Ramblin' Fingers," as he was called for his manic barrelhouse style, settled in Houston. He released a single, "Blues at Sunrise," in 1942 on his own Ivory label which grew legs and danced through Texas, the Southwest, and California, so Hunter headed to Berkeley to check out the jump blues scene out there. Wartime sanctions short-circuited the label, but Hunter stayed busy: He met and played with Johnny Moore and the Blazers during that period, and was subsequently introduced to the great blues pianist Charles Brown, who became a significant influence.

Though Hunter utilized a standard jump-blues combo, he mixed his smooth-as-fog, make-the-women-swoon vocals on lovely ballads with the up-tempo style that was becoming rhythm and blues, and started a second label, Pacific Records, for which he released several singles. He also recorded for 4 Star, King, and Excelsior, but it wasn't until the late forties and early fifties, when he had major-label gigs with first MGM and later Atlantic, that Hunter scored with three huge hits: "I Almost Lost My Mind, "Since I Met You Baby" (both number 1), and "I Need You So."

At that point, with a quantifiable R&B movement emerging and radio formats bridging the gap in white and black music, Hunter began to broaden his stylistic scope even further. He heavily worked the R&B and pop markets, and even recorded a number of gospel sessions. By his death in 1974, Hunter had spray-painted wildly across the canvas of music, and though detractors point to his seemingly opportunistic work ethic, it's undeniable that he was a terrific artist responsible for some truly fine and prototypical moments in the burgeoning R&B market. He was one of the first to cross over to a white audience, he appeared on *The Ed Sullivan Show*, and no less than Nat King Cole and Elvis Presley covered his material. The curious should check out *Seventh Avenue Boogie* (Route 66) and King Records' *Ivory Joe Hunter: 16 of His Greatest Hits.*

Vocalist Percy Mayfield was another veteran of the California jump blues movement, though once he hit his stride, his work was rarely of the straight blues variety. His forte was tender-voiced soul balladry, his reputation for which was only exceeded by his status as a songwriter.

His material was covered by a virtual hall of fame of blues and R&B artists, including Lowell Fulson, John Lee Hooker, Jimmie Dawkins, and Ray Charles—the latter for whom Mayfield wrote under contract.

He was born in Linden, Louisiana, in 1920, and set out in his formative years in Houston to be a songwriter. He worked at various nonmusic gigs and also as a club singer, then moved to L.A. in 1942 to pitch songs. Mayfield eventually sold "Two Years of Torture" to execs at Specialty Records. They were as impressed with his vocal style as with the song, recorded Mayfield doing the tune, and after a few more sessions, the singer had a national hit with "Please Send Me Someone to Love" b/w "Strange Things Happening."

His multifaceted career seemed limitless until a horrible auto wreck in 1952 left the handsome singer grotesquely disfigured and his voice significantly altered. Still, with the courage and dignity suggested by the eloquent, positive, and often spiritually inspired material he wrote, Mayfield persevered and played the cruel hand dealt him.

He quietly continued to record his own stuff—terrific, haunting, and creatively structured pop/soul songs. In the early fifties, he charted seven top ten singles for Specialty Records, and more than fans were listening. Other artists began to clamor to record Mayfield's compositions, and at the end of the fifties, Mayfield signed a contract to write exclusively for Brother Ray Charles. Between 1962 and 1964 alone, for example, Mayfield cranked out "Danger Zone," "But on the Other Hand," "Tell Me How Do You Feel," and, of course, the immortal "Hit the Road, Jack."

In the meantime, Mayfield recorded several solid albums for Charles's own Tangerine label. Though the rock 'n' roll volcano of the sixties effectively slowed Mayfield's surge, he managed to record more sides for the Brunswick, Atlantic, and RCA labels.

He remained active, recording and performing, and toured Europe shortly before his death in 1982. In a genre rife with nicknames—some ludicrous, some bizarre, and some merely convenient—Mayfield's tag, "The Poet Laureate of the Blues," was remarkably appropriate.

Several excellent collections are yet available of his work, among them *My Jug and I* (Tangerine), *Poet of the Blues* (Specialty), and *My Heart Is Always Singing Sad Songs* (Ace).

JOE TEX (BORN IN ROGERS, TEXAS, IN 1933), ALSO SPENT MUCH of his South Texas youth singing gospel music in church and more secular material in clubs on weekends. His earliest musical successes came as a songwriter, inasmuch as he cranked out curious hybrid tunes utilizing the standard blues structures but with a narrative lyrical form most closely associated with country-and-western music.

After winning a Baytown talent contest which took him to New York City, he won another talent contest—this one at the famed Apollo Theatre in Harlem—and scored a four-week engagement at the venue. While he continued to write songs (and occasionally place them with actual recording artists), Tex was also developing his own style, an exhorting, work-the-chautauqua cross between Little Richard and Elmer Gantry.

Starting in 1955, Tex recorded for labels like King and Ace without ever making much headway. But in 1961, James Brown covered Tex's "Baby You're Right" and the young singer began to get a reputation. A Nashville

C&W manager, Buddy Killen, signed Tex and created the Dial label (distributed by Atlantic) so the singer would have a sympathetic record company. And, starting in 1965, when Tex broke through with "Hold What You've Got" (number 5), he had a string of funky, schizophrenic tunes (in which Tex gleefully championed the "my brain's in my loins" philosophy or sang weepy, cautionary warnings against doing your baby wrong) including two number 1 R&B hits: "I Want to Do Everything (For You)" and "A Sweet Woman Like You."

In 1967, Tex's status grew even more with another huge hit, "Skinny Legs and All," and Atlantic Records came up with the idea of the Soul Clan, a proposed early supergroup culled from its artist roster, which included Tex, Otis Redding, Wilson Pickett, Don Covay, Ben E. King, and Solomon Burke. However promising the concept may have been, Redding's death hampered plans, and though Arthur Conley stepped in for Pickett and one single was released, the Soul Clan never really got going.

In the late sixties, Tex's momentum slowed a bit, but he recovered in 1972 long enough for the irritating, quasi-novelty disco staple, "I Gotcha" (number 1 R&B, number 2 pop). Though he recorded for a variety of labels for the rest of the decade, and had a lamentable final success with 1977's "Ain't Gonna Bump No More (With No Big Fat Woman)," he finally managed to resolve the inner conflicts so often mirrored in his material: He became a Muslim minister and was known as Joseph Hazziez until his death in 1981. The 1988 Rhino collection *I Believe I'm Gonna Make It* is probably the best of the records still in print, though the Curb *Greatest Hits* set is fairly representative.

Fort Worth's King Curtis (born Curtis Ousley in 1934) is essentially the man who brought the saxophone to the forefront of R&B instrumentation. Fascinated as a child by the sounds of sax men Lester Young and Louis Jordan, Curtis took up the horn in junior high and kicked so much ass that, after graduation, he turned down several college musical scholarships to join Lionel Hampton's road band.

Based in New York starting in 1952, Curtis became *the* tenor saxophonist of choice in Big Apple session work, appearing on myriad recordings by hundreds of top artists ranging from Wilson Pickett and Sam and Dave to Andy Williams and Connie Francis to the Allman Brothers and Simon and Garfunkel (it's Curtis's burping horn on the Coasters' 1957 hit "Yakety-Yak").

But all along Curtis had been developing a career as a featured performer, too. In the late fifties, after forming his own band, Soul, Inc., he was signed to the tiny Enjoy label. From 1962 to 1963 Curtis charted three R&B hits, "Soul Serenade," "Monkey Shout," and "Soul Twist," the latter of which spent several weeks at number 1.

With Soul, Inc., Curtis hit the road, slowly building a fan base by working West Coast clubs and the southern chitlin circuit. He attracted the attention of Capitol Records, who signed him and released two albums (including

1964's *Soul Serenade* and 1965's *King Curtis Plays the Hits of Sam Cooke*) before Curtis jumped to Atco.

With his signature horn blowing nasty, wonderful squonks, Curtis covered a variety of pop and soul material as well as his own songs, and was able to instantly transform it all into what was indelibly King Curtis music.

Suddenly, the grassroots legion of fans Curtis had worked on for so long swelled over, and what had been primarily black audiences and in-awe musicians blossomed into a mainstream acceptance by white pop audiences. He was a featured draw at mainstream jazz and rock festivals. Too, Curtis mastered guitar, began singing his own songs, and even took on label exec responsibilities at Atco.

Unfortunately, in 1971, just as it had all come together for him, Curtis was stabbed to death on a New York street, the victim of a rumored romantic imbroglio. Prestige's *Soul Meeting* and Collectibles' *Soul Twist and Other Golden Classics* are more than adequate introductions to King Curtis's work.

BUT THE NEW RANKS OF TEXAS R&B STARS WERE BY NO MEANS A Men Only club. "Little" Esther Phillips and Barbara Lynn were both among the pioneers.

Phillips, who was born Esther Mae Jones in Galveston in 1935, fell in love early on with singers like Dinah Washington, Billie Holiday, and Sarah Vaughan. Her family lived in both Houston and Los Angeles during her wonder years, when Phillips honed what was obviously, even at that age, an incredible gospel voice in church choirs. At thirteen, she entered a talent competition at the Barrelhouse Club in Watts where an audience member, who happened to be Johnny Otis, was completely astounded by her talent.

For the next three years, she toured as the featured vocalist in Otis's band, which is where she got the nickname "Little" Esther Phillips and where she began her recording career. With Otis, Mel Walker, and on her own, on both the Savoy and King/Federal labels, Phillips recorded a string of top ten R&B hits (including "Cupid Boogie," "Double Crossin' Blues," "Little Esther," and "Weddin' Boogie").

In 1952, at the wizened age of seventeen, Phillips embarked on a solo career, and scored an immediate hit single with "Ring-A-Ding-Doo" for the Federal label. Her career was incredibly promising, but she developed chronic problems with drugs and alcohol, and spent the bulk of the fifties back in Houston in various recuperative therapies.

In the early sixties, having temporarily tamed her dragons, she signed with Lenox Records and had another smash with the "Release Me" single, a funked-up rendition of the C&W classic. While most of the States remained clueless, Phillips had a significant British following, including the Beatles, on whose 1965 BBC television special she appeared.

Phillips's remarkable voice was indeed a versatile thing, and the wide swath she was able to cut through various blues, soul, jazz, and R&B tunes resulted in a worldwide audience. She signed with Atlantic in 1965, had another big hit with her take on a Beatles hit, "And I Love Him," appeared at the Newport Jazz Festival, and recorded a batch of LPs during the period, of which 1966's *Confessin' the Blues* is a genuine classic.

A 1970 release, *Live at Freddie Jett's Pied Piper*, furthered her critical acclaim, and appearances at the Monterey and various other jazz festivals were lauded. She jumped to Columbia, then Kudu, Mercury, Muse, CBS, and Columbia again for a patchwork collection of records, including 1972's *From a Whisper to a Scream* (Kudu, with a harrowing version of Gil Scott-Heron's "Home Is Where the Hatred Is," a fierce antidrug song that was cruelly ironic given Phillips's heroin addiction).

As the disco era heated up, Phillips was even able to conquer that arena, charting the dance favorite "What a Difference a Day Makes," but though she continued to record with moderate success, her long abuse problems eventually resulted in kidney and liver problems that couldn't be overcome. She passed away in 1984. Despite the tragedy of her life, her voice remains an astonishing thing to hear. Several of her LPs are still available; Columbia's *The Best of Esther Phillips* and the aforementioned *From a Whisper to a Scream* are must-own records.

Beaumont's Barbara Lynn Ozen (born 1942) became a star at a tender, comparable age to Phillips. Along with a bluesy, after-midnight voice, she grew up cultivating a prowess for guitar. A left-handed player with considerable chops, Lynn (she billed herself as Barbara Lynn) was a twenty-year-old staple in Louisiana blues clubs when discovered by famed Houston producer Huey Meaux. Utilizing a poem Lynn wrote when she was sixteen, they recorded a song called "You'll Lose a Good Thing," which was imbued with a mournful N'Awlins feel as intoxicating as one of those embalming fluid-flavored Bourbon Street hurricanes. The song made Lynn a star virtually overnight (going straight to number 1 on the R&B charts and hitting number 8 in popland).

She followed with a like run of New Orleans–recorded hits for Jamie Records, all produced by Meaux, then recorded briefly (and with little success) for his Tribe label before jumping to Atlantic in 1968. Over the next three years, she hit the R&B Top 40 twice with "This Is the Thanks I Get" (number 39) and "(Until Then) I'll Suffer" (number 31). The Rolling Stones covered her "Oh! Baby (We Got a Good Thing Goin')" on their *Rolling Stones Now!* LP, but, though Lynn continues to record and perform, she's exceedingly s-l-o-w about it.

She issued a 1976 album on Oval, *Here Is Barbara Lynn*, a 1988 LP on Ichiban titled *You Don't Have to Go*, recorded briefly for Antone's, and, in 1994, released the critically applauded *So Good* for Bullseye Blues. Why Lynn has never equaled the success hinted at by her early hits is a mystery—she's a captivating performer, a helluva singer, a rock-the-house guitarist, and a superb songwriter. Proof is available on a fine import collection, Oval's *Here Is Barbara Lynn*.

Linden, Texas's Marie Adams is another gospel-trained R&B belter who sang for Johnny Otis. Discovered in her teens by Don Robey, she had an immediate top ten hit on the R&B charts in 1952 with "I'm Gonna Play the Honky Tonks."

This success enabled Adams to spring to plum gigs like the Johnny Otis Show, and one of his supplemental acts, Three Tons of Joy, so named because of the heft of the featured female singers. (Adams weighed in at 260 pounds.) Three Tons of Joy topped the British charts with "Ma, He's Making Eyes at Me" in 1957, and Adams and Otis went top twenty in 1958 with "Bye Bye Baby."

Though she resurfaced in the early seventies for a series of Otis reunion dates, Adams subsequently retreated into a private-citizen existence.

Scarcity of output has never been a problem for Lubbock's Delbert McClinton, the tireless White Knight of Texas R&B. He was born in 1940, moved with his family to Fort Worth in 1951, and like a lot of musicians who spent impressionable years in that Where the West Begins community, assimilated a rich chili of musical influences.

After collecting country, rockabilly, and blues albums during his early teens, McClinton took up guitar and began singing in various bands he assembled for roadhouse purposes. One of his better groups, the Straitjackets, was the only white band that played the great Fort Worth R&B rooms like the Skyliner Ballroom, Jack's, and, later, the Tracer Club.

Heavily influenced by Jimmy Reed, McClinton added harmonica to his repertoire. It paid off early on when he played the instrument on Bruce Channel's hit "Hey Baby," and a British tour followed in which McClinton got to tutor John Lennon on the nuances of the harmonica. Back in the States, McClinton kept busy on the Texas club circuit and doing session work, then relocated to California.

After releasing a pair of LPs on the Clean label with pal Glen Clark, McClinton went solo. He scored a deal with ABC, which was interested in McClinton's country side. In 1975, he released the all-original *Victim of Life's Circumstances*, then followed the next year with *Genuine Cowhide* (which mixed in a few R&B covers and shifted McClinton's focus a bit more in that direction), and *Love Rustler* the year after that.

When ABC went out of business, McClinton signed with Capricorn during the twilight of that label's first run, and managed to squeeze out two respectably selling LPs (1978's *Second Wind* and 1979's *Keeper of the Flame*; a tune from that period, "Two More Bottles of Wine," later became a number 1 hit for Emmylou Harris) before Capricorn went bankrupt. Finally, inking a deal with Capitol's Muscle Shoals imprint, MSS, McClinton recorded a Top 40 1980 album called *The Jealous Kind*, which had an actual hit single, the number 8 "Givin' It Up for Your Love."

When *that* label went belly up, McClinton decided the fates were trying to tell him something, and he headed back to Fort Worth to straighten out a growing drug problem and to see if he could restructure his career.

He remains a true sweat-slingin', ass-kickin' road dog, grinding out hard-core R&B for anyone who'll listen, and with a clean bill of health, Mc-Clinton's managed to keep product in the marketplace. He's since recorded for Alligator, MCA, Polygram, and most recently Curb (which has rere-leased many of his earlier efforts as well as a series of retrospective collec-tions). His most recent studio LPs have all been solid works, and his national profile has been bolstered by a 1991 Grammy for his duet with Bonnie Raitt on "Good Man, Good Woman," as well as by a duet with Tanya Tucker on the single "Tell Me About It," which was a Grammy nominee for Best Country Vocal Collaboration.

Billy Preston, who is probably most famous for his work with the Beatles on the *Abbey Road, Let It Be,* and *The Beatles* sessions, as well as session/performance gigs with the Rolling Stones, has also had a substantial career in gospel/soul. Born in Houston in 1946, Preston learned piano growing up in Los Angeles, and was playing in Little Richard's band by his sixteenth birthday.

He later replaced Leon Russell on television's *Shindig,* recorded briefly for Sam Cooke's Sar label, and played a stint in Ray Charles's road band. Preston then met the Beatles, recorded with them, and was signed to their Apple label. *That's the Way God Planned It* was released in 1969, reaching number 11 on the British pop charts, then Preston hopped to A&M, where he charted three top ten hits, including a number 1 single in 1973, "Will It Go Round in Circles."

He continued to do prominent session dates, then signed with Motown for the *Fastbreak* soundtrack LP (which included another top five hit, a duet with Syreeta called "With You I'm Born Again"). Since then, Preston's output has been decidedly religious in flavor (including 1982's full-gospel album, *Behold*), and most of his time these days is invested in various spir-itual projects.

Tracy Nelson, the Wisconsin chick who ravaged Austin and San Fran-cisco in the late sixties and early seventies as the volcanic singer for the funk/rock Mother Earth, has also continued a career that dabbles heavily in blues and R&B.

When she left Mother Earth, Nelson moved to Nashville and recorded for Flying Fish Records. The albums were difficult to pigeonhole, being as they were intriguing mutations of country, folk, blues, and R&B. But after a decade of reflection, she bounced back at the dawn of the nineties with a trio of popular LPs for Rounder (1993's *In the Here and Now,* 1995's *I Feel So Good,* and 1996's *Move On*), all of which explore the fertile territory between straight blues and soul-flavored R&B. In 1998, she joined up with Marcia Ball and New Orleans' wonderful Irma Thomas for a delightful three-way vocal extravaganza called "Sing It," which correctly topped nu-merous critics' best-of lists.

Leonard Victor Ainsworth isn't the sort of name that rolls resonatingly off the tongue, so when Leonard decided he wanted to make it as a soul singer, he became Dobie Gray. Born in Brookshire, Texas, in 1942, Gray (as we'll refer to him at every stage of his life) was born into sharecropper stock and, early on, figured plant life wasn't as interesting as singing.

He headed to Los Angeles in 1963, responded to a radio ad seeking singers, and went down and auditioned for a guy named Sonny Bono who was representing Specialty Records. Bono liked what he heard, and a first single, "Look at Me," did well enough to release a second—which happened to be "The In Crowd," a 1965 smash that went to number 13 and was written by a friend of Gray's based on an anecdote related by the singer.

He recorded throughout the sixties but couldn't equal the success of "In Crowd" and eventually enrolled in prelaw classes. He also milked the hit-song status, appearing with a group called Pollution sporadically, and eventually sought work as an actor.

After a few increasingly prestigious Broadway roles, Gray was cast in *Hair*, with which he toured for two years before trying once more, at the urging of Paul Williams's brother, Mentor, to jump-start his singing career. After a lengthy negotiation process, Gray scored a deal with MCA records and recorded one of Mentor's songs called "Drift Away," which went top five. (The album of the same name was one of the big successes of 1973.) A follow-up single, "Loving Arms," also sold well.

In 1975, Gray signed with Capricorn, a Georgia-based label, and spent time helping Jimmy Carter's election campaign. He relocated to Nashville, has continued to record for a variety of labels, and his smooth baritone sounds more than comfortable working an easy style of country/soul.

Dobie Gray Sings for In-Crowders (Collectables, 1987) is a definitive collection.

AND THEN, OF COURSE, THERE'S THE TIGHTEN UP. WITH THAT one bit of "We're Archie Bell and the Drells from Houston, Texas" intro repartee at the start of the song, the whole country became aware of the Bayou City—or at least anyone who listened to Top 40 radio, anyway.

Formed in the mid-sixties by Bell and Huey "Billy" Butler, Joe Cross, and James Wise (Butler and Cross were later replaced by Wilie Parnell and Lee Bell), the dance/soul band signed to Atlantic in 1968 and ignited dance floors across the country with the staccato groove of "Tighten Up," which went to number 1 on both the pop and R&B charts. Oddly enough, "Tighten Up" was actually the B-side of the single; the intended hit was called "Dog Eat Dog."

Their next song, "I Can't Stop Dancing," was probably a reference to their first tune, and also went top ten. But after Archie served a stint in Vietnam, their career momentum had been disrupted. After a dance-floor hit with "Here I Go Again" in 1972, and a few minor R&B chart successes since then, the group settled into a cult status and could probably have worked black showcase rooms into the next century if they'd been so inclined. Instead, Bell went solo at the start of the eighties, releasing *I Never Had It So Good* in 1981 on the Becket label.

It's not cynical to suggest the group may yet re-form; it's a living, after all. Besides, two questions remain unanswered: How *does* one do the Tighten Up, and just what the hell is a "Drell," anyway?

If Houston seemed to foster a preponderance of truly big shot, early R&B stars from Texas, Dallas certainly has more than its share of guys that *should* be stars.

Arzell "Z. Z." Hill, of course, was a star—but it wasn't one of those protracted, David Bowie/Let's Summer In Monaco types of stardom. Born in Naples, Texas, in 1935, Hill was an itinerant bluesman of infinite taste and skill who wrung his sweat on the dance floors across the South and in L.A., leaving a sporadic and difficult-to-find recorded legacy (blues, soul, even country) on a variety of small and frequently forgotten labels.

In 1980, Hill signed with Malaco, and a bizarre thing happened. After a well-received, self-titled debut for the label in 1981, his next record, *Down Home*, which came out the following year, featured the title cut as a single—and it didn't just take off, it erupted. The song, an infectious enough slice of blues/soul, quickly became a jukebox standard in every blues bar in the world, and *Down Home* went on to become one of the largest-selling blues albums ever recorded.

CRIMINALLY OVERLOOKED ARTIST
Bobby Patterson

Music isn't just a cruel mistress; she can take on decidedly Lorena Bobbitt overtones, and no one knows that more than Bobby Patterson—though it should be quickly pointed out that we're talking figuratively, here. Patterson, who was born in Dallas in 1944, was one of the great hopes of early soul.

A talent who was playing guitar and drums by the age of ten, Patterson was only thirteen when his first band, the Royal Rockers, won a contest that took them to California to record a single for Liberty Records. For a variety of reasons (which should have served warning to the youngster), the record never came out, but Patterson was not deterred. His attitude was more than remarkable: By the time he was out of high school, he went to Arlington College mornings, played country music in the afternoons, and frequented the R&B clubs at night. Along the way he mastered keyboards and saxophone, started writing songs and discovered he had an amazing, soul-twisting, King Hell of a voice.

Patterson signed with a Dallas label, Abnak, and released a 1962 single called "You Just Got to Understand," which did well enough that Abnak created a new, soul-oriented label called Jetstar. Thus began a six-year relationship in which Patterson wrote, recorded, produced, and performed virtually anything Jetstar might require.

With his band, the Mustangs, Patterson had several moderate hits during that time, including "T.C.B. or T.Y.A. (Take Care of Business or Turn Yourself Around)," but in 1969 the label went under. Patterson simply wrote and recorded a masterful solo disc in 1971, *It's Just a Matter of Time*, which in turn led to a contract with Jewel/Paula (where Patterson served a similar function for the record company—which is to say he wrote and produced other artists as well as himself, among whom were Little Johnny Taylor, Bobby Rush, and the Montclairs).

Again, there were several perfect R&B gems crafted by Patterson during his Jewel/Paula years, songs like "How Do You Spell Love? (M-O-N-E-Y)," "Quiet! Do Not Disturb (While I'm Making Love)," and "She Don't Have to See You (To See Through You)," which demonstrated not just his songwriting acumen but an affinity for parenthetical expressions.

But, for whatever reason, Patterson never hit like he deserved to, and he found himself back in Dallas for the bulk of the seventies, working the clubs and in lesser capacities for local record companies—and always staying pleasant and positive.

Though artists like the Fabulous Thunderbirds and Albert King covered Patterson's material, he'd long since abandoned any hopes of actual stardom—until 1995, when a young alterna-retro, reborn honky-tonk bunch of upstart supergroupers called Golden Smog (including members from the Jayhawks, Soul Asylum, and Wilco, among others) covered "She Don't Have to See You (To See Through You)" on their *Down by the Old Mainstream* CD.

A high-profile set by the band at the 1996 South-by-Southwest conference culminated with a guest appearance by Patterson, and *mucho* national media attention ensued. All of this vastly overdue activity is fortuitously timed: In early 1996, Patterson released *Second Coming* on Dallas's Proud Records, and has been making a series of plum club dates throughout Texas.

While, of all people, Patterson knows better than to count on anything, his new chance at the stardom he always deserved has got to be rewarding—perhaps as much so as the music itself.

Though he recorded one more fine CD for Malaco, 1983's *The Rhythm and the Blues*, Hill, in the one career move that could short-circuit his zooming career, died of a sudden heart attack the following year. The *In Memoriam* collection is certainly representative, but all the Malaco LPs are worthy.

* * *

R. L. GRIFFIN AND ERNIE JOHNSON ARE TWO OTHER HARDCORE
Dallas soulsters whose careers, perhaps, haven't been as successful as they
deserved to be—not that they're necessarily complaining.

Johnson, born in Winnsboro, Louisiana, well before any of the members
of Oasis were old enough to think of blowing snot on-camera at the MTV
Awards show, grew up in Dallas, and was recording on a variety of regional
labels like Paula and Malaco before he was twenty.

Blessed with a gravelly but soaring, Joe Tex–sings-gospel voice and an
ultrahip onstage grace, Johnson settled into the chitlin circuit by the late
sixties. Throughout the years he has continued to record for small companies, and his 1993 CD for Paula, *It's Party Time*, is a genuine groove cas-
serole. In 1995, Johnson released the terrific *In the Mood* (Waldoxy
Records), a continuous celebration of perfectly crafted R&B and soul.

R. L. Griffin, who holds down the symbolic fort represented by the South
Dallas blues/R&B community from his wonderful Blues Palace Club, is a
wonderful singer/songwriter/curator who—at fifty-eight—has just recorded
his first CD, which is due on the Italian Black Grape label in 1996.

Several other veterans and Young Turks of the Dallas soul/R&B scene
deserve to be mentioned. Tutu Jones, a mere "youngster" who grew up
playing drums for Griffin from the time he was ten, has become a blues/
R&B guitarist/vocalist/songwriter of incredible verve and wit, and his 1996
debut on the Bullseye Blues label, *Blue Texas Soul*, is absolutely genuine.

Al "TNT" Braggs is, along with Griffin, a true godfather of Texas R&B.
From his earliest days singing doo-wop, Braggs has been incontrovertibly
involved with music. He recorded singles for Chess and Peacock and has
written songs that have been covered by everyone from Bobby Blue Bland
and Aretha Franklin to Freddie King and Kenny Rogers (and more often
than not Braggs got hosed out of the royalties).

Though he toured with Bland, Braggs is most impressive as the featured
performer with his own revue; he's an amazing singer whose ignite-the-room
penchant for onstage flips, cart-wheeling across tables, and trouser-ripping
splits was the genesis of his TNT nickname.

Though his own recording career has never panned out the way it should
have, Braggs continues to make his own records sporadically, and also pro-
duces lovingly crafted, classic soul records for other artists on small mom-
and-pop labels that actually give a damn about product. He also hosts an
award-winning radio program devoted to vintage R&B.

Others pioneers of merit are Curly "Barefoot" Miller, Little Joe Blue,
Charley Roberson, Vernon Garrett, L. C. Clark, and two members of the
Coasters (Tyler's Carl Gardner and Itasca's Billy Guy).

Though many would argue that the advent of rap has essentially destroyed soul music and rhythm and blues (not to mention Earth as well),
both soul and R&B are grounded in something far too strong to ever be
erased or eliminated—good songs.

☆Two: Disco, Gospel, and the Poetry of the 'Hood

A T FIRST GLANCE, THERE IS LITTLE TO CONNECT DISCO, GOS-
pel, and rap music, unless one stretches a bit and thinks of disco as
the gospel music of the feet and loins, or rap as the gospel of disenfranchised
inner-city youth (which, in turn, becomes the gospel of suburban white kids
who menacingly cruise shopping malls).

It's probably not necessary to complete the ludicrous analogy by calling
gospel "disco music for the soul" or saying that gospel is "rap for the celes-
tially secure." Gospel is, well, gospel—but even that's splintered into various
Protean shapes.

What can be said is that all three are principally black in origin and
execution, which will have to serve as the tenuous umbilical cord thematically uniting them for the purposes of this chapter.

Disco is an essentially harmless phenomenon, a sort of seventies backlash
against live bands in which prerecorded, beat-heavy music was played in
clubs for the singular purpose of dancing—and whatever narcotic or alcoholic infusions enhanced the experience (or helped free the inhibitions for
any wrought-of-Caligula activities that might follow) were heartily encouraged.

So great was the response from the record-buying public that the backlash
was eventually felt in all forms of music, from new wave to rap and hip-
hop. But, in the beginning, there was the beat.

Johnny "Guitar" Watson, who was born in Houston in 1935 and was the
nephew of blues great Frankie Lee Sims, grew up as accomplished on piano
as he was on guitar. Not surprisingly, then, long before there was disco,
Watson was a highly respected and influential blues player.

Watson made his way to Los Angeles and was a featured sideman by
the time he was fifteen years old. Within two years, he was signed to Federal Records as a solo artist. Billed as Young John Watson, he released
ahead-of-his-time singles like "Highway 60" and "Space Guitar" before signing with the Modern label. He then became Johnny "Guitar" Watson, and

if massive record sales eluded him, his development as a stage performer did not.

He became a huge draw on the basis of his showmanship and technique—his act was a dizzying blend of feedback, T-Bone Walker antics, and an electrical storm. After a short stint with Modern, Watson signed with King Records and, in the late fifties and early sixties, released several respectably selling and musically important singles ("Three Hours Past Midnight," "Cuttin' In," and "Those Lonely Lonely Nights"), including some of the first known recordings of feedback. In fact, by then, Watson was such a guitar force that everyone from Joe Ely and Steve Miller to Jimi Hendrix and Frank Zappa reverentially sopped up his shtick.

In the meantime, Watson was signed to the CBS subsidiary Okeh by producer/keyboardist Larry Williams. They cowrote "Mercy Mercy Mercy" with Josef Zawinul and toured internationally for a few years before Watson returned to solo status for blues/funk LPs like *Bad* and *Two for the Price of One*.

As his style continued to evolve in a decidedly groove-oriented direction, Watson moved to Fantasy Records and, in 1973, released the seminal *Gangster of Love* LP. In 1975 he was slotted to sing on the Frank Zappa masterwork *We're Only in It for the Money*, then scored his first disco hit with the 1976 single "I Don't Want to Be a Lone Ranger," from the *I Don't Want to Be Alone, Stranger* LP.

He then started his own label, DJM Records, and flooded the discos with a succession of witty, beat-saturated albums: *Ain't That a Bitch* (1976), *A Real Mother for Ya* and *Funk Beyond the Call of Duty* (1977), *Giant* (1978), and *What the Hell Is This?* (1979). "I Need It," "It's Too Late," and the title track from *A Real Mother for Ya* were all disco staples, and Watson reached the peak of his success.

But as disco began to segue into the next musical fad, Watson's commercial appeal began to wane. He continued to record for both Mercury and A&M, but spent most of the eighties in a vacation/retirement mode. After a fourteen-year silence, a period during which he listened to countless rappers sample his grooves, Watson went back into the studio and recorded the Grammy-nominated *Bow Wow* (Bellmark Records, 1994), and was on a tour of the Far East when he died onstage—where he belonged—of a heart attack. Several excellent collections are available, but for genuine funk, *A Real Mother for Ya* is hard to argue with.

Johnnie Taylor is another disco star who'd actually started in gospel (see, you *knew* this would all connect), then spent years as a moderately successful blues/R&B artist before striking it rich in the seventies. The Dallas-based singer was born in Crawfordsville, Arkansas, in 1935, and by 1954 was singing with a doo-wop outfit called the Five Echoes. He then joined up with the gospel group the Highway QCs before replacing Sam Cooke in the Soul Stirrers, a terrifically significant gospel group.

In 1963, after a short-lived stint in the ministry, Taylor went secular and signed with Cooke's SAR label. Utilizing a sweet-but-sandpapery voice and a roller-coaster delivery, Taylor had a hit with "Rome Wasn't Built in a Day," and eventually signed with Stax in 1966. For the next six years he hit the charts regularly with tunes like "Who's Making Love" (number 5), "Take Care of Your Homework" (number 20), "Testify (I Wanna)" (number 36), "Jody's Got Your Girl and Gone" (number 28), "I Believe in You" (number 11), "Cheaper to Keep Her" (number 15), and you get the idea.

Despite his obvious success as a soul singer, Taylor was dealt a curious hand of fate when Stax went bankrupt in 1976. With obvious commercial appeal, Taylor had no trouble signing with Columbia—at which time he recorded the decidedly non–gospel-titled *Eargasm*. A single off the album, "Disco Lady," went to number 1 like a heat-seeking missile, pulsing smoothly out of every stereo speaker in every disco in the world—and, along the way, becoming the first single ever to go platinum.

Never mind that the rest of the LP was essentially the same soul material Taylor had always recorded—it is for that one tune that Taylor will always be remembered, and as such he will be eternally pigeonholed as a disco artist. In fact, after "Disco Lady" hit, he was more or less honor-bound to attempt to replicate the success, and the three records that were cranked out immediately following *Eargasm*, *Rated Extraordinaire* and *Disco 9000* (1977) and *Ever Ready* (1978), were of the dance-floor ilk.

Taylor also toured for several years on the strength of "Disco Lady," and the irony is that, only after the hoopla died down and disco self-destructed did Taylor sign with a small label (Malaco) and go back to recording the same wonderful soul music he'd made in the first place. *I Know It's Wrong, But I . . . Just Can't Do Right*, from 1991, and 1994's *Real Love* are sterling later efforts, and two Stax LPs, *Taylored in Silk* (1973) and *Chronicle* (1977), capture the essence of this marvelously talented crooner—without any disco.

WHEREAS JOHNNY WATSON DELIVERED HIS DISCO WITH DOSES of tongue-in-cheek humor and hard-edged guitar funk, and Johnnie Taylor sort of fell into disco by accident, there is every indication that Galveston's Barry White grew with the movement, approaching disco as an art form and, fashioning it in his own image, made it a far, far better thing than it had ever been (if cornier).

White, who is certainly the Orson Welles of disco, took the early-seventies grooves and orchestrations of Isaac Hayes and Curtis Mayfield, added a husky, spoken-word carnality to the proceedings, and established himself as not only a record industry visionary and consistent number 1 hitmaker, but a substantially girthed and most unlikely sex symbol as well.

As a session pianist from the time he was eleven, White joined a Los

Angeles R&B band called the Upfronts when he was sixteen, and got arrangement credits on Bob and Earl's minor-hit version of "The Harlem Shuffle" and Jackie Lee's "The Duck" two years after that.

He further honed various production and session skills, scored a gig as an A&R man for Mustang Records, and then signed a female vocal group called Love Unlimited. In 1972, he took Love Unlimited to Uni Records and produced their first gold single, "Walking in the Rain with the One I Love." White then set up his own production company, signed on as the manager for Love Unlimited, got himself a deal with 20th Century–Fox in 1973—and it was hit time.

For the next five years, everything White recorded was a success, and one doesn't doubt that, had he released a tape of himself eating lunch, it would've climbed the charts, too (as it is, most of his singles sound like White was recording his bedroom love-play sessions and releasing them as singles). Instantly familiar White songs from that period include "I'm Gonna Love You Just a Little More Baby" (number 1), "Never, Never Gonna Give Ya Up (number 2), "I've Got So Much to Give (number 5), "Can't Get Enough of Your Love, Babe" (number 1), "You're the First, the Last, My Everything" (number 2), and "What Am I Gonna Do with You" (number 8)—and those are just the *top ten* hits! (White had several more routinely rocket into the Top 40.)

In the meantime, he expanded Love Unlimited to the Love Unlimited Orchestra, for whom he penned the number 1 "Love's Theme" right out of the box, as well as other hit singles and LPs. It would take Bill Gates and Stephen Hawking, both laced with caffeine and Yellow Dog speed, working for days on end to calculate the number of gold/platinum records, and more important, the cash Barry White generated during peak disco years in the mid-seventies.

Oddly enough, when the craze was over and the appeal of White's music had lessened considerably, the singer/songwriter continued to work. Where lesser folk would've packed a few suitcases with large-denomination bills and purchased an island (though preferably not in Marlon Brando's neighborhood), White kept recording.

In 1979, he started his own label, Unlimited Gold (a CBS imprint), which surely recouped investments over the next few years, and in 1987 he signed with A&M Records. From then on, White has at least partially regained his touch. He's charted several Top 40 R&B hits, including "Sho' You Right" (number 17), "I Wanna Do It Good to You" (number 26), and the number 2 hit, "Put Me in Your Mix."

White has also appeared as a featured vocalist on the 1990 Quincy Jones collaboration "The Secret Garden (Sweet Seduction Suite)" (number 1) and on Big Daddy Kane's 1991 single, "All of Me."

As late as 1994, the irrepressible White was still digging it all the way to the bedroom: His *The Icon Is Love* CD was a number 1 R&B hit and featured a number 1 single, "Practice What You Preach." Then, surprisingly,

White reassembled the Love Unlimited Orchestra for 1999's rewardingly nostalgic *Staying Power*.

Dallas's Calvin Yarbrough and Alisa Peoples, friends from childhood who sang together for the first time in their church, became a brief if intense force in the R&B charts when a 1981 single, "Don't Stop the Music," went to number 1. Three years later, they charted again with "Don't Waste Your Time." They released the Guilty album in 1986, but have since kept a (presumably) happily married low profile.

Miss Lavelle White (no relation to Barry) is a secret Texas R&B treasure. A Louisiana native who moved to Houston at the age of fifteen, White started out singing on that city's awesome blues circuit and was signed to the immortal Duke Records label in 1958.

Over the next two decades, she released a few regionally successful singles ("Stop These Teardrops," "Yes I've Been Crying") and touring with the likes of Bobby "Blue" Bland, Junior Parker, B. B. King, Sam Cooke, the Isley Brothers, Aretha Franklin before relocating to Chicago in 1978. She was house vocalist at Kingston Mines for eight years before returning to Texas, first to Houston, and then to Austin, where she signed with Antone's Records.

Her debut CD for the label, *Miss Lavelle*, was nominated for three W. C. Handy Blues awards, and her huge popularity in France garnered her an Otis Redding Award from the Academy of Jazz. Her latest album, *It Hasn't Been Easy*, is another masterful effort.

No other Texans experienced much success during the disco era, but both Jennifer Holliday and a Dallas vocal group called the MAC Band landed nationally in that thin radio soul corridor between the end of disco and the runaway onslaught of rap.

Holliday, born in Houston in 1960, spent her childhood singing in church and attending drama school. At twenty-two, she landed a part in the Broadway musical *Dreamgirls;* her recording of that production's song "And I Am Telling You I Am Not Going" was a top twenty-five hit and resulted in a recording contract for Holliday with Geffen Records.

Her first LP, *Feel My Soul* (1983), was produced by Maurice White of Earth, Wind and Fire and went to number 31. A second Geffen release, *Get Close to Your Love*, followed two years later, but, as with subsequent efforts like *Dream with Your Name on It* (1988, Ariola) and *I'm on Your Side* (1991, Arista), sales just weren't cutting it. Critics applauded her world-class pipes but theorized that her thespian's delivery of pop material was perhaps a bit too grandiose.

Geffen released a greatest hits package in 1994 which is just that.

Dallas's MAC Band worked a smooth soul groove in the mid-eighties, borrowing heavily from acts like the Dazz Band and Kool and the Gang. Though they released two LPs on MCA, *Love U 2 the Limit* and *The MAC Band Featuring the McCampbell Brothers* (the latter produced by L. A. Babyface), sales couldn't justify another album. They released a third record in the early nineties, *Real Deal* (on Ultrax), but no further recordings have been forthcoming.

Certainly the biggest success story of late belongs to Erykah Badu, a graduate (like jazz trumpeter Roy Hargrove and rock vocalist Edie Brickell) of Dallas's Arts Magnet High School. Creating a blend of traditional soul and smooth jazz with the vibe and technology of hip-hop, Badu has done what seemed impossible: created a new form of R&B.

Her debut CD, *Baduism*, assaulted the *Billboard* charts in a blitzkrieg fashion reminiscent of country youngster (and fellow Dallas kid) LeAnn Rime's success, selling over one hundred thousand units a week upon its release. Her first single, "On and On," went to number 1, and her Billie Holiday Wakes-Up in the Nineties take on soul music is riveting. That Badu also wrote essentially all the material is important, too, inasmuch as her message is determined and spiritual.

Oddly enough, her second CD was an in-concert document called *Erykah Badu Live*. Though some of the material is from the debut album—which was only released months before—the live arrangements proved Badu to be a dynamic and forceful performer. A new song, the powerful "Tyrone," and some imaginative covers made the CD much more of a sure bet than an eyebrow-raising strategy.

After taking time to have a baby in 1999, the Grammy-nominated, Soul Train award-winning artist commenced work on a new CD and also started an acting career by appearing in *The Ciderhouse Rules*.

Essentially, the real threat to classic R&B/soul is that the new generation isn't exposed to it; they all want to be rap artists. That having been said, there *are* two bright hopes on the horizon: Quindon Tarver and Tevin Campbell.

At fourteen, Waxahachie native Campbell, already a mature R&B crooner, was discovered by Quincy Jones and soon thereafter had a song, "Round and Round," on Prince's *Purple Rain* soundtrack.

The next year, he released T.E.V.I.N. for the Reprise label, scored a second hit with "Tell Me What You Want Me to Do," and encored with the *I'm Ready* CD in 1993. After a hiatus to finish school, Campbell, at 19, released *Back to the World* on Warner Brothers.

Tarver, billed simply as Quindon, was thirteen in 1996 when he came out with his first album, a self-titled opus for the Virgin label. A nicely received disc, it featured sweet soul melodies with a contemporary hip-hop feel.

THE EIGHTIES AND NINETIES HAVEN'T BEEN OTHERWISE DE-void of R&B traditionalists, though the ranks have thinned. Bands like Elvis T. Busboy and the Blues Butchers, Joe McBride, Junior Medlow and Tornado Alley, Hamilton, Miss Molly and the Whips, Maylee Thomas and Texas Soul, and Extreme Heat are representative.

It is less fortunate that the state's first legitimate rap star was Vanilla Ice. Though the Carrollton, Texas, native was once complimented by Public Enemy's Chuck D for his dancing ability, it is nevertheless true that Ice is the greatest embarrassment in rap history—and probably responsible for the fact that it is now almost impossible for a white person to get any respect at all in the genre.

Born Robbie Van Winkle in Miami in 1968, he grew up in the Dallas suburb of Carrollton, a fact conveniently overlooked when he was discovered by a Dallas club owner named Tommy Quon and presented to the American public as a child of Miami's mean streets, a white kid affectionately nicknamed "Vanilla" by the black kids he ran with and with whom he learned the nuances of rhyme, dance, and inner-city chicanery—all of which is a bit of speculative fiction rivaling Ray Bradbury's *Dandelion Wine* for pure imagination.

In fact, though, Vanilla Ice (as he'd come to be billed) *could* dance and somehow managed to string together some postadolescent, rhyming-dictionary raps. And with the sort of chiseled good looks and ultrahip haircut that impress pubescent girls, Ice secured a recording contract with SBK and, in 1990, released *To the Extreme*. In addition, Vanilla Ice scored an opening slot on a lucrative tour with MC Hammer, who, at that time, was the hottest rapper in the world.

During the course of the tour, Ice's first single, "Ice Ice Baby," was released—and blew the lid off the radio world. MC Hammer was presumably astounded as well: The upstart white kid sold seven million copies of the record and knocked Hammer out of the *Billboard* number 1 slot he'd held for twenty-one weeks.

The hit, a slick and infectious tune featuring a riff lifted straight from the David Bowie/Queen single "Under Pressure," resulted in a nightmarish period of American history when we were besieged by a genuine Vanilla Ice frenzy. He was everywhere: popping up in Teenage Mutant Ninja Turtle movies, releasing a live LP, endorsing Coke and Nike, hanging with Madonna . . .

Slowly, though, as the truth about Van Winkle's nondescript suburban upbringing came out, and his cardboard personality began to benumb fans through radio and television exposure, the Ice Man began to melt.

An ill-advised starring role in a truly awful feature film called *Cool as Ice* (in which the star delivered neo–*Twelfth Night* dialogue like, "Drop that zero, get with the hero"), further chipped away at the façade, and Ice retreated while his management's damage control people presumably called Gary Hart to see if salvage was possible.

Cautiously, four years after *To the Extreme*, Vanilla Ice put out another album, *Mind Blowin* (1994), a desperate effort to sound tough and aggressive. It failed miserably, and had Ice wandered into Houston's Fifth Ward, for example, in an attempt to push the record off on some genuine gangstas, he would've been gunned down in his tracks.

As it is, apparently nothing will kill His Iceness. Pursuant to the sort of white-boy-rapper-meets-millennial-metal being churned out by acts like Limp Bizkit or Kid Rock, VI actually scored yet another record deal and, in 1998, came out with the oh-so-imaginatively titled *Hard to Swallow*.

Speaking of Houston's Fifth Ward, it's home to Texas's *real* bad-asses of rap, the Geto Boys and their sundry offshoots. The group was formed in 1986 by James "Li'l J" Smith, then twenty-two years old, who hand-picked members Scarface (Brad Jordan, born in Houston, 1969), Bushwick Bill (Richard Shaw, born in Kingston, Jamaica, 1966), and Willie D. (Willie Dennis, born in Houston, 1966) as the flagship group for his Rap-a-Lot Records.

The Geto Boys are diametrically opposite of Vanilla Ice: Actual inner-city street *denizens* whose violent, misogynistic, and racist tunes boil with rage and hatred—and if they frequently go straight for the shock value quotient, let it never be said that the emotions aren't born of genuine anger, frustration, and despair. Their first efforts were so antagonistic, radical, and socially irresponsible—in the tradition of 2 Live Crew and Ice-T—that the phrase "horrorcore" was invented to describe their music.

The first two albums, 1988's *Making Trouble* and 1990's *Grip It! On That Other Level* (both on Rap-a-Lot), on which the three Geto Boys took turns spinning sinister tales and issuing calls to arms over slick production grooves, propulsive church organs, and incessant beats, spawned a huge fan base and seized the collective imagination of young black men across the United States. Everyone else, though, was repulsed by songs like "Let a Ho Be a Ho" and "Trigger Happy Nigga," and the Geto Boys' solution seemed to be either rape it or kill it (or both, in no particular order).

In 1990, the Geto Boys signed with Rick Rubin's Def Jam label and recorded *We Can't Be Stopped*, which was refused for shipment by Geffen Records (Def Jam's distributor) on the grounds that the material was acutely offensive to, well, every human on earth except young black males. The decision further enraged the Geto Boys, with some justification, since Geffen had no problem distributing Def Jam's Andrew "Dice" Clay, a white "comic" guilty of the exact same lyrical offenses leveled at the Geto Boys— just from a white perspective.

In any case, Virgin agreed to distribute the CD, which climbed to number 24. A single, "Mind Playing Tricks on Me," a slice of urban paranoia written by Scarface which *The Source* described as "four of the most chilling minutes of hip-hop," became something of an anthem. The group seemed on the verge of superstardom, even as Willie D. bowed out and was replaced by Big Mike (Mike Barnett, born in New Orleans in 1971); it's true that none of the original three got along particularly well. They were, after all, assembled by Smith for the purpose of recording, and had no prior friendships on which to build their success.

Perhaps because of that lack of camaraderie, all three of the original Boys had dabbled in solo work anyway. Though the individual CDs were rarely as impressive as Geto Boys stuff, they each had their moments. On his 1992 CD, *Little Big Man*, Bushwick Bill, who at four feet six is a dwarf, described in elaborate detail the circumstances that resulted in his persuading his seventeen-year-old girlfriend to shoot one of his eyes out (in an anecdote of suicidal drunkenness and emotional extortion that is almost unbelievable—even considering the source).

Scarface has been the most prolific, releasing several CDs through the nineties (many of them platinum), including *Mr. Scarface Is Back, The Diary*, a collaborative effort with pals like Too Short, Tupac, and Master P called *My Homies*, and the *The Untouchable*.

And Willie D. released *Controversy* (1989) and, after leaving the group, *I'm Goin' Out Lika Soldier* (1992), *Play Wicha Mama* (1994, Wize Up/Wrap), and, with Sho, 1993's *Trouble Man*. Willie D. did okay for himself, but was perennially faced with the inevitable "When are you getting back with the Boys?" questions.

In the meantime, after Rap-a-Lot rushed out a Geto Boys greatest hits package (*Uncut Dope*, 1992), Big Mike made his debut on 1993's *Till Death Do Us Part*, a record that seemed largely to tread conceptual water, though some of the backing grooves displayed the technological advances of the times. Ditto for their 1994 effort, *Makin' Trouble*, which seemed to indicate that, although Big Mike was adept with a rhyme and sympathetic to the Geto Boys cause, and Bushwick Bill could still think of plenty to say about his penis, the group didn't have the inspiration or energy to come up with anything new.

After a few years off, though, Willie D. was welcomed back into the fold for 1996's freshly creepy *The Resurrection*, a CD that still contains all the group's standard gangsta shock tactics, but includes a surprisingly mature take on ghetto existence. One still doesn't want the Geto Boys (Men?) hosting one's children's Halloween party, but there's a glimmer of responsibility to their seething anarchy. It would be interesting to see what it would sound like if the Geto Boys recorded an album ten years from now.

In the meantime, the Boys reunited once more—this time without Bushwick Bill—for *Da Good Da Bad & Da Ugly*. Reviews were mixed despite truly interesting moments (use of a harpsichord, for example, or a pretty cool cover of Deniese Williams's "Free"). (Big Mike, by the way, is still signed with Rap-a-Lot and released a solo CD called *Something Serious*.)

WITH THE SUCCESS OF THE GETO BOYS WAS THE EMERGENCE of a so-called Gulf Coast hip-hop scene that absolutely rivals both the East Coast and West Coast scenes (besides Houston, New Orleans, Memphis, and Atlanta are all true breeding grounds of a whole new generation of hip-hop innovators).

The Houston Sound is very much part of the Gulf Coast contingent but also constitutes quite a style unto itself. Out from under the shadow of Rap-a-Lot are several burgeoning artists and record labels. Tony Draper, the CEO of Suave House Records, has demonstrated a business and artistic acumen to turn his label into a giant player.

With a Memphis duo (since moved to Houston) called Eightball and MJG, and two early CDs, *Coming Out Hard* and *On the Outside Looking In*, which sold between them a half-million records, the indie label inked a deal with Relativity. The next Eightball and MJG CD, 1995's *On Top of the World*, went gold, and the next one, 1998's triple disc Lost, went double platinum and saw the rappers hobnobbing with Busta Rhymes, the Goodie Mob, and Master P. The duo's distinctively Southern view of race, drugs, and hatred is always intriguing.

And speaking of Master P, the New Orleans rapper and head of the No Limit label lived a while in Houston and recently signed the town's grade-school rappers, Lil' Soldiers.

Mr. Mike is another popular and Houston-based Suave House signee, inked on the strength of a single, "Where Ya Love At?"

Lil' Keke is another massive Houston export. An indie CD for the Jam Down label contained a hit single in "Don't Mess Wit Texas," which sold over fifty thousand copies on the Gulf Coast alone and led to a major label deal with Island. By adding several new tunes to the existing CD, called *The Commission*, the label scored big-time success and seems assured that Lil' Keke's wizened gangsta-isms will result in long-term stardom.

DJ DMJ, a Port Arthur native now in H-Town, rode a collaborative indie hit (recorded with pals Lil' Keke and the late Fat Pat) called "25 Lighters" and the 1997 CD on which it appeared, *Twenty-Two: P.A. World Wide*, into a deal with Elektra Records.

And Lil' Troy—are any of these people Big?—the founder and CEO of Short Stop Records, released a debut CD called *Sittin' Phat Down South* that sold over 117,000 copies and garnered a distribution deal with Universal Records. And a rapper called Gangsta Nip out of Houston's South Park, working an obvious theme through indie CD's *South Park Psycho and Psychic Thoughts*—between them moving 180,000 units—has recently released *Psychotic Genius*.

But Houston isn't the only hotbed of activity. A Dallas act, Nemesis, has also made a national impression. Formed in 1990 by Big D natives MC Aziz, DJ Snake, Big Al, and Joe Macc, the group lavished thick, oozing bass lines over traditional funk grooves and quickly signed with Profile Records.

They've since released four CDs, *To Hell and Back* (1990), *Munchies for Your Bass* (1991), *Temple of Boom* (1993), and, after Ron C replaced Aziz, 1995's *Tha People Want Bass*—the titles of which indicate the emphasis Nemesis places on dance-floor accessibility.

D. O. C. is another Dallas rapper who's made international inroads. He was discovered by Dr. Dre while a member of the Dallas group Fila Fresh Crew, and shortly thereafter split and headed solo to California. He worked with the likes of Dr. Dre, Ice Cube, and Easy E, and collaborated on some of the material on NWA's all-important *Straight Outta Compton* album.

In 1989, Dr. Dre produced D. O. C.'s first LP, *No One Can Do It Better* (Ruthless Records), which boasted two hit singles, "The Formula" and "Funky Enough," that pushed the album to number 1 on the Black Music charts.

Shortly thereafter, an auto accident severely damaged D. O. C.'s vocal chords and cut short his performing career, though he's still active in production and writing.

El Paso was the birthplace of B. Fats, an earlier rapster who enjoyed a bit of fame in the mid-eighties. He released only one album, *Music Maestro* (1986, Orpheus Rex), but a single from the record, "Woppit," spurned a kooky dance craze called "the Wop," which could be observed in dance clubs until the turn of the decade—which meant it lasted longer than B. Fats's career.

Robert Lee Green, Jr., of Bryan, Texas, is a rapper known as Spice 1. He grew up in Oakland and rapped his way through high school, shortly thereafter attracting the attention of noted porno-rapper Too Short, who signed Spice 1 to his Dangerous Music label. Spice 1 appeared as a guest rapper on a few LPs, but it wasn't until he jumped to Jive Records that he recorded his first album, a self-titled 1992 release that promptly went gold.

Another act on the Jive roster is Beaumont's Underground Kingz (UGK). Originally comprised of Bun B, Pimp C, and Bird, the trio first came to attention on a 1992 Big Tyme Records album called *Too Hard to Swallow*, a rather obvious title. The record resulted in a contract with Jive and, after the defection of Bird, UGK recorded 1994's *Super Tight* with a variety of guest artists. The CD garnered plenty of good press, as has their 1996 effort, *Ridin' Dirty*, another package of pleasantly deviant jams about infinite carnal possibilities.

Dallas's Mad Flava is another rapper who seems large with potential. His 1994 Restless Records album, *From the Ground Unda*, is a high point in Metroplex gangsta-isms.

From another direction, where plenty of alternative rock acts follow the examples of the Red Hot Chili Peppers, Faith No More, or 311, and utilize rap characteristics within their rock/funk structures, only Dallas's MC 900 Ft. Jesus has actually gained significant notoriety as a successful purveyor of rap hybrids—and that he's included in the rap section here will no doubt frustrate him (he once told the author, "If someone hears what I do and calls it rap, it's okay. But to describe it as rap to someone who's never heard it would be incorrect.").

The Really Tall Savior is actually the persona of a Dallas-based artist named Mark Griffin, who grew up playing trumpet in Ohio, graduated with a music degree from Morehead State University, then migrated to Texas to further his musical studies at the renowned North Texas State University.

He eventually settled in Dallas and became a leading participant on the avant-garde edge of the Deep Ellum alternative scene.

Griffin began to get into sampling and, calling himself MC 900 Ft. Jesus, released an EP that featured a jazzy/world beat/cerebro-rap song called "Too Bad." Surprisingly, the song became a dance hit, and Nettwerk Records offered a two-album deal.

The first, 1991's *Hell with the Lid Off*, was an innately catchy collection of ruminations from a delightfully twisted mind, under which Griffin diced up early-nineties dance trends, house music sounds, and Talking Heads–style structures, then reglued them to his own warped specifications.

In 1993, he released *Welcome to My Dream*. Another dance hit, "The City Sleeps," a disturbing tune about an arsonist, propelled the record to very acceptable sales levels, and the Mountain-Sized Jeez signed with Rick Rubin's American Recordings label. In 1994, MC 900 Ft. Jesus released *One Step Ahead of the Spider*, a critical triumph which nevertheless assimilated so many styles and surrounded Griffin's neobeat poetry with what cretins can only infer is free jazz, that he's probably aimed well over the head of the average hip-hop/alt-rock fan.

IN THE HISTORY OF TEXAS GOSPEL, ONE PROBABLY WON'T FIND too many artists crowing about sexual battery or murdering police. But in an odd way, given that the music is rooted in salvation, tribulations, and survival, gospel has at least casual similarities to rap—if nothing else.

In any event, Texas does have a sprinkling of formidable names in the long line of gospel heavyweights.

"Blind" Arizona Dranes, who sounds like a blues star, is acknowledged as the first gospel pianist anywhere, for any reason. She reportedly lost her eyesight in an influenza epidemic in Texas in the early 1900s (though it's not precisely known where or when in the state she was born), but nevertheless became an accomplished pianist and church song leader in the COGIC movement (Church of God in Christ).

Described as an innovator of the "sanctified style" of piano playing, in which the musician's zeal for performance should rock mightily yet not detract from the choir's enthusiastic vocal work, Dranes was one of the gospel performers signed to Okeh Records during the twenties—a heyday for blues and gospel "race records."

Another of her stylistic innovations is now known as the "gospel beat," a bit of a ragtime/barrelhouse innovation in which Dranes emphasized the "two" and the "four" beats with left-handed octaves while kicking out the jams with single-note right-handed runs and chordal improvisations. Her shrill but operatic voice could cut like tin-snips through church din, and a 1928 recording, "I Shall Wear a Crown," is emblematic of yet another Dranes gospel modification: the reliance on ¾time, which has endured through the years in old-time gospel composition.

Washington Phillips, another native Texan who also happened to be a blind gospel pianist, recorded extensively for a variety of race labels also. A noted preacher as well as a gospel artist, Phillips wrote much of his own material and brought a stern but fatherly tone to his musical sermonizing.

Two other pianists were significant players in the gospel saga: Dave Carl Weston and Jessy Dixon. Weston, who was born in Lufkin, Texas, in 1923, graduated from Prairie View A&M and moved to Santa Monica, California, in 1942. There he played gospel piano and formed his own gospel group, the Dave Weston Singers, which toured with the likes of the Jordanaires. Eventually he returned to California and became a minister of music.

San Antonio native Jessy Dixon (born in 1938) attended St. Mary's College as a music major with hopes of becoming a concert pianist. He grew increasingly attracted to gospel music, though, and eventually aborted his college plans (well, let's just say he quit college early) to become an accompanist for Brother Joe May. He later joined James Cleveland's Gospel Chimes, with whom he toured for five years before forming his own group, the Jessy Dixon Singers, in 1960. Dixon actually sang in that outfit, utilizing a booming baritone and alternating it with a shrieking falsetto. The group recorded for the Savoy label and, in the seventies, Light Records.

At that point, Dixon's material took on contemporary overtones—which is to say it sounded like modern-day R&B with spiritual lyrics. He's also famous as the composer of such gospel favorites as "The Failure's Not in God" and "Bring the Sun Out."

There is a solid vocal tradition in Texan gospel, too. Sister Jessie Mae Renfro, who was born in Waxahachie in 1921, was raised in a Dallas COGIC organization, decided early on to forgo a secular singing career and, by the mid-forties, had joined the Sallie Martin Singers. By 1950, she went solo and recorded for a number of gospel labels, attracting a substantial following as a "hard gospel" performer (hard gospel being that strident, Hit the Absolute Top of Your Range in Celestial Rapture on Every Phrase style).

A compatriot, Madame Emily Bram, born somewhere in Texas around 1919, was another hard-gospel vocalist who also happened to be a practicing evangelist. Her vocal style incorporated rabid growls and slow but aggressive melodic ascensions until, presumably, only religious dogs could hear her.

Houston's Thurston Frazier (born in 1930) sang in gospel choirs throughout his youth and, after his family relocated to California, studied music, gospel repertoire, and conducting with the noted J. Earle "Not Fatha" Hines.

As the director of the Voices of Hope Choir, Frazier became famous as the composer of "We've Come This Far by Faith," which became the equivalent of a bar-band standard—sort of a gospel "Cat Scratch Fever," if you will.

Relying on many of the harmonic innovations found in contemporary rhythm and blues, Frazier's work remained fresh, whether he was conducting a four-piece gospel group or a hundreds-strong choir.

At the forefront of gospel popularity, of course, is the singing group—and Texans featured prominently in two of the most famous: the Soul Stirrers and the Pilgrim Travelers.

The Soul Stirrers are arguably the coolest and most innovative gospel group ever, and they formed in Houston in the early 1920s. Original members were Edward R. Rundless (lead), Walter LeBeau (tenor), Silas Roy Crain (baritone), and O. W. Harris (bass).

The group first recorded in 1936, under the direction of noted musicologist John Lomax in sessions for the Library of Congress. But it wasn't until 1937, when they added first tenor Rebert H. Harris, that the group really became innovative.

Harris, born in 1916, was gospel-bound from the crib, apparently. He penned his first hit, "Everybody Ought to Love His Soul," at the age of eight, and wrote what would be another gospel classic, "I Want Jesus to Walk Around My Bedside," a year later. Before he hooked up with the Soul Stirrers, he formed a family group, the Friendly Five, in his hometown of Trinity, Texas. After attending seminary for two years, he joined the Soul Stirrers and they blithely went about changing gospel music. For one thing, they added a certain rapturous delivery to the traditionally staid form, and group members actually began to move about onstage in time to the music, in contrast to the still-as-statues routines theretofore inherent in gospel. They also came up with the "swing lead" concept, in which two vocalists might sing lead on the same tune.

Overnight, the Soul Stirrers became major draws, hosted their own popular Sunday morning radio show, and throughout the forties toured the United States to consistently ecstatic audiences. Harris bowed out in 1950, replaced by an equally charismatic singer named Sam Cooke, who fronted the group in performance and on several Specialty LPs until 1956, when he headed for secular stardom. He in turn was succeeded by Johnnie Taylor, the Texas soul star discussed earlier in this chapter.

Despite several personnel changes over the years, the Soul Stirrers, well into their third quarter-century of existence, continue to roll on. Most of the surviving recordings feature Sam Cooke (of which *Jesus Gave Me Water*, 1992, Specialty, is a good primer), but Specialty's *Shine On Me* emphasizes the brilliant Harris years.

Directly inspired by the Soul Stirrers was a Houston quintet called the Pilgrim Travelers, which formed in 1936. After winning several regional contests, the group actually toured with the Stirrers and, after several personnel changes, settled in Los Angeles and, in 1946, began recording with a more-or-less permanent lineup which included James "Woodie" Alexander (group leader and tenor), Kylo Turner and Keith Barber (leads), Jesse Whitaker (baritone), and Rayford Taylor (bass).

In 1948, the Pilgrims had two huge hits, "Thank You, Jesus" and "Jesus," and recorded consistently excellent records until the mid-fifties. Specialty Records has released three collections of Pilgrim material.

Like any other music, gospel has evolved with the times and incorporated characteristics of contemporary music. As such, there are country/gospel bands, Christian metal and rock bands, soul/gospel artists, even Christian rap performers—and Texas is represented in just about every fashion.

Twentysomething Kirk Franklin is surely going to be one of the biggest gospel stars ever—if he's not already. A product of Fort Worth's Riverside ghetto, in which he actually dabbled in gangs and drug experimentation, Franklin managed through a loving great-aunt and a passion for God and music to avoid darker urban temptations.

A gifted singer and pianist who was his church's minister of music at the age of eleven, Franklin studied gospel history the way premed students absorb comparative anatomy texts, attended an arts magnet high school and, at seventeen, was an ordained minister.

In 1992, Franklin recorded a demo tape that attracted the attention of GospoCentric, a small label started on a shoestring budget in an effort to provide kids with an alternative to contemporary secular music. Sympathetic to their purpose, Franklin signed. In 1993, Franklin released *Kirk Franklin and the Family*, a completely catchy, skip-the-tightrope amalgamation of hip-hop and slick R&B, infused with positive messages and the J-word.

It's since sold millions of albums, topped the *Billboard* gospel chart, and sped up the secular R&B charts, eventually lodging in the top ten there. (It eventually became only the third gospel record ever to go platinum; predecessors were Elvis Presley and Aretha Franklin.) "Why We Sing," the single from the CD, scored massive air time on non-Christian radio, too, which is all but unheard-of for gospel artists.

He won two Dove awards for *Kirk Franklin and the Family*, and has since released a Christmas LP, which refuses to leave the gospel charts, and a second mainstream gospel record, *Whatcha Lookin 4* (1995), which effortlessly jetted to number 1.

Franklin has made it cool to be Christian and to sing about it, which, in an age when the Geto Boys address the same problems with decidedly more depressing answers, is something indeed. Offshoot projects, including the eponymously monikered God's Property (more uplifting and uptempo contempo gospel) and the Nu Nation Project (also self-titled, and a slightly odd disc complete with a mock courtroom trial in which the validity of Franklin's hip-hop-tinged "gospel" is brought into question) have Roman-candled their ways to the top of the charts. Franklin also published an autobiography called *Church Boy*.

Other Texans making headway in gospel and contemporary Christian music are doing so in a variety of different ways.

The Bronx-born, Dallas-raised MC Ge Gee is surely one of the first female Christian rappers. Austin's One Bad Pig is a Christian punk/thrash band (however *that* works out). Gary Chapman (aka the former Mr. Amy Grant) is in his own right a successful Christian songwriter with several LPs (as well as writing credits for secular artists like Kenny Rogers and T. G. Sheppard). Susan Ashton, also from Texas, is another singer in the MOR/ Amy Grant mold with several albums out on the Sparrow label. And Joyful Noyze, a Dallas-based gospel-funk outfit, recently signed with Word Records.

☆ Part 7: Easy Listening, New Age, and Classical

☆ One: Opera (Not Soap or Oat), Classical, and Musical Theater

LET'S FACE IT: TEXAS REPRESENTS MANY INTRIGUING AND EX-otic things to people all over the world. Opera, however, is not one of them. Pausing on the public television channel to watch Domingo, Carreras, and Pavarotti shake the walls of some twelve-thousand-year-old opera house on the Continent decidedly does *not* bring to mind images of the Alamo or the Astrodome—or, for that matter, George Jones.

Nevertheless, there are great opera singers who've hailed from the Lone Star state, just as there are great classical musicians and musical theater stars. Hey: there was a Van Cliburn a long time before there was a Van Halen.

In fact, Fort Worth's Van Cliburn is not just a Texas hero, he's ten fingers of *serious* piano wizardry; this ain't Liberace here. Cliburn was actually born in Shreveport in 1934, and showed virtually a natal aptitude for piano. His mother, Rilda Bee Cliburn, a terrific pianist in her own right who studied under Arthur Friedheim, gave her son extensive lessons until he was seventeen, at which time he entered Juilliard.

By that time, Cliburn was already accustomed to performance; he'd won his first competition, the Texas State Prize, at thirteen, and appeared as a soloist with the Houston Symphony Orchestra the same year. In 1948, Cliburn won the National Music Festival Award; in 1952, the Dealy Award and the Kosciuszko Foundation Chopin Prize (which, despite titular appearances, was not a spelling contest).

It was in 1958, though, several contest and festival triumphs down the road, that Cliburn accomplished something all the spies in the history of espionage could not have done: He thawed the frozen hearts of the Soviet people at the height of the Cold War when he went to Moscow and won the First International Tchaikovsky Competition. The victory made Cliburn an international star and an American hero (upon arrival back in the States, Cliburn was treated to a New York ticker-tape parade, the sort of thing normally reserved for cultural icons like baseball players).

For the next twenty years, Cliburn was a global household name. He was in demand for the creamiest symphony orchestra gigs, at any and all head-of-state ceremonies, a millions-selling recording artist—and the namesake of Fort Worth's Van Cliburn International Piano Competition (first held in 1962), which is now the premiere such event in the world, drawing the top young players to compete.

In 1978, Cliburn withdrew from the concert stage, content to oversee a variety of philanthropic pursuits, providing scholarships at several universities and international conservatories as well as serving on the board of trustees for Interlochen Arts Academy. In addition, Cliburn's time has been heavily mortgaged just keeping up with the honorary degrees he's (deservedly) chalked up.

In 1987, Cliburn emerged from self-exile to perform for President Reagan, and appeared two years later in Moscow at the invitation of Mikhail Gorbachev. He went on to play the opening of the one hundredth anniversary season at Carnegie Hall, and has since maintained a rather exuberant performance schedule.

In commemoration of Cliburn's return to the concert stage, BMG Classics has recently reissued eight classic Cliburn releases as a collected set entitled *The Van Cliburn Collection*. He remains one of the better classical pianists in the world, a technically dazzling performer whose pristine technique is flavored with a subtle twist of Romantic melodicism.

WITHOUT QUESTION, VAN CLIBURN IS THE BIG STAR OF TEXAS classical music. But other artists should also be mentioned. Several pianists from across the globe who have participated in the Cliburn competitions have moved permanently to the Fort Worth area, including Alexei Sultanov and Jose Feghali, while Russian-born duo pianists Valentina Lisitsa and Alexei Kuznetsoff now call Dallas home.

On the other hand, Olga Somaroff, a world-renowned piano teacher, wasn't from Russia—she was from Texas. In fact, her name wasn't really Olga Somaroff, it was Lucy Hickenhooper. Understandably, she thought her real name didn't sound enough like an instructor of classical piano, and thus invented the Russian moniker. It worked—though she must've had substantial talent to go along with the nom de keyboard.

There are several classical stars who achieved fame on instruments other than piano. Lynn Harrell, the son of opera great Mack Harrell, is a world-class cellist. Though he was born in New York City in 1944, he grew up in Dallas, studying in Big D with Gregor Piatigorsky. He was the first cellist with the Cleveland Orchestra, and has been a corecipient of the Avery Fisher Prize. Since 1971, Harrell's divided his time between performance and teaching; a former faculty member at Juilliard, he was appointed to the Piatigorsky Chair at the University of Southern California School of Music. In the meantime, his rendition of Dvořák's *Concerto for Cello* is the stuff of dreams.

Ballinger, Texas's David Gujon (born in 1892), a composer of some note, studied with Leopold Godowsky in Vienna during his youth, then returned to the United States to teach.

Eventually, he landed back in Texas, where he was commissioned to write *Cavalcade of America* for the state's centennial in 1936. He spent several years arranging American folk music, all the while composing both ballet and orchestral suites. He passed away in 1981.

Victor Alessandro, it can be said with some certainty, is probably the only human from Waco who became a nationally renowned symphony conductor. Born in 1915, he studied French horn early on, then studied composition, first at New York's Rochester School of Music and later at the Accademia di Santa Cecilia in Rome. Back in America, he was the conductor of the Oklahoma Symphony Orchestra for thirteen years, and in 1951 became conductor of the San Antonio Symphony Orchestra. He died in 1976.

More than a few opera stars have crawled out of the Lone Star soil, too. Arguably the greatest was San Saba's Thomas Stewart. Born in 1928, Stewart attended Baylor University, studying in that prerequisite field for all opera aspirants: electrical engineering. Somehow he ended up at Juilliard as a voice major, and shortly thereafter sang bass roles with the Metropolitan and Chicago operas. After receiving a Fulbright scholarship in 1957, he moved to Berlin and signed on as a baritone with the Stadtische Oper, where he sang for seven years (also appearing in other European productions).

Stewart returned to New York in 1966 and made his debut at the Metropolitan Opera as Ford in Verdi's *Falstaff*. He graduated to lead roles in lucrative productions across the country, appearing as Don Giovanni, Escamillo in *Carmen*, *Otello*'s Iago, and other meaty parts. His wife is opera star Evelyn Lear, with whom he appeared numerous times. The two have retired to Texas.

An early instructor of Stewart's was Mack Harrell, who was born in Celeste, Texas, in 1909. Another alumnus of Juilliard, where he studied violin and voice, Harrell had an acclaimed career as a baritone. He joined the staff of the Metropolitan Opera in 1939, where he remained for six years, and continued to appear there periodically for another decade. Harrell, who also became an instructor at Juilliard, died in 1960, and is survived by his son, Lynn, the acclaimed cellist.

There are several significant Texas divas as well, and Thomas Stewart's wife, Evelyn Lear, was a world-class soprano. She was born in New York in 1926 to a musical family, and grew up studying piano and horn.

At seventeen, she married Dr. Walter Lear, and though the marriage was short-lived, she maintained the surname throughout her professional career. She developed an interest in singing opera fairly late in life, took vocal lessons with baritone John Yard, and later studied at Juilliard—where she met her second husband, Thomas Stewart.

The couple obtained Fulbright grants and moved to Germany, where they appeared at the Stadtische Oper. Upon receiving an opportunity to sing the intimidating title role in *Lulu* (Berg's opera, not the large woman on "*Hee Haw*") in Vienna in 1960, Lear "kicked major league ass," as opera-meisters like to say. From there, she became a major attraction at the Metropolitan Opera in New York City, where she remained a star until 1985.

Lear was so talented that a number of her roles are now permanently associated with her: Irma Arkadina in *The Seagull* and Magda in *Minutes to Midnight*, for example. As noted above, she and her husband have retired in Texas.

Two contemporary divas experiencing terrific success are also from Texas: Austin's Lella Cuberli and Pampa's Mary Jane Johnson.

Cuberli, who grew up in El Paso and started playing piano at seven, went to SMU to study voice and planned on a career in symphonic and chamber music. After she married, though, her husband played opera around the house continually and Cuberli eventually became hooked on the stuff. By the time she graduated from college, she'd sung a number of small parts at the Dallas Civic Opera and won a grant from the National Opera Institute.

Cuberli utilized the grant money to study three years in Italy—where she became sort of a Chicago Bulls of international opera competitions, winning regularly. After performing terrifically in a few last-minute, high-pressure substitution gigs, her reputation and career took off. She began singing at La Scala in feature roles, and by the early eighties was renowned for her acuity at Mozart, Rossini, and Handel.

She returned to the States, debuted at Carnegie Hall with Marilyn Horne, and has since starred at various European festivals and across the country—and her reputation as one of the premier sopranos of the world is beyond question. Though she's recently decided to cut back on her hectic performance schedule, there is little doubt that Cuberli will draw capacity crowds the world over whenever she feels like singing.

A predecessor to Cuberli and Johnson who warrants mention is Yvonne de Treville (born Edyth La Gierse in Galveston in 1881). Treville studied in New York City, then went to Europe, where she sang in Madrid, Brussels, Vienna, Budapest, and Russia before returning to America in 1913. Back home, she toured the country several times before passing away in 1954.

And two other performers should be mentioned: Opera singers Gary Lakes and William Blankenship.

In terms of civic opera and symphony orchestras, the state is well provided for, and most communities of even average size offer various chamber groups, orchestras, choral groups, and derivations thereof.

The opera companies in the state's three largest cities. Dallas (Dallas Opera), Houston (Houston Grand Opera), and San Antonio (San Antonio Opera Company) are reputable. Similarly, each city boasts strong symphony orchestras: the Dallas Symphony (under the direction of Andrew Litton and associate conductor Keri-Lynn Wilson), the Houston Symphony (headed up by executive director David M. Wax and music director Christopher Eschenbach), and the San Antonio Symphony (with music director Christopher Wilkins).

Also, schools such as S.M.U., the University of Texas, Texas Tech, and in particular, the University of North Texas offer top-of-the-line music departments.

In addition, the United States Air Force Band of the West is, like all of the service bands, a particularly strong outfit, providing classically trained musicians job opportunities with actual salaries and benefits—considerations often lacking in civic orchestras (or at least they're far less lucrative).

FINALLY, THERE IS A BIT OF MUSICAL THEATER TRADITION IN Texas that is worthy of note. Not only was the film *State Fair* made in Dallas, but Harvey Schmidt and Tom Jones, who wrote *The Fantasticks, Colette, I Do! I Do!*, and several other Broadway hits, are Texas guys. Both met at the University of Texas, collaborated on zany college shows, and after serving in World War II, moved to New York City, where they hit the big home run with *The Fantasticks*.

Other Texans who've had success writing for the musical theater (though one might not want, necessarily, to hear them sing) are Joshua Logan, who won a Pulitzer Prize for *South Pacific*, and Larry King, who cowrote *The Best Little Whorehouse in Texas*.

Ann Miller, who's from Chinero, was born Lucille Ann Collier in 1923 and took the famous stage name when breaking into musical dance in the thirties. She then began to star in low-budget Hollywood musicals and eventually found fame and major respect as the Broadway star of *Mame* and *Sugar Babies*.

Waco's Jules Bledsoe, born in 1898, starred on Broadway in *Show Boat* before dying prematurely in 1943.

Tommy Tune, the noted musical-meister who starred in *My One and Only* and *Bye Bye Birdie* and has directed several Broadway smashes, is also a Texas kid—as is Betty Buckley. She's the versatile star of stage, screen, television, and musical theater who's best remembered for her Tony Award–winning role as Grizabella in Andrew Lloyd Webber's *Cats*.

Buckley's sister-in-law, Candy, who starred at the Dallas Theatre Center for years, has also gone on to some nice musical roles in the New York theater district.

And a former New Yorker turned Dallasite, folk/blues guitarist Josh Alan, has written a musical called *The Worst!* (previously noted). Based on the life of B-movie director Ed Wood, and conceptually predating Tim Burton's film on the same subject, Alan's soundtrack premiered with Burton's film in London, and plans are tentatively under way to produce the musical in Europe in the not too distant future.

LUDICROUSLY OVERLOOKED ARTIST
Mary Jane Johnson
☆

Mary Jane Johnson, whose sterling career in opera is decidedly more glamorous than her other gig (running a bed and breakfast in Amarillo), is a consummate Texas artist: fun-loving, brassy, bold, and beautiful—and immensely talented. She's probably a bit of an anomaly in the somewhat stodgy world of opera, but as her performances in the world's finest opera houses and with the likes of Luciano Pavarotti testify, she's a super talent.

She grew up studying ballet, singing gospel every Sunday in the black church she attended with the family maid. A high school cheerleader in the football-happy plains of West Texas, Johnson was probably the least likely opera star in the solar system when she enrolled at Texas Tech as a music major.

She married a Tech basketball player and, after graduation, settled in Amarillo to raise a family while she pursued a master's degree in performance at West Texas State University and directed the school's opera workshop.

She next won the regional competition of the Metropolitan Opera's Auditions for Young Singers, though she didn't make it to the finals. Still, bolstered by a local bank loan, Johnson moved to New York to study; then, in 1981, she was chosen by Pavarotti as one of sixteen winners in his inaugural International Voice Competition.

Johnson turned pro. Gradually, she landed bigger and bigger roles, mastering along the way increasingly difficult challenges including plum Puccini, Strauss, and Wagner parts.

While she now performs internationally and has done SRO concerts with her benefactor, Pavarotti, Johnson still faces problems many Texans associate with, say, trying to vacation in Colorado—call it Texaphobia. Her accent is decidedly provincial, her steam engine delivery has been described as being too shrill, and, as recounted in *Texas Monthly*, Johnson's decision to appear topless for a seven-plus-minute dance in Strauss's *Salome* (rather than wear a cheesy body stocking) is admittedly the decision born of a Lone Star state of mind.

But, hey, if her voice is good enough for Luciano . . . and furthermore, if a world-class soprano is going to sing topless, it's probably a shrewd idea that she's a former Texas high school cheerleader rather than one of the corpulent divas whose wails signal the end of operas.

☆ Two: Easy Listening (My Parents Love This Stuff!) and New Age

NOT TO DEMEAN EASY LISTENING MUSIC, BUT WHICHEVER MAR-
keting tsar coined that phrase did the genre's practitioners no great
service. Would someone cool like Nicolas Cage walk into a record store
and ask, "Can you show me where your Easy Listening section is?"

No. Even if he *worships* Burt Bacharach and Mantovani, Nicolas Cage is
not going to walk into a record store and ask for "easy listening." And you're
probably not, either.

Why? Well, not to demean easy listening artists, but where is the lore
behind the music? Where is the sense of *history*? We have our images of
Beethoven, courageously denying the rising tide of his deafness even as he
continued to create through genius and sheer will; we've heard the legends
of the Delta bluesmen, jamming for days and nights on end in backwater
Mississippi juke joints, impervious to time under the soul-stealing spell of
the music; and Jimi Hendrix *slept* with his guitar—but not until he was
exhausted from playing it till his fingers bled.

But where are the anecdotal nuggets from the great scrapbook of easy
listening? Where are the tales of crazed after-hours sessions at Ray Conniff's
pad, where Ferrante and Teicher, Zamfir, Shirley Bassey, and Lawrence
Welk would hammer cold ones and vamp for hours on "Theme from a
Summer Place"?

The deal, of course, is that in all probability, no one set out to be an
"easy listening" artist (with the possible exception of Wayne Newton, who
may have been *told* by various Sicilians that, yes, he *would* have a career in
easy listening). But all of the other unfortunates who've been lumped under
this corny, mellow umbrella are nothing more than musicians, singers, and/
or songwriters who performed what was at the time contemporary pop music
but has come to be called "easy listening" over the course of the years (much
as Buddy Holly—once a pioneering, outlaw musical forerunner—is now
referred to as a "golden oldie" artist or Bad Company called a "classic rock"
band; just as, someday, Pearl Jam will be nothing more than confetti'd

fodder in the shaky brains of gray-haired codgers whose tattoos have faded and become grotesque in crinkled folds of skin).

So cut easy listening some slack: like anything else, there are good easy listening artists and there are bad ones and, on the whole, those from Texas are a pretty kick-ass lot.

CONSIDER MAC DAVIS. HIS 1994 COLUMBIA/NASHVILLE ALBUM is called *Will Write Songs for Food*, which either means the Lubbock-born entertainer (1941) blew the millions he earned writing songs for himself, Elvis Presley, Dolly Parton, and others, or he's just kidding about cranking out tunes for chow. It's probably the latter, because he's sold more records than Evan Dando ever thought about. (Who's Evan Dando? Well, that's a case in point.)

Anyway, Davis spent his boyhood learning guitar, working on his uncle's ranch, singing in church, and listening to the varied sounds of West Texas radio. After attending college in Georgia, he parlayed sales manager/music publishing gigs at record labels on both coasts into a career as a burgeoning songwriter, selling early tunes to Lou Rawls and Glen Campbell. Then that Elvis man heard some of Davis's songs and began recording them. One tune, "In the Ghetto," became a top ten seller for the King, then Bobby Goldsboro had a hit with Davis's "Watching Scotty Grow" and Kenny Rogers and the First Edition scored with another Davis song, "Something's Burning." By then, the young songwriter's already bright reputation redshifted to luminescent.

Eventually, Davis decided he wanted to maneuver his career to where *he* was the entertainer. He began singing his own material, and had a number of successful appearances on television variety programs like *The Tonight Show* and those hosted by Red Skelton, David Frost, Glen Campbell, Johnny Cash, and the Smothers Brothers. He was a popular guest; in point of fact, Davis is as witty a personality and as virtuoso a guitarist as he is adept at songwriting. In 1971, he recorded his first album, *I Believe in Music* (Columbia), a solid set of hummable, clever tunes that established Davis as the friendly next-door neighbor of song. The title cut has probably sold more copies than there are people in Calcutta, and has been covered by more than fifty artists.

Davis began to headline Vegas showrooms and college concert tours, and 1972's number 1 hit, "Baby Don't Get Hooked on Me" (off the LP of the same name), was the first in a string of hit singles and albums which included songs like "Rock and Roll (I Gave You the Best Years of My Life)," "One Hell of a Woman," "Everybody Loves a Song," "Beginning to Feel the Pain," and "Stop and Smell the Roses."

In 1974, Davis began to host his own network variety program, *The Mac Davis Show*. Throughout the rest of the decade, though his recording momentum slowed, he continued to sell records on both the country and pop charts (including "Forever Lovers" and "Texas in My Rear View Mirror"), and in 1979 starred in the film version of the Pete Gent novel about the Dallas Cowboys, *North Dallas Forty*.

It could be easily argued that, since then, Davis has shifted his career emphasis from singer/songwriter to professional guest—but considering everyone wants him, what's wrong with that? He did release the *Will Write Songs for Food* LP, and there will doubtless be others, but anything at this point is probably done more for Davis's own entertainment than anything else.

EL PASO HARDLY SEEMS THE SORT OF TOWN THAT COULD CALL itself "the Home of the Easy Listening Queens," and though Debbie Reynolds and Vicki Carr were both born there, there's no record of them slipping into Juárez together to drink tequila and regale the natives with Spanish-language renditions of Hoagy Carmichael songs.

For one thing, Reynolds is older by several years, and for another, despite their West Texan births, both actually grew up in southern California (Reynolds in Burbank and Carr in Rosemead). Reynolds's career as a songstress was actually a by-product of her film stardom, which began when she won a celebrity impressions contest as a teenager, which resulted in a movie contract.

In an age when almost every movie star recorded albums at one time or another (check out the mellifluous singing of Jimmy Durante sometime), Reynolds actually had the innocuous, sweetened-tea voice you'd want her to have. Against a velveteen backdrop of orchestral strings and gloppy arrangements, she recorded a series of albums in the fifties and sixties, and in fact released a 1957 single called "Tammy" that went to number 1—knocking Buddy Holly's "That'll Be the Day" out of the top spot.

Obviously, though, the movie biz was her priority, and the essence of her singing career can be found on either of two greatest hits collections (one on Capitol Records and a newer LP from Curb).

Vicki Carr was born Florencia Bisentta de Casillas Martinez Cardona, which is admittedly a lot of syllables for any concert hall marquee or album cover. Florencia realized that and became Vicki Carr (a marketing strategy that apparently failed to impress a promising early nineties Dallas pop group called Last One Dead Has the Paws of a Cheetah—and they wonder why they didn't make it).

Carr, however, *did* make it. A tomboy who didn't get interested in music until high school, Carr became the featured vocalist in the Pepe Callahan Mexican/Irish Band, which played weekends in resort towns like Reno and Las Vegas.

Then, after recording a solo demo, she signed with and cut a few singles for Liberty Records in the early sixties. Though domestic sales were disappointing, she had an Australian hit with "He's a Rebel," after which sales in Britain picked up briskly. Still, in the States, she was forced to work as a bookkeeper until new management landed her a featured spot on television's *Ray Anthony Show*. With her powerful voice, almost operatic range, and wholesome good looks, guest appearances on the Steve Allen and Jerry Lewis shows soon followed. By 1964, a debut Liberty LP, *Color Her Great*, was released, which featured the single "San Francisco."

Though rock 'n' roll was beginning to dominate the airwaves, Carr managed to land on the charts with several albums throughout the rest of the sixties, including 1964's *Discovery!*, 1966's *Discovery! Volume 2*, 1965's *Anatomy of Love*, and 1968's *It Must Be Him* (the title song of which was a number 3 hit). She became a huge club attraction in America, and remained a significant star in England (where she performed before Queen Elizabeth at a Royal Command Performance in 1968).

By the turn of the decade, though, when Carr wasn't invited to perform at Woodstock, it might've been taken as a sign that such music wasn't particularly hip anymore. Suprisingly, though, she inked a new deal with Columbia, and charted LPs for the next several years (including 1971's *Superstar* and 1973's *Ms. America*).

Since 1980, Carr has returned to her roots, shifting into a Latin musical direction with the massively popular *Vikki Car y el Amor*. Her success has been steady since then, and in 1991 she won a Grammy for Best Latin Pop Album for *Cosas del Amor*.

Another Latin American Texan to wield the bat of easy listening is Dallas's Trini Lopez. Born in 1937, Lopez began to learn Mexican folk songs as a child. He formed a street corner band at the age of eleven, playing for the coins of passersby, and was singing in Latin nightclubs by sixteen.

After exhausting the Texas club circuit, he headed to Los Angeles and steadily worked larger and larger rooms until he was awarded a contract with Reprise Records. With a smile as powerful as a klieg light, a folksy voice, and a mastery of binational folk songs and contemporary hits, Lopez's debut, *Trini Lopez at P. J.'s*, hit the charts and remained there for two years. Featuring a rendition of "If I Had a Hammer" on which Lopez made work sound like a Brazilian carnival, the album went gold, "If I Had a Hammer" was a number 1 single in sixteen countries, and two other songs, "La Bamba" and "A-mer-ri-ca," logged heavy airplay.

Shrewdly knowing a winning concept when they heard it, Reprise rushed out *More Trini Lopez at P. J.'s*, which included hit singles "Kansas City" and "Green Green," and Lopez toured the world.

He had released fourteen LPs by 1972 (as many as three in a year), and almost all included at least one hit. His best-known song is probably the 1965 smash "Lemon Tree," and by the late sixties his fame was such that he blossomed into film roles and a substantial part in the popular war movie *The Dirty Dozen* (although he portrayed a homicidal GI who conveniently happened to be a guitar-strumming crooner; too bad Oliver Stone didn't attribute Sergeant Barnes's villainy in *Platoon* to his frustrations as a folksinger—Lopez could well have earned an Oscar nomination in that context).

Though Lopez hosted his own variety show for a while and remained a hot club attraction, his recording production dropped off as the seventies wore on. Still, he's anything but overlooked: Warner Brothers, Reprise, and Bella Musica have all released greatest hits packages that include new material, unreleased tracks, and remixed masters. Lopez will go down as having cross-pollinated folk with rock and Mexican traditionals, and brought a wealth of rich musical heritage to millions of listeners.

HOUSTON CAN BOAST ITS SHARE OF EASY LISTENING HEROES: B. J. Thomas, Kenny Rogers, and Johnny Nash all spent their childhoods there. Rogers, of course, has achieved astounding crossover success in the pop and C&W fields, and is probably best known as a country star (for purposes of this book, in fact, he's primarily discussed in the country section), but his brand of music is so decidedly Lite that he could go to a Halloween party dressed normally, tell everyone he came as an easy listening singer, and he'd win first place in the costume contest.

Johnny Nash (born in 1940) is probably more famous for bringing reggae to the attention of American audiences than for serenading the Ward and June Cleaver generation with sing-along ditties. But his biggest hit, 1972's "I Can See Clearly Now," which made it to number 1 on the pop charts, and has since surfaced (with altered lyrics) as a particularly irritating optical clinic commercial, is very much a staple of contemporary easy listening.

Nash, who grew up singing all forms of music—gospel, pop, C&W, calypso—experienced recording success by the late fifties. One indicative song, a 1959 number 29 hit called "The Teen Commandments," was recorded along with Paul Anka and George Hamilton IV—and no one was about to mistake that trio for Cream.

After only dubious recording achievements in the States, though, Nash spent a lot of time in the sixties in Jamaica and England, working reggae and pop styles with more success, and also starring in European films. Even after "I Can See Clearly Now" erupted, his subsequent "hit" output was sporadic, though he maintains a high British profile. His 1972 Epic LP, *I Can See Clearly Now*, remains the best of his generic pop efforts, while Epic's 1993 release, *The Reggae Collection*, showcases his more international vibes, mon.

B. J. Thomas, who was born in Hugo, Oklahoma, in 1942, before his family moved to Texas, is probably the essence of the easy listening male vocalist. Or he was, anyway, for the better part of the seventies. He'd played in rock bands growing up in Houston, but scored his first success with a 1966 version of Hank Williams's "I'm So Lonesome I Could Cry."

A handsome guy who looks a bit like a genetic crossing of Mel Gibson and Ricky Nelson, Thomas moved mainstream with the title single from his 1970 ABC debut, "Raindrops Keep Falling on My Head," a number 1 hit that also appeared on the soundtrack to the film *Butch Cassidy and the Sundance Kid*. Several like-tempo'd songs and albums followed, all landing in the middle of the charts, but Thomas spun back in a C&W direction for a country chart-topper with 1975's "(Hey Won't You Play) Another Somebody Done Somebody Wrong Song."

Shortly thereafter, Thomas, who'd publicly discussed being the victim of child abuse, and admitted to substance abuse as an adult, became a born-again Christian. Most of his recorded work since then has been either pop/gospel or secular country (his first gospel LP, 1976's *Home Where I Belong*, went platinum), and, to date, he's won two Dove and five Grammy awards.

One really shouldn't forget that, while neither were born in Texas, both Pat Boone and John Denver did spend enough time within her borders to merit inclusion here. Boone, whose white-shoed glory has most recently been tainted by his truly eerie album of heavy metal rearrangements, was born in Florida but attended some college at Denton's North Texas State University.

It was during that period that he won a succession of talent shows and scored a recording contract for his ability to "whiten-up" black R&B music. In fact, several of his over fifty charted hits were crossover versions of songs already recorded by black artists such as Little Richard or Fats Domino.

While it's true that, in a sense, he was making scads of cash utilizing black artists' material, it's also important to remember that, by doing so, he brought several black artists and musical styles to the myopic vision of white American. Most of his hits appeared between 1955 and 1962, and included such number 1 smashes as "Ain't That a Shame," "Don't Forbid Me," "Love Letters in the Sand," and "April Love."

Of course, at the time, Boone was a rock 'n' roll star—a contemporary of Buddy Holly and Roy Orbison. Somehow, though, even then, his next-door-neighbor-turns-evangelist image seemed so contrary to the concept of rocker-as-rebel that he was forever destined to the land of easy listening.

John Denver, too, started out as one of those folky kinds of rock people that were possible in the early seventies. Like Boone, he was born out of state (New Mexico) and attended college in Texas (at Texas Tech). He first gained fame when he replaced Chad Mitchell in the Chad Mitchell Trio, and scored his own recording contract in 1969. He wrote "Leaving on a Jet Plane," which was a hit for Peter, Paul and Mary, and his second album featured "Take Me Home, Country Roads," his own first hit and the tune that launched his popularity as a performer.

Quickly thereafter, "Annie's Song," "Rocky Mountain High," "Thank God I'm a Country Boy," and "I'm Sorry" followed, and Denver's reputation as a sorta hip guy who was a little goofy but would probably smoke herb with you accelerated into a major schlockmeister.

Eventually, his ability to move massive units for record companies all but

CRIMINALLY OVERLOOKED ARTISTS
The Turtle Creek Chorale
☆

Dallas's Turtle Creek Chorale, under the direction of Dr. Timothy Seelig, is an inspiring and talented male chorus that has released several independent CDs of material encompassing classical, pop, and show tunes (including 1990's *From the Heart: Live,* 1991's *Peace,* 1992's *Testament,* 1993's *When We No Longer Touch,* 1994's *Postcards,* and 1995's *The Times of Day,* the latter a world premiere recording on Reference Records of Richard Strauss's *Die Tageszeiten*). While an excellent group whose work would (should) stand on its own merit, the TCC is also famous for having been the focus of a PBS documentary called *After Goodbye: An AIDS Story.*

The Chorale, many of whose members are gay, and which has lost over sixty members to the AIDS virus since its inception, is as much a therapeutic endeavor as it is an artistic one, and its achievements to both ends are substantial.

As such, it is easy to praise the TCC out of sheer sympathy to the ongoing tragedy that is inextricably linked with their existence. But that would cheapen their talents, and since the LPs are uniformly engaging, masterfully crafted, and Byronic in scope, it's enough to say the Turtle Creek Chorale is a terrific ensemble.

Though all the CDs are at once poignant and exhilarating, *When We No Longer Touch,* a concept CD about the stages of grief based on Peter McWilliams's book *How to Survive the Loss of Love,* is a gorgeous testimonial to the concept of music as a healing property, and a melodic and heartfelt tribute to anyone who's known protracted sorrow.

dissolved, but he remained active in charitable causes until his death in 1997.

Also deserving mention here is Mason Williams, who was born in Abilene, Texas, in 1938. He's a superb guitarist and comedy writer whose most memorable song is undeniably the wonderful instrumental guitar piece, "Classical Gas," which is featured on his 1970 Warner Brothers LP, *Hand Made.* Williams has also recorded several other albums of whimsical and compelling acoustic guitar material.

In the annals of Texas easy listening, Dallas's Vocal Majority definitely deserves mention. The twenty-five-year-old close harmony men's chorus has entertained with a variety of traditional favorites, inspirational material, show tunes, et cetera. They've released several albums, including their latest, *How Sweet the Sound.*

* * *

NEW AGE MUSIC IS A RELATIVELY RECENT MUSICAL DEVELOP-
ment which might also be described as a form of easy listening; one cynic
calls it elevator tunes for the postacid set. In fact, new age is kinda difficult
to differentiate from light jazz, acoustic pop, or starter-kit classical.

And, as performed by stars like George Winston, William Ackerman, Liz
Story, Kitaro, John Tesh, Tangerine Dream, and Yanni, "new age" is a
hardly adequate term to describe a body of music which is actually quite
stylistically expansive and diverse.

George Winston, the godfather of new age, for example, is a Professor
Longhair freak whose solo piano exercises are typically quite inventive,
evocative, and memorable. And Tangerine Dream, whose soundtrack work-
sheets are probably second only to John Williams's in quantity and quality,
have composed music so nightmarish (1974's *Phaedra*) as to qualify them as
the crown princes of Anti–New Age.

In any case, Texas has a bona fide new age star—Fort Worth's Danny
Wright, whose solo piano work is decidedly of the George Winston school.
Wright, who showed an aptitude for piano from infancy, studied classically
throughout his school years and at Texas Christian University.

After leaving college fifteen hours shy of a degree, he was biding his
time, figuring out how to earn a living as a musician, earning some bucks
playing standards and Broadway classics in an Italian restaurant. An appreciative couple, Dori and Bob Nichols, who enjoyed his work and found
themselves returning to the restaurant again and again, as much for Wright's
playing as for the spaghetti sauce, struck up a friendship with the young
pianist. They offered to finance and produce a recording, which became an
album of show tunes called *Black and White* (1985 on their Nichols/Wright
label).

The album was originally offered on consignment in Fort Worth record
stores, and eventually sold enough to justify a second release. This time,
the songs were Wright's original compositions. The CD was called *Time
Windows*, and the set of pretty, melancholy solo piano tunes was so popular
that a Pacific Northwest distributor asked to carry the record. Wright (and
the Nicholses) have never looked back.

Since then, Wright's recorded nine more CDs (roughly divided between
the *Black and White* series, Christmas records, and his original, solo piano
material) and sold over *three million* records. The label's now called Moulin
D'Or Recordings, and Wright, who looks a bit like a sheepish Val Kilmer,
definitely doesn't have to play happy-hour gigs in restaurants anymore.

His records have shown up regularly on the *Billboard* New Age charts,
and he's now a featured performer with symphony orchestras across the
United States. While his show tune and Christmas recordings are expertly
done and display a proper enthusiasm, his own compositions are more intriguing. Like a lot of the writers working within the parameters of new age,

his melodies are occasionally so pretty as to be vapid, and are often so light as to float out of one's memory.

But Wright's a damned fine player, too, and when he hits an inspired melody line or chord progression, most notably on material from *Phantasys*, *Autumn Dreams*, and *Day in the Life*, he is a credit to a beleaguered genre.

Again, while the following artists probably cringe at the prospect of being mentioned as new age artists, they certainly compose music that is at least pleasant to listen to. Besides, there's nothing *wrong* with new age music— if it's *good* new age music.

That having been said, there are two harpists (by harp I refer to the angel type—not the gritty blues harmonicas) who are particularly compelling, both of whom could just as easily be said to practice light jazz: Cindy Horstman (whose *Fretless* album on Seahorse records is well worth the cash) and Carlos Guedes (*Toda America* on Heads Up is an invigorating sample of his work). Jon Dahlander, a spokesman for the Dallas Independent School District, is a clever and adroit pianist whose two albums for Carpe Diem (*piano landscapes, v. 1 and v. 2*) are tasty, melancholy efforts from the Spencer Brewer School. And pianist Carl Cluney, whose work is unfortunately not released, is a genuine cross between Lyle Mays and George Winston. Why these people are not famous is puzzling.

☆ Part 8: Jazz

☆ One: Scott Joplin, Charlie Christian, and the Piano and Guitar Giants

O THAT POPULACE ORIGINALLY TARGETED BY P. T. BARNUM—
the demographic heart of our nation that now clusters around TV sets
to feast hungrily at the intellectual buffet provided by *Married . . . with
Children* or NASCAR races—jazz is an arcane musical universe characterized by unlistenable "music" performed by incomprehensible players—except for that cute Kenny G. guy.

This is the same audience to whom Scott Joplin is famous (if at all) as
one of those one-hit wonder people like Gilbert O'Sullivan ("Alone Again
[Naturally]") and Milli Vanilli ("Girl You Know It's True"). They remember
Joplin's smash, "The Entertainer," a catchy piano ditty that became a huge
success when it was renamed "The Sting" and included as the title song for
that Academy Award–winning film.

But reality is different. For one thing, jazz is wonderful music. For another, Gilbert O'Sullivan actually had a second hit ("Clair"), and, third,
Scott Joplin was, by the time of *The Sting*, a long-dead pianist of Texas
extraction who was not only a superlative composer but a pioneer of that
early jazz called ragtime.

JOPLIN WAS BORN IN TEXARKANA IN 1868 AND BEGAN TEACH-
ing himself piano at an early age, stepping up his progress at eleven with
lessons from a German instructor known as "The Professor." The cross-
referencing of his southern black upbringing (and its attendant musical
forms like gospel and blues) with the European/classical/opera influences of
his formal instruction had a substantial long-term effect on Joplin.

He soon thereafter formed the Texas Medley Quartet (which included
his brother Will, and which later became a quintet with the addition of
another brother, Robert). They played briefly around northeast Texas, performing what was probably a stylistic smorgasbord of minstrel tunes,
marches, and early blues.

The first edition of Texas Medley was short-lived, though, as Joplin sought musically freer pastures. He moved to St. Louis and began playing in saloons and whorehouses in the notorious Chestnut Valley district, help- ing refine the burgeoning ragtime form, a dance music which was, as a precursor to jazz proper, heavily reliant on syncopated, bubbly piano lines. Joplin's original rags became staples in the clubs throughout the red-light district, and gave the composer perhaps his first inkling that he was on to something.

After several years, Joplin relocated to Chicago and organized a group in time to perform on the fringes of the 1894 Chicago World's Columbian Exposition. From there he moved to Sedalia, Missouri, re-formed the old Texas Medley band with his brothers, and began touring extensively.

In 1895, Joplin began to see the fruits of his musical scholarship: He published his first tunes ("A Picture of Her Face" and "Please Say You Will"), resulting in a financial situation not afforded most young ragtime innovators because they couldn't write music. The following year, after a tour of Texas, Joplin disbanded the Texas Medley and settled in Sedalia, studying piano, theory, and composition for four years at George Smith College. It was there that Joplin's material began to be published by John Stark and Son, whose work on the composer's behalf was particularly effi- cient.

In 1899, Stark and Son published Joplin's "Maple Leaf Rag," which sold one hundred thousand copies in its first year alone and would eventually sell hundreds of thousands of copies. The tune would become the most popular ragtime song of all time—or at least until "The Entertainer" became famous in *The Sting*. The agreement between John Stark and Joplin was groundbreaking for a few reasons: One because the publisher was white and Joplin was black, and that sort of thing just didn't happen all that often at that point in time; and two, because as a result of the agreement Joplin began to earn quite a bit of royalty cash for "Maple Leaf Rag" and other similar pieces, and was able to turn his compositional efforts to longer, more serious works. He was completely committed to ragtime as a musical form, and began attempting to expand the genre's creative parameters with a variety of experimental compositions.

In 1899, Joplin wrote *The Ragtime Dance*, a folk ballet comprising ten dance themes which basically confused most of the listening public (no doubt the forefathers of those earlier-cited fans of Al and Peg Bundy) and sold poorly. Four years later, Joplin finished *A Guest of Honor*, a one-act ragtime opera which is considered a "lost property" inasmuch as it was never produced and no one can find an existing score.

Though the limited acclaim of these more ambitious efforts was demor- alizing to the pianist, he continued to have success with shorter pieces— "Easy Winners," "Original Rags," "Sugar Cane Rag," "Elite Syncopations," and "The Entertainer" among them. Besides, Joplin was planning his mas- terpiece: a three-act opera called *Treemonisha*, on which he worked dili- gently from 1907 until the end of his life.

Unfortunately, Joplin had contracted syphilis by this point and began having difficulty with certain physical activities like speaking and playing the piano. Furthermore, he'd split from Stark and Son in a royalty rate disagreement, though he had enough money to underwrite his own production of *Treemonisha* in 1915. That the opera was a critical and commercial failure was a spiritually fatal affront to the already physically devastated Joplin; he was admitted to a hospital and died in 1917.

Though Joplin's brand of ragtime was too structurally rigid to have a long-lasting impact on the development of jazz, his influence on several early jazz giants like Fats Waller, Earl "Fatha" Hines, Louis Armstrong, King Oliver, and "Jelly Roll" Morton was substantial.

AUSTIN'S TEDDY WILSON (1912–1986), THE SECOND OF THE GREAT Texas jazz pianists, was arguably the greatest swing pianist ever ("swing" denoting that danceable style of jazz most commonly associated with the big band era).

He grew up in Alabama, where his parents had obtained academic posts at Tuskegee Institute. Wilson showed musical inclinations at a young age, received training on piano and violin while growing up, and was later a music theory major at Talladega College.

An early visit to Chicago turned him on to the music of trumpeter Bix Beiderbecke and cornet player King Oliver, and Wilson blew off school to pursue a career in jazz. Within a year, the gentle and urbane Wilson joined Speed Webb's band, then quickly built a reputation as a pianist and arranger with Jimmy Noone, Louis Armstrong, Art Tatum, Budd and Keg Johnson, and Benny Carter, recording his first dates with the latter's Chocolate Dandies band.

Wilson also began to record solo (including the instrumental chart-topper "You Can't Stop Me from Dreaming"), with a variety of his own small groups, and frequently with a troubled but brilliant vocalist named Billie Holiday. He also backed Ella Fitzgerald, Lena Horne, and a variety of other prominent vocalists. But the pianist really blew the doors open when he became the first black to play in clarinetist Benny Goodman's trio. The group, with the addition of Lionel Hampton on vibraharp, made jazz history with the recording of their Carnegie Hall concert of 1938, and Wilson subsequently made several more recordings with Goodman in both the trio and big band formats before forming his own big band in 1939.

Though that excellent group was short-lived, Wilson's reputation had by that time grown exponentially. His status as the preeminent swinging pianist, whose discipline and good taste were matched only by his skills at improvisation, was assured. Throughout the forties, he led a triumphant sextet, recorded with Sarah Vaughan, and into the fifties continued to perform selected dates with Goodman, head his own trio, host his own radio show, and teach music at Juilliard.

During the sixties, Wilson honed his reputation as a superb solo performer, imbuing classic tunes with signature interpretation and embarking on improvisational odysseys highlighted by his starburst right-hand runs. Though his later performances were occasionally criticized for containing a creeping "cocktail lounge" flavor, Wilson remained a visionary force in jazz piano until his death in 1986. Several of his recordings are still available, and Smithsonian's *Statement and Improvisations (1934–1942)*, any of the Classics solo releases, and the Giants of Jazz's *Gentleman of the Keyboard* are excellent introductions to Wilson's sorcery.

WILLIAM "RED" GARLAND ROUNDS OUT TEXAS'S TRIUMVIRATE of truly great jazz pianists, and his work as a bebop innovator (a generally faster-tempo'd, free-flowing jazz than swing, usually performed by smaller combos) is assured. He was born in Dallas in 1923 and studied clarinet (under the guidance of Buster Smith, no less) and alto sax until he joined the army and discovered the possibilities of the piano. After the service, he returned to Texas and played professionally in clubs, honing his new chops as he gleaned mightily from the works of Count Basie and Nat "King" Cole.

Interestingly, Garland was "discovered" by fellow Dallasite Oran "Hot Lips" Page when the famous trumpeter passed through Texas on tour. He asked Garland to join up, and after an extended series of road dates, the young pianist found himself in New York. Garland immediately secured a series of club dates, meanwhile soaking up the sounds of Erroll Garner, Bud Powell, Art Tatum, and, not much later, Ahmad Jamal. Boasting a crashing, mutated approach to block-chord voicings and a smooth way with a run that sounded like the tinkling of bells, Garland quickly carved out a singular, sought-after style of playing.

For the better part of a decade, starting in 1946, Garland worked steadily in the Philadelphia and New York areas, supporting such varied artists from both the swing and bop eras as (fellow Texan) Eddie "Cleanhead" Vinson, Coleman Hawkins, Ben Webster, Billy Eckstine, Lester Young, Charlie Parker, and Fats Navarro.

It was in 1954, though, that Garland joined up with the Miles Davis Quintet, becoming part of a world-class rhythm section that included drummer Philly Joe Jones and bassist Paul Chambers, with John Coltrane on sax rounding out the group. Until 1958, that band was arguably one of the finest groups ever assembled in the bop idiom. In 1956 alone, they cut such classics as *Workin'*, *Steamin'*, and *Cookin'* (all for Prestige)—with Garland's piano work coming in for a heavy dose of critical acclaim. The band became a sextet, then players began drifting in and out and, unfortunately, Davis eventually dissolved the unit because of the vast appetite for narcotics that the members had collectively developed.

During and subsequent to the Davis years, Garland recorded solo albums and records with John Coltrane, worked with his own trio as well as a quartet, and while his performances never reached the level he achieved with Davis, Garland was nevertheless a huge force in bebop piano. He shifted his base of operations to Philadelphia for a short time, then, in 1968, to care for his ill mother, he returned to Dallas. He was essentially retired for fifteen years, though he enjoyed stopping by—always incognito—a small jazz club called the Recovery Room.

Whenever he showed up, Garland would sit in—he steadfastly refused any payment other than beer and cigarettes—with the house band, which frequently featured tenor sax players Marchel Ivery and James Clay or visiting stars like Buddy Rich. (Dozens of tapes of some very amazing performances from those gigs exist on cassette, and are being culled through for eventual release by Dallas's upstart jazz label, Leaning House Records.)

In 1978, Garland came out of "retirement" and returned to New York, where he recorded several more records for Galaxy before he passed away in 1984. Aside from the Davis Quintet albums, his work on Red Alone (Moodsville), All Mornin' Long (Prestige), and Crossings (Galaxy) demonstrates the remarkably varied facets of the great man's career.

SEVERAL OTHER PIANISTS MADE SIGNIFICANT MARKS IN THE storied history of jazz. John Dickson "Peck" Kelley, who was born in Houston in 1898, was a pianist and bandleader of great talent and taste—such is his reputation. It turns out that, though he made appearances in Louisiana and Missouri early in his career, union red tape and work permit problems frustrated the gentle bandleader, and he returned to Texas and resisted all subsequent efforts to get him to travel or record. (Kelley finally did record in the late fifties.)

Fortunately, history has been reasonably generous in chronicling his early exploits. He first became famous as the leader of a mid-twenties Houston-area band called Peck's Bad Boys, a unit that included at various times trombonist Jack Teagarden, trumpeter Louis Prima, clarinetist/sax man Pee Wee Russell, and others. While all of those musicians went on to the national spotlight, the pianist insisted on staying home (more than one sought to bring Kelley along, and other stars like the Dorsey brothers, Rudy Vallee, and Bing Crosby courted his talent unsuccessfully).

Despite his best efforts at anonymity, Kelley remained famous; more than one national article was written about the reclusive genius, and it's said the hit song "Beat Me Daddy, Eight to the Bar" was penned about him. Kelley continued to lead bands until the late forties, when he began to work essentially as a solo pianist. Finally, in 1957, with Dick Shannon's quartet, the nearly blind artist recorded what has been released as Peck Kelley Jam Vols. 1 and 2 on Commodore—the only recordings he ever made. Kelley passed away in 1980.

Another Houston-born (1934) pianist is Horace Tapscott, known primarily as a proponent of free and postbop jazz creation. Though Tapscott didn't seriously take up the piano until he was in an auto accident in the early fifties, his mother was a jazz musician and Tapscott played trombone in high school bands with classmates like Eric Dolphy and Don Cherry after his family moved to southern California in the mid-forties. As a member of an armed forces band Tapscott first began tinkering with the piano.

After the service, Tapscott toured with Lionel Hampton and, postaccident, settled in Los Angeles as a pianist. In 1961 he formed the Pan Afrikan Peoples Arkestra, a big-band free-jazz ensemble whose avant-garde performances were closely tied to the artist's heavily involved community activism. Tapscott's stature as a composer grew as well, and contributed significantly to saxophonist Sonny Criss's groundbreaking 1968 LP, *Sonny's Dream: The Birth of New Cool.*

Tapscott also recorded extensively on his own Nimbus label, but the originality of the music and the limitations of his indie label resources for years kept a significant audience from appreciating Tapscott's work.

He has since recorded as a solo pianist and as the leader of a trio, and though his material isn't easy to obtain, it's probably worth the effort for those interested in the outer fringe possibilities of jazz. *Dark Trees: Vols. 1 and 2* (Hat Art) are current representations.

Dallas's Cedar Walton, also born in 1934, has had a long, star-crusted career as the premier accompanist in postbop piano. As a boy, he was taught piano by his mother, learned clarinet and played in R&B bands around Texas before heading to the University of Denver to pursue the study of piano. Just as a Northwestern business school grad would emigrate to Wall Street, Walton then headed to New York to begin a career in jazz. Though interrupted briefly by a stint in the army, Walton then set about establishing himself throughout the fifties as a versatile talent, evolving a powerful melodic and percussive style, performing in succession with Kenny Dorham, J. J. Johnson, the Jazztet, and Art Farmer.

In 1961 he then settled in for three years as a member of Art Blakey's Jazz Messengers (which also included Freddie Hubbard and Wayne Shorter). He became a much in-demand session player for both the Prestige and Blue Note labels, and also backed Abbey Lincoln. Throughout these prestigious dates, Walton headed up his own traditional bop quartet, which eventually became known as Eastern Rebellion. Foremost among the frequently evolving personnel was drummer Billy Higgins, who has continued to work with Walton in a variety of intriguing situations, frequently as a duo.

Walton rejoined Blakey for a Far East tour in 1973, then toyed with various fusion and funk/rock elements in first Soundscapes and then Mobius before returning to lead more traditional trios and quartets (with Higgins constantly in tow). Finally, since the eighties, Walton has recorded with the Timeless All-Stars, formed a quintet, done festivals, and continued to write and record for a variety of artists and labels.

While his status as a sideman is probably Walton's claim to fame, his work as a writer, solo performer, and leader is substantial. Prestige's *Plays*

Cedar Walton is an excellent sampling of the pianist's late-sixties original material and performances, and the two-volume *Night at Boomer's* is recommended. Walton also appeared in the film *Round Midnight* with the likes of Freddie Hubbard, Herbie Hancock, Dexter Gordon, and others. He's appeared as a session player on an almost countless list of important records, in addition to solo work and heading up his own quartet. And he's not done, either, as evidenced by 1999's *Roots*, out on the Astor Place label.

The preeminent keyboardist of the Texas fusion/funk set would have to be Joe Sample, who was born in Houston in 1939 and grew up listening to Clifton Chenier and Louis Armstrong. In his teens, Sample studied music at Texas Southern University and formed a group that pioneered the "Gulf Coast Sound," a mixture of blues and funk with instrumental jazz overtones. The band included, besides Sample, Wayne Henderson on trombone, Wilton Felder on tenor sax, and Stix Hooper on drums. They moved to Los Angeles in 1960, eventually became the Jazz Crusaders, and were not only pioneers of the soul/jazz movement, but probably its finest practitioners.

Sample, who added electric piano and organ to his piano riffs, was particularly adept at holding down sinuous funk rhythms while scattering melodious right-hand runs over the band's thick grooves. In addition to the Jazz Crusaders, Sample worked extensively in the sixties with a variety of similarly inspired artists like Tom Scott's L.A. Express and Bobby Hutcherson and Harold Land's group.

In the early seventies, the Jazz Crusaders shortened their name to simply the Crusaders, added guitarist Larry Carlton, and slicked up their sound to a West Coast studio sheen. As jazz, their stuff was fairly lightweight and far closer to straight funk, but it definitely sported some tasty chops. Though Hooper and Henderson eventually abandoned ship, Sample continued to work, principally as a session man for artists like B. B. King, Joe Cocker, Anita Baker, and Marvin Gaye. He's now active as a solo artist, (*Old Faces, Old Places*; *The Song Lives On*; and *Sample This*) and indicates an interest in retrospective performances showcasing the likes of Scott Joplin and Jelly Roll Morton.

Necessary Crusaders albums would include *Street Life* and *Those Southern Knights* (both available from MCA).

Lyle Mays should also be mentioned. Although the Wisconsin-born pianist resided in Texas only during his years of study at North Texas State University (now the University of North Texas), his contributions to their world-class music department are historic. While a member of their prestigious One O'Clock Lab Band, he scored and notated an album which, in 1975, became the first by a college group to win a Grammy.

Mays has since gone on to stardom as pianist/synthesist/composer with the Pat Metheny Group and on his own albums. *As Falls Wichita, So Falls Wichita Falls* (ECM), a duet album with Metheny, and his album of trio pieces, *Fictionary* (Geffen), are terrific.

Other Texas jazz pianists who should be remembered include: James Polk (writer/arranger for Ray Charles), Lloyd Glenn (Kid Ory, Joe Turner), Hersal Thomas (recorded with Louis Armstrong and Sippie Wallace), Joe Gallardo (Arnett Cobb), Norma "Yes I'm a" Teagarden, Bob Torough, Cedrick Haywood, and Knocky Parker. Others to study include Dave Palmer, Fred Sanders (*East of Vilbig*, Leaning House), and Joe LoCascio (*Silent Motion, A Charmed Life*, both on Heart Music).

IN A SIMILAR FASHION TO PIANO, TEXAS HAS HAD SEVERAL significant jazz guitarists who easily rate as major players. But three—Charlie Christian, Eddie Durham, and Herb Ellis—truly stand out as major dudes.

At twelve or thirteen, in his parents' backyard, Charlie Christian coaxed amazing sounds and chord clusters from a guitar he'd constructed from a cigar box. But his skill and promise went far beyond science fair project wizardry.

Christian was destined to give jazz a stylistic facelift; Frederick Grunfeld, in his book *The Art and Times of the Guitar*, described Christian's artistry as "the great divide of the jazz guitar: there is the guitar before Christian and the guitar after Christian, and they sound virtually like two different instruments."

Born in Dallas in 1919, Christian moved with his family to Oklahoma City while he was still young. Though he is thought to have studied trumpet, string bass, and possibly even piano, his love of and affinity for guitar were established quickly. Early influences most certainly included Blind Lemon Jefferson, Eddie Lang, and Lonnie Johnson, and it is thought that saxophonist Lester Young profoundly flavored Christian's instinctive knowledge of theory and harmony.

By the mid-thirties, Christian was playing string bass in Alphonso Trent's sextet. When he was overheard practicing on an amplified guitar, he was quickly switched to the guitar slot, and a chance meeting in Oklahoma City with Eddie Durham (whose early solo and electric guitar conceptions opened the door for Christian's genius) was fortuitous.

It wasn't long before blues/jazz historian and talent scout John Hammond convinced a recalcitrant Benny Goodman to give Christian a chance. An inaugural attempt with the Goodman Orchestra on "Rose Room"—a tune Christian had never heard before—turned into a lengthy and breathtaking jam that changed jazz history.

Christian is frequently credited with being the first modern jazzman to utilize single-string solos on electric guitar—which we know was probably the work of his pal and quasi-mentor, Durham, but what Christian did with his solos was integral in the creation of bebop (the phrase itself is something many experts also credit Christian with coining).

Though he was only with Goodman (the orchestra and the sextet) from September 1939 until his death of tuberculosis in March 1942, Christian's drive, spontaneity, phrasing, and sophisticated fire remain the stuff of pure genius. While his recorded output is regrettably small, and all available discs are excellent, *Genius of the Electric Guitar* and *With the Benny Goodman Sextet and Orchestra* (both Columbia) are particularly representative.

HERB ELLIS IS ANOTHER GIFT FROM GUITAR HEAVEN. BORN IN Farmersville, Texas, in 1921, he started out playing banjo and, at eight, switched to guitar when he came across a book called *How to Play the Guitar in Five Minutes*. Though the actually mastery of the instrument took a bit longer (Ellis would say it's a perpetually ongoing process), he was by his college years at North Texas State University quite accomplished; fellow students included tenor man Jimmy Giuffre and arranger Gene Roland.

After school, Ellis migrated to Kansas City, played awhile with Glen Gray's Casa Loma Orchestra, then scored a gig with the Jimmy Dorsey Band. In the late forties, Ellis formed the Soft Winds band with pianist Lou Carter and bassist/violinist Johnny Frigo. The group was a Nat "King" Cole–inspired trio that recorded for Majestic and authored the Billie Holiday hit "Detour Ahead," as well as "I Told Ya I Love Ya Now Get Out." Further success was limited, though, and in 1953 Ellis replaced Barney Kessel with Oscar Peterson's trio.

It was during his six-plus years with Peterson that Ellis became famous for his swinging lines, a Christian-influenced stylist with deep blues roots and an attention to space as much as speed. He followed up his Peterson experience as an accompanist to Ella Fitzgerald, then settled into a secure and creative period as a session player. He was also featured in club and recording dates with Joe Pass, Ray Brown, and Ben Webster, and formed the Great Guitars with Charlie Byrd and Barnie Kessel.

Of late, Ellis has regrouped the Soft Winds trio, which recorded live during a cruise tour. Results of those sessions, in conjunction with recently discovered "lost" tapes of the group from the forties and fifties, were scheduled to be released in 1996 as *Soft Winds Then and Now*.

Nothin' But the Blues (Verve), *Soft and Mellow*, and *Seven Come Eleven* (the latter two on Concord Jazz) represent Ellis's varied talents.

Oscar Moore and Larry Coryell are two other Texas guitarists who've made significant inroads into the jazz legacy. Bop guitarist Moore, born in Austin in 1916, was another player heavily influenced by Charlie Christian, as well as a pioneer in the integration of guitarists into the jazz combo structure. He solidified that role with Nat "King" Cole, having joined the singer's quartet in 1937 for a residency at Santa Monica's Swanee Inn.

He toured and recorded with Cole for ten years, then did sessions with the likes of Art Tatum, Illinois Jacquet, and Lionel Hampton, and starting in 1945, won the *Down Beat* Readers Poll as Best Guitarist four years running. Moore then joined up with his brother Johnny's Three Blazers (an outfit famous for the contributions of pianist Charles Brown) but, inexplicably, after three albums with the group, the guitarist quit to become a brick

Criminally Underrated Guitarist
Eddie Durham

Jazz guitar wouldn't be jazz guitar—at least the way we know it—and Charlie Christian probably wouldn't have played like Charlie Christian if it hadn't been for San Marcos's Eddie Durham.

A virtual prodigy, Durham, born in 1906, showed promise on trombone, banjo, and guitar by ten, at which point he thought it prudent to learn theory. Since his oldest brother, Joe, played bass for Nat "King" Cole, he was only too happy to help the kid out, and taught him the rudiments of three-part harmony. Eddie took it from there and taught himself five-and six-part harmony as well as composition, and would eventually come up with the concept of adding sixths and ninths to existing song arrangements, an idea so madcap in its ingenuity that it would change the face of jazz.

First, though, Durham had to get through his teens. He was on the road by eighteen, playing guitar and trombone for acts like the 101 Ranch Brass Band and Gene Coy's Happy Black Aces. By twenty-two, he'd joined Walter Page's Blue Devils, a blues/jazz outfit which happened to include trumpeter Oran "Hot Lips" Page and altoist Buster Smith (both prominent Texans) as well as a pianist called Count Basie.

It was at that point that Durham became one of the first jazzmen to play electric guitar. In doing so, a few things happened that had lasting repercussions: 1. on an October 1929 recording of "New Vine Street Blues," Durham's guitar solo alternated single-note lines with modulating chords—something that had never been done and would open the door for single-line soloing in the future; 2. Durham's 1935 solo on "Hittin' the Bottle" was one of the first attempts anywhere at recording an electric solo; and 3. in 1937 Durham met Charlie Christian. Durham's advice and innovations (which, among other things, included advice on down-strokes with his plectrum hand) heavily influenced Christian, who, as has been noted, blasted off from there.

And though it's probably true that Eddie Durham will be remembered more in the great musical scheme of things for his innovative and blistering arrangements in swing (and possibly for his trombone playing) than for his contributions to jazz guitar, the latter aspect cannot be overemphasized. If his own solos and rhythm work aren't enough (check out the early Count Basie or Bennie Moten recordings), then remember him every time you enjoy Charlie Christian.

layer. Though he emerged periodically to perform or record (including a tribute album to Cole, no longer available), his time in the spotlight was essentially over. He died in 1981; suggested listening would include any of the Nat King Cole sessions from their time together, or *The Oscar Moore Quartet* (Tampa).

Of a more modern era, representing the jazz/rock fusion period, is Galveston's Larry Coryell (born in 1943). Essentially a self-taught guitarist, Coryell played in various rock bands in his teen years and throughout his time as a journalism student at the University of Washington.

Opting for six strings over a typewriter, he moved to the Big Apple after bailing out of college and played first with Chico Hamilton, then helped form one of the earliest of the fusion groups, Free Spirits. He then triple-jumped from Gary Burton's band to Herbie Mann to his own band, Foreplay.

In 1970, with John McLaughlin, Chick Corea, Miroslav Vitous, and Billy Cobham, Coryell recorded the groundbreaking fusion album *Spaces*, which served as the blueprint for Coryell's next conceptual band, Eleventh House (which included Randy Brecker and Alphonse Mouzon). Eleventh House achieved the sort of status afforded rock stars, touring the world and selling *beaucoup* LPs to young musical illuminati obsessed with the new jazz/rock gumbo that was stirring.

Since the heyday of fusion passed—some say mercifully—Coryell has remained busy in a slightly more traditional sense, though still seasoning his music with a variety of world-flavored styles. He's worked extensively in an acoustic format, touring solo, with Philip Catherine, and in trio with John McLaughlin and Paco De Lucia.

He's also recorded with Sonny Rollins, Charles Mingus, Stephane Grappelli, John Scofield, and Steve Khan—not to mention his myriad adventuresome solo albums. Coryell is an inventive, quicksilver-fast player who intermingles flashbulb snatches of humor, melody, and mathematics in his fretboard excursions.

He continues to stylistically sample the world, generally adding to our musical understanding even as he erases boundaries. *Spaces* and *Eleventh House* are both recommended and available from Vanguard, and Act's *Twin House* is a fine set of duet performances with Catherine.

As usual, in the Texas context, there is no shortage of other guitarists who are terrific jazz musicians, and the names Jimmy Wymble, Don Gilliland, Roger Boykins, Zachary Breaux, Clint Strong, Joe Lee, Roy Gaines, Mitch Watkins, Al Hendrickson, Fred Hamilton, Monty Montgomery, and Nick DeGenero should all be fastened to the refrigerator with a magnet.

☆ Two: Ornette Coleman, the Texas Tenors, and Various Single-Reed Men

IN THE SINGULARLY CRUEL UNIVERSE CALLED "HIGH SCHOOL life," marching band members are accorded the same societal respect we give to real-world lepers and sin-eaters. Imagine, though, a high school marching band that simultaneously included future jazz heroes like Ornette Coleman, Prince Lasha, Dewey Redman, and Charles Moffett. It would be the musical equivalent of having William Faulkner, Alexander Solzhenitsyn, Toni Morrison, and Bret Harte on the same yearbook staff, or Ted Williams, Roberto Clemente, Robin Yount, and Carl Yastrzemski on the same prep baseball team.

The thing is, though, that Coleman, Lasha, Redman, and Moffett *were* in the same high school band together at Fort Worth's I. M. Terrell—and we can all be grateful that this happened at a time before they would have been required to play Chicago's "Colour My World" at halftime of the homecoming football game.

Coleman went on to change modern jazz with his concept of harmolodics, Moffett is a drummer who's worked with Archie Shepp in addition to Coleman, and Lasha became an alto sax man and flutist of some repute. As for Redman, he comprises part of that phenomenon known throughout music as "the Texas Tenors," a three-generation aggregate of brilliant tenor saxophonists from the Lone Star State which also includes Illinois Jacquet, Jimmy Giuffre, James Clay, Marchel Ivery, Budd Johnson, Herschel Evans, and Arnett Cobb, to name just a few. All these players were (are) world-class talents with disparate and incredible abilities who nevertheless boasted a similarity of tone and style that was as identifiable as fingerprints—or, as described by one Texas musician, while they each have their individual styles, it's as though they play their horns with a Texas accent.

The collective contribution to jazz by all these men is truly staggering, and the conundrum of the Texas connection and the whys and hows of its evolution remains as puzzling as the state's propensity for cranking out guitar geniuses.

* * *

ORNETTE COLEMAN IS CLEARLY THE MOST FAMOUS AND CON-
troversial of the Texas jazzers because of his theory of harmolodics and its
subsequent contribution to the development of "free jazz"—a movement
that not only altered the face of music but created a huge rift between
musicians as well as critics as to whether Coleman was a visionary genius
or a minimally talented hoaxer. Born in Fort Worth in 1930, Coleman
willed his way through a tragic boyhood, shined shoes to earn money to
buy a saxophone, and found a respite in music.

He started on alto sax at fourteen, became infatuated with bebop and
Charlie Parker and switched to tenor shortly thereafter. Within three years,
Coleman was backing any number of big-time jazz, blues, western swing, and
R&B stars who came through town. After stints in a minstrel show and with
Big Joe Turner, Coleman joined up with Pee Wee Crayton, where his in-
creasingly obscure musical ideas began to get him into trouble. He was once
beaten up outside a nightclub because of his weird playing, and another time
his sax was destroyed on the bandstand by the sort of irate crowd one associates with the torch-bearing mobs advancing on Dr. Frankenstein's castle.
(The latter episode, in fact, precipitated Coleman's return to alto sax.)

Coleman was eventually abandoned by Crayton in Los Angeles, where,
after a brief and temporary return to Fort Worth, he began to infuse an
intense study of theory and harmony into his own compositional ideas.

When he began to incorporate these concepts into performance, Coleman succeeded mostly in either baffling or infuriating other musicians, if
for no other reason than it seemed to them that Coleman's harmolodics
constituted nothing less than antimusic.

Simply expressed (or maybe not), Coleman seeks to spin jazz away from
reliance on conventional chord structures, principal soloists, and a singular
melody. To best accomplish these things, Coleman tossed away the alternating, swinging soloist tradition and tossed into the mix asymmetrical lines,
odd rhythmic emphasis, and the freedom for any instrumentalist to pursue
melodic tangents with and/or against the tangents simultaneously improvised by other players.

It might *sound* like it's completely chaotic, but there is form to the music.
Coleman's blues training is frequently evident in his quasi-structures, and
there are dalliances within the standard AABA format; it's just that the
cacophonous improvisation over those vaguely observed building blocks su-
persedes the norm and creates confusion—and freedom. Think of Coleman's
core idea as a musical camping trip in which Verse and Chorus, Lead and
Rhythm, and Beginnings and Endings all take acid and gather round the
campfire to make gumbo—just in time for a category 5 hurricane to shred
through the campground.

But not everyone thought Coleman was a kook. A bassist named Red

Mitchell was sufficiently impressed that he was able to engineer for Coleman a recording contract with Contemporary Records. The resultant two LPs, 1958's *Something Else* and 1959's *Tomorrow Is the Question*, had the admirable effect of absolutely polarizing the entire jazz community—and marked the start of the Free Jazz era.

John Lewis of the Modern Jazz Quartet arranged for Coleman to go to New York, where a contract with Atlantic Records was signed. Working with what would become his standard quartet (trumpeter/cornetist Don Cherry, bassist Charlie Haden, and drummer Billy Higgins), and utilizing a variety of guest artists, Coleman released *The Shape of Jazz to Come* in 1959, and over the next three years recorded several more albums, including 1960's *Free Jazz: A Collective Improvisation*, for the label. All have since become landmark works in the saga of jazz (and are now available in a remarkable boxed set from Rhino Records called *Beauty Is a Rare Thing: The Complete Atlantic Recordings*).

Coleman then took a few years off from recording and performing and taught himself to play trumpet and violin. In the late sixties, he emerged with first a trio and later a variety of quartets, recording as well with old schoolmate Dewey Redman. All told, Coleman recorded for ESP, Blue Note, RCA, and Atlantic during that period, and while his ideas continued to stimulate the open-minded, he was never what one might call a big commercial draw.

Since the early seventies, Coleman began to further diversify his musical palette, defining "harmolodics" as a philosophy and a lifestyle as well as an ever evolving musical idea. He's recorded with a variety of different artists, in peculiar configurations, and he began working within what might be described as jazz/rock structures, forming a group called Prime Time which utilized alto in conjunction with a "double trio" concept: two electric guitarists, two electric bassists, and two drummers. He's also recorded with Moroccan musicians and, in 1985, recorded the *Song X* album with Pat Metheny, which was a high visibility point for both players. Since then, he has continued to compose prodigiously and perform in a variety of frameworks, jamming with the Grateful Dead, releasing *Tone Dialing*, *Colors* (with Joachim Kuhn), and *Town Hall 1962*, and running his own Harmolodics studio/label. The recent recipient of a MacArthur Fellowship, the brilliant enigma known as Ornette Coleman shows no sign of creative abatement. And the rest of us will either get it or not.

ANOTHER MASSIVE TALENT AT ALTO SAX WAS HENRY "BUSTER" Smith, who was born near Ennis in 1904 and took up the clarinet in his childhood. Largely self-taught, he played with a variety of Dallas-area bands before switching to alto sax in 1923 for a decade-long stint with Walter Page's famous Blue Devils group.

In the thirties, he played with Bennie Moten and coheaded the Count

Basie/Buster Smith Barons of Rhythm, carving out a significant niche as an arranger as well as an innovative player who utilized his Texas blues roots in friendly counterpoint to his machine gun–fingered sheets of notes.

He then moved to New York and began to lead his own groups, one early edition of which included a seventeen-year-old Charlie Parker—upon whom Smith was a massive influence. As a long-term leader, though, Smith had a more frustrating time, and more and more he turned to arranging as a primary source of income. (He is generally credited with cowriting "One O'Clock Jump" and arranging the tune.)

In 1941, Smith returned to Dallas and headed up a variety of small combos. Apparently, he abandoned the alto sax in the late fifties and, though he continued to play until his death in 1991, his instruments of choice were piano, guitar, or double bass.

While his recording career was frustratingly unjust (jump on Atlantic's *Legendary Buster Smith*, if you can find it), his innovative, linear style was the stuff of giants, his skill as an arranger top-notch, and, above all, his influence on Charlie Parker was absolutely vital to the Bird's development.

Three other superb alto sax players, John Handy, Eddie "Cleanhead" Vinson, and Julius Hemphill, should be discussed before undertaking the massive legacy of the Texas Tenors.

Vinson, a Houston native born in 1917, picked up an alto sax in his early teens and, by the time he was twenty, had established a reputation as a soul/jazz honker in Chester Boone's group, Milt Larkin's band, and with Floyd Ray. He picked up his nickname after an overdose of hair straightener necessitated a head-shaving session—and the look stuck. After touring the chitlin circuit as vocalist for Big Bill Broonzy and Lil Green, he signed up in 1942 with Cootie Williams's orchestra in a lead singer/alto sax capacity.

After hit songs with "Cherry Red" and "Somebody's Got to Go," Vinson had a national reputation as a blues shouter with a winsome, ironic, and self-deprecating style. He led his own bands in the late forties (including a septet with Red Garland and John Coltrane), and had another massive smash with "Kidney Stew Blues."

He recorded for several labels, frequently in a blues capacity, and established a workhorse reputation for the next twenty years. His alto work eventually gained the same notoriety as his singing, for many of the same reasons: His playing was coarse and playful, vibrant and bluesy.

In the late sixties, touring in a strict jazz capacity with Jay McShann, Vinson's career took an upswing. Throughout the seventies he worked high-profile blues and jazz sessions for Count Basie, Johnny Otis, Roomful of Blues, Arnett Cobb, and Buddy Tate. He also composed steadily, including "Tune Up" and "Four," both of which have been incorrectly attributed to Miles Davis.

Vinson played actively until his death in 1988; Black and Blue's *Kidney Stew* is a fine primer, as is *Live at Sandy's* (Muse).

John Handy, a Dallas native born in 1933, was, like Buster Smith, a self-

taught clarinetist, was a champion amateur boxer and, at sixteen, took up
the alto sax when his family relocated to California. After the service,
Handy played in a variety of blues bands in the San Francisco area, then
moved to New York and joined Charles Mingus's band.

In 1959 he started his own group, toured Europe, then moved back to
northern California to study theory. Throughout the sixties he worked with
a variety of artists on a variety of projects, including symphonies and opera
and with Mingus again. He then formed a new ten-piece band, which recorded a knockout bop performance at the 1965 Monterey Jazz Festival.

In 1970, in conjunction with the San Francisco Symphony Orchestra,
Handy performed his own *Concerto for Jazz Soloist and Orchestra*. His subsequent work has been varied and ambitious indeed. He's worked with Ali
Akbar Khan in the jazz/Indian outfit called Rainbow (*not* the Rainbow
formed by ex–Deep Purple misanthrope Ritchie Blackmore), experimented
with jazz/rock fusion, performed regularly with a group of Mingus veterans
called Mingus Dynasty, recorded a pop hit called "Hard Work," and worked
extensively as a teacher.

Besides the *Live at Monterey* CD (Columbia), his work on the seminal
Mingus Ah Um album (Columbia) is highly suggested.

Julius Hemphill, a 1940 addition to the Fort Worth census, was a childhood pal of John Carter and, in a broken-record recitation, learned clarinet
at North Texas State and played in a variety of R&B groups.

He played with Ike Turner for a while, then moved to St. Louis and
joined the Black Artists Group in 1968. An ardent composer and disciple
of the free jazz movement, Hemphill started his own band in 1972, Mbari,
a platform from which he engineered a variety of conceptual pieces involving dance, theater, poetry, and music.

Heading for New York, Hemphill worked with Lester Bowie, Anthony
Braxton, and Kool and the Gang, participated in the "loft jazz" concept,
and, most important, cofounded the World Saxophone Quartet.

A player of conviction and wild imagination, Hemphill continued to
work, both with the WSQ and in a variety of studio and group configurations, despite poor health which resulted in the amputation of one leg.
Eventually, his illnesses caused him to retire from the World Saxophone
Quartet in spite of their substantial international popularity, and he passed
away in 1995.

The *Julius Hemphill Big Band* (Elektra Musician) and *Steppin' with the
World Saxophone Quartet* (Black Saint) are good introductions.

The balance of Texas alto saxophonists who had noteworthy careers in
jazz includes: Jimmy Ford, Ernie Caceres, Leo Wright, Clifford Scott, and
"Shorty" Clemmons.

As for the myriad sax kings who opted for stardom in the tenor arena,
Herschel Evans, born in 1909 in Denton, was a forerunner of the Texas
Tenor movement. He started out in the Troy Floyd Band in San Antonio,

playing both tenor and alto, then played with Lionel Hampton and Buck Clayton in California before landing with Bennie Moten (who may as well have billed himself as the One-Man Finishing School for Budding Texas Jazzers).

Evans also freelanced for a number of years, honing his one-in-a-million tenor persona: Though influenced by Coleman Hawkins, his sound was so effortless, so naturally smooth that it frustrated countless musicians who assumed, listening to Evans, that the tenor sax must be on a "difficulty" par with playing a comb wrapped in a Kleenex.

In 1936, Evans joined Count Basie's orchestra in the midst of a post–Buster Smith reorganization. Though Smith had been an alto star, Evans, in conjunction with fellow tenor-meister Lester Young, more than replaced the absent alto in a most remarkable tandem. Evans's engaging, all-encompassing swing style contrasted winningly with Young's upstart, soon-to-be-bop meanderings.

For almost three years, Evans was a star with the Basie group. Unfortunately, his shimmering possibilities were never fully realized; a heart ailment felled him in 1939. Though he died prematurely, his influence on artists such as Buddy Tate (who replaced him in the Basie orchestra), Illinois Jacquet, Arnett Cobb, and other substantial tenors is without debate. Evans can be heard in full glory on Count Basie's The Original American Decca Recordings.

Only a year younger than Evans was his Dallas-born contemporary Budd Johnson, who was also younger than trombonist Keg Johnson—who happened to be his brother. A supreme woodwinds man and arranger, Budd was equally adept on drums, clarinet, and tenor, baritone and alto saxes, and early on played with his brother in a variety of Texas bands before hooking up with Terrence Holder's Twelve Clouds of Joy.

In 1932 he moved to Chicago, where he played with both Louis Armstrong and Earl "Fatha" Hines among others, also arranging for a variety of stars including Buddy Rich, Woody Herman, and Billy Eckstine. While arranging was a primary occupation into the forties, Johnson also played for Eckstine, Dizzy Gillespie, and Sy Oliver during those years. It was most significant that Johnson wrote and arranged a massive amount of material that was integral in the great shift in jazz from swing to bop.

In the fifties, he was particularly active in the production and arrangement of a kooky new phenomenon called rock 'n' roll, though he continued to play jazz (with Benny Goodman, Gil Evans, Cab Calloway, Quincy Jones, and Count Basie).

It was only in these later years that Johnson's talent as a pioneer bop saxophonist came to the fore. Though his rippling lines could be reminiscent of Lester Young, Johnson had a singular cheery, cool, bubbling style.

In his latter years, he performed with his own small combos and in Earl Hines reunions, at several international festivals, and with the New York

Jazz Repertory Company. He died in 1984. Riverside's *Budd Johnson and the Four Brass Giants* and Prestige's *Let's Swing* are solid introductions to his work.

IF JEAN BAPTISTE ILLINOIS JACQUET SOUNDS MORE LIKE A guy from Louisiana than the Billy Bob Tuckers one associates with Texas, well, it's because Jacquet *is* from Louisiana. (On the other hand, does that mean someone named Louisiana would presumably be from Illinois?) In any case, Jacquet was born in Broussard, Louisiana, in 1922, though his family moved shortly thereafter to Houston, where he grew up.

As a member of a consummately musical clan (brother Russell was a superb trumpet player), Jacquet was tap dancing in a family act by the time he was ten, and quickly graduated to the study of soprano and alto sax. But it was on tenor sax that young Illinois would make music history. In the late thirties, he played with Lionel Proctor and Milt Larkin, then headed to the West Coast as a member of the Floyd Ray Orchestra.

When Lionel Hampton offered him a job, Jacquet climbed aboard, and his 1942 solo on the song "Flying Home" made him a household name and established the sound that would become associated with the Texas Tenor phenomenon: clusters of high-register notes like the beatings of humming-bird wings, freaky harmonics, and a solid underpinning of down-home Lone Star blues (it should be noted that the improvised sixty-four-bar solo on "Flying Home" was incorporated note for note into subsequent arrangements of the tune).

Over the next decade, Jacquet led his own bands, played with Count Basie, Jazz at the Philharmonic, Cab Calloway, and, along with Lester Young, was featured prominently in the film *Jammin' the Blues* (1944).

As a masterful innovator as comfortable in blues and soul as he was in swing and bebop, Jacquet became a figurehead player. After a high-profile gig as the principal soloist for Jazz at the Philharmonic, he signed with Verve Records in 1950 and began to record his own albums regularly, as well as dates with Kenny Burrell, Ben Webster, and Count Basie.

Throughout the decade, the Jacquet mystique only intensified as he toured internationally. In the sixties, fulfilling a passion for the music of his youth, he recorded a number of soul and R&B dates, and formed with Arnett Cobb and Buddy Tate a band called, appropriately enough, the Texas Tenors.

Later on, settling in New York, Jacquet formed a big band and worked clubs regularly, popping up on sessions by Eddie "Lockjaw" Davis, Dizzy Gillespie, and Gerry Mulligan—and even loaned his sax to President Bill Clinton. As a performer, musician, and disciple of the tenor saxophone, Illinois Jacquet absolutely qualifies as one of the greatest jazz musicians ever. *The Cool Rage* is an exciting sampling of Jacquet's Verve years, while Black Lion's *The Comeback*, the Classic Jazz album *Blues from Louisiana*, and 1999's

Birthday Party offer other excellent representations of the artist's vast repertoire.

Jacquet's pal, Arnett Cobb, was no slouch either. The Houston native (born 1918) learned piano, violin, and trumpet before taking up the tenor sax, then, as had Jacquet, played with Milt Larkin and Floyd Ray, before actually replacing Jacquet in the Lionel Hampton band in 1942.

Featuring a sound that splintered high and low notes indiscriminately, with an earthy street tone anchoring the confettied notes pouring forth, Cobb managed to mix all that had historically gone on before in the realm of sax with his own unique conceptions of the future.

In 1947, he formed his own band and signed with the Apollo label, a maneuver which should have boded great things; unfortunately, spinal surgery, followed a few years later by a serious auto accident, retarded Cobb's development. He persisted, however, managing a Houston club and leading his own small band. In the early seventies, he performed a well-received New York date that recast him in the limelight.

From that point, Cobb was frequently featured as soloist for Hampton as well as with his own bands, touring the European festival circuit as a member of the Texas Tenors. While much of his later work appealed to R&B fans, his ability within the jazz realm was forever respected and admired. He died in 1989. Jazz Legacy offers *The Complete Apollo Sessions*, and Prestige's *Blue and Sentimental* showcases work with Texas piano giant Red Garland.

Dallas's Jimmy Giuffre is the fifth of the truly great Texas Tenors. He was born in 1921 and managed, in his time on our planet, to master, in addition to tenor sax, the clarinet, baritone and soprano sax, flute, and bass flute. In other words: he was the Woodwind King of sax players.

As might be suspected, Giuffre is a consummate *player*; his virtuosity is almost frightening, and as a proponent of that jazz we call "cool," a purposefully understated conception which nonetheless does not preclude chops, he was a true pioneer. He was also an eager student. After receiving his bachelor's in music from NTSU, he continued to pursue formal musical education wherever his professional travels carried him—which was a substantial itinerary indeed.

He blasted out of college for a rapid series of one-year stints with Jimmy Dorsey, Buddy Rich, and Woody Herman, then settled on the West Coast with the Lighthouse All-Stars. By the mid-fifties, he was leading and recording with a variety of trios, all the while developing a prime reputation as a composer (in addition to cool, Giuffre was more than conversant during those years with bebop).

By the end of the decade, he was teaching jazz at the Lenox School of Jazz and recording heavily for a variety of major labels (including Verve, Columbia, Capitol, and Atlantic).

In 1961, a radical stylistic shift to free jazz was achieved by Giuffre's new trio with Steve Swallow and Paul Bley—a movement for which he proselytized for several years across the States and throughout Europe, with a variety of outfits.

Finally, in the mid-seventies, he hopscotched again, flavoring his compositions with Asian and African influences, ultimately returning to the early bop/cool style from whence he sprang. In 1978, he signed on as a professor at the New England Conservatory of Music, and continues to record and perform with the inspiration and aplomb that has marked his long, adventuresome career. In a strictly "sax" sense, his playing is invigoratingly all over the map—yet refined within a Giuffre signature by its own wackiness and taste that it's instantly identifiable to fans.

There are numerous Giuffre albums in print, representing myriad phases of his ambitious career, but PolyGram's *1961* is a daring look at free jazz experimentation, while Soul Note's *Dragonfly* offers a contemporary glimpse of the master's accumulated knowledge.

WHILE THOSE MUSICIANS REPRESENT THE ABSOLUTE FINEST OF the Texas Tenors tradition, they are by no means all of the club. There is a second tier just below these artists, an extensive group of players spanning several decades of excellent performance and contribution.

Fort Worth's Tex Beneke (born 1914) came to national awareness as a singer/sax double threat for Glenn Miller in the late thirties. As the singer of "Chattanooga Choo Choo" and other hits, Beneke became a poll-winning vocalist whose voice often overshadowed his more than adequate sax skills.

He appeared in several films and, after postwar appearances with the Modernaires, was asked by Miller's estate to take over the leadership of the Glenn Miller Orchestra. It was a post Beneke has filled admirably through the eighties and into the present decade.

Houston's Billy Harper (born in 1943) represents one of the latter-day Texas Tenors. He graduated from North Texas State with a major in saxophone and theory, and worked in New York with Gil Evans, Art Blakey's Jazz Messengers, and Elvin Jones at the end of the sixties.

He developed a strident, attacking hard-bop sound invigorating in its raw energy, and shifted in the early seventies from Max Roach to the Thad Jones/Mel Lewis orchestra and, ultimately, his own quintet. Harper continues to perform and compose actively, and has entertained a heavy teaching schedule at a variety of colleges and universities.

Dallas's James Clay, who was born in 1935, moved to tenor sax from alto and flute, graduated from Huston-Tillotson, worked awhile at a lead smelter and as a blaring R&B stylist in a variety of regional soul bands before heading to L.A., where he dove headfirst into the jazz scene as a hard-bop/free stylist with the Jazz Messiahs, one of the earliest of Ornette Coleman's harmolodic experiments.

After playing with Ray Charles and Fathead Newman in the sixties, Clay

CRIMINALLY OVERLOOKED ARTIST
Marchel Ivery
☆

A relatively anonymous wizard from Ennis, Texas (born in 1938), Ivery, like James Clay, intentionally avoided the spotlight (and madness) of big-time jazz—for the most part, anyway—which is certainly his prerogative. But it doesn't mean the rest of us shouldn't get the pleasure of listening to him.

Ivery came up blasting hard bop and, after military service in the late fifties, performed with Bud Powell. In the mid-sixties, he joined fellow Texan Red Garland for a stint. But Ivery preferred the security of family life and missed Texas, so he returned home and worked a straight gig, freelancing occasionally with R&B groups.

In the early eighties, he was called by his old pal Red Garland, and began working with him at a Dallas jazz spot called the Recovery Room. Garland dragged Ivery to a date in New York at the Village Vanguard, where Ivery's blistering solos and menthol balladry resulted in a rave review in The New York Times.

Which in turn brought Ivery to the attention of Art Blakey. Ivery was flown to New York to become a member of Blakey's Jazz Messengers, rehearsed successfully with the group and, for reasons only Ivery understands, the talented tenor decided to return to Texas to handle "other responsibilities."

Finally, in 1994, Ivery signed with Dallas's upstart Leaning House Jazz label and recorded the astonishing Marchel's Mode with another old friend on piano, Cedar Walton (and a bop-happy group of sidemen). The CD more than evidences that Ivery, whose blues-based, impassioned bop runs blow white-hot or ice-cream cool, is a lost treasure. Fortunately, a recent session with organist Joey DeFrancesco—called Marchel Ivery Meets Joey DeFrancesco and released on Leaning House in early '97—is a remarkable CD, and Marchel Ivery 3 was scheduled for release by Halloween 1999. That's good news indeed.

dropped out of sight for several years—his desire to feed and provide for his family required, he felt, a steadier financial situation than proffered by jazz—before resurfacing in a quartet context with pianist Cedar Walton and, later, with Roy Hargrove. Even more recently, he'd recorded several fine traditional albums for the Antilles label and appeared headed toward a belated but permanent reputation as one of the greats. Unfortunately, he passed away in early 1995.

Following the prescribed path to Tenordom, Fort Worth's Dewey Redman (born 1931) learned clarinet and alto sax first, played in that magical high school band with Ornette Coleman, Prince Lasha, and Charles Moffett, then shifted to tenor while studying at Prairie View A&M. After earning his master's from NTSU in 1959, Redman headed west, worked with Pharoah Sanders and Wes Montgomery, and finally caught up in New York with Don Cherry and Coleman, working those mystical free-jazz experiments.

Into the seventies, he worked with a variety of liberating artists, from Carla Bley to Keith Jarrett, scoring periodic studio time along the way as a leader (recording LPs for Freedom, Impulse, and Galaxy). In 1976, he cofounded Old and New Dreams with Cherry, Charlie Haden, and Ed Blackwell, a sort of Son of Coleman conception that recorded well into the next decade.

Though he's taken somewhat of a backseat to son Joshua in recent years, Father Redman remains active, he continues to record for Enja and Black Saint, and his razor-sharp, guttural squonks are brilliant representations of the Texas Tenor tradition.

Booker Ervin, Denison, Texas's contribution to jazz greatness, was born in 1930. A committed and flamboyant celebrant of all things tenor, Ervin started out steeped in blues, first picking up the trombone before moving to the sax while in the air force.

He studied music after the service, then played R&B with Ernie Fields before playing in Charles Mingus's Jazz Workshop. He also worked with the Playhouse Four before starting to record as a leader for several Prestige albums. Ervin's grandiose and exuberant style was a continual and rich aural buffet; unfortunately, he died at the age of forty.

David "Fathead" Newman, so named as a student by a frustrated music teacher incensed over a blown Newman arpeggio (rather than any perpetual swelling of the occipital bone), was born in Dallas in 1933. While his bebop forays are uniformly excellent, he's established an enviable track record as a soul and R&B enthusiast.

He started his pro career with the bands of Red Connors, Lowell Fulson, and T-Bone Walker, then hit the big time as featured sax king in Ray Charles's band. The success of his work for Brother Ray led to a prolonged stint as a session player for Atlantic, for whom he recorded with a variety of stars from Dr. John to Aretha Franklin.

Newman also found time to record his own dates—wildly varied experiments involving everything from weird jazz to ballads drenched in saccharine string arrangements—but settled down to his R&B-flavored jazz musings. While recording several of his own excellent LPs for Prestige, Atlantic, and Milestone, he also worked wonders for Stanley Turrentine and Hank Crawford sections.

Of all the Texas Tenors, Newman was probably the most at home in the R&B and soul arena, and his playing reflected that, but when he ventured into bop and free jazz, he was definitely not out of his league.

One of the pioneers of Texas jazz who should not be overlooked is Sherman's Buddy Tate, who was born in 1913. A deceptively smooth player with a monstrous tone, Tate turned pro at fourteen, did time with Mc-Cloud's Night Owls and the St. Louis Merrymakers, and by the early thirties could boast Count Basie, Terrence Holder, and Andy Kirk on his résumé.

In 1939, he returned to Basie to replace the suddenly deceased Herschel Evans; the relationship with Basie happily lasted for almost a decade. After freelancing around New York, Tate formed his own band, which held down the house gig at Harlem's Celebrity Club for over twenty years.

Later, when Tate's stint there had outlasted cruel fashion, he hit the European circuit with Buck Clayton, Jay McShann, and his own groups. He also did a lot of prime session work through the seventies, and co-led some fine live groups with Paul Quinichette, Al Grey, and Bobby Rosengarden. Though he was seriously burned in a shower accident at the dawn of the eighties, he recovered and toured with Illinois Jacquet's Texas Tenors, stayed active in the European festival circuit, and continues to record. (Several of his records are still available on a variety of labels.)

While these several musicians represent the finest of the Texas Tenor tradition, they are by no means all of them. Several other artists, past and present, deserve to be listed on this august roster, including Don Wilkerson, Shelley Carrol, Jesse Powell, Wilton Felder, Eddie Wasserman, Gene Hall, Harold Land, John Hardee, multi-instrumentalist Tony Campise (check out his *Strange Beauty* CD on the Heart Music label), and Campise's label mate, Elias Haslanger (*Kicks Are for Kids* and *For the Moment*).

It would be easy, in final analysis and consideration of the myriad brilliant alto and tenor sax giants, to overlook the baritone sax. After all, Budd Johnson, Ernie Caceres, and Jimmy Giuffre all played the baritone sax as second instruments, and it should be mentioned that Leroy "Hogg" Cooper and Claude Johnson—both Texans, both baritone sax players, both talents—were baritone players of some notoriety. That the latter two didn't select a more plum instrument, from the glory aspect, shouldn't obscure their accomplishments.

☆ Three: Trumpet Kings, a Trombone Meister, and Miscellaneous Virtuosos

As evidenced by the likes of Charlie Christian and Scott Joplin, it was possible to be a Texas jazz star before the evolution of the Texas Tenors—and trumpeters Oran "Hot Lips" Page and Harry James and trombonist Jack Teagarden went so far as to establish early on a tradition of greatness on instruments other than the saxophone.

Teagarden, who was born in Vernon, Texas, in 1905, was the oldest of four siblings who made their marks in jazz, and was also the one whose legacy remains the most significant. Not only was he a consummately gifted player, Jack Teagarden was the most innovative jazz trombonist ever to pick up the instrument.

Schooled by his mother Helen on piano, he shifted to the ever popular baritone horn and, at ten, the trombone. He went pro in his teens, and quickly established a reputation in the twenties when he joined up with Peck Kelley's Bad Boys—where his talent so intimidated trombonist Pee Wee Russell that Russell asked for a ticket back to his home in St. Louis. From there Teagarden played with the Original Southern Trumpeters and Doc Ross's Jazz Band before joining Ben Pollack in 1928 (ultimately replacing Glenn Miller). By then, Teagarden had refined a variety of innovations, including a legendary series of close-to-the-chest slide positions, the execution of which largely remains a mystery.

Teagarden also played with a great emphasis on tone and dynamics, two concepts that were at that point relatively rare in the technique department, and utilized rounded notes and a phrasing that was heavily adapted from the blues he grew up listening to in his home state. In addition, he was a terrific singer, and the resultant Teagarden package was unique indeed; he was subsequently able to freelance substantially in addition to any band duties (recording with Fats Waller and Eddie Condon, among others).

In 1933 he became a featured player in Paul Whiteman's group (though it's said he wasn't a big fan of Whiteman's material). Through radio appearances and lead instrumental and vocal status, Teagarden attained near-superstar status. At the same time, he'd begun working on projects with his brothers (trumpeter Charlie in the Three T's with Frankie Trumbauer, and drummer Cub backing a Hoagy Carmichael film). In the late thirties, Teagarden began leading his own bands. Though they weren't financially successful, and the trombonist experienced personal problems with the bottle and some dishonest business partners, Teagarden's sextets were popular and his recording career continued to blossom. (He had hits with "A Hundred Years from Today" and, with Bing Crosby and Mary Martin, "The Waiter and the Porter and the Upstairs Maid.")

In 1947, Teagarden became an even more high-profile guy when he signed on with Louis Armstrong's All-Stars. They recorded a number of memorable albums for both Decca and RCA, and Armstrong remained convinced that Teagarden was the greatest trombonist of all time. In 1951, Teagarden went solo again, headed up a variety of his own successful sextets and Dixieland bands, and continued as a mightily in-demand session player until his death in 1964.

As a popular vocalist and a visionary instrumentalist, Jack Teagarden made a reputation as a player with style, taste, emotion, and humor. A three-disc boxed set from XFL, *Columbia Special Products*, Jazz Band's *Jack Teagarden's Sextet Live in Chicago 1960–61*, and RCA's *The Indispensable Jack Teagarden* are all recommended.

WHILE JACK TEAGARDEN IS WITHOUT QUESTION THE greatest of the Texan jazz trombonists, Wayne Henderson, Eddie Durham, Tyree Glenn, and Keg Johnson were all wonderful players, too.

Durham, of course, has also been discussed for his marvelous contributions to guitar, but his abilities on the horn were just as inspiring—not to mention his work as a composer, arranger, and banjoist. He worked as an arranger for no less than Glenn Miller and Artie Shaw, and his trombone talent was particularly noted in his work with Buddy Tate and the Harlem Blues and Jazz Band.

Evans "Tyree" Glenn was born in Corsicana, Texas, in 1912, and worked in a variety of bands in Texas, Virginia, Washington, D.C., and on the West Coast before catching on with artists like Benny Carter, Lionel Hampton, and Cab Calloway.

It was with the latter, from 1939 to 1946, that Glenn led a trombone section that featured Quentin Jackson, Claude Jones, and fellow Texan Keg Johnson. Afterward, he played with Don Redman, then joined Duke Ellington in the early fifties. Settling in New York, Glenn hopscotched from recording session to recording session, played on radio, and headed up his own quartets and quintets. In the latter years of his life, Glenn performed with both Louis Armstrong and Ellington (often, with the latter, on his second instrument, the vibes), and died only a few days after the Duke in 1974.

A trombonist who, like Teagarden, had decided blues imprints in his playing,

Glenn was a very singular musician, utilizing the plunger for pristine runs and an exuberant wah-wah tone. Though his own recordings for the Roulette label are out of print, Glenn's work is terrific on CBS French's *The Complete Duke Ellington (1947–1952)*.

Frederic "Keg" Johnson was the son of a clarinetist/choir director father and the older brother of tenor great Budd Johnson. He was born in Dallas in 1908, was tutored by both his father and noted teacher Portia Pittman (the daughter of Booker T. Washington), and performed with his brother in a Texas/Oklahoma band called the Blue Moon Chasers before moving with his brother to Kansas City (for a stint with Jesse Stone) and then Chicago.

There they played with Louis Armstrong, and Keg began his recording career. After two years, Satchmo's orchestra disbanded and Keg migrated to New York for gigs with Benny Carter and Fletcher Henderson before landing with Cab Calloway, with whom he played and recorded for almost fifteen years. He then headed to California, working with Gil Evans and Ray Charles as well as his brother, before passing on in 1967.

Keg Johnson was a terrific sideman, even if critics' main complaint about his work was that it was *too* derivative of Teagarden. Though the Johnson Brothers released one album together in 1960, *Let's Swing*, the record is long out of print—and the curious should decidedly *not* race out of music stores clutching CDs by the seventies funk act called the Brothers Johnson. Indeed, it's not easy to find Keg Johnson on record; Gil Evans's *Out of the Cool* (MCA) features Johnson in a shining support role.

Wayne Henderson, the youngest of the significant Texas trombonists, came to fame in the Houston-based Jazz Crusaders outfit. He was born in Houston in 1939 and grew up playing with fellow Crusaders Joe Sample, Wilton Felder, and "Stix" Hooper. The group moved to the West Coast and became famous as a funk/soul/jazz outfit with a batch of radio-ready tunes.

As a matter of fact, it was Henderson's ability on his trombone that gave a decided jazz kick to the group's recordings, particularly on *Scratch* (1975, MCA) and *Freedom Sounds* (Atlantic, 1969), and when he split the group to go into solo performance and production in the mid-seventies, the on-going sound of the Crusaders leaned more significantly in a smooth soul direction. After leaving the band, Henderson has released some nice LPs, particularly *Big Daddy's Place* (ABC) and, as Wayne Henderson and the Next Crusade, *Sketches of Life* (Paramount).

There are numerous other trombonists who managed to scurry out from the substantial shadow of Jack Teagarden and achieve notoriety in the ever-competitive world of jazz: Dan Minor, Herbie Harper, Warren Smith, Allen Durham, Henry Coker, Joe Gallardo, and Matthew Gee are all notable players.

* * *

IF TEAGARDEN IN FACT BROUGHT THE TROMBONE TO THE FORE of jazz music, trumpet was already established as a "lead instrument" in the genre, and a cross-section of great Texas trumpeters spans the century, from Oran "Hot Lips" Page and Harry James to Kenny Dorham and onward to Roy Hargrove.

James is probably the biggest name of these artists. Born in Albany, Georgia, in 1916, James learned drums and trumpet from his father and played in the old man's circus band from an early age. When not blowing under the big top, James attended high school in Beaumont, Texas, and at fourteen won a statewide solo contest.

Shortly thereafter, he played with acts like the Old Phillips Friars, Herman Waldman, and Ben Pollack. With the latter, he began to gain a national reputation, not only for the wit, technique, and aggression of his playing, but for writing the tune "Peckin," which became a dance sensation along the lines of the Macarena or the Hustle. In spite of that, James prospered; he recorded with a number of stars of the age and, in 1937, was asked to join Benny Goodman's band.

In a manner of speaking, James's chops and stage persona could be likened to Jimi Hendrix's in his showy inventiveness, and it wasn't long before James split Goodman's orchestra to head up his own big band. From that point forward, James worked as a leader, and his excellent ensembles (which included at various times Frank Sinatra, Helen Forrest, Sam Donahue, Vido Musso, and Corky Corcoran) were tightly constructed units designed to superbly back the trumpeter in a series of increasingly difficult and "out-there" pieces like "Flight of the Bumblebee," "Concerto for Trumpet," and the band's theme song, "Ciribiribin," all of which amply spotlit his virtuosity. During this period, James recorded heavily, toured the United States and Europe, appeared in several films, married Betty Grable and, in general, became the sort of star people today would associate with Quentin Tarantino—though without the "hipster" cultural references about fast food or bad radio. Though the postwar evolution in jazz music threw the trumpeter for a bit of a loss, he rebounded admirably, countering the new bebop era with the formation of the Music Makers (featuring Buddy Rich), then stubbornly re-formed his big band and made it work through sheer force of will and talent.

For the remaining decades of his life, James—a brilliant and distinctive, cocky and winsome artist—played the game as he wanted it to be played, which is to say he invented any rules he felt necessary to enliven jazz. Most of the time, he was on the money; Hindsight has released a six-volume set called Uncollected Harry James and His Orchestra which is a comprehensive study of his work. He passed away in 1983.

Oran "Hot Lips" Page may not have equaled James's fireworks luminosity, but the trumpeter/vocalist/mellophonist, born in Dallas in 1908, made a huge name for himself as a Louis Armstrong–inspired horn man of quantifiable brilliance.

He grew up in the same Corsicana High School as Budd Johnson, listening to and playing in blues bands, and early on toured in support of such blues belters as Ma Rainey, Bessie Smith, and Ida Cox. He graduated to bigger regional acts like Walter Page's Blue Devils and Bennie Moten's band, honing along the way a giddy, sizzling melodic style built for improvisation and the after-hours jam sessions Page loved.

After a brief stint with Count Basie, the effervescent and devilishly good-looking young player thought he'd hit it big when he signed a personal contract with Louis Armstrong's manager, Joe Glaser, who was worried that Satchmo's career would be permanently stalled by a lip condition.

As most of the galaxy knows, Armstrong healed and Page was tied up in a contract that relegated him to second-string priority status. Not that Page wasn't a star in his own right: From 1937 through the fifties, Hot Lips worked with his own groups as well as with Artie Shaw, recording several fine solo records including hits like "St. James Infirmary" and "Blues in the Night" (with Shaw) and "Baby It's Cold Outside" (with Pearl Bailey).

He continued to record and tour the States and Europe, appearing at many prestigious festivals, until his untimely death in 1954. Page's cross-pollination of traditional jazz trumpet with bluesy vocals was a unique and wonderful sound, indeed, but ill-fated managerial experiences and bad luck probably limited his potential. Classics Records is periodically issuing recommended archival discs from their ongoing *The Chronological Hot Lips Page* series.

Bop trumpeter Kenny Dorham (born McKinley Howard Dorham in Fairfield, Texas, in 1924) was another artist brought up in a completely musical family, and proved adept at both piano and trumpet by the time he finished high school (and tenor sax a short time later). After studying music, chemistry, and physics at Wiley College, the versatile Dorham joined the army, where he was a member of the boxing team. Someone in that capacity must've knocked some sense into the youngster, and he came out of the service with the realization that playing the trumpet was probably a lot more fun than any career forays into pugilism or complex mathematics.

In any case, he certainly pursued music with a fervor; from 1943 to 1948 he played with Russell Jacquet, Frank Humphreys, Dizzy Gillespie, Billy Eckstine, Lionel Hampton, the Bebop Boys (with Sonny Stitt and Bud Powell), and Mercer Ellington, among others.

While that pedigree is certainly impressive enough, Dorham next made the big move from more swing-oriented material to hard bop, replacing Miles Davis in the Charlie Parker quintet. He then freelanced in New York at the dawn of the fifties, recording as a leader on sessions for Charles Mingus's and Max Roach's Debut label in 1953 before signing on as a cofounder of Art Blakey's Jazz Messengers a year later.

Dorham then formed his own similar group, the Jazz Prophets, which was over too quickly, and then switched over to Max Roach's quintet from 1955 to 1958. For the next fifteen years, Dorham made the rounds, working with his own groups, touring, doing sessions (with such giants as John Coltrane, Hank Mobley, Thelonious Monk, Sonny Rollins, and Horace Silver) and even scored motion pictures. Such was his reputation as a bebop forerunner—a musician whose speed and chops were at once playful and madcap within his improvisational context—that he is renowned as a true pioneer of bop trumpet.

In the sixties, Dorham recorded with both Joe Henderson and Muhal Richard Abrams, as well with his own sextet, before succumbing to kidney failure in 1972. While he was never *the* premier trumpeter in any particular decade of his career, Dorham's virtuosity and humanism were the stuff of greatness. He leaves a rich recorded legacy, of which the Blue Note material is superlative (particularly *Trompeta Toccata*).

Roy Hargrove, the Texas *wunderkind* of modern jazz, was discovered while a student at Dallas's Arts Magnet High School. Born in Dallas in 1969, Hargrove was playing Freddie Hubbard licks in his bedroom while most of the neighborhood kids were puzzling over the metaphysical intricacies presented by "Scooby Doo."

His skill and otherwordly instincts earned him the tutelage of Dizzy Gillespie and a scholarship to Berklee when he was sixteen, and by the time he was twenty he'd nailed a recording contract with RCA/Novus. The next year, he released his debut CD, *Diamond in the Rough*, which more than indicated that the hype was justified. As with other youngsters heralded in the competitive and cruel world of jazz (Harry Connick, Jr., and the Brothers Marsalis spring to mind), Hargrove has his detractors, particularly those who indicate that his soloing is overly derivative, but these critics seem to have backed off as Hargrove's CDs indicate a rapid maturation and emerging style.

An enthusiastic champion of retro-bop, Hargrove has a fluid, round tone with a fetching way of alternating spaces and atmospheric phrasing with spatterings of exuberant notes. His balladry is surprisingly tender for one so young, and as his reputation solidifies within the musical community, look for him to expand his horizons in terms of both performance and production.

Diamond in the Rough and *Of Kindred Souls* are excellent bookends demonstrating his development, and a recent interest in the Cuban jazz scene lead him to record *Habana* with an 11-piece Cuban-American Puerto Rican band he's formed called Crisol.

IN FAME'S TEMPLE, JUST UNDER THE TIER AFFORDED THE ABOVE musicians, are seven other Texas trumpeters. Milt Larkin, born in Houston in 1910, was a self-taught player who also came to relative prominence as a bandleader and singer.

He got his start with the Chester Boone band in 1934, and two years later formed his own big band in Houston. The orchestra routinely kicked

the hell out of national bands coming through Houston's Harlem Square
Club, then toured throughout the Midwest, prominently in Chicago and
Kansas City, even landing at the Apollo Theatre in Harlem. Probably the
weirdest thing about Larkin's group was that, inasmuch as it included Eddie
"Cleanhead" Vinson, Illinois Jacquet, Arnett Cobb, and Wild Bill Davis,
Larkin's own skills were frequently overshadowed by the geniuses he em-
ployed to work for him.

In 1943, Larkin disbanded the group to enter the service during World
War II, where he learned trombone and played in the army band. After the
war, though he reformed his band, he could not replicate his earlier successes. He shifted to a sextet format and settled in at the Celebrity Club in
New York City until he retired in the mid-seventies. Unfortunately, Larkin's
recorded legacy is virtually nonexistent.

Two other famous trumpeters who would yet be more famous if their
respective brothers weren't bigger bad-asses were Charlie Teagarden and
Russell Jacquet.

Jacquet, the older brother of tenor king Illinois, was born in St. Martin-
ville, Louisiana, in 1917, and grew up with his seriously musical family in
Texas. At seventeen, he played with his brothers (a second brother, Linton,
was a drummer) in the California Playboy Band, then did short stints with
Floyd Ray and Milt Larkin before studying music at both Wiley College
and Texas Southern University. After his schooling, he moved west with
brother Illinois's swing band, and shortly thereafter headed up his own group
as trumpeter and singer.

From 1945 to 1949, they were the house band at Hollywood's Cotton
Club, and recorded several LPs for the King label (now unavailable) before
Russell rejoined Illinois's group in the late forties. Russell stayed with his
brother's outfit until 1954, touring Europe and recording various albums,
but thereafter set up shop in Oakland, California, where he once more led
his own, smaller units through the sixties.

Eventually, Russell returned to Houston, where he played with Arnett
Cobb and, only rarely, on New York dates with his brother. While he was
a terrifically competent musician, easily able to traverse both swing and bop
territories, Russell Jacquet's playing never seemed to burn with the fires of
genius. He passed away in 1990. His work can be heard on a variety of
Illinois Jacquet recordings, but, unfortunately, all of his stuff as a leader is
out of print.

Charlie Teagarden, not to be confused with brother Clois (drums), sister
Norma (piano), mother Helen (piano), and certainly not brother Jack (god
of trombone), was nevertheless a substantially musical carrier of the family
surname.

Born in Vernon, Texas, in 1913, the trumpet wielder of the Family T
studied, like all his siblings, with his mother, and kicked off his professional
career with a variety of regional bands before hooking up with Ben Pollack
in New York in 1929.

After recording with Pollack and Red Nichols, Charlie joined Jack in Paul Whiteman's orchestra, and seemed thereafter to shadow bro Jack's professional footsteps—frequently in the older brother's bands. Still, Charlie's only crime is that he didn't have Jack's intuitive flair and inventive genius; as a pure technician, Charlie had a smooth, luxuriant style and, as a singer, he had a perfectly capable voice.

From the mid-forties on, Charlie split his time and talent, briefly heading his own group, working with Jack's smaller combos, and also performing with Harry James, Jerry Gray, Ray Bauduc, Jess Stacy, Bob Crosby's Bobcats, and Benny Goodman. He was a popular hotel entertainer and worked more than his share of recording studio and television sessions.

As his career wound down, Charlie Teagarden grew more and more active in work with the musicians' union in his adopted state of Nevada. He died in 1984, probably unaware that, among his peers, he was regarded as a consummate swinging trumpet player. Samples of his work can be found on selected Jack Teagarden albums, as well as Jimmy Dorsey's *Muscat Ramble* (Swing House).

Galveston's Richard "Notes" Williams (born 1931), a hard-bop trumpeter, originally targeted the fertile tenor sax territory before shifting hornward under the inspirational ebb of Fats Navarro and Charlie Parker. After playing in various coastal bands and earning a music degree from Wiley College, Williams spent four years in the air force before joining up with Lionel Hampton's band as the orchestra's principal soloist in 1956.

Back in the States, Williams took a master's degree from the Manhattan School of Music, then, from 1959 till the mid-sixties, freelanced around New York, most notably with Quincy Jones, Slide Hampton, Duke Ellington, Roland Kirk, Eric Dolphy, and Charles Mingus at the Mingus Workshop. His recorded work, particularly with Mingus, established Williams as a fiery, brilliant soloist with the confidence to pull off the most frenzied attempts and the quirkiness of thought to surprise.

At that point, Williams caught on with the Thad Jones–Mel Lewis Orchestra, touring Europe and the Far East. Blasting into the seventies, he teamed up again with Mingus in the Mingus Dynasty, performed in Gunther Schuller's *Journey into Jazz*, then worked at various times with Clark Terry, Gil Evans, Sam Jones, and his own quartet. He passed away in 1985, considered by most jazz cognoscenti a brilliant and underrated player. His best work is probably found on the Imperial album *Mingus, Mingus, Mingus, Mingus*, which is, not surprisingly, a Charles Mingus record. As a leader, Williams was outstanding on Candid's *New Horn in Town*.

Lammar Wright, Sr., is another Texas alumnus of Bennie Moten's band. He was born in Texarkana in 1907, was raised in Kansas City, and had joined Moten by the time he was sixteen. A stylistic descendant of King Oliver, Wright then traveled to New York as a member of a group called the Cotton Club Orchestra (which became the Missourians). The outfit was taken over by Cab Calloway, and Wright stayed on as principal soloist for the next decade and a half, lending his spectacular and frenetic solo work to several recording sessions.

In the Calloway aftermath, though he occasionally led his own groups, Wright was highly sought after as a soloist guaranteed to kick relentless blizzards of nutty scalar notes into the night air. During those years he played with Louis Armstrong, Cootie Williams, Lucky Millander, Don Redman, and Claude Hopkins. Wright also got into teaching and session work as the fifties and sixties blew through, though he continued to perform live with, variously, George Shearing, Arnett Cobb, Count Basie, and Perez Prado. Both of Wright's sons, Elmon and Lammar Junior, followed their father's inspired path as trumpeters, though not as spectacularly. Either of the first two of Classics' Cab Calloway collections, *1930–31* or *1931–32*, are blistering reference points for Wright's Vesuvius-like horn eruptions (the former including "Minnie the Moocher," the "hi-de-hi-de-hi-de-hi" song familiar to most pro basketball fans from those idiotic over-the-P.A. cheerleading ploys prevalent in arenas throughout the NBA).

Smithville, Texas's Marvin "Hannibal" Peterson was a free spirit who creatively expanded the boundaries of big band jazz. Born in 1948, Peterson grew up absorbing the piano work of his mother and the singing of his sister, learned his way around a cornet and a trap kit, and was playing in neighborhood combos from the time he was fourteen. He switched to trumpet while a student in the prestigious music department at North Texas State University (inspired by everyone from Coltrane to T-Bone Walker), and landed a New York City gig with Rahsaan Roland Kirk after college.

In the 'round-the-Monopoly-board itinerant gig status common to most jazzers, Peterson quickly shared his rangeroving, upper-register solos with a variety of jazz kings, among them Gil Evans, Pharoah Sanders, Roy Haynes, and Elvin Jones. Eventually, in 1974, Peterson formed a band, the Sunrise Orchestra, to perform one of his own compositions, a piece called *Children of the Fire*, and he persisted in composing, leading his own groups in contrapuntal activity, and doing solo and session work.

Indeed, his own material was exploratory, thoughtful, and archival, encapsulating a history of black music, including folk and blues traditions as well as jazz. Though he recorded this material extensively, the bulk of it was for hard-to-come-by European labels, and it's easier to find his seventies work on studio dates for the likes of Dewey Redman, Oliver Lake, Billy Hart, and George Adams.

While the foregoing comprise the greatest of the Texas trumpeters, Harry Lawson, Joe Keyes, Martin Banks, Harry "Money" Johnson, Dennis Dotson, Pete Cooley, "Bunny" Scurry, John Buckner, Clyde Hurley, and Gene Rowland should all be mentioned as nationally recognized jazz trumpeters.

Bobby Bradford

Bobby Bradford, a Mississippi native who was born in 1934 and brought up in Dallas, hung out and jammed throughout his early years with schoolmates Cedar Walton and Fathead Newman. While this no doubt gave him a solid jazz background, it could in no way indicate that Bradford would become one of the pioneers who helped Ornette Coleman usher in his age of harmolodics.

Bradford met Coleman and Eric Dolphy in Los Angeles in 1953, becoming an immediate coconspirator in their early experiments. Interestingly, Bradford's solo style infuses a sense of humor and uncommon melodicism within the accepted contexts of the free-jazz movement. After a hitch in air force bands, Bradford wound up replacing Don Cherry in the Coleman quartet in the early fifties, then earned a music degree from Huston-Tillotson College.

He returned to L.A. and formed the New Art Jazz Ensemble with Fort Worth clarinetist/composer John Carter, a friend of Coleman's from their high school days who's been a frequent partner of Bradford's ever since. The New Art Jazz Ensemble was a creative extension of Coleman's musical theories, and recorded four albums (all out of print) of fresh, experimental, and generally intriguing free jazz.

Starting in the mid-sixties, Bradford began a part-time career teaching (and has taught at all levels from elementary school to college), lived briefly in England, and has since played with David Murray, Charlie Haden, and John Stevens, as well as with Carter and his own group, Mo'tet. He continues to play and teach today, and his son, Dennis, was a founding member of the Jeff Lorber Fusion. A superlative work with Carter, *Flight for Four*, is available from Flying Dutchman, and Soul Note's *Lost in LA* and *One Night Stand* are emblematic of Bradford's wit, sophistication, and melodic virtuosity.

HAVING ALLUDED BEFORE TO BOBBY BRADFORD'S LONGTIME association with John Carter, it seems a prudent opportunity to discuss the state's clarinetists—of whom Carter is without question the finest.

Born in Fort Worth in 1929, Carter was another in the staggeringly talented musical student body at I. M. Terrell High School. He studied composition and alto sax as well as clarinet, received a music degree from Lincoln University and a master's from the University of Colorado, and, like Bradford, has taught school (from the late forties till the early eighties).

Also in the late forties, Carter began playing with Ornette Coleman, through whom he met Bradford. He was primarily a teacher in those years,

though, in the Fort Worth school district, and while he did perform in
bands and record sporadically, it wasn't until he relocated to the West Coast
in 1961 that his career became a bit more high-profile.

He founded the Wind College in Los Angeles, which is decidedly *not* a
Hollywood P.R. instructional school. He also wrote five suites called *Roots
and Folklore: Episodes in the Development of American Folk Music*, a project
commemorating the African-American experience and ancestry, beginning
with the dawn of slavery in Ghana and continuing to present-day America,
thematically covering the whole of black music, comprised of five LPs recorded over a seven-year period. The albums in the collection, *Dauwhe*,
Castles of Ghana, *Dance of the Love Ghosts*, *Fields*, and *Shadows on a Wall*,
comprise a massively ambitious series, gracefully executed and poetically
envisioned. The entire project (available on Gramavision) goes so far beyond the idea of dashing through an arrangement of "Take the A-Train"
that it may be pitched over the head of the average person.

If he'd never written his five suites, Carter would be remembered as a
versatile musician equally at home in hard bop, swing, pop, and the more
liberated free jazz marinating in the brains of Coleman and Bradford. His
work with Bradford in the New Art Jazz Ensemble is probably recognized
as the most highly visible of Carter's output, or perhaps his work as the
founder of the Clarinet Summit quartet, but his whole body of work as a
musician, teacher, and humanitarian should never be overlooked.

If Carter was far and above the finest of the Texas clarinetists, it should
not be to the exclusion of Ernesto Caceres, Clarence Hutchenrider, Deane
Kincaide, and Bob McCracken—all of whom at least deserve mention.

While the clarinet has an honored tradition in jazz music—particularly
when one thinks of Dixieland, or meandering down Bourbon Street to the
Pete Fountain-esque sounds lilting out of dark tavern doorways—the flute
is perhaps not so historically revered. In many ways, purists can blame rock
star Ian Anderson for forever ruining the flute, and even jazz apologists have
a hard time with one of their own, Herbie Mann, going disco in the seventies.

Fortunately, Texan Hubert Laws upholds the dignity of the flautist role
in jazz. Born in Houston in 1939 and the brother of tenor saxophonist
Ronnie Laws, Laws is another of the Harris County bunch that ultimately
became the Crusaders.

After leaving the Jazz Crusaders in the early sixties, Laws jumped full-
bore into an international music scene, performing at one time or another
with Mongo Santamaria, Sergio Mendes, Lena Horne, and Clark Terry, as
well as several groups of his own design.

He's also established a superb reputation as a classical musician, and in
the late sixties and early seventies performed with both the New York Philharmonic and the Metropolitan Opera Orchestra. He's adapted many classical pieces for jazz, and also experimented with jazz/rock fusion.

Though it's true Laws is clearly Texas's preeminent jazz flautist, it should be remembered that tenor wizards James Clay and Fathead Newman have both worked extensively and impressively in the realm of the flute, and Dallasite Bobbi Humphrey records for the prestigious Blue Note label and has won *Billboard*'s Best Female Instrumentalist award.

Texas has also spawned a few jazz vocalists of note, though admittedly no one like a Nat King Cole or a Frank Sinatra. Still, the mysterious and reclusive Ella Mae Morse, who recorded for Capitol and actually turned the label on to Cole, is certainly noteworthy. The Mansfield-born Morse (1926) lied about her age and won a gig with the Jimmy Dorsey band. She later joined up with ex-Dorsey pianist Freddie Slack, scored the Capitol deal, and had a chart-topping, million-selling hit with "Cow Cow Boogie." Though she had other hits, appeared on *The Ed Sullivan Show* and numbered among her fans artists like Sammy Davis, Jr., and Elvis Presley, Morse settled down in her thirties to raise children. She continued to sing in a small trio for years, but seemingly welcomed the anonymity of family life. The Capitol Collectors Series has reissued a set of her work.

Tyler's Don Shelton, who was born in 1934, was a vocalist of some renown who also played a variety of saxes, as well as flute and clarinet. He started singing professionally in the mid-fifties, working on the CBS *Rusty Draper Show*, then later with Bob Florence and other acts.

Kay Starr, born in Oklahoma in 1922 and raised in Dallas, sang at the start of her career with Glenn Miller, Bob Crosby, and Joe Venuti's orchestra. She achieved early stardom as the singer for Charlie Barnett in the early forties, which blossomed for a while as she recorded for Capitol, Victor, and Liberty.

Ernestine Irene Anderson is another Texas vocalist who had big moments. Born in Houston in 1928, she played with Russell Jacquet, Johnny Otis, and Lionel Hampton before becoming a European star on tour with Rolf Ericson. Back in the States, she won the *Down Beat* Critics Poll in 1959. Meanwhile, young Hunter Sullivan is a youngster with enormous talent in the new-Sinatra vein, and Carmen Bradford, daughter of Bobby, sang nine years with Count Basie's orchestra and has a solo album, *Finally Yours*. And Carla Helmbrecht's *One for My Baby* is a fine debut.

FREQUENTLY OVERLOOKED IN THE SOLO-HAPPY WORLD OF JAZZ are the rhythm sections. In Texas, both drummer Gus Johnson and bassist Gene Ramey are positively world-class players.

Ramey, who was born in Austin in 1913, was a double bassist of frightening skill who came to the instrument only after precollegiate experiments with tuba, trumpet, and sousaphone. In 1932, he moved to Kansas City to attend Western University and took bass lessons from the great Walter Page. Ramey was a great pal of Charlie Parker's—and is in some quarters credited with influencing the Bird to seriously pursue jazz as a career. Ramey himself became an immediate force in the studio sessions realm and, while not

CRIMINALLY UNDERRATED BAND

Little Jack Melody and His Young Turks

☆

Though this ambitious and rewarding—and frequently amusing—musical quilt of an outfit could probably fit in most any section of this book, Denton's Little Jack Melody and His Young Turks will be placed in the jazz section for many reasons, not the least of which are instrumentation and a profound sense of adventure.

Headed up by Little Jack (former Schwantz Lefantz bassist Steve Carter) the outfit is a sort of cabaret group as envisioned by Charles Bukowski, a lunatic musical campout between Kurt Weill, Tom Waits, Bertold Brecht, and Randy Newman, with perhaps Jim Morrison and John Kennedy Toole to read them bedtime stories round the toasty fire. Driven by Eastern European oom-pah rhythms, In the Wee Small Hours of My Brain jazz, and a Spike Jonesian sense of fun, LJM & HYT are absolutely unique—and very, very good.

There's an inherent sadness to Melody's muse—perhaps the realization that his band is far too smart and accomplished to appeal to Wal-Mart Nation, but in the end that only adds to the band's magic.

Thus far, there are two available recordings, *On the Blank Generation* and *World of Fireworks*, and rumors of a live CD called *Noise and Smoke* surround us. It'll be a fine day when it comes out.

noted as a soloist, was a veritable bedrock support system. After settling in New York, he sided for an impressive potpourri of talent, including Ben Webster, Coleman Hawkins, Eartha Kitt, Miles Davis, Tiny Grimes, Charlie Parker, and Lester Young.

Ramey also led his own bands, then toured extensively with first Art Blakey, then Buck Clayton, Muggsy Spanier, and Teddy Wilson. He also worked intermittently throughout his career with Jay McShann, and was a jazz mainstay until the mid-seventies, when he moved back to Texas. He passed away in 1984; unfortunately, there are no LPs in print with Ramey as a leader, though he can be found on some of the comprehensive Mc-Shann releases.

Henry Babasin is another significant bassist. A Dallas native born in 1921 and raised in Vernon—not far from that wacky Teagarden family—Babasin studied cello and double bass at North Texas State University, then traveled with Gene Krupa, Boyd Raeburn, and Benny Goodman. Babasin is remembered as the first to introduce pizzicato on cello, which is best summed up for the layman as *not* something to eat.

After touring extensively with Woody Herman, Babasin worked steadily as a West Coast session player and for radio and television. He also formed his own band, the Jazzpickers, appeared as an actor in a few films, and started his own Nocturne record label. After receiving a master's degree in composition from San Fernando Valley College, Babasin went back to playing, appearing with Harry James, Barney Kessel, and Phil Moody.

Chuck Rainey, who lives in the Fort Worth suburb of Bedford, is maybe the most recorded bassist in the universe. The roster of artists he's done sessions for would in itself be longer than this book, and include a variety of jazz, R&B, and rock musicians from Cannonball Adderly and Louis Armstrong to Aretha Franklin and Marvin Gaye to Little Feat and Steely Dan.

His personal preference is Latin fusion, though, and among his own very fine solo recordings are such CDs as *Oneness and the Happy Spirit* (A&M), *The Chuck Rainey Coalition* (Skye/Buddha), and *The Walker/Rainey Band* (Japan's Toys/Lexington Records).

Other bassists to be remembered include Louis Spears, Ray Leatherwood, Morty Corb, Don Payne, Arthur Edwards, and Buddy Mohmed.

Of the drummers who've made their mark, Tyler's Gus Johnson is truly outstanding. He was known as a child prodigy growing up in Houston, mastering piano, bass, and drums. Like many other Texas jazzers, Johnson went to Kansas City for a collegiate education, learning at the (hands and) feet of Jo Jones. Like bassist Ramey, Johnson played with Jay McShann. After World War II, Johnson meandered between Chicago and New York, playing with Cleanhead Vinson, Cootie Williams, and Earl "Fatha" Hines in his last big band before hooking on with Count Basie.

After recording several seminal albums with the Count (including the *Dance Session* LP), he freelanced through the mid-fifties, then spent substantial time supporting first Lena Horne and then Ella Fitzgerald. He also continued to work the session circuit prodigiously throughout the sixties (with Woody Herman, Stan Getz, Gerry Mulligan, and Johnny Hodges, among luminous others), and finally retired in Denver in the early seventies.

Aside from the Basie records, Johnson can be heard on Verve's *Gerry Mulligan Quartet*.

Fort Worth's Charles Moffett, born in 1929, grew up jamming with Leo Wright, Ornette Coleman, and Dewey Redman and, after teaching school in New York City for years, signed on with Coleman's trio in 1961. He also played with Sonny Rollins and formed his own group, which included Pharoah Sanders and Carla Bley. He continues to perform and lead a variety of groups that include his students and children as well as more famous jazz pals. His son Charnett, a double bass player, has worked with both Branford Marsalis and Stanley Jordan.

Stix Hooper, whose given name is Nesbert, was born in Houston in 1938, and would probably come up with a nickname even if his proclivity for drums hadn't lent itself to the "Stix" moniker. As has been documented herein several times, Hooper was one of the school chums who formed the Jazz Crusaders, headed to L.A., and became famous as the soul/funk/jazz aggregate the Crusaders. He's recorded his own solo material, and in 1983 retired from the band to work in television.

Granville Theodore Hogan, Jr., who goes by "G. T.," is another superb drummer who was born in Galveston in 1929. He played his early years in R&B bands, then headed to New York and played with a variety of artists, most significantly Kenny Dorham, Charles Mingus, and, in Paris, Bud Powell.

California-born Ed Soph (1945) grew up playing drums in Houston, jamming with Arnett Cobb, then went to North Texas State. He subsequently played with Stan Kenton and Ray McKinley, graduating to Woody Herman's group and later the bands of Clark Terry and Joe Henderson. Of late, Soph has turned up in Dallas, working sessions with tenor sax genius Marchel Ivery.

Ray McKinley, born in Fort Worth in 1910, was a drummer/singer/leader of no small repute. As one of the finest of the swing and Dixieland drummers, he graduated from regional bands to the Dorsey Brothers, then formed his own big band with trombonist Will Bradley. He later joined Glenn Miller's orchestra, taking over its leadership with Jerry Gray after Miller's death.

After a decade, McKinley formed another band, featuring his vocals as prominently as his percussion work. He essentially retired in the late sixties, though he surfaced occasionally to front a Miller tribute band. He passed away in 1995.

Yet another Fort Worth magician, Ronald Shannon Jackson, born in 1940, grew up honing his drum and flute chops in a variety of Texas R&B units, then became an early innovator in the jazz/rock fusion movement. In the sixties, in New York to pursue a college degree, he played with a hall of fame of jazz stars, including Charles Mingus, Betty Carter, Stanley Turrentine, McCoy Tyner, and Kenny Dorham, then moved in a free-jazz direction with Albert Ayler.

He then went on a five-year hiatus in which he did nothing but practice (though some argue he also slept and ate occasionally), emerging as a prime force in Ornette Coleman's jazz/rock experiment, Prime Time. He also played with James "Blood" Ulmer and Cecil Taylor, then formed his own band, Decoding Society, which cross-sections heroes from the worlds of jazz, funk, and rock. He remains an innovative force on the creative jazz scene.

Drummers who have also caused ripples in the great pond of jazz are: Paul Guerrero, Walter Winn, Clois "Cub" Teagarden, Carl Lott, Sebastian Whittaker, Raymond Bauduc, and Earl Harvin, a remarkably versatile drummer (he's toured with and written for rock star Seal, among other things), whose three records for Leaning House, *Earl Harvin Trio/Quartet*, *Strange Happy* (with pianist Dave Palmer), and *The Earl Harvin Trio—At the Gypsy Tea Room*, are remarkably fresh and interesting efforts.

It should also be mentioned here that vibes/percussionist Ed Hagen was a fine musician.

Finally, because it's not his fault that the noble tuba isn't a really dynamic instrument, and because he was actually good at it, Bill Stanley (born in Hull, Texas, in 1923) is the final musician to be mentioned in this book. Though it's true he never hauled his great brass ax over to Mingus, Bird, Miles, or Monk's pads to break out the cookies and hot chocolate and help them explode the crystalline and made-to-be-broken parameters of jazz, Stanley can take solace in the knowledge that, insofar as Texas jazz tuba dudes are concerned, he was a seriously honkin' guy.

☆ Bibliography and Sources

Interviews

Subjects were either interviewed directly for the purpose of this book, responded to questionnaires, or both. I have also utilized material from interviews I've conducted in preparation for various articles, when applicable. When the subject was a musician, he/she is identified by his/her most prominent associations.

Vinnie Abbott. Musician (Pantera).
Josh Alan. Musician/Journalist.
Tim Alexander. Musician (solo artist, Asleep at the Wheel).
Rocky Athas. Musician (Lightning, Black Oak Arkansas).
Moe Bandy. Musician.
Vince Bell. Musician.
Davis Bickston. Musician (Spot, Mildred).
Doyle Bramhall, Jr. Musician (solo artist, ARC Angels).
Brannon Brewer. Musician (Diablo Sol).
Nick Briscoe. Musician (Fever in the Funkhouse/solo artist).
Clarence "Gatemouth" Brown. Musician.
Junior Brown. Musician.
Stephen Bruton. Musician/Producer.
Sumter Bruton. Musician, Owner (Record Town).
Richard Buckner. Musician.
Sarah Elizabeth Campbell. Musician.
Olin Chisolm. Journalist.
Jeff Clark. Musician (Too Smooth).
Kevin Coffey. Journalist.
Bruce Corbitt. Musician (Rigor Mortis).
John Croslin. Musician (The Reivers/Zeitgeist).
Rodney Crowell. Musician.
Mary Cutrufello. Musician.
Mike Daane. Musician (Ugly Mus-tard, Andy Timmons Band)/Producer.
Kim Davis. Musician (Point Blank).
Ronnie Dawson. Musician.
Tim Delaughter. Musician (Tripping Daisy).
David Dennard. Record Label Owner (Dragon Street Records)/A&R Head (Steve Records)/Musician (Gary Myrick and the Figures).
King Diamond. Musician.
Robert Ealey. Musician.
Shaune Edwardes. Manager (Vibrolux, Tablet).
Mark Elliot. Record Label Owner (Leaning House Records).
Joe Ely. Musician.
Emily Erwin Robison. Musician (Dixie Chicks).

Roberta Evans. Manager (Absu).
Carl Finch. Musician (Brave Combo), Producer.
Sue Foley. Musician.
Donnie Ray Ford. Musician.
Denny Freeman. Musician.
Jimmie Dale Gilmore. Musician.
George Gimarc. Author, radio personality.
Nanci Griffith. Musician.
Earl Harvin. Musician (solo artist, rubberbullet).
Bugs Henderson. Musician.
Kim Herriage. Musician (Feet First, the Cartwrights).
Aden Holt. Musician (Caulk, record label owner (One Ton Records)
Stephen Holt. Musician (Tablet).
Flaco Jimenez. Musician (solo artist, Texas Tornados).
Eric Johnson. Musician.
Mark Jones. Musician (the Blue Johnnies).
Patrick Keel. Producer (Dragon Street Records)/Musician (the Pool).
Robert Earl Keen. Musician.
Barry Kooda. Musician (the Nervebreakers, Yeah! Yeah! Yeah!, the Cartwrights).
Chris Layton. Musician (Double Trouble, ARC Angels, Storyville).
Natalie Maines. Musician (Dixie Chicks).
M.C. 900-Foot Jesus. Musician.
Sam McCall. Musician (Brutal Juice) /Producer.
Pat McKanna. Musician (The Trees/Lockjaw).
Ron McKeown. Publisher (BUDDY Magazine).
Casey Monahans. Director (Texas Music Office).
Ian Moore. Musician.
Milton Moore. Journalist.
Tommy Morrell. Musician (solo artist, Time-Warp Tophands).
Ernie Myers. Musician (the Elements).
Sam Myers. Musician (Anson Funderburgh and the Rockets Featuring Sam Myers).
Salim Nourallah. Musician (the Moon Festival).
Jack O'Neill. Musician (Jackopierce).
Rob Patterson. Journalist.
Jonathon Pell. Director (Dallas Opera).
Lucky Peterson. Musician.
Lee Pickens. Musician (Bloodrock).
Cary Pierce. Musician (Jackopierce).
Joe Priesnitz. Manager (Eric Johnson, Chris Duarte).
Leon Rausch. Musician (solo artist, Texas Playboys).
Redbeard. Deejay/Program Director (KTXQ/Q102, Dallas).
Johnny Reno. Musician (solo artist, Sax Maniacs, Chris Isaac).
Alan Restrepo. President (Carpe Diem Records).
Mike Rhyner. Radio personality/journalist.
Bruce Robison. Musician.
Mark Rubin. Musician (Bad Livers, Rubinchik's Orkestyr).
Chad Rueffer. Musician (Spot, Mildred).
Reggie Rueffer. Musician (Spot, Mildred).
Keith Rust. Producer.
Tim Schuller. Journalist.
Marty Seidell. Musician (Dixie Chicks).
Chris Shull. Journalist.
Jim Suhler. Musician (Monkey Beat).
Mario Tarradell. Journalist.
Craig "Niteman" Taylor. Musician (Killbilly), disc jockey.

Jess "Guitar" Taylor. Musician.
Teye. Musician.
Andy Timmons. Musician (solo artist, Danger Danger).
Michael Tusa. Professor of Music History (University of Texas, Austin).
Turner Scott Van Blarcum. Musician (Pump'n Ethyl, Sedition).
Jimmie Vaughan. Musician (solo artist, Fabulous Thunderbirds).
Matt Weitz. Journalist.
John Wheat. Professor/archivist (Center for American History, University of Texas).
Van Wilks. Musician.
Alan Wooley. Musician (Killbilly, the Cartwrights).
Danny Wright. Musician.
Miles Zuniga. Musician (Fastball).

Books

Abernethy, Francis E. *Singin' Texas*. Denton: University of North Texas Press, 1994.
Ancelet, Barry Jean. *The Makers of Cajun Music*. Austin: University of Texas Press, 1984.
Antone, Susan. *Antone's: The First Ten Years*. Austin: Blues Press, 1986.
Barthel, Norma. *Ernest Tubb: The Original E. T.* Roland, OK: Ernest Tubb Fan Club Enterprises, 1969.
Blayney, David. *Sharp-Dressed Men: Z.Z. Top—Behind the Scenes from Blues to Boogie to Beards*. New York: Hyperion Press, 1994.
Bond, Johnny. *The Tex Ritter Story*. New York: Chappell Music, 1976.
Booth, Stanley. *Rhythm Oil: A Journey Through the Music of the American South*. New York: Vintage Books, 1993.
Boyer, Horace Clarence. *How Sweet the Sound: The Golden Age of Gospel*. Washington, D.C.: Elliot & Clark Publishing, 1995.
Bufwack, Mary A., and Robert K. Oermann. *Finding Her Voice: The Illustrated History of Women in Country Music*. New York: Henry Holt and Company, 1993.
Cackett, Alan, Roy Thompson, and Douglas B. Green. *The Harmony Illustrated Encyclopedia of Country Music*. New York: Harmony Books, 1986.
Carlisle, Dolly. *Ragged but Right: The Life and Times of George Jones*. Chicago: Contemporary Books, 1984.
Carr, Ian, Digby Fairweather, and Brian Priestly. *Jazz: The Rough Guide—The Essential Companion to Artists and Albums*. London: Penguin Books, 1995.
Carr, Joe, and Alan Munde. *Prairie Nights to Neon Lights*. Lubbock: Texas Tech University Press, 1995.
Clayson, Alan. *Only the Lonely: Roy Orbison's Life and Legacy*. New York: St. Martin's Press, 1989.
Collins, Ace. *The Stories Behind Country Music's All-Time Greatest 100 Songs*. New York: Boulevard Books, 1996.
Collins, Ace. *Tanya*. New York: St. Martin's Paperbacks, 1995.
Cooper, Daniel. *Lefty Frizzell: The Honky-Tonk Life of Country Music's Greatest Singer*. New York: Little, Brown and Co., 1995.
Dance, Helen Oakley. *Stormy Monday: The T-Bone Walker Story*. New York: Da Capo Press, 1987.
Erlewine, Michael, with Scott Bultman, eds. *All Music Guide*. San Francisco: Miller-Freeman Books, 1992.
Erlewine, Michael, with Chris Woodstra and Vladimir Bogdanov, eds. *All Music Guide 2nd Edition*. San Francisco: Miller-Freeman Books, 1994.
Erlewine, Michael, with Vladimir Bogdanov, Chris Woodstra, Stephen Thomas Erlewine, Richie Unterberger, and William Ruhlmann, eds. *All Music Guide to Rock*. San Francisco: Miller-Freeman Books, 1995.
Ewen, David. *Popular American Composers from Revolutionary Times to the Present*. New York: The H. W. Wilson Company, 1962.

Feather, Leonard. *The Encyclopedia of Jazz.* New York: Da Capo Press, 1960.

Flint, Joe, and Judy Nelson. *The Insiders Country Music Handbook.* Salt Lake City: Gibbs-Smith Publisher, 1993.

Friedman, Myra. *Buried Alive: The Biography of Janis Joplin.* New York: Bantam Books, 1974.

Frith, Simon, with Andrew Goodwin, eds. *On Record: Rock, Pop and the Written Word.* New York: Pantheon Books, 1990.

Gammond, Peter. *Scott Joplin and the Ragtime Era.* New York: St. Martin's Press, 1985.

Garvin, Richard M., and Edmond G. Addeo. *The Midnight Special: The Legend of Leadbelly.* New York: B. Geis Associates, 1971.

Gillett, Charlie. *Sound of the City: The Rise of Rock 'n' Roll.* New York, 1983.

Ginell, Cary, with Roy Lee Brown. *Milton Brown and the Founding of Western Swing.* Urbana: University of Illinois Press.

Goldrosen, John, and John Beecher. *Remembering Buddy Holly: The Definitive Biography of Buddy Holly.* New York: Viking Penguin, 1986.

Govenar, Alan. *Meeting the Blues: The Rise of the Texas Sound.* New York: Da Capo Press, 1988.

Gregory, Hugh. *Soul Music A–Z.* London: Blandford, 1991.

Hanousek, Ladislav, ed. *CD World Reference Guide.* Milwaukie, OR: CDI Publishing Corporation, 1993.

Haralambos, Michael. *Soul Music, the Birth of a Sound in Black America.* New York: Da Capo Press, 1974.

Harris, Craig. *The New Folk Music.* Crown Point: White Cliffs Media Corporation, 1991.

Harris, Sheldon. *Blues Who's Who.* New York: Da Capo Press, 1979.

Haskins, James, with Kathleen Benson. *Scott Joplin.* New York: Scarborough Books, 1980.

Hentoff, Nat. *Listen to the Stories: Nat Hentoff on Jazz and Country Music.* New York: HarperCollins, 1995.

Herzhaft, Gérard. *Encyclopedia of the Blues.* Fayetteville: The University of Arkansas Press, 1992.

Howard, John Tasker. *Our American Music.* New York: Thomas Y. Crowell Company, 1965.

Hume, Martha. *Kenny Rogers: Gambler, Dreamer, Lover.* New York: Plume Books, 1980.

Jacobs, Arthur. *The Penguin Dictionary of Musical Performers.* New York: Penguin Books, 1990.

Jones, Tom, and Harvey Schmidt. *The Fantasticks: The 30th Anniversary Edition.* New York: Applause Theatre Book Publishers, 1990.

Jones, K. Maurice. *Say It Loud: The Story of Rap Music.* Brookfield: The Millbrook Press, 1994.

Larkin, Margaret. *Singing Cowboys: A Book of Western Songs.* New York: Alfred A. Knopf, 1931.

Leigh, Keri. *Stevie Ray: Soul to Soul.* Dallas: Taylor Publishing Company, 1993.

Lomax, Alan. *The Land Where the Blues Began.* New York: Pantheon Books, 1993.

Lomax, John. *Cowboy Songs and Other Frontier Ballads.* New York: Macmillan & Co., 1938.

Malone, Bill. *American Music, Southern Music.* Lexington: University of Kentucky Press, 1979.

Malone, Bill. *Country Music U.S.A.* Austin: University of Texas Press, 1985.

Marsh, Dave, with John Swenson, eds. *The Rolling Stone Record Guide.* New York: Random House/Rolling Stone Press, 1977.

Martin, Suzanne. *Awesome Almanac Texas.* Walworth: B&B Publishing, Inc. 1995.

Martino, Dave. *Singer-Songwriters.* New York: Billboard Books, 1994.

May, Robin. *A Companion to the Opera.* New York: Hippocrene Books, Inc., 1977.

McCloud, Barry, and contributing writers. *Definitive Country: The Ultimate Encyclopedia of Country Music and Its Performers.* New York: Perigee Books, 1995.

McCoy, Judy. *Rap Music in the 1980s.* Metuchen, NJ: Scarecrow Press, 1992.

Monahan, Casey, ed. *Texas Music Industry Directory, 1996 Edition.* Austin: Office of the Governor, State of Texas, 1996.

Moore, Frank Ledlie, ed. *Crowell's Handbook of World Opera.* New York: Thomas Y. Crowell Company, 1961.

Nelson, Willie, with Bud Shrake. *Willie: An Autobiography.* New York: Simon & Schuster, 1988.

Obrecht, Jas, ed. *Blues Guitar: The Men Who Made the Music.* San Francisco: GPI Books, 1990.

Oliphant, Dave. *Texan Jazz.* Austin: The University of Texas Press, 1996.

Patoski, Joe Nick, and Bill Crawford. *Stevie Ray Vaughan: Caught in the Crossfire.* Boston: Little, Brown and Company, 1993.

Peña, Manuel. *Tex-Mex Conjunto: The History of a Working-Class Music.* Austin: University of Texas Press, 1985.

Pike, Jeff. *The Death of Rock 'n' Roll: Untimely Demises, Morbid Preoccupations, and Premature Forecasts of Doom in Pop Music.* New York. Faber & Faber, 1993.

Pride, Charley, with Jim Henderson. *The Charley Pride Story.* New York: William Morrow, 1994.

Ramos, Mary G., ed. *1996–1997 Texas Almanac.* Dallas: The Dallas Morning News, Inc., 1996.

Reid, Jan. *The Improbable Rise of Redneck Rock.* Austin: Heidelberg Publishers, Inc., 1974.

Richards, Tad, and Melvin B. Shestack. *The New Country Music Encyclopedia.* New York: Fireside Books, 1993.

Romanowski, Patricia, with Holly George-Warren and Jon Pareles, eds. *The New Rolling Stone Encyclopedia of Rock & Roll.* New York: Fireside Books/Rolling Stone Press, 1983, 1995.

Russell, Ross. *Jazz Style in Kansas City and the Southwest.* Berkeley, CA: University of California Press, 1971.

Sallis, James. *The Guitar Players.* Lincoln: University of Nebraska Press, 1982.

Shank, Barry. *Dissonant Identities: The Rock 'n' Roll Scene in Austin, Texas.* Hanover: Wesleyan University Press/University Press of New England, 1994.

Shaw, Arnold. *Honkers and Shouters: The Golden Years of Rhythm and Blues.* New York: Collier Books, 1978.

Slovimsky, Nicolas, ed. *Baker's Biographical Dictionary of Musicians, Eighth Edition.* New York: Schirmer Books, 1992.

Smith, Jay, and Leonard Guttridge. *Jack Teagarden: The Story of a Jazz Maverick.* New York: Da Capo, 1976.

Smith, Richard D. *Bluegrass.* Chicago: a cappella books, 1995.

Stambler, Irwin. *Encyclopedia of Pop, Rock and Soul.* New York: St. Martin's Press, 1974.

Suskin, Steven. *Show Tunes 1905–1991: The Songs, Shows and Careers of Broadway's Major Composers.* New York: Limelight Editions, 1993.

Sweeney, Philip. *The Virgin Directory of World Music.* New York: Owl Books, 1991.

Tosches, Nick. *Country: The Biggest Music in America.* New York: Stein and Day, 1977.

Townsend, Charles R. *San Antonio Rose: The Life and Music of Bob Wills.* Urbana: University of Illinois Press, 1976.

Trim, Laura. *Short Trips in and Around Dallas.* Dallas: LDT Press, 1984.

Walker, Dave. *American Rock 'n' Roll Tour.* New York: Thunder's Mouth Press, 1992.

White, Timothy. *Rock Lives.* New York: Henry Holt & Co., 1990.

Willoughby, Larry. *Texas Rhythm, Texas Rhyme: A Pictorial History of Texas Music.* Austin: Texas Monthly Press, 1984.

Wolfe, Charles. *Lefty Frizzell: His Life, His Music*. Bremen, Germany: Bear Family, 1984.

Wynn, Ron, with Michael Erlewine and Vladimir Bogdanov, eds. *All Music Guide to Jazz*. San Francisco: Miller-Freeman Books, 1994.

Articles

Acosta, Belinda. "The Return of Manuel "Cowboy" Donley—Beautiful Songs and Good, Heavy Sounds." *The Austin Chronicle*, November 27, 1998.

Adzgery, Sandy. "What Matters Most: Although He's Finally Obtained Success in Country Music, Ty Herndon Hasn't Lost Sight of What's Important in Life." *Tune-In*, May 1995.

Allen, Bob. "Rick Trevino Stands Out." *Country Music*, July/August 1995.

Allen, Bob. "Review: Steve Earle's *Train a Comin'*." *Country Music*, July/August 1995.

Ardoin, John. "Lisitsa and Kuznetsoff Are Doubly Delightful." *The Dallas Morning News*, August 11, 1996.

Arlo. "An Interview with Shawn Phillips." Internet web site (http: dipl.ee.uct.ac.z . . . wn docs/arlo/inter.html).

Ayres, Keith. "Interview: James McMurtry." *Texas Beat*, September 1992.

Ayres, Keith. "Interview: Tish Hinojosa." *Texas Beat*, December 1992.

Ayres, Keith. "King's X—Ty Tabor Revisited." *Texas Beat*, August 1991.

Ayres, Keith. "Women in Texas Music." *Texas Beat*, August 1993.

Bell, Vince. "One Man's Music." *Leak*, Fall 1995.

Bentley, Bill. "At the Starting Gates of the Seventies: Austin Music as the Decades Changed." *The Austin Chronicle*, September 3, 1993.

Bessman, Jim. "Earle, Partner Link Venture with WB." *Billboard*, January 6, 1996.

Black, Judy. "Darden Smith: Taking Notes on the Human Condition." *Cleveland Scene*, April 1993.

Bleestein, Rob. "Joe Ely's Letter Is Gonna Get to You." *Gavin*, August 4, 1995.

Bond, Eric. "Soul Hat Does Its Tricks on Sixth." *The Daily Texas*, November 7, 1991.

Boyd, D. "In the Spotlight: Too Smooth." *Sundown Magazine*, January 1977.

Bradford, Colleen. "Breakin' the Rules: Brutal Juice." *BUDDY Magazine*, November 1992.

Bradford, Colleen. "They're Back: the Buck Pets." *BUDDY Magazine*, April 1993.

Bradley, Bob. "In the High Country: Rose Flores and Friends in Aspen." *The Journal of Country Music*, Vol. 17, No. 2.

Burns, Stoney. "Lou Ann Barton Is Old Enough." *BUDDY Magazine*, March 1982.

Burr, Ramiro. "Tejano Awards Invite Controversy, Not Excellence." *Houston Chronicle*, March 24, 1996.

Cadena, Andi. "Joel Nava." *Mike's Feedback*, March 1996.

Caligiuri, Jim. "West Coast Meets South of Texas." *The Austin Chronicle*, September 18, 1998.

Carr, Patrick. "George Jones Survives the Country Wars." *Country Music*, July/August 1995.

Cartwright, Gary. "Asleeping Beauty." *Texas Monthly*, November 1995.

Celeste, Eric. "Mystery Train: Wayne Hancock Emerges from the Ghetto as a Major Country Talent." *The Met*, November 1, 1995.

Chappell, Jon. "Eric Johnson: The Incredible Tone Master Returns." *Guitar*, September 1996.

Chrissoupoulos, Philip. "The Offspring: Dallas' Punk Bands Resurrect the Spirit of the '70s." *Dallas Observer*, November 2, 1995.

Christensen, Thor. "Out of the Blue: Denton Band Deep Blue Something Feeds Off Top 10 Success of 'Breakfast at Tiffany's.'" *The Dallas Morning News*, January 21, 1996.

Coffey, Kevin Reed. "Floyd Tillman: Architect of Honky-Tonk." *The Journal of the American Academy for the Preservation of Old-Time Country Music*, December 1995.

Coffey, Kevin Reed. "The Light Crust Doughboys: Western Swing Training Ground." *The Journal of the American Academy for the Preservation of Old-Time Country Music,* June 1995.

Coffey, Kevin Reed. "Steel Colossus: The Bob Dunn Story." *The Journal of Country Music,* Vol. 17, No. 2.

Cohen, Jason. "Butch Hancock: 'It's Just Life, Y'Know.' " *Option,* March/April 1992.

Coleman, Ornette. "Tone Dialing." *Bomb,* Summer 1996.

Cooper, Daniel. "Tanya Tucker: Almost Grown." *The Journal of Country Music,* Vol. 17, No. 1.

Corcoran, Michael. "The Morse Code: Texan Ella Mae Influenced Rock, Then She Crawled Under One." *Dallas Observer,* March 21, 1996.

Crawford, Bill. "The Artistic Afterlife: Stevie Ray Vaughan." *The Austin Chronicle,* October 6, 1995.

Cuellar, Catherine. "Campbell's Soup: Waxahachie's Tevin Campbell Survives Teen Stardom." *The Dallas Morning News,* July 11, 1996.

Dalton, Nick. "Hugh Moffatt: Whatever You Do, Don't Mention 'That Song.' " *Country Music International,* August 1995.

Dalton, Nick. "Smith and Weston: Darden Smith Insists He's Still Not a Country Act." *Country Music International,* July 1994.

DeLuca, Dan. "An Austin Songwriters' Tour at the Tin Angel." *The Philadelphia Inquirer,* October 22, 1993.

DeLyons, William. "Up Jumped the Devil: Dallas Cat Rocker Ronnie Dawson Is as Unique as Ghost Riders Get—Cause He Ain't Dead Yet." *The Met,* January 26, 1995.

Dingus, Anne. "Texans Never Cry and 25 Other Great Moments in Texas Movie History." *Texas Monthly,* April 1990.

Dixon Harden, Lydia. "Brooks & Dunn Side Step Stones in the Road." *Music City News,* July 1996.

Draper, Robert. "The Real Buddy Holly." *Texas Monthly,* October 1995.

Drozdowski, Ted. "Not Your Father's Delta Blues." *Musician,* April 1996.

Dunn, Jancee. "Q: Gibby Haynes of the Butthole Surfers." *Rolling Stone,* May 2, 1996.

Dunn, Jancee. "Q: Willie Nelson." *Rolling Stone,* March 9, 1995.

Eig, Jonathon. "Joe Sample: Hard Hands, Sweet Soul." *JAZZIZ,* July 1996.

Eig, Jonathon. "Youngster's Jazz Career Continues on a Rising Note." *The Dallas Morning News,* April 6, 1996.

Evans, Paul. "The Cool Flame: Boz Scaggs' *Some Change.*" *Rolling Stone,* May 5, 1994.

Evans, Rush. "Home with the Armadillo: Austin's Legendary Armadillo World Headquarters." *DISCoveries,* March 1996.

Ferguson, Ben. "King in Kansas: Maybe . . . Almost . . . Yes, He Made It!" *BUDDY Magazine,* March 1975.

Flanagan, Bill. "Ragged Company: Steve Earle and Townes Van Zandt, A Musician Forum." *Musician,* August 1995.

Flippo, Chet. "Hot Tamales, Cold Beer, and Austin's Own Country Music." *The Austin Chronicle,* January 14, 1994.

Flippo, Chet. "Listening for the First Austin Sound: The Essential Cosmic Cowboy Albums." *The Austin Chronicle,* January 21, 1994.

Flippo, Chet. "Sixties Upside Down Is Nineties: Sir Douglas Quintet." *The Austin Chronicle,* March 18, 1994.

Flores, Chuck. "Lord of the Highway: Joe Ely." *BUDDY Magazine,* September 1992.

Forte, Dan. "Eric Johnson's Home Studio." *Guitar Player,* March 1996.

Forte, Dan. "Stevie Ray Vaughan: The Triple-Crown Bluesman Talks Technique, Equipment and Soul." *Guitar Player,* October 1984.

Fricke, David. "Alejandro Escovedo: The Austin, Texas, Songwriting Legend Has Made Music His Life. Now He'd Like to Make It His Living." *Rolling Stone,* May 2, 1996.

Fromholz, Steven. "Discovering Austin on the 'Tour of Heaven': A Cosmic Cowboy Remembers." *The Austin Chronicle*, January 21, 1994.

Gabriel, Rashiel. "The Urban Underground: The DIY Aesthetics of Hip Hop." *The Austin Chronicle*, April 19, 1996.

Geary, Susan. "Buried Alive in Blues: Janis Fled Texas and Went On to Become Another Lone Star." *BUDDY Magazine*, March 1975.

Gershuny, Diane. "Sue Foley's Young Girl Blues." *Guitar Player*, August 1992.

Giddens, C. D. "Mary Cutrufello's Guitar Not for the Weak." *Country Nights*, November 1993.

Goad, Kimberly. "Joe Ely: This Texas Troubador Rocks to His Own Beat." *The Dallas Morning News*, September 10, 1995.

Goldstein, Deborah. "Lizards Work Too Hard." *Austin American-Statesman*, June 1, 1995.

Green, Tony, "Perms, Science Fiction, and Hip-Hop." *Vibe*, June/July 1999.

Gubbins, Teresa. "Diversity Rules on Denton Music Scene." *The Dallas Morning News*, January 21, 1996.

Gubbins, Theresa. "The Mighty Quindon: At 13, Plano's Quindon Tarver Seems Headed for Stardom." *The Dallas Morning News*, June 13, 1996.

Hagelberg, Kymberli. "Lord Tracy Speaks: An Interview with Terry Lee Glaze." *Speed of Sound*, January 1990.

Hample, Henry. "Leadbelly." *Vibe*, February 1995.

Handelman, David. "Sold on Ice: He's Being Touted as the Elvis of Rap. Can 5 Million Vanilla Ice Fans Be Wrong?" *Rolling Stone*, January 10, 1991.

Haneiko, Laura. "The Fabulous Thunderbirds." *Music News*, December 1995.

Hardwig, Jay. "American's Ethnic Music Mantle." *The Austin Chronicle*, October 30, 1998.

Hardwig, Jay. "Rhythm Is King." *The Austin Chroncile*, June 25, 1999.

Hardwig, Jay. "Roots, Reckonings, and Resolution." *The Austin Chronicle*, November 27, 1998.

Harvey, Phil. "Little Jack Melody: A Lesson in Alternative Music." *The Grind*, September 15, 1996.

Hattersly, Craig. "The Armadillo Brings It All Together." *The Austin Chronicle*, January 21, 1994.

Hernandez, Dennis. "Review: *King's X* by King's X." *BUDDY Magazine*, May 1992.

Hernandez, Raoul. "Satin Dolls: The Ladies of Austin Jazz." *The Austin Chronicle*, June 7, 1996.

Hess, Christopher. "Soul Man W. C. Clark—Confessin' the Blues." *The Austin Chronicle*, July 31, 1998.

Hess Christopher. "Teye's Viva Flamenco—La Guitarra de Callajera." *The Austin Chronicle*, July 9, 1999.

Hewitt, Bill, with Joseph Harmes and Bob Stewart. "Before Her Time." *People Magazine*, April 17, 1995.

Hilburn, Robert. "Through the Ring of Fire: Country Renegade Steve Earle Has Overcome Drug Addictions, a Stint in Jail and a Four-Year Songwriting Block to Return to the Acclaim of His 1986 Nashville Breakthrough." *Los Angeles Times*, February 18, 1996.

Hillis, Craig. "The Music That Put Austin on the Map: What Is Progressive Country?" *The Austin Chronicle*, January 14, 1994.

Holden, Stephen. " 'Country Hoot' Ends Festival at Carnegie Hall." *The New York Times*, May 2, 1994.

Hooper, Country Roger. "Not Your Ordinary Ten-Gallon Barroom Singer: Neal McCoy Works a Crowd Like a Flyrod." *BUDDY Magazine*, September 1992.

Hooper, Country Roger. "Pickin' the Bluegrass Blues." *BUDDY Magazine*, August 1993.

Hooper, Country Roger. "Review: Billy Joe Shaver's *Tramp On Your Street*." *BUDDY Magazine*, October 1993.

Hooper, Dave. "End of the Line: The Passing of Grey Ghost." *The Austin Chronicle*, July 26, 1996.

Hopkins Clark, Renee. "Zen and the Art of Country Music: Jimmie Dale Gilmore." *BUDDY Magazine*, October 1993.

Hyatt, Tommy. "Austin Veterans Fuse New Sound: Storyville Band Members Can Truly Be Called a Super-Group." *BUDDY Magazine*, July 1996.

Hyatt, Tommy. "King's X Deserves Grunge Credit." *BUDDY Magazine*, June 1996.

Jones, James T. IV. "Chillin' with the Lord: Gospel's Franklin Is a 'Crossover Miracle.' " *USA Today*, March 8, 1995.

Jones, Lisa C. "New Gospel Sensation: Kirk Franklin." *Ebony*, October 1995.

Jones, Scott Kelton. "Obstacle Course: An Uncertain Label Situation Makes Waiting the Hardest Part for Course of Empire." *The Met*, June 26, 1996.

Jones, Sharon. "The Ultimate Cow-Punk: Dale Watson," *Mike's Feedback*, March 1996.

Johnston, Richard. "Death Steals the Gangsta." *Guitar Player*, October 1996.

Kenneally, Tim. "Electric Leary—Are the Butthole Surfers Fugitives in Alternative Nation?" *Guitar Player*, October 1996.

Kienzle, Rich. "Review: Rodney Crowell's *Jewel of the South*." *Country Music*, July/August 1995.

Koster, Rick. "A Braver New Direction: Jimmie Dale Gilmore's Latest CD Is a Triumph of New Authenticity." *BUDDY Magazine*, October 1996.

Koster, Rick. "A Fiddle, Bob Wills and Thou: The Young Persons' Guide to Western Swing." *BUDDY Magazine*, April 1995.

Koster, Rick. "A Life in the Day: The Myriad Adventures of Andy Timmons." *BUDDY Magazine*, September 1994.

Koster, Rick. "Border Tripping: The Quixotic Story Behind Joe Ely's *Letter to Laredo*." *BUDDY Magazine*, December 1995.

Koster, Rick. "Can Jim Suhler *Shake* the Blues?" *BUDDY Magazine*, March 1995.

Koster, Rick. "Can Josh Alan Crack Broadway?" *BUDDY Magazine*, December 1994.

Koster, Rick. "Cut the Cards, Ante Up: Spot Reshuffles the Deck." *Dallas Observer*, August 22, 1996.

Koster, Rick. "Class Is in Session: Blues Clubs Turn the Stage into a School." *Dallas Observer*, January 20, 1994.

Koster, Rick. "DFW Music Scene Uncovered: Why Are Major Labels Looking to the Metroplex with Such Interest?" *BUDDY Magazine*, October 1995.

Koster, Rick. "Do-It-Yourself Secrets Revealed: Local Artists Get the Music Out with Their Own Labels." *BUDDY Magazine*, November 1995.

Koster, Rick. "The Evolution of the Tone Man: The Long-Awaited *Venus Isle* LP Takes Eric Johnson Beyond All the Rest." *BUDDY Magazine*, September 1996.

Koster, Rick. "The Gospel According to MC 900 Ft. Jesus." *BUDDY Magazine*, June 1993.

Koster, Rick. "His Work Is Never Done: Robert Earl Keen Would Like Nothing Better Than to Save Country Music." *Dallas Observer*, June 13, 1996.

Koster, Rick. "Jacko Wins: The Hometown Redemption of Jackopierce." *BUDDY Magazine*, June 1996.

Koster, Rick. "Intergalactic C&W: Junior Brown." *BUDDY Magazine*, September 1995.

Koster, Rick. "Jimmie Sings! *Strange Pleasures* Is Not Only His Debut Solo Album, Also Is a Spiritual Healing for Vaughan." *BUDDY Magazine*, June 1994.

Koster, Rick. "Magnets and Steel: Eric Johnson's Move to the Mainstream." *BUDDY Magazine*, April 1978.

Koster, Rick. "The Maitre d' of R&B: Elvis T. Busboy Drives His Soul Train into the Future." *Dallas Observer*, June 27, 1996.

Koster, Rick. "Man of Many Musical Hats: Stephen Bruton." *BUDDY Magazine*, May 1994.

Koster, Rick. "Metal's Crimson King: The Mellow Satanism of King Diamond." *Dallas Observer*, October 23, 1996.

Koster, Rick. "Pantera Springs Eternal." *BUDDY Magazine*, May 1996.

Koster, Rick. "Photographer Archived Deep Ellum Scene." *BUDDY Magazine*, October 1996.

Koster, Rick. "The Portable Ian Moore." *BUDDY Magazine*, August 1995.

Koster, Rick. "The Reverend's Happy Hour Heaven: It's Always *Martini Time* with the Reverend Horton Heat." *BUDDY Magazine*, July 1996.

Koster, Rick. "Review: James McMurtry's *Candyland*." *BUDDY Magazine*, September 1992.

Koster, Rick. "Review: Bobby Patterson's *Second Coming*." *BUDDY Magazine*, July 1996.

Koster, Rick. "Review: Poi Dog Pondering's *Volo Volo*." *BUDDY Magazine*, September 1992.

Koster, Rick. "Review: Texas Tornados' *Hangin' On by a Thread*." *BUDDY Magazine*, June 1993.

Koster, Rick. "A Rockabilly Original: Ronnie Dawson." *BUDDY Magazine*, December 1994.

Koster, Rick. "Rocky's Road: One of Dallas's Most Promising Guitarists Might Get His Break—After 20 Years." *Dallas Observer*, November 18, 1993.

Koster, Rick. "The Sage of the Stomach Steinway: Flaco Asks, 'What Is *Conjunto?*' It's Pretty Amazing, and There Will Be a Test Later." *BUDDY Magazine*, June 1993.

Koster, Rick. "Texas' Newest Guitar Hero: Ian Moore." *BUDDY Magazine*, October 1993.

Koster, Rick. "There Is Life After Stevie: Chris Layton Moves to Storyville." *BUDDY Magazine*, July 1994.

Koster, Rick. "Tripping Daisy Goes Pyrotechnic." *BUDDY Magazine*, July 1995.

Langer, Andy. "Antone's Ch-ch-ch-changes." *The Austin Chronicle*, September 3, 1993.

Langer, Andy. "Galactic Cowboys." *Texas Beat*, October 1991.

Langer, Andy. "Suicide Is No Solution: The S.I.N.S. Foundation." *The Austin Chronicle*, June 28, 1996.

Langer, Andy. "Who's Got the Hootie? Comparin' Austin's and Dallas' 1995 Output." *The Austin Chronicle*, January 19, 1996.

Lindsey, Craig D. "Discman—DJ DMD goes national with his continental. Houston-based rap style." *Houston Press*, June 10, 1999.

Lindsey, Craig D. "Rap Space—Will hip-hop ever find a home in Houston?" *Houston Press*, June 3, 1999.

Lindsey, Craig D. "That's the Breaks—Houston rap labels and their artists look for that big deal." *Houston Press*, February 11, 1999.

Littlepage, Mary Susan. "Temple's Tejano Sensation: Little Joe y La Familia." *Texas Our Texas*, October 1995.

Malindrone, Scott. "Profile: Ty Tabor." *Guitar Player*, May 1996.

Mansfield, Brian. "Doug Supernaw Survives the Controversy and Misunderstanding." *New Country*, December 1995.

Martin, Kim. "Walker's Found a Home: Jerry Jeff Walker Took the Long Road to Texas." *BUDDY Magazine*, March 1975.

Mayo, Corey Michael. "Brutal Juice Goes Nationwide." *BUDDY Magazine*, May 1995.

Mayo, Corey Michael. "Between Heaven and Las Vegas: Reverend Horton Heat's Bassist Jimbo Wallace Is a Stand-Up Guy." *BUDDY Magazine*, August 1994.

Mayo, Corey Michael. "If Shakespeare Played Guitar: Guy Clark Influenced Two Generations of Songwriters." *BUDDY Magazine*, April 1995.

Mayo, Corey Michael. "Lisa Loeb—The Poetess of Gen X." *BUDDY Magazine*, December 1995.

Mayo, Corey Michael. "The Year of the Toad: Fort Worth's Toadies Leap into the Big Leagues." *BUDDY Magazine*, September 1994.

McCall, Michael. "The Strait Edge." *New Country*, January 1996.

McClain, Buzz. "No Need for Nashville: These Four Pay Their Roadhouse Blues." *The Dallas Morning News*, April 26, 1996.

McGuire, Steve. "The Making of the Austin Music Club Scene." *The Austin Chronicle*, September 10, 1993.

McLeese, Don. "Don Walser: Best New Artist?" *The Journal of Country Music*, Vol. 17, No. 2.

McLeese, Don. "Duarte's 'Magik' Ax." *Austin American-Statesman*, December 1, 1994.

McLeese, Don. "Pierce Collects Praises on Tribute." *Austin American-Statesman*, December 3, 1992.

McVey, Richard II. "Charley Pride." *Music City News*, July 1996.

Milano, Brett. "Cult Icon Daniel Johnston Goes Major Label, While Fellow-Austinite K. McCarty Turns Johnston's Songs into an Indie-Label Masterpiece." *Pulse!* December 1994.

Milkowski, Bill. "Mr. Freeze: Telecaster Master Albert Collins Stands at the Forefront of a New Blues Revival." *Guitar World*, September 1990.

Miller, Ed. "Past Meets Present at Longhorn: From Bob Wills in the 40s to Ray Wylie Hubbard in the 70s." *BUDDY Magazine*, March 1975.

Miller, Ed. "The Rise and Fall of the Texas Progressive Country Movement." *BUDDY Magazine*, October 1990.

Miller, Ed. "Rockabilly: Past, Present and Future." *BUDDY Magazine*, May 1992.

Mills, Fred. "All in the Family: Alejandro Escovedo." *Magnet*, April/May 1996.

Milner, Jay. "The New Jerry Jeff Walker?" *Texas Music*, June 1976.

Milner, Jay. "Outlaws Love Texas." *Texas Music*, May 1976.

Minutaglio, Bill. "Flaco Jimenez: Squeezing Out Fame, Fortune and Music in South Texas." *The Dallas Morning News*, August 11, 1996.

Minutaglio, Bill. "Roland Swenson: SXSW Co-Founder Helped Put Austin on the Pop-Music Map." *The Dallas Morning News*, March 17, 1996.

Minutaglio, Bill. "Soul Stirrer: It Took Years, But Ernie Johnson Paid His Dues." *The Dallas Morning News*, October 12, 1995.

Minutaglio, Bill. "Soul Survivor: New Generation Discovers Bobby Patterson's Blues." *The Dallas Morning News*, May 2, 1996.

Minutaglio, Bill. "Texas Flood: Capitol Blues Collection Highlights Lone Star Talent." *The Dallas Morning News*, August 3, 1995.

Mitchell, Joe. "Folk Kerrvision." *The Austin Chronicle*, May 24, 1996.

Mitchell, Rick. "Bush Has Secure Footing Among Two-Steppers." *Houston Chronicle*, July 28, 1994.

Mitchell, Rick. "Eric Taylor Not a Secret Any Longer." *Houston Chronicle*, September 21, 1995.

Mitchell, Rick. "The Royal Guardsman: Don Walser Quits His Day Job of 45 Years and Creates Some of the Sweetest Texas Music Imaginable." *New Country*, May 1996.

Monahan, Casey. "Lou Ann Documents Ultimate Barroom Set." *Austin American-Statesman*, July 6, 1989.

Monroe, Larry. "King Tears for Walter: the Passing of Walter Hyatt." *The Austin Chronicle*, May 17, 1996.

Morris, Chris. "Strehli's Bay Blues." *Billboard*, October 9, 1993.

Morthland, John. "Blues Brothers." *Texas Monthly*, July 1999.

Morthland, John. "Wasted Days." *Texas Monthly*, October 1995.

Moser, Margaret. "The Scene Is Gone but Not Forgotten: The Evolution of Austin's White Blues." *The Austin Chronicle*, August 9, 1996.

Moser, Margaret. "Too Smooth: A Smooth Trot." *Austin Sun*, November 18, 1977.

Nichols, Lee. "Conflicts and Contradictions: the Choices of Terry Allen." *The Austin Chronicle*, February 16, 1996.

Nicholas Lee. "The Guy Is Everywhere." *The Austin Chronicle*, November 8, 1966.

Nichols, Lee. "Same Train, a Different Time: Austin's Country Music Scene Regenerates." *The Austin Chronicle*, May 10, 1996.

Obrecht, Jas. "Eric Johnson: An Underground Legend Surfaces." *Guitar Player*, May 1986.

Obrecht, Jas. "Eric Johnson: Confessions of a Tone Freak." *Guitar Player*, May 1996.

O'Brien, Patti. "Pure, Simple Style: Kelly Willis: Country Waif." *Rolling Stone*, September 2, 1993.

O'Connor, Colleen. "Lella Cuberli: A Passion for Opera Fuels Her Jet-Setting Career." *The Dallas Morning News*, March 3, 1996.

Oermann, Robert K. "Guitar Slinger: Bluesy Lee Roy Parnell Takes Rockin' Roadies into Studio." *The Tennessean*, October 21, 1996.

Oppel, Pete. "Bob Wills Is Still the King." *BUDDY Magazine*, June 1975.

Ornish, Laurel. "Interview: Kinky Friedman." *BUDDY Magazine*, July 1979.

Palmer, Robert. "Black Snake Moan: The History of Texas Blues." *Guitar World*, September 1996.

Pan, Arnold. "Welcome to Hell's Lobby: The Area's Best—Maybe Only—Real 'Music Scene' Can Be Found in Denton." *Dallas Observer*, July 27, 1995.

Pareles, Jon. "A Nostalgic Mix of Tex-Mex Styles." *The New York Times*, September 30, 1990.

Pareles, Jon. "The Sounds of Texas in New York." *The New York Times*, May 8, 1995.

Pascal, Tomas. "An Independent Label Report." *Metal Maniacs Magazine*, March 1995.

Patoski, Joe Nick. "The Big Twang." *Texas Monthly*, July 1994.

Patoski, Joe Nick. "Dirty Dancing: A New Musical from a Group of Lubbock Expatriates Celebrates West Texas' Bawdy Past." *Texas Monthly*, July 1994.

Patoski, Joe Nick. "Hit Picker." *Texas Monthly*, June 1995.

Patoski, Joe Nick. "The Queen Is Dead." *Texas Monthly*, May 1995.

Patoski, Joe Nick. "Reaching for Rock & Roll's Brass Ring: True Believers." *The Austin Chronicle*, March 18, 1994.

Patoski, Joe Nick. "Roky Road." *Texas Monthly*, March 1995.

Patoski, Joe Nick. "Sex, Drugs and Rock & Roll." *Texas Monthly*, May 1996.

Patoski, Joe Nick. "The Sweet Song of Justice." *Texas Monthly*, December 1995.

Patterson, Rob. "Austin's Real Lounge Lizards: Down South, It Don't Mean a Thing If It Ain't Got That Swing." *The Dallas Observer*, December 6, 1995.

Patterson, Rob. "Austin's Country Limits: Can The Live Music Capital of the World Become Country Music's Second City?" *New Country*, May 1996.

Patterson, Rob. "Back on the Bus: HighTone's Roadhouse Tour Revives Rock and Roll Caravan." *Dallas Observer*, February 15, 1996.

Patterson, Rob. "The Chief of Conjunto: Santiago Jimenez Jr. Maintains His Father's Historic Musical Legacy." *The Dallas Observer*, November 2, 1996.

Patterson, Rob. "The Marketing of Tejano Post-Selena." *Request*, September 1995.

Paul, Alan. "Bearded Glory: Z.Z. Top, Boogie Rock's Premier (Facial) Hair Band, Returns to Form with the Raw and Rowdy *Rhythmeen*." *Guitar School*, October 1996.

Pellecchia, Michael. "Cowtown Lament: Candid Comment by Delbert McClinton and Stephen Bruton on Texas Music." *Texas Music*, June 1976.

Pellecchia, Michael. "Cowtown Refrain: 'Yeah, It Always Feels Like It's Fixing to Happen in Fort Worth.' " *Texas Music*, May 1976.

Peña, Bob. "Shelly Lares: Li'l Miss Dynamite Poised for New CD Release." *DFW's Tejano Review*, December 20, 1995.

Perry, Claudia. "Brave New World Music: Brave Combo and Its Sound Mature." *The Houston Post*, December 9, 1990.

Point, Michael. " 'Girl Group' Collaboration Offers Old-Fashioned R&B." *Austin American-Statesman*, November 11, 1990.

Point, Michael. "Omar Overcomes All Obstacles: Undersung Howlers Mark 20th Year with Release of Quintessential Album *World Wide Open*." *Austin American-Statesman*, January 20, 1996.

Price, Michael H. "Bramhall and the Blues." *Fort Worth Star-Telegram*, March 3, 1994.

Primack, Bret. "Herb Ellis: Signature Artistry." *Jazz Times*, August 1996.

Randall, Mac. "Charlie Sexton: Returning Riffs." *Musician*, October 1995.

Ramsey, Doug. "Riffs on Roy." *Texas Monthly*, May 1996.

Ray, Paul. "The Band That Gave Austin the Blues: Yes, Yes, Yes, I Dig the Storm." *The Austin Chronicle*, September 3, 1993.

Reid, Jan. "The Cult of Keen." *Texas Monthly*, April 1996.

Reid, Jan. "LaFave Rave." *Texas Monthly*, August 1995.

Reynolds, J. R. "Virgin Gets a Head Start Marketing Quindon Tarver." *Billboard*, May 11, 1996.

Rhyner, Mike. "The Willie Charisma." *BUDDY Magazine*, June 1975.

Rogers, Tex. "Eric Taylor: On His Own Terms . . ." *Columbus Weekly*, August 30, 1995.

Rollins, Lisa. "Following in the Possum's Footsteps: Bubba Never Shoots the Jukebox During a Mark Chestnutt Song." *BUDDY Magazine*, November 1992.

Rollins, Lisa. "Parnell Slides to Success." *BUDDY Magazine*, October 1994.

Rollins, Lisa. "Rooted in Texas: Hal Ketchum." *BUDDY Magazine*, April 1993.

Rowland, Hobart. "The Color of Money." *Houston Press*, October 29, 1998.

Rowland, Hobart. "Never too Old to Rock 'n' Roll." *Houston Press*, June 5, 1997.

Saenz Harris, Joyce. "Emilio: Tejano's Low-Key King Reaches for Country Music Stardom." *Dallas Morning News*, December 3, 1995.

Salas, Abel. "The Derailers Are Just Downright Delightful." *Austin American-Statesman*, April 27, 1995.

Salas, Abel. "The Soul of Conjunto: Flaco Jimenez and the Conjunto Dream Team." *The Austin Chronicle*, July 5, 1996.

Schilling Fields, Jamie. "Magic Johnson." *Texas Monthly*, August 1996.

Schnackenberg, Karen. "Musical Appliances: Café Noir." *International Musician*, November 1993.

Schuller, Tim. "Anson Examined." *BUDDY Magazine*, September 1992.

Schuller, Tim. "Back to the Future: Sumter Bruton's Brand of Retro Blues Makes Nostalgia Sound Subversive." *The Met*, November 24, 1995.

Schuller, Tim. "Bugs Henderson Bares His Guitarist's Soul." *BUDDY Magazine*, August 1993.

Schuller, Tim. "Has Brave Combo Gone Too Far?" *BUDDY Magazine*, June 1995.

Schuller, Tim. "The Johnson Testimony: Truth from the Tall Man of Texas R&B." *BUDDY Magazine*, December 1995.

Schuller, Tim. "Soul Trained." *The Met*, July 27, 1995.

Schuller, Tim. "W. C. Clark Opens the Books." *BUDDY Magazine*, October 1994.

Schuller, Tim. "Where's the Smoke . . . Smokin' Joe Kubek Reveals Rule-Breaking Tactics Behind Fourth Bullseye CD." *BUDDY Magazine*, April 1995.

Schuller, Tim. "The James Clay Story." *BUDDY Magazine*, May 1995.

Shull, Chris. "Pretty Persuasion: Classical Guitarist Carlo Pezzimenti Refines the Virtuosity of Restraint." *The Met*, August 7, 1996.

Shull, Chris. "Scene Unheard: Three Diverse Dallas Players Shine on Recent CD Releases." *The Met*, July 20, 1995.

Shull, Chris. "Texas Jazz." *The Met*, August 28, 1996.

Sloan, Bill. "Groomsman: Dewey Groom Turned His Love for Music into 30 Years of Brown Bags at the Longhorn Ballroom." *The Met*, December 20, 1995.

Smedley. "Rappin' with Lightnin' Hopkins—or . . . You're Never Too Old to Be a Groupie." *BUDDY Magazine*, August 1973.

Smith, Russell. "The Elements of Rock 'n' Roll: Local Award-Winning Band Hopes to Change Its Low Profile." *The Dallas Morning News*, June 14, 1984.

Stegall, Tim. "Aces High: The Return of the Texas Tornados." *The Austin Chronicle*, July 5, 1996.

Stegall, Tim. "Fiddles, Not Violins: The Secret to Ray Price and *San Antonio Rose*." *The Austin Chronicle*, August 23, 1996.

Stegall, Tim. "No Flies on Waylon: An Outlaw Who's Not Angry?" *The Austin Chronicle*, July 26, 1996.

Stegall, Tim. "Twisted Williemania: On the Bus Again with Willie Nelson." *The Austin Chronicle*, February 9, 1996.

Stern, Adam Keane. "Ornette Coleman." *Seconds*, Issue 35.

Stowers, Carlton. "Hip Hop Hallelujah." *FW Weekly*, July 4, 1996.

Strauss, Neil. "Poetry, Monsters and Metal in the Dark World of Vince Bell." *The New York Times*, June 27, 1995.

Tarradell, Mario. "Domestic Bliss: Putting a Fresh Spin on Music of the Past, Domestic Science Club Can Really Cook." *The Dallas Morning News*, April 18, 1996.

Tarradell, Mario. "Out of the Darkness: Texas Roots Help Light the Way for Kimmie Rhodes' Slice of *Heaven*." *The Dallas Morning News*, May 9, 1996.

Tarradell, Mario. "Ray Wylie Hubbard." *The Dallas Morning News*, July 18, 1999.

Tarradell, Mario. "Sexy Image Prevails in the Marketing of Tejano Women." *The Dallas Morning News*, March 17, 1995.

Tarradell, Mario. "Tejano King Emilio Leads a Crossover to Country." *The Dallas Morning News*, October 29, 1995.

Tarradell, Mario. "Tracy Marches: Evolving Lawrence Stretches His Style to New Heights." *The Dallas Morning News*, August 15, 1996.

Tarradell, Mario. "Up and Coming: Nominee Selena Wins Big at Tejano Music Awards." *The Dallas Morning News*, February 12, 1995.

Thompson, Helen. "Little Boy Lost: Charlie Sexton." *Texas Monthly*, February 1996.

Thorpe, Helen. "Darkness Audible: Shawn Colvin, the Latest Pop Emigré to Land in Austin, Sets the Record Straight on Her Long and Difficult Road to Stardom." *Texas Monthly*, April 1995.

Toland, Michael. "Standing on the Shoulders of Giants." *Pop Culture Press*, Fall 1991.

Tosches, Nick. "The Devil in George Jones." *Texas Monthly*, July 1994.

Townsend, Charles R. "The Light Crust Doughboys—Yesterday and Today." Pamphlet: Saratoga Springs, New York, Summer 1994.

Tyler, Brad. "Houston Scene: Taking a Glance at the Spectrum." *The Austin Chronicle*, March 18, 1994.

Von Zenicht, Mark. "Living in a Dream: The ARC Angels are the Hottest New Group Out of Texas." *BUDDY Magazine*, May 1992.

Warden, Jerry. "Review: Geto Boys' *Til Death Do Us Part*." *BUDDY Magazine*, April 1993.

Warnock, Kirby F. "Tres Decades: Z.Z. Top." *BUDDY Magazine*, October 1994.

Warnock, Kirby F. "Will the Real Blues Brothers Please Stand Up? Groovin' with the Thunderbirds." *BUDDY Magazine*, December 1978.

Watkins, Gerry, and George Watkins. "Those Swingin' Cowboy Poets: Red Steagall's Swing Festival." *Texas Our Texas*, October 1995.

Weitz, Matt. "Fond Farewell." *The Dallas Morning News*, July 11, 1999.

Weitz, Matt. "Mo' Townes: Townes Van Zandt Continues to Find Optimism in Despair." *The Met*, January 24, 1996.

Weitz, Matt. "Setting Sail Once More: Shakespeare's Again at the Ship of Vibes." *Dallas Observer*, August 15, 1996.

Weitz, Matt. "Thank Heaven for Little Country Girls." *Dallas Observer*, August 29, 1996.

Williams, Frank "P-Frank." "Live from the Geto: The Reunion of the Original Geto Boys Sparks Hope in the Hearts of Hip-Hop Purists." *The Source*, June 1996.

Wills, Rosetta. "Review: Bob Wills' *Encore*." *Music City Texas*, November 1995.

Wilonsky, Robert. "Blues for James: Local Jazzer James Clay Leaves Remarkable Legacy." *The Dallas Observer*, January 12, 1996.

Wilonsky, Robert. "Rhythm and Jews: The Modern-Day Klezmer Revival Jazzes Up the Music of Tradition." *The Dallas Observer*, December 21, 1995.

Wilonsky, Robert. "A Royal Treat: Café Noir's *Waltz King* Is Music That Transcends Simple Definition." *The Dallas Observer*, March 16, 1995.

Wilonsky, Robert. "Scene, Not Heard: Deep Ellum's Still Got the Good Bands, But Where's the Crowd?" *Dallas Observer*, November 18, 1993.

Wilonsky, Robert. "Star Maker: Can Interscope Do for Local Bands What It Did for Nine Inch Nails and Snoop Dogg?" *Dallas Observer*, June 8, 1996.

Wilonsky, Robert. "Swingin' the Blues: Big Al Dupree Makes His Recording Debut After 72 Years." *Dallas Observer*, September 7, 1995.

Wilonsky, Robert. "T.C.B. or T.Y.A. Bobby Patterson, Dallas' Great Unsung Soul Singer, Gets His *Second Chance*." *Dallas Observer*, February 1996.

Wilonsky, Robert. "Toadies vs. the World." *Dallas Observer*, August 11, 1996.

Wilonsky, Robert. "Whose Young Turks?" *Dallas Observer*, December 7, 1995.

Wilson, Mandy. "Up-Close: Tracy Byrd." CMA *Close Up*, January 1996.

Wolfe, Charles. "Vernon Dalhart: Country's First Million-Seller." *The Journal of the American Academy for the Preservation of Old-Time Country Music*, June 1995.

Woolley, Bryan. "Don Walser: By Eschewing Commercialism, He's Found a Purer Brand of Country." *The Dallas Morning News*, December 17, 1995.

Yates, Don. "Review: *Milton Brown and the Musical Brownies, The Complete Recordings of the Father of Western Swing*." *No Depression, The Alternative Country (Whatever That Is) Quarterly*, Summer 1996.

☆ Index

LaVergne, TN USA
23 October 2009

161831LV00001B/8/A